Index to
the New World
Recorded Anthology
of American Music

Index to the
New World Recorded
Anthology of
American Music

A User's Guide to the
Initial One Hundred Records

PREPARED BY
Elizabeth A. Davis

W·W·NORTON & COMPANY

NEW YORK   LONDON

FIRST EDITION

Copyright © 1981 by Recorded Anthology of American Music, Inc.
Published simultaneously in Canada by George J. McLeod Limited, Toronto
Printed in the United States of America

LIBRARY OF CONGRESS CATALOGING IN PUBLICATION DATA

Davis, Elizabeth A.
Index to the New World Recorded anthology of American music.
1. Recorded anthology of American music–Indexes.
2. Music–United States–Indexes. 3. Music–United States–
Discography. I. Title.
ML156.9.D38   016.7899'12773   81-2500
ISBN 0-393-95172-3   AACR2

W. W. Norton & Company, Inc.   500 Fifth Avenue, New York, N.Y. 10110
W. W. Norton & Company Ltd.   25 New Street Square, London EC4A 3NT

1 2 3 4 5 6 7 8 9 0

94277

Contents

Preface   vii

Index to Recorded Material   121

Index to Printed Material   191

Index to Genres and Performing Media   205

Chronological Index   231

Preface

The idea that was to become New World Records dates back to the mid-1960s. The newly created Arts Division of The Rockefeller Foundation began to explore the possibility of a record series offering concert music by American composers—a series which was destined to become part of the Bicentennial celebration.

Through a decade of planning, this idea was researched, refined, and expanded. In 1975, New World Records was incorporated as the first nonprofit company devoted exclusively to recording American music.

In the three and one-half years from 1975 to 1978, with funds provided by The Rockefeller Foundation, New World Records produced the Recorded Anthology of American Music: 100 discs comprising not only concert art music, but everything from marching bands to bebop, film music to field hollers, symphonies to theater songs—in short, music of every genre, spanning well over 200 years of America's history and cultural heritage. The Anthology was distributed, as a gift, to almost 7,000 schools, libraries, nonprofit radio stations, and other educational institutions in the United States and throughout the world.*

Its 100 record programs were designed to augment the American repertoire already recorded on other labels. Almost one-half of the New World Records comprise unique compilations of archival material made available through the generosity of a large number of commercial record companies; the remaining discs present music that had never before been recorded.

The Anthology is the result of an unparalleled confluence of talent. An Editorial Committee of fifteen composers, musicologists, performers, writers, and historians shaped the overall project, and hundreds of experts meticulously programmed and annotated the

---

*New World Records is presently entering its sixth year and continues to release recordings of American music. Since the completion of the first phase—the 100-record Anthology—an additional nine recordings have been released.

records. Double-fold album packages, with over 500 pages of liner notes, bibliographies, discographies, and original American artwork on the covers, offer extensive information on the history and the music.

The Anthology has sought to avoid the pitfalls of being merely entertaining or merely educational; it has sometimes attempted the controversial and the unexplored. Its long-range effect on our consciousness of our own heritage has yet to be measured. But it stands as a most remarkable body of American sounds, a testament to America's ingenuity and spirit. New World Records set out to present a history of America's people through their music; in so doing, it has made a unique and lasting contribution to America's discography.

It would be impossible to thank everyone who contributed to New World Records and this Index, for the Anthology is the collective work of many hundreds of people. New World would have remained only an idea without the faith, guidance, and fortitude of Howard Klein, Director of the Arts for The Rockefeller Foundation, who, with his predecessor Norman Lloyd, shaped the original project. It could never have been realized without the talents of the Editorial Committee (listed below) and a dynamic and dedicated staff, headed by Herman Krawitz (President), my predecessor Andrew Raeburn (Director, Artists and Repertoire), and Michael Sonino (Art Director and Literary Editor).

The Index is the result of tireless work on the part of Elizabeth Davis of W. W. Norton, who, with Music Editor Claire Brook, has given such careful attention to detail and format, making the Index both usable and useful. Thanks also go to Grace Sowerwine, for her preliminary work of breaking up the Anthology into individual entries, and to David Hamilton, for reading, guiding, and advising.

This volume consists of a Master Index and four subsidiary indices. Not only an indispensable guide to the contents of the Anthology, it is also a detailed discographic source and a major research tool for the study of American music, even if the recordings are not readily at hand.

The Master Index, arranged consecutively by record number, gives all pertinent information about each disc: record title; liner note author; composer, title, and performers for each individual selection; and data on the jacket cover art. The remaining indices are concerned respectively with all the music (recorded material), all the printed material (liner notes and record jackets), and all the musical genres (e.g., cantatas, marches, jazz, songs, etc.). Finally, there is a chronology, arranged by date of composition, of the recorded selections. The reader is referred to the introductory paragraph at the beginning of each index, where the function and structure of the index is explained and suggestions given for its most effective use.

Elizabeth Ostrow, Vice President
Director of Artists & Repertoire

The Editorial Committee

(listed with professional positions held during the planning and execution of the Anthology)

Don Roberts—Chairman: Music Librarian, Northwestern University; Former President, Association of Recorded Sound Collections

Milton Babbitt—Composer; Conant Professor of Music, Princeton University

David Baker—Composer; Professor of Music; Director, Institute of Jazz Studies, Indiana University

Neely Bruce—Choral Director and Associate Professor of Music, Wesleyan University

Richard Crawford—Musicologist; Professor of Music, University of Michigan

Ross Lee Finney—Composer; Professor Emeritus, University of Michigan

Richard Franko Goldman—Conductor, Composer; President (Emeritus), Peabody Conservatory of Music

David Hamilton—Music Critic, "The Nation"

H. Wiley Hitchcock—Professor of Music, Brooklyn College, CUNY; Director, Institute for Studies in American Music

Cynthia Hoover—Curator, Division of Musical Instruments, Smithsonian Institution

Herman E. Krawitz—Professor (Adjunct), School of Drama, Yale University

Gunther Schuller—Composer, Conductor; President, New England Conservatory of Music

Mike Seeger—Performer, Teacher, Collector of Traditional Mountain Music

Michael Steinberg—Director of Publications, Boston Symphony Orchestra; (Former) Music Critic, "The Boston Globe"

Warren Susman—Historian; Chairman, Department of History, Rutgers University

(For further information about these recordings, please contact New World Records, 231 East 51st Street, New York, N.Y. 10022.)

Index to
the New World
Recorded Anthology
of American Music

Master Index

The *Index to the New World Recorded Anthology* consists of a Master Index and four subsidiary indices. The Master Index provides a systematic description of each record arranged in numerical order. Included with the album number is its title, the author of the liner notes, the artist and title of the cover art, and the title of each recorded work in the album with its creator(s) and performers. This is the only place where you will find the names of the record producers and the publisher of each selection as well as individual timings.

In the other four indices, the reader is referred back to the Master Index by record number, with sides and bands where appropriate; e.g., 288/89 indicates the entire album which consists of two records, or 298:s1/4 refers to a selection on album number 298, side 1, band 4. C indicates the composer, L the lyricist.

201 Cecil Taylor

LP
1946

Notes by Spencer Richards and Ramsey Ameen.
Producer: Sam Parkins. Cover art: David X. Young,
Hounfor. On all selections: Jimmy Lyons, also saxo-
phone; Raphé Malik, trumpet; Ramsey Ameen, violin;
Sirone, bass; Ronald Shannon Jackson, drums. All
selections published by Mayflower Music.

s1/1	*Idut* (Cecil Taylor, C).	14:40
s1/2	*Serdab* (Cecil Taylor, C).	14:13
s2	*Holiday en Masque* (Cecil Taylor, C).	29:41

202 Songs of the Civil War

LP
1668

Notes by Charles Hamm. Producer: Andrew Raeburn.
Cover art: Winslow Homer, *Songs of the War*. All
selections except s2/1 published by Dover Press.

s1/1	*I Wish I Was in Dixie's Land* (Dan D. Emmett, C/L). Alan Baker, baritone; The Harmoneion Singers; Lawrence Skrobacs, piano.	2:58
s1/2	*All Quiet Along the Potomac Tonight* (John Hill Hewitt, C; Ethel L. E. Beers, L). John Aler, tenor; Lawrence Skrobacs, piano.	5:30
s1/3	*We Are Coming, Father Abra'am* (Luther O. Emerson, C; John Sloan Gibbons, L). Alan Baker, baritone; The Harmoneion Singers; Lawrence Skrobacs, piano.	4:13
s1/4	*Mother, Is the Battle Over?* (attrib. Benedict Roefs, C). Bonnie Hamilton, soprano; Lawrence Skrobacs, piano.	3:14
s1/5	*Tenting on the Old Camp Ground* (Walter Kittredge, C/L). Alan Baker, baritone; The Harmoneion Singers; Lawrence Skrobacs, piano.	4:54
s1/6	*The Drummer Boy of Shiloh* (William Shakespeare Hays, C/L). John Aler, tenor; Lawrence Skrobacs, piano.	7:41
s2/1	*Beauregard's Retreat from Shiloh* (Anon.). Tony Randall, narrator; The Harmoneion Singers; Lawrence Skrobacs, piano.	7:12
s2/2	*Jeff in Petticoats* (Henry Tucker, C; George Cooper, L). John Aler, tenor; The Harmoneion Singers; Lawrence Skrobacs, piano.	4:00

202 (continued)

s2/3	*Weeping, Sad and Lonely* (Henry Tucker, C; Charles Carroll Sawyer, L). Bonnie Hamilton, soprano; The Harmoneion Singers; Lawrence Skrobacs, piano.	5:29
s2/4	*I'm A Good Old Rebel* (attrib. R. Bishop Buckley, C). Alan Baker, baritone.	1:53
s2/5	*When Johnny Comes Marching Home* (Louis Lambert, pseud. of Patrick S. Gilmore, C). Bonnie Hamilton, soprano; The Harmoneion Singers; Lawrence Skrobacs, piano.	1:57
s2/6	*We Are Coming from the Cotton Fields* (J. C. Wallace, C). Alan Baker, baritone; The Harmoneion Singers; Lawrence Skrobacs, piano.	4:11

203 **Sound Forms for Piano: Experimental Music by**
LP   **Henry Cowell, John Cage, Ben Johnston, and**
1535 **Conlon Nancarrow**

> Notes by Charles Hamm. Producer: Sam Parkins. Cover art: Elaine Sherer Cox. On all selections (except s2/5-7): Robert Miller, piano.

s1/1	*The Banshee* (Henry Cowell, C). Associated Music, pub.	2:20
s1/2	*Aeolian Harp* (Henry Cowell, C). Associated Music, pub.	1:27
s1/3	*Piano Piece (Paris 1924)* (Henry Cowell, C). Associated Music, pub.	3:59
s1/4	Sonata I (John Cage, C). C. F. Peters, pub.	2:56
s1/5	Sonata V (John Cage, C). C. F. Peters, pub.	1:23
s1/6	*Second Interlude* (John Cage, C). C. F. Peters, pub.	4:24
s1/7	Sonata X (John Cage, C). C. F. Peters, pub.	3:45
s1/8	Sonata XII (John Cage, C). C. F. Peters, pub.	3:44
s2/1-4	Sonata for Microtonal Piano (Ben Johnston, C). Smith Publications, pub.	
	Movement I	2:43
	Movement II	1:38
	Movement III	3:55
	Movement IV	2:45
s2/5-7	*Studies for Player Piano* (Conlon Nancarrow, C).	
	Study #1	2:00
	Study #27	5:32
	Study #36	4:02

204 *Loxodonta Africana*: The Jazz Sound of Ricky Ford

LP
1881

Notes by Gunther Schuller. Producer: Michael Cuscuna. Cover art: Romare Bearden, *Ritual Bayou*.

s1/1	*Loxodonta Africana* (Ricky Ford, C). Ricky Ford, tenor saxophone; Oliver Beener and Charles Sullivan, trumpets; Bob Neloms, piano; Richard Davis, bass; Dannie Richmond, drums. Jazz Workshop, pub.	4:38
s1/2	*Ucil* (Ricky Ford, C). Ricky Ford, tenor saxophone; James Spaulding, alto saxophone; Oliver Beener and Charles Sullivan, trumpets; Janice Robinson, trombone; Jonathan Dorn, tuba; Bob Neloms, piano; Richard Davis, bass; Dannie Richmond, drums. Jazz Workshop, pub.	5:07
s1/3	*Blues Peru* (Ricky Ford, C). Ricky Ford, tenor saxophone; Oliver Beener and Charles Sullivan, trumpets; Bob Neloms, piano; Richard Davis, bass; Dannie Richmond, drums. Jazz Workshop, pub.	5:00
s1/4	*Dexter* (Ricky Ford, C). Ricky Ford, tenor saxophone; Oliver Beener and Charles Sullivan, trumpets; Bob Neloms, piano; Richard Davis, bass; Dannie Richmond, drums. Jazz Workshop, pub.	5:38
s2/1	*My Romance* (Richard Rogers, C; Lorenz Hart, L). Ricky Ford, tenor saxophone; Oliver Beener and Charles Sullivan, trumpets; Bob Neloms, piano; Richard Davis, bass; Dannie Richmond, drums. T. B. Harms, pub.	8:24
s2/2	*One Up, One Down* (John Coltrane, C). Ricky Ford, tenor saxophone; James Spaulding, alto saxophone; Oliver Beener and Charles Sullivan, trumpets; Janice Robinson, trombone; Jonathan Dorn, tuba; Bob Neloms, piano; Richard Davis, bass; Dannie Richmond, drums. Jowocol Music, pub.	4:18
s2/3	*Aerolinos* (Ricky Ford, C). Ricky Ford, tenor saxophone; Oliver Beener and Charles Sullivan, trumpets; Bob Neloms, piano; Richard Davis, bass; Dannie Richmond, drums. Jazz Workshop, pub.	6:50

205 White Spirituals from *The Sacred Harp*

LP
1736

Notes by Alan Lomax. Assistant producer: N. W.
Pearson. Cover art: Charles Burchfield, *Tall White Sun*.
On all selections: The Alabama Sacred Harp Convention.
All selections published by Sacred Harp Publishing
except s1/10, s2/5, 7, 12.

s1/1	*Sherburne* (Daniel Read, C).	1:52
s1/2	*David's Lamentation* (William Billings, C/L).	1:08
s1/3	*Melancholy Day* (H. S. Rees, C; Isaac Watts, L).	2:08
s1/4	*Soar Away* (A. M. Cagle, C/L).	3:15
s1/5	*Commentary* (attrib. Alexander Means, text). Spoken by Joyce Smith.	1:25
s1/6	*Wondrous Love* (Anon., C; attrib. Alexander Means, L). Joyce Smith, vocal.	2:51
s1/7	*Traveling On* (S. M. Denson and J.S. James, C).	1:49
s1/8	*New Harmony* (M. L. A. Lancaster, C).	2:43
s1/9	*Hallelujah* (William Walker, C).	2:16
s1/10	*Prayer for Recess*	:58
s1/11	*Loving Jesus* (B. F. White, L; Searcy, C).	1:51
s2/1	*Greenwich* (Daniel Read, C; Isaac Watts, L).	2:19
s2/2	*Milford* (John Stepheson, C).	1:41
s2/3	*Baptismal Anthem* (B. F. White, C).	2:23
s2/4	*Amsterdam* (James Nares, C; Robert Seagrave, L).	1:40
s2/5	*Montgomery* (David Morgan, C; Isaac Watts, L).	2:09
s2/6	*North Port* (R. Osborne, C; John Cennick, L).	1:46
s2/7	*Memorial Service*	:34
s2/8	*Cusseta* (John Massengale, C).	1:44
s2/9	*The Last Words of Copernicus* (Sarah Lancaster, C/L).	1:55
s2/10	*The Morning Trumpet* (B. F. White, C/L).	1:18
s2/11	*Homeward Bound* (Howard Denson, C).	1:55
s2/12	*Closing Prayer*	1:33
s2/13	*Northfield* (Jeremiah Ingalls, C; Isaac Watts, L).	2:06

206 Malcolm Frager Plays Adolph Martin Foerster,
LP Henry F. Gilbert, Henry Holden Huss, Ethelbert
1915 Nevin, Horatio Parker, Edward MacDowell, John
Knowles Paine

> Notes by Richard Jackson. Producer: Horace Grenell.
> Cover art: Frederic Edwin Church, *Our Banner in the
> Sky*. On all selections: Malcolm Frager, piano.

s1/1	*Etude in Form of a Scherzo*, Op. 18, No. 2 (Ethelbert Nevin, C). Boston Music, pub.	3:57
s1/2	*Prelude II*, Op. 17, No. 2 (Henry Holden Huss, C).	1:54
s1/3	*Fuga Giocosa*, Op. 41, No. 3 (John Knowles Paine, C).	1:27
s1/4	*Romance*, Op. 12 (John Knowles Paine, C).	6:22
s1/5	*Mazurka* (Henry F. Gilbert, C). Wa-Wan Press, pub.	1:55
s1/6	*On the Sea* (Adolph Martin Foerster, C).	4:13
s1/7	*Valse Gracile*, Op. 49, No. 3 (Horatio Parker, C).	2:20

s2	*Twelve Virtuoso Studies*, Op. 46 (Edward MacDowell, C). Associated Music Publishers, pub.	
	No. 1 *Novellette*	2:04
	No. 2 *Moto Perpetuo*	1:30
	No. 3 *Wild Chase*	2:15
	No. 4 *Improvisation*	2:02
	No. 5 *Elfin Dance*	3:19
	No. 6 *Valse Triste*	2:53
	No. 7 *Burlesque*	2:13
	No. 8 *Bluette*	1:40
	No. 9 *Träumerei*	2:40
	No. 10 *March Wind*	1:55
	No. 11 *Impromptu*	1:34
	No. 12 *Polonaise*	3:40

207 Country Music in the Modern Era 1940s–1970s
LP
1667

> Notes by William Ivey. Producer: William Ivey. Cover
> art: Thomas Hart Benton, *Youth Music*.

s1/1	*Bouquet of Roses* (S. Nelson, B. Hilliard, C). Eddy Arnold, vocal. Unichappell Music, pub.	2:32
s1/2	*Never No More Blues* (J. Rodgers, C; E. McWilliams, L). Lefty Frizzell, vocal. Peer International, pub.	3:03
s1/3	*Much Too Young to Die* (Rusty Gabbard, C). Ray Price, vocal. Acuff-Rose Publications, pub.	2:04

207 (continued)

s1/4	*Squid Jiggin' Ground* (A. R. Scammel, C). Hank Snow, vocal.	3:06
s1/5	*There's Poison in Your Heart* (Zeke Clements, C). Kitty Wells, vocal. Unichappel Music, pub.	2:32
s1/6	*Try Me One More Time* (E. Tubb, C). Ernest Tubb, vocal. Unichappel Music, pub.	2:19
s1/7	*Love Letters in the Sand* (J. Fred Coots, Charles and Nick Kenny, C). Patsy Cline, vocal. Bourne, pub.	2:22
s1/8	*Jean's Song* (Marguerite Monnot, C). Chet Atkins, vocal. Chappell, pub.	2:13
s1/9	*Mystery Train* (Herman Parker, Sam Phillips, C). Elvis Presley, vocal. Hi Lo Music, pub.	2:25
s2/1	*Little Ole You* (Dave Burgess, Jim Reeves, C). Jim Reeves, vocal. Singletree Music, pub.	2:22
s2/2	*Jimmy Martinez* (M. Robbins, C). Marty Robbins, vocal. Unichappell Music, pub.	2:27
s2/3	*I'm a Honky-Tonk Girl* (L. Lynn, C). Loretta Lynn, vocal. Sure Fire Music, pub.	2:15
s2/4	*Lorena* (arr. C. Williams). Johnny Cash, vocal.	1:53
s2/5	*Don't Let Her Know* (Buck Owens, Don Rich, Bonnie Owens, C). Buck Owens, vocal. Central Songs, pub.	2:32
s2/6	*All I Love Is You* (R. Miller, C). Roger Miller, vocal. Alrhond Publishing, pub.	2:12
s2/7	*Sing a Sad Song* (W. Stewart, C). Merle Haggard, vocal. Owen Publications, pub.	2:31
s2/8	*Coat of Many Colors* (D. Parton, C). Dolly Parton, vocal. Owepar Publishing, pub.	3:01
s2/9	*Help Me Make It Through the Night* (Kris Kristofferson, C). Kris Kristofferson, vocal. Combine Music, pub.	2:23

208 Heinrich: *The Ornithological Combat of Kings*
Gottschalk: *Night in the Tropics*

LP
1947

The Ornithological Combat of Kings: Notes by David
Barron. Producer: Andrew Raeburn.
Night in the Tropics: Notes by Richard Jackson.
Producer: Horace Grenell.
Cover art: Frederic Edwin Church, *Trees in Jamaica*.

s1/1-4 *The Ornithological Combat of Kings* or *The
Condor of the Andes and the Eagle of the
Cordilleras* (Grand Symphony) (Anthony
Philip Heinrich, C). Syracuse Symphony
Orchestra, Christopher Keene, conductor.
    The Conflict of the Condor in the Air
    (Allegro, ma moderato)   7:06
    The Repose of the Condor (Andante
    sostenuto, quasi adagio)   5:38
    The Combat of the Condor on Land
    (Allegro)   6:10
    Victory of the Condor (Finale: vivace
    brillante)   6:17

s2   *Night in the Tropics* (two-piano arrangement)
(Louis Moreau Gottschalk, C; arr. by John
Kirkpatrick, based on the unfinished arrange-
ment for two or three pianos by N. R.
Espadero). Anthony and Joseph Paratore,
pianos.   16:40
    1 Andante
    2 Allegro moderato

209 New Music for Virtuosos

LP
1733

Notes by Eric Salzman. Producer: Sam Parkins. Cover
art: David Smith, *Untitled II*.

s1/1   *Phonemena* (for soprano and piano) (Milton
Babbitt, C). Lynne Webber, soprano; Jerry
Kuderna, piano. C. F. Peters, pub.   4:55
s1/2   *Phonemena* (for soprano and tape) (Milton
Babbitt, C). Lynne Webber, soprano.
C. F. Peters, pub.   4:12
s1/3   *Fancies for Clarinet Alone* (William O. Smith,
C). William O. Smith, clarinet. MJQ Music,
pub.   7:18

209 (continued)

s1/4   *Reflections* (for piano and synthesized tape)
(Milton Babbitt, C). Robert Miller, piano.
C. F. Peters, pub.   10:12

s2/1   *Music for Saxophone and Piano* (Leslie
Bassett, C). Donald Sinta, saxophone; Ellen
Weckler, piano. C. F. Peters, pub.   8:56

s2/2   *Post-Partitions* (Milton Babbitt, C). Robert
Miller, piano. C. F. Peters, pub.   3:30

s2/3   *Bassoon Variations* (Charles Wuorinen, C).
Donald MacCourt, bassoon; Susan Jolles, harp;
Gordon Gottlieb, timpani. C. F. Peters, pub.   12:05

210 Salvatore Martirano: *Mass*
L P   **Donald Martino:** *Seven Pious Pieces*
18 43

Notes by Edwin London. Producer: Andrew Raeburn.
Cover art: Lauren MacIver, *Red Votive Lights*.

s1/1-3   *Mass* (Salvatore Martirano, C). The Ineluctable
Modality, Edwin London, conductor. Belwin-
Mills, pub.
    Kyrie   4:08
    Gloria   9:07
    Credo   12:12

s2/1   *Sanctus & Benedictus*   6:52
s2/2   *Agnus Dei*   3:58
s2/3   *Seven Pious Pieces* (Donald Martino, C;
Robert Herrick, L). The John Oliver Chorale,
John Oliver, conductor. E. C. Schirmer Music,
pub.   16:48
    To his ever-loving God
    Mercy and Love
    His Ejaculation to God
    The Soule
    Eternitie
    Teares/To Death/Welcome what comes
    No coming to God without Christ

211 Winds of Change: Music for Wind Ensemble

LP
1749

Notes by John P. Paynter. Producer: Andrew Raeburn. Cover art: John Covert, *Brass Band*. On all selections: The Northwestern University Symphonic Wind Ensemble, John P. Paynter, conductor.

s1/1	*Pageant* (Vincent Persichetti, C). Carl Fischer, pub.	7:24
s1/2	*Expansions* (Hale Smith, C). Edward B. Marks Music, pub.	8:17
s1/3	*Verticals Ascending* (Henry Brant, C). Clifford Colnot, conductor. MCA Music, pub.	9:31
s2/1	Concerto for Alto Saxophone and Orchestra of Wind Instruments (Ross Lee Finney, C). Frederick L. Hemke, saxophone. C. F. Peters, pub. Moderato; Allegro energico	13:14
s2/2	*Symphonic Songs for Band* (Robert Russell Bennett, C). Chappell, pub. Serenade; Spiritual; Celebration.	13:29

212 Andrew Imbrie: String Quartet No. 4
Gunther Schuller: String Quartet No. 2

LP
1916

Notes by Phillip Ramey, Andrew Imbrie, and Gunther Schuller. Produced by Elizabeth Ostrow. Cover art: Laszlo Moholy-Nagy, *Untitled Abstraction*. On all selections: The Emerson String Quartet: Philip Setzer, first violin; Eugene Drucker, second violin; Lawrence Dutton, viola; Eric Wilson, cello.

s1	String Quartet No. 4 (Andrew Imbrie, C). Malcolm Music, pub.	
	I	7:23
	II	6:16
	III	6:13
s2	String Quartet No. 2 (Gunther Schuller, C). G. Schirmer, pub.	
	I	4:09
	II	9:08
	III	5:50

213 Works by Arthur Farwell, Preston Ware Orem, Charles Wakefield Cadman

LP
1748

Notes by Gilbert Chase. Producer: Horace Grenell.
Cover art: Ferdinand Burgdorff, *Canyon de Chelly*.

s1/1	*Three Indian Songs*, Op. 32 (Arthur Farwell, C). William Parker, baritone; William Huckaby, piano. G. Schirmer, pub.	
	Song of the Deathless Voice	2:06
	Inketunga's Thunder Song	2:45
	The Old Man's Love Song	3:17
s1/2	*American Indian Rhapsody* (Preston Ware Orem, C). Peter Basquin, piano. Theodore Presser, pub.	7:59
s1/3	*The Old Man's Love Song*, Op. 102, No. 2 (Arthur Farwell, C). The New World Singers, John Miner, conductor. G. Schirmer, pub.	6:46
s2/1	*Navajo War Dance*, Op. 102, No. 1 (Arthur Farwell, C). The New World Singers, John Miner, conductor. G. Schirmer, pub.	3:23
s2/2	*Navajo War Dance* (for piano) (Arthur Farwell, C). Peter Basquin, piano. G. Schirmer, pub.	2:18
	Pawnee Horses (Arthur Farwell, C). Peter Basquin, piano. G. Schirmer, pub.	1:12
s2/3	*Four American Indian Songs*, Op. 45 (Charles Wakefield Cadman, C). William Parker, baritone; William Huckaby, piano. Edwin H. Morris, pub.	
	From the Land of the Sky-Blue Water	1:46
	The White Dawn Is Stealing	1:53
	Far Off I Hear a Lover's Flute	2:37
	The Moon Drops Low	2:55

214 Harry Partch—John Cage

LP
1948

Notes by Ben Johnston. Producer (Side 1): Danlee Mitchell. Cover art: John Cage, *Seventeen Drawings by Thoreau*. All compositions on Side 1 by Harry Partch and published by the Harry Partch Foundation. Both compositions on Side 2 by John Cage and published by Henmar Music.

s1/1	*The Rose*. Harry Partch, intoning voice and Adapted Guitar II; Ben Johnston, Diamond Marimba.	1:38

214 (continued)

s1/2   *The Wind*. Harry Partch, intoning voice and
Harmonic Canon I; Ben Johnston, Bass
Marimba.   1:38

s1/3   *The Waterfall*. Harry Partch, intoning voice
and Adapted Guitar II; Ben Johnston,
Diamond Marimba.   1:03

s1/4   *The Intruder*. William Wendlandt, intoning
voice; Harry Partch, intoning voice and
Adapted Viola.   1:09

s1/5   *I Am a Peach Tree*. William Wendlandt,
intoning voice; Harry Partch, intoning voice
and Adapted Viola.   1:23

s1/6   *A Midnight Farewell*. William Wendlandt,
intoning voice; Harry Partch, intoning voice
and Adapted Viola.   1:15

s1/7   *Before the Cask of Wine*. William Wendlandt,
intoning voice; Harry Partch, intoning voice
and Adapted Viola.   2:10

s1/8   *The Street*. Harry Partch, intoning voice and
Harmonic Canon II; Ben Johnston, Bass
Marimba.   2:39

s1/9   *The Dreamer That Remains*. Harry Partch,
intoning voice and narrator; Mark Hoffman,
Brash Musician; Danlee Mitchell, Second
Musician; Jon Szanto, The Voice; Katherine
Bjornson, Alexis Glattly, Michael Crosier and
the following instrumentalists and chorus: Ron
Caruso, Gourd Tree; David Dunn, Adapted
Viola; Dennis Dunn, New Harmonic Canon I;
Jean-Charles Françoix, Quadrangularis
Reversum; Jonathan Glasier, New Harmonic
Canon I; Randy Hoffman, Eucal Blossom and
Mbira Bass Dyad; Danlee Mitchell, New
Kithara I; Emil Richards, Cloud-Chamber
Bowls; Jon Szanto, Ektara and Boo II; Duane
Thomas, Harmonic Canon II; Francis Thumm,
Chromelodeon; Jack Logan, conductor.   10:27

s2/1   *Music of Changes Part III*. David Tudor,
piano.   10:19

s2/2   *Music of Changes Part IV*. David Tudor,
piano.   11:48

215 Follies, Scandals, and Other Diversions: From Ziegfeld to the Shuberts

LP
1747

> Notes by George Oppenheimer. Cover art: Joseph Urban, *Bath Scene*.

s1/1	*The Moon Shines on the Moonshine*, from *Broadway Brevities of 1920* (Robert Hood Bowers, C; Francis De Witt, L). Bert Williams, vocal. Shapiro, Bernstein, pub.	3:01
s1/2	*Second-Hand Rose*, from *Ziegfeld Follies of 1921* (James F. Hanley, C; Grant Clarke, L). Fanny Brice, vocal. Shapiro, Bernstein/Fred Fisher Music, pub.	3:16
s1/3	*Mister Gallagher and Mister Shean*, from *Ziegfeld Follies of 1922* (Ed Gallagher & Al Shean, C/L). Ed Gallagher and Al Shean, vocals. E. Gallagher and A. Shean, pub.	3:09
s1/4	*I'll Build a Stairway to Paradise*, from *George White's Scandals of 1922* (George Gershwin, C; B. G. DeSylva & Ira Gershwin, L). Paul Whiteman and His Orchestra. New World Music, pub.	3:13
s1/5	*A Cup of Coffee, a Sandwich and You*, from *Charlot's Revue of 1926* (Joseph Meyer, C; Billy Rose and Al Dubin, L). Gertrude Lawrence and Jack Buchanan, vocals. Warner Bros. Music, pub.	3:07
s1/6	*Doin' the New Low-Down*, from *Blackbirds of 1928* (Jimmy McHugh, C; Dorothy Fields, L). Bill "Bojangles" Robinson, vocal; Don Redman and His Orchestra. Mills Music, pub.	2:33
s1/7	*Moanin' Low*, from *The Little Show* (Ralph Rainger, C; Howard Dietz, L). Libby Holman, vocal. Warner Bros. Music, pub.	3:10
s2/1	*Shine On, Harvest Moon*, from *Ziegfeld Follies of 1931* (Nora Bayes and Jack Norworth, C/L). Ruth Etting, vocal.	2:46
s2/2	*On the Sunny Side of the Street*, from *The International Revue* (Jimmy McHugh, C; Dorothy Fields, L). Harry Richman, vocal; Jack Golden, conductor. Shapiro, Bernstein, pub.	3:06
s2/3	*Hoops*, from *The Band Wagon* (Arthur Schwartz, C; Howard Dietz, L). Fred and Adele Astaire, vocals; Leo Reisman and His Orchestra. Harms, pub.	2:49

215 (continued)

s2/4   *Paree*, from *At Home Abroad* (Arthur
Schwartz, C; Howard Dietz, L). Beatrice
Lillie, vocal. Chappell, pub.   3:57

s2/5   *Anatole of Paris*, from *The Straw Hat Revue*
(Sylvia Fine, C/L). Danny Kaye, vocal.
Sylvia Fine, pub.   2:57

s2/6   *Are You Havin' Any Fun?*, from *George
White's Scandals of 1939* (Sammy Fain, C;
Jack Yellen, L). Ella Logan, vocal. DeSylva,
Brown, & Henderson, pub.   2:30

s2/7   *South American Way*, from *Streets of Paris*
(Jimmy McHugh, C; Al Dubin, L). Carmen
Miranda, vocal. Harms, pub.   2:51

216 *Mirage*: Avant-Garde and Third-Stream Jazz

*LP
1732*

Notes by Gunther Schuller. Cover art: Gabor Peterdi,
Angry Sky.

s1/1   *Summer Sequence* (Parts 1, 2, 3) (Ralph
Burns, C). Woody Herman and His Orchestra:
Sonny Berman, Cappy Lewis, Conrad Gozzo,
Pete Candoli, and Shorty Rogers, trumpets;
Ralph Pfeffner, Bill Harris, Ed Kiefer, and
Lyman Reid, trombones; Woody Herman,
clarinet; Sam Marowitz and John LaPorta,
clarinets and alto saxophones; Flip Phillips
and Mickey Folus, tenor saxophones; Sam
Rubinowitch, baritone saxophone; Ralph
Burns, piano; Chuck Wayne, guitar; Joe
Mondragon, bass; Don Lamond, drums. Edwin
H. Morris, pub.   8:40

s1/2   *The Clothed Woman* (Duke Ellington, C).
Duke Ellington and His Orchestra: Harold
Baker, trumpet; Johnny Hodges, alto saxo-
phone; Harry Carney, baritone saxophone;
Duke Ellington, piano; Junior Raglin, bass;
Sonny Greer, drums. Mercer K. Ellington, pub.   2:53

s1/3   *Yesterdays* (Jerome Kern, C; Otto Harbach,
L). Lennie Tristano Quartet: Lennie Tristano,
piano; Billy Bauer, guitar; Arnold Fishkin,
bass; Harold Granowsky, drums. T. B. Harms,
pub.   2:48

216 (continued)

s1/4   *Mirage* (Pete Rugolo, C). Stan Kenton and His
Orchestra: Buddy Childers, Maynard Ferguson,
Shorty Rogers, Chico Alvarez, and Don
Paladino, trumpets; Milt Bernhart, Harry Betts,
Bob Fitzpatrick, Bill Russo, and Bart Varsalona,
trombones; John Graas and Lloyd Otto, French
horns; Gene Englund, tuba; Art Pepper, clarinet
and alto saxophone; Bud Shank, flute and alto
saxophone; Bob Cooper, tenor saxophone, oboe,
and English horn; Bart Cardarell, tenor saxo-
phone and bass clarinet; George Kast, Jim
Cathcart, Lew Elias, Earl Cornwell, Anthony
Doria, Jim Holmes, Alex Law, Herbert Offner,
Dave Schackne, and Carl Ottobrino, violins;
Stan Harris, Leonard Selic, and Sam Singer,
violas; Gregory Bemko, Zachary Bock, and Jack
Wulfe, cellos; Stan Kenton, piano; Laurindo
Almeida, guitar; Don Bagley, bass; Shelly Manne,
drums and timpani. Leslie Music, pub.   5:00

s1/5   *Eclipse* (Charles Mingus, C). Charles Mingus
Octet, with Janet Thurlow, vocal; Willie Dennis,
trombone; Eddie Caine, alto saxophone and
flute; Teo Macero, tenor saxophone; Danny
Bank, baritone saxophone; Jackson Wiley, cello;
John Lewis, piano; Charles Mingus, bass;
Kenny Clarke, drums. Jazz Workshop, pub.   2:56

s2/1   *Egdon Heath* (Bill Russo, C). Stan Kenton and
His Orchestra: Buddy Childers, Vic Minichiello,
Sam Noto, Stu Williamson, and Don Smith,
trumpets; Bob Fitzpatrick, Frank Rosolino,
Milt Gold, Joe Ciavardone, and George Roberts,
trombones; Lee Konitz, Dave Schildkraut, and
Charlie Mariano, alto saxophones; Bill Perkins
and Mike Cicchetti, tenor saxophones; Tony
Ferina, baritone saxophone; Stan Kenton,
piano; Bob Lesher, guitar; Don Bagley, bass;
Stan Levey, drums. Benton Publications, pub.   3:53

s2/2   *Concerto for Billy the Kid* (George Russell, C).
George Russell and His Smalltet: Art Farmer,
trumpet; Hal McKusick, alto saxophone; Bill
Evans, piano; Barry Galbraith, guitar; Milt
Hinton, bass; Paul Motian, drums. Russ-Hix
Music, pub.   4:44

216 (continued)

s2/3 *Transformation* (Gunther Schuller, C).
Brandeis Jazz Festival Ensemble: Jimmy
Knepper, trombone; Jimmy Buffington,
French horn; John LaPorta, clarinet;
Robert DiDomenica, flute; Manuel Zegler,
bassoon; Hal McKusick, tenor saxophone;
Teddy Charles, vibraphone; Margaret Ross,
harp; Bill Evans, piano; Joe Benjamin, bass;
Teddy Sommer, drums. Malcolm Music, pub.   5:58

s2/4 *Piazza Navona* (John Lewis, C). John Lewis
and His Orchestra: Melvin Broiles, Bernie
Glow, Al Kiger, and Joe Wilder, trumpets;
Dick Hixon and David Baker, trombones;
Gunther Schuller, Al Richman, Ray Alonge,
and John Barrows, French horns; Harvey
Phillips, tuba; John Lewis, piano; George
Duvivier, bass; Connie Kay, drums. MJQ
Music, pub.   6:27

s2/5 *Laura* (David Raksin, C; Johnny Mercer, L).
Jeanne Lee, vocal; Ran Blake, piano.
Robbins Music, pub.   5:10

217 *Jammin' for the Jackpot*: Big Bands and Territory Bands of the 30s

LP
1694

Notes by J. R. Taylor. Cover art: Romare Bearden,
Jazz 1930s: The Savoy.

s1/1 *Caravan* (Juan Tizol, Duke Ellington, and
Irving Mills, C). Edgar Hayes and His
Orchestra: Henry Goodwin, Vernie Flood,
and Leonard Davis, trumpets; Robert Horton,
Clyde Bernhardt, and Joe Britton, trombones;
Rudy Powell, clarinet and alto saxophone;
Crawford Wethington, clarinet and tenor sax-
ophone; Roger Boyd, alto saxophone; Joe
Garland, tenor saxophone; Edgar Hayes,
piano; Andy Jackson, guitar; Elmer James,
bass; Kenny Clarke, drums. American
Academy of Music, pub.   3:03

217 (continued)

s1/2   *Casa Loma Stomp* (Gene Gifford, C). Casa
Loma Orchestra: Joe Hostetter, Frank
Martinez, and Bobby Jones, trumpets; Walter
"Pee Wee" Hunt and Billy Rauch, trombones;
Glen Gray and Ray Eberle, clarinets and alto
saxophones; Pat Davis, clarinet and tenor sax-
ophone; Joe Hall, piano; Gene Gifford, guitar;
Stanley Dennis, bass; Tony Briglia, drums.
Morley Music, pub.   3:16

s1/3   *Dallas Blues* (Hart Wand, Lloyd Garrett, C/L).
Andy Kirk and His Twelve Clouds of Joy:
Billy Massey, vocal; Harry Lawson and Edgar
Battle, trumpets; Allen Durham, trombone;
John Harrington, clarinet and alto saxophone;
John Williams, alto and baritone saxophone;
Lawrence Freeman, tenor saxophone; Mary
Lou Williams, piano; William Dirvin, banjo;
Andy Kirk, tuba; Edward McNeil, drums.
Edwin H. Morris, pub.   2:41

s1/4   *Madhouse* (Earl Hines, C; arr. James Mundy).
Earl Hines and His Orchestra: Charlie Allen,
George Dixon, and Walter Fuller, trumpets;
James "Trummy" Young, Louis Taylor, and
William Franklin, trombones; Darnell Howard,
clarinet and alto saxophone; Omer Simeon,
clarinet and alto and baritone saxophone;
Cecil Irwin, clarinet and tenor saxophone;
Jimmy Mundy, tenor saxophone; Earl "Fatha"
Hines, piano; Lawrence Dixon, guitar; Quinn
Wilson, tuba; Wallace Bishop, drums. Edwin H.
Morris, pub.   2:45

s1/5   *Heebie Jeebies* (Boyd Atkins, C). Chick Webb
and His Orchestra: Louis Bacon, Shelton
Hemphill, and Louis Hunt, trumpets; Jimmy
Harrison, trombone; Benny Carter and Hilton
Jefferson, clarinets and alto saxophones;
Elmer Williams, clarinet and tenor saxophone;
Don Kirkpatrick, piano; John Trueheart,
guitar; Elmer James, bass; Chick Webb, drums.
Leeds Music, pub.   3:00

217 (continued)

s1/6   *Pickin' the Cabbage* (Dizzy Gillespie, C). Cab
Calloway and His Orchestra: Dizzy Gillespie,
Mario Bauza, and Lammar Wright, trumpets;
Tyree Glenn, Quentin Jackson, and Keg
Johnson, trombones; Jerry Blake, clarinet and
alto saxophone; Hilton Jefferson, alto saxophone; Andrew Brown, alto and baritone saxophone; Chuck Berry and Walter Thomas,
tenor saxophones; Bennie Paine, piano; Danny
Barker, guitar; Milton Hinton, bass; Cozy Cole,
drums. John Gillespie, pub.   2:45

s1/7   *Ebony Silhouette* (Benny Payne and Milt
Hinton, C; arr. Andy Gibson). Same group as
the preceding. Pub. unknown.   2:35

s1/8   *Jammin' for the Jackpot* (Eli Robinson, C).
The Mills Blue Rhythm Band: Lucky Millinder,
leader; Charlie Shavers, Carl Warwick, and
Harry Edison, trumpets; Alfred Cobbs and
Wilbur DeParis, trombones; Tab Smith, alto
saxophone; Eddie Williams, Ben Williams, and
Harold Arnold, tenor saxophones; Billy Kyle,
piano; Danny Barker, guitar; John Williams,
bass; Lester Nichols, drums. Pub. unknown.   2:30

s2/1   *Toby* (Eddie Barefield and Buster Moten, C).
Bennie Moten's Kansas City Orchestra: Oran
"Hot Lips" Page, Joe Keyes, and Dee Stewart,
trumpets; Eddie Durham, trombone and guitar;
Dan Minor, trombone; Eddie Barefield, clarinet
and alto saxophone; Jack Washington, alto and
baritone saxophone; Ben Webster, tenor saxo-
phone; Count Basie, piano; Leroy Berry, guitar;
Walter Page, bass; Willie McWashington, drums.
Pub. unknown.   3:26

s2/2   *Blues of Avalon* (Anon., C). Boots and His
Buddies: Charles Anderson, G. H. Jones, Percy
Bush, and L. D. Harris, trumpets; George
Corley, trombone; Alva (or Alvin) Brooks and
Artie Hampton, alto saxophones; Baker Millian
and David Ellis, tenor saxophones; A. J.
Johnson, piano; Jeff Thomas, guitar; Walter
McHenry, bass; Boots Douglas, drums.
Pub. unknown.   3:25

217 (continued)

s2/3   *Sensational Mood* (Henri Woode, Reuben
Floyd, C). Hunter's Serenaders: Lloyd Hunter,
Reuben Floyd, and George Lott or Ted Frank,
trumpets; Elmer Crumbley or Joe Edwards,
trombone; Horace "Noble" Floyd and Archie
Watts, alto saxophone; Harold Arnold or Dick
Lewis, tenor saxophone; George Madison,
piano; Herbert Hannas (or Hannah), banjo;
Robert Welch (or Welsh) or Wallace Wright,
bass; Pete Woods or Jo Jones, drums. Southern
Music Publishing, pub.   3:14

s2/4   *Original Dixieland One-Step* (J. Russell
Robinson, George Crandall, D. J. (Nick)
La Rocca, Joe Jordan, C). Grant Moore and
His New Orleans Black Devils: Robert Russell
and Ellis Whitlock, Sylvester Friel, or Bill
Martin, trumpets; Elmer Crumbley and Thomas
Howard, trombones; Earl Keith and Grant
Moore, alto saxophones; Willard Brown, tenor
saxophone; J. Norman Ebron, piano; Harold
Robbins, banjo; Lawrence Williams, tuba;
Harold Flood (or Floyd) or Jo Jones, drums.
Edward B. Marks Music, pub.   2:40

s2/5   *Atlanta Low Down* (Henry Mason, C).
J. Neal Montgomery and His Orchestra:
Henry Mason and Karl Burns, trumpets;
unidentified, trombone; George Derigotte and
(unknown) Puckett, clarinets and alto saxophones; (unknown) Brown, clarinet and tenor
saxophone; J. Neal Montgomery, piano;
unidentified, banjo; Jesse Wilcox, tuba; Ted
Gillum, drums. Pub. unknown.   3:03

s2/6   *Auburn Avenue Stomp* (Henry Mason, C). Same
group and recording data as the preceding.   3:00

s2/7   *West End Blues* (Joe Oliver and Clarence
Williams, C). Zach Whyte's Chocolate Beau
Brummels: Sy Oliver, Bubber Whyte, and
Henry Savage, trumpets; Floyd Brady, trom-
bone; Earl Tribble, "Snake" Richardson, and
Clarence Page, alto saxophones; Al Sears, tenor
and baritone saxophone; Herman Chittison,
piano; Zach Whyte, banjo; Montgomery
Morrison, tuba; William Benton, drums. MCA
Music, pub.   3:10

s2/8   *Good Feelin' Blues* (Anon., C). Same group as
the preceding, except Fred Jackson, tenor
saxophone, and Charlie Anderson, banjo.
Pub. unknown.   2:54

218 Chamber Works by Arthur Shepherd, Henry Cowell, Roy Harris

LP
1842

Notes by Bruce Archibald. Producer: Elizabeth A. Ostrow. Cover art: Jack Levine, *Quartette*.

s1/1-3   *Three Variations on a Theme* (String Quartet No. 2) (Roy Harris, C). The Emerson String Quartet: Eugene Drucker, violin; Philip Setzer, violin; Masao Kawasaki, viola; Eric Wilson, cello. G. Schirmer, pub.

Variation I	5:42
Variation II	5:09
Variation III	7:22

s2/1   *Quartet Euphometric* (Henry Cowell, C). The Emerson String Quartet. C. F. Peters, pub.   1:55

s2/2-4   *Triptych, for High Voice and String Quartet* (Arthur Shepherd, C; Rabindranath Tagore, L). The Emerson String Quartet; Betsy Norden, soprano. Theodore Presser, pub.

He It Is	6:08
The Day Is No More	4:27
Light, My Light	3:53

219 Choral Works by Randall Thompson, Elliott Carter, Seymour Shifrin

LP
1880

Notes by Robert Morgan. Producer: Andrew Raeburn. Cover art: Richard Smith, *Soft Pack*. On all selections: The University of Michigan Chamber Choir, Members of the University of Michigan Symphony Orchestra, Thomas Hilbish, conductor.

s1/1-5   *Americana* (Randall Thompson, C; texts from *American Mercury*). E. C. Schirmer, pub.

May Every Tongue	:53
The Staff Necromancer	5:08
God's Bottles	1:44
The Sublime Process of Law Enforcement	7:02
Loveli-Lines	3:14

s1/6   *To Music* (Elliott Carter, C; Robert Herrick, L). Peer International, pub.   9:01

s2/1-2   *The Odes of Shang* (Seymour Shifrin, C; Ezra Pound, L). C. F. Peters, pub.

Part I	7:18
Part II	10:20

220 *Angels' Visits*: and Other Vocal Gems of Victorian
LP **America**
1691

Notes by Richard Jackson. Producer: Andrew Raeburn.
Cover art: Daniel Huntington, *Mercy's Dream*.

s1/1	*Sweet By and By* (J. P. Webster, C; S. F. Bennett, L). The Harmoneion Singers; Lawrence Skrobacs, piano.	3:37
s1/2	*Willie's Grave* (J. P. Webster, C; H. D. Webster, L). Raymond Murcell, baritone; The Harmoneion Singers; Lawrence Skrobacs, piano.	4:36
s1/3	*We are Happy Now, Dear Mother* (I. B. Woodbury, C/L). The Harmoneion Singers; Lawrence Skrobacs, piano.	2:27
s1/4	*Flee as a Bird* (Anon.). Rose Taylor, mezzo-soprano; Lawrence Skrobacs, piano.	3:10
s1/5	*Shall We Know Each Other There?* (Rev. R. Lowry, C/L). Jacqueline Pierce, soprano; Rose Taylor, mezzo-soprano; The Harmoneion Singers; Lawrence Skrobacs, piano.	4:11
s1/6	*Trusting* (C. A. White, C/L). Kathleen Battle, soprano; Curtis Rayam, tenor; Lawrence Skrobacs, piano.	4:07
s1/7	*Rock of Ages* (Dudley Buck, C; A. M. Toplady, L). Maeretha Stewart, soprano; The Harmoneion Singers; Lawrence Skrobacs, harmonium.	3:55
s2/1	*Angels' Visits* (Claude Melnotte, pseud. of Charles Kunkel, C; Charles Spooner, L). Kathleen Battle, soprano; Lawrence Skrobacs, piano.	4:18
s2/2	*Oh, You Must Be a Lover of the Lord* (J. N. S., C; Isaac Watts, L). Howard Crook, tenor; Raymond Murcell, baritone; The Harmoneion Singers; Lawrence Skrobacs, piano.	3:08
s2/3	*Put My Little Shoes Away* (Charles E. Pratt, C; S. N. Mitchell, L). Rose Taylor, mezzo-soprano; The Harmoneion Singers; Lawrence Skrobacs, piano.	5:16
s2/4	*I Love To Tell the Story* (William G. Fischer, C; Kate Hankey, L). Rose Taylor, mezzo-soprano; Raymond Murcell, baritone; The Harmoneion Singers; Lawrence Skrobacs, piano.	3:21

220 (continued)

s2/5   *The Last Hymn* (J. W. Hicks, C; Marianne
Farningham, pseud. of Marianne Hearn, L).
Rose Taylor, mezzo-soprano; Raymond
Murcell, baritone; The Harmoneion Singers;
Lawrence Skrobacs, harmonium.   7:57

s2/6   *The Babe of Bethlehem* (Rev. J. W. Dadmun,
C/L). The Harmoneion Singers; Lawrence
Skrobacs, piano.   3:08

221 *I Wants to Be a Actor Lady*: and Other Hits from Early Musical Comedies

LP
1911

Notes by Deane L. Root and Stanley Green. Producer:
Andrew Raeburn. Cover art: Everett Shinn, *Revue*. On
all selections: Cincinnati's University Singers and
Theater Orchestra, Earl Rivers, director; Ron Byrnside,
orchestrator.

s1/1   *Amazon's March*, from *The Black Crook*
(Guiseppe Operti, C).   2:45

s1/2   *The Yankee Doodle Boy*, from *Little Johnny
Jones* (George M. Cohan, C/L). Richard
Perry, vocal.   2:30

s1/3   *My Heart*, from *Evangeline* (Edward E. Rice,
C; J. C. Goodwin, L). Carol Sweeney-Sparrow,
vocal.   1:53

s1/4   *Buckets of Gore*, from *The Corsair* (John
Braham, C; Henry E. Dixey, L). Philip Yutzy,
vocal.   2:31

s1/5   *I Wants to Be a Actor Lady*, from *In Dahomey*
(Harry Von Tilzer, C; Vincent Bryan, L).
Renée Crutcher, vocal.   2:19

s1/6   *The Heidelberg Stein Song*, from *The Prince
of Pilsen* (Gustav Luders, C; Frank Pixley, L).
Ronald Campbell, vocal.   3:14

s1/7   *How'd You Like to Spoon with Me?*, from
The Earl and the Girl (Jerome Kern, C;
Edward Laska, L). Kim Criswell and Joel
Imbody, vocals.   2:25

s1/8   *May Irwin's "Bully" Song*, from *The Widow
Jones* (Charles E. Trevathan, C). Teresa
Bowers, vocal.   4:00

221 (continued)

s2/1	*Sex Against Sex*, from *The Passing Show* (Ludwig Englander, C; Sydney Rosenfeld, L). Carol Sweeney-Sparrow and Michael van Engen, vocals.	3:03
s2/2	*A Pretty Girl*, from *Wang* (Woolson Morse, C; J. Cheever Goodwin, L). Thomas Mariner, vocal.	2:22
s2/3	*Reuben and Cynthia*, from *A Trip to Chinatown* (Percy Gaunt, C; Charles H. Hoyt, L). Gina Ferraro and William Schaeffer, vocals.	1:24
s2/4	*The Broadway, Opera and Bowery Crawl*, from *The Black Crook* (Guiseppe Operti, C; Philip Stoner, L). Thomas Bankston, vocal.	3:04
s2/5	*Song of Brown October Ale*, from *Robin Hood* (Reginald De Koven, C; Harry B. Smith, L). Michael van Engen, vocal.	2:34
s2/6	*Lullaby*, from *Fritz, Our Cousin German* (Joseph K. Emmet, C; arr. Charlie Baker). Frank Kelley, vocal.	3:20
s2/7	*The Bowery*, from *A Trip to Chinatown* (Percy Gaunt, C; Charles H. Hoyt, L). Richard Perry, vocal.	2:57
s2/8	*I Can't Do the Sum*, from *Babes in Toyland* (Victor Herbert, C; Glen MacDonough, L). Kim Criswell, vocal.	3:21

222 *Praise the Lord and Pass the Ammunition*: Songs of World Wars I and II

LP 1879

Notes by Carl H. Scheele. Cover art: Samuel Greenburg, *For Freedom*.

s1/1	*When the Lusitania Went Down* (Nat Vincent, C; Charles McCarron, L). Herbert Stuart (Albert Wiederhold), vocal. Leo Feist, pub.	3:00
s1/2	*I Didn't Raise My Boy to Be a Soldier* (Al Piantadose, C; Alfred Bryan, L). Morton Harvey, vocal. Leo Feist, pub.	2:58
s1/3	*Let's All Be Americans Now* (Irving Berlin, George W. Meyer, C; Edgar Leslie, L). American Quartet, vocals. Irving Berlin Music, pub.	2:58
s1/4	*Over There* (George M. Cohan, C/L). Nora Bayes, vocal. Leo Feist, pub.	2:54

222 (continued)

s1/5   *Hello, Central! Give Me No Man's Land* (Jean
Schwartz, C; Sam M. Lewis, Joe Young, L).
Al Jolson, vocal. Mills Music, pub.   3:18

s1/6   *There's a Vacant Chair in Every Home Tonight*
(Ernest Breuer, C; Alfred Bryan, L). The
Shannon Four, vocals. Shawnee Press, pub.   2:52

s1/7   *I've Got My Captain Working for Me Now*
(Irving Berlin, C/L). Al Jolson, vocal. Irving
Berlin Music, pub.   2:41

s1/8   *My Dream of the Big Parade* (Jimmy McHugh,
C; Al Dubin, L). Peerless Quartet, vocals.
Mills Music, pub.   3:25

s2/1   *Der Fuehrer's Face* (Oliver Wallace, C).
Spike Jones and His City Slickers. Southern
Music, pub.   2:37

s2/2   *He's 1-A in the Army and He's A-1 in My
Heart* (Redd Evans, C). Betty Bonney, vocal;
Les Brown and His Orchestra. Redd Evans
Music, pub;   3:04

s2/3   *Stalin Wasn't Stallin'* (A Modern Spiritual)
(Willie Johnson, C). Golden Gate Quartet,
vocals. MCA Music, pub.   3:07

s2/4   *We Did It Before and We Can Do It Again*
(Cliff Friend, Charles Tobias, C). Dick
Robertson, vocal. Warner Bros. Music, pub.   2:24

s2/5   *I Left My Heart At the Stage Door Canteen*
(Irving Berlin, C/L). Kenny Baker, vocal.
Irving Berlin Music, pub.   2:38

s2/6   *Goodbye, Mama (I'm Off to Yokohama)*
(J. Fred Coots, C). Dick Robertson, vocal.
Chappell Music, pub.   2:36

s2/7   *No Love, No Nothin'* (Harry Warren, C; Leo
Robin, L). Patti Dugan, vocal; Johnny Long
and His Orchestra. Bregman, Vocco & Conn,
pub.   2:57

s2/8   *Praise the Lord and Pass the Ammunition*
(Frank Loesser, C). Glee Club, vocals; Kay
Kyser and His Orchestra. Famous Music, pub.   2:31

s2/9   *My Guy's Come Back* (Mel Powell, C; Ray
McKinley, L). Helen Forrest, vocal. Shapiro,
Bernstein, pub.   3:00

223 *I'm on My Journey Home*: Vocal Styles and Resources in Folk Music

LP
1917

Notes by Charles Wolfe. Cover art: Stow Wengenroth, *Untamed*.

s1/1	*Hollerin'*. Leonard Emanuel, vocal.	:30
	Whooping. "Red" Buck Estes, vocal.	2:23
	Eephing. Jimmie Riddle, vocal.	1:07
	Ringing the Pig. Lindy Clear, vocal effects.	:57
s1/2	*Spelling From the Old Blue-Back Speller*. Ben Rice, vocal.	:54
	Tobacco Auctioneering. Two unknown auctioneers, vocals.	3:16
s1/3	*Turkey in the Straw*. Neil Morris, dance calls; Charlie Everidge, mouthbow.	2:49
	Risselty Rosselty. Ray R. Denoon, vocal.	1:38
s1/4	*Bold McCarthy, or The City of Baltimore*. Bill Cramp, vocal.	3:17
	Sweet Wine. Mrs. Goldie Hamilton, vocal.	2:46
s1/5	*Barbara Allen*. I. N. (Nick) Marlor, vocal.	6:01
s1/6	*Late One Evening*. Barry Sutterfield, vocal.	3:30
s2/1	*Hanging Johnny*. Captain Leighton Robinson, lead vocal; Alex Barr, Arthur Brodeur, and Leighton McKenzie, vocals.	2:08
s2/2	*Bright and Morning Star*. Walter and Lola Caldwell, vocals and guitar.	3:53
s2/3	*The Black Sheep*. Darby and Tarlton: Tom Darby, vocal and guitar; Jimmie Tarlton, vocal and Hawaiian guitar.	3:09
s2/4	*Hey Hey, I'm Memphis Bound* (Alton and Rabon Delmore, C/L). The Delmore Brothers: Alton Delmore, vocal and guitar; Rabon Delmore, vocal and tenor guitar.	2:39
s2/5	*Don't Put Off Salvation Too Long*. Southland Ladies Quartette, vocals.	2:35
s2/6	*Been a Long Time Traveling Here Below*. Grandpa Isom Ritchie's church congregation, vocals.	2:18
s2/7	*I'm on My Journey Home*. The Denson Quartet, vocals.	3:19
s2/8	*I Am O'ershadowed by Love*. Members of the Stamps-Baxter School of Music, vocals.	2:55

224 *Brighten the Corner Where You Are*: Black and White
LP Urban Hymnody
1902

> Notes by Anthony Heilbut and Harry Eskew. Cover art:
> George Bellows, *Billy Sunday*.

s1/1   *God Shall Wipe All Tears Away* (Antonio
Haskell, C). The Kings of Harmony: Carey
Bradley, lead; Eugene "Pop" Strong, second
lead; Marion Thompson, tenor; Walter
Latimore, baritone; Bill Morgan, bass.   2:54

s1/2   *Canaan Land* (A. H. Windom, C). The Famous
Blue Jay Singers: Charlie Bridges, lead; Silas
Steele, second lead; Jimmy Veal, tenor; James
Hollingsworth, baritone; Dave Parnell, bass.   3:17

s1/3   *Walk Around* (R. H. Harris, C). The Soul
Stirrers, including R. H. Harris, lead; S. R.
Crain, tenor; Mozelle Franklin, baritone;
Reverend Rundless, baritone; J. J. Farley, bass.   2:51

s1/4   *Tree of Level* (traditional). The Fairfield Four:
Sam McCrary, tenor; Edward Thomas, second
tenor; Willie Lewis, baritone; Dicky Freeman,
bass.   2:15

s1/5   *Yield Not to Temptation* (Horatio Palmer, C).
The Roberta Martin Singers: Delores Barrett,
lead; Roberta Martin, contralto and piano;
Norsalus McKissick, tenor; Eugene Smith and
Willie Webb, baritones.   3:00

s1/6   *Daniel in the Lion's Den (He Locked the
Lion's Jaw)* (traditional). Rosetta Tharpe,
vocal and guitar; Katie Bell Nubin, vocal;
Sammy Price, piano; Billy Taylor, Sr., string
bass; Herbert Cowans, drums.   2:42

s1/7   *Give Me Wings* (D. B. Hardy, C). Willie Mae
Ford Smith, vocal; Bertha Smith, piano;
Gwendolyn Cooper, organ.   2:36

s1/8   *They Led My Lord Away* (traditional).
Marion Williams, vocal.   2:03

s2/1   *We're Marching to Zion* (Robert Lowry, C;
Isaac Watts, L). Congregation of the Ridgecrest (N.C.) Baptist Conference Center.   3:19

s2/2   *Jesus Is All the World to Me* (Will L.
Thompson, C). Congregation of the Ridgecrest (N.C.) Baptist Conference Center.   3:10

s2/3   *The Ninety and Nine* (Ira D. Sankey, C;
Elizabeth C. Clephane, L). George Beverly
Shea, vocal; Ira Sankey, reed organ.   2:47

224 (continued)

s2/4   *To God Be the Glory* (William Howard Doane, C; Fanny Jane Crosby, L). Billy Graham London Crusade Choir.   2:13

s2/5   *Brighten the Corner Where You Are* (Charles H. Gabriel, C; Ina Duley Ogdon, L). Homer Rodeheaver, vocal, and brass band. Rodeheaver Co., pub.   3:04

s2/6   *In the Garden* (C. Austin Miles, C). Mrs. William Asher and Homer Rodeheaver, vocals. Rodeheaver Co., pub.   3:16

s2/7   *Nearer, My God, To Thee ("Bethany")* (Lowell Mason, C; Sarah Flower Adams, L). Oscar Seagle and unidentified quartet, vocals.   2:58

s2/8   *Saved by Grace* (George Coles Stebbins, C; Fanny Jane Crosby, L). Gipsy Smith, vocal.   3:42

s2/9   *Just as I Am, Without One Plea ("Woodworth")* (William B. Bradbury, C; Charlotte Elliott, L). Billy Graham Australian Crusade Choir.   3:06

225 *Hills and Home*: Thirty Years of Bluegrass

LP
1669

Notes by Neil V. Rosenberg. Producer: William Ivey. Cover art: Edward Hopper, *The Railroad*.

s1/1   *Why Did You Wander?* (L. Flatt, B. Monroe, C). Bill Monroe and His Blue Grass Boys: Lester Flatt, lead vocal and guitar; Bill Monroe, tenor vocal and mandolin; Earl Scruggs, banjo; Chubby Wise, fiddle; Howard Watts ("Cedric Rainwater"), bass.   2:31

s1/2   *Blue Ridge Cabin Home* (Louise Certain, Gladys Stacey, C). Lester Flatt, Earl Scruggs, and the Foggy Mountain Boys: Lester Flatt, lead vocal and guitar; Curley Seckler, tenor vocal and mandolin; Earl Scruggs, banjo; Paul Warren, fiddle; Buck ("Uncle Josh") Graves, dobro; Jake Tullock, bass. Golden West Melodies, pub.   2:53

s1/3   *Daniel Prayed* (G. T. Speer, C). The Stanley Brothers and the Clinch Mountain Boys: Carter Stanley, lead vocal and rhythm guitar; Bill Napier (?), baritone vocal and mandolin; Ralph Stanley, tenor vocal and banjo; Al Eliot, bass; Ralph Mayo (?), bass vocal. La-Car Publishing, pub.   2:24

225 (continued)

s1/4 *Love Please Come Home* (Leon Jackson, C).
Don Reno, Red Smiley, and the Tennessee Cut
Ups: Red Smiley, lead vocal and guitar; Ronnie
Reno, mandolin; Don Reno, tenor vocal and
banjo; Mac Magaha, fiddle; John Palmer, bass.
Fort Knox Music, pub. 2:15

s1/5 *You'd Better Wake Up* (J. Eanes, C). Mac
Wiseman and the Country Boys: Mac Wiseman,
lead vocal and guitar; Kenneth Burns (?),
mandolin; Ed Amos (?), banjo; unidentified
fiddles and bass. Austin Division of Atlantic
Music, pub. 2:28

s1/6 *Your Old Standby* (J. Eanes, W. Perry, C).
Jim Eanes and the Shenandoah Valley Boys:
Jim Eanes, lead vocal and guitar; Arnold Terry,
baritone and vocal and "sock" rhythm guitar;
Allen Shelton, banjo; Roy Russell, tenor vocal
and fiddle; unidentified bass. Stone Age
Publishers, pub. 2:22

s1/7 *Twenty-One Years* (Bob Miller, C). The Lonesome Pine Fiddlers: Paul Williams, vocal and
guitar; Rex Parker, mandolin; Ray Goins,
banjo; Curley Ray Cline, fiddle; Ezra Cline,
vocal and bass. MCA Music, pub. 2:22

s1/8 *Springhill Disaster* (M. Ruddick, B. Clifton,
P. Clayton, C. G. Pembroke, C). Bill Clifton
and the Dixie Mountain Boys: Bill Clifton,
lead vocal and lead guitar; Jimmy Self,
baritone vocal and rhythm guitar; Johnny
Clark, tenor vocal and banjo; Tommy Jackson
and Tommy Vaden, fiddles; Joe Zinkan, bass.
Fort Knox Music, pub. 3:00

s1/9 *Old Age* (Dave Woolum, C). Dave Woolum
and His Kentucky Mountain Boys: Dave
Woolum, vocal and guitar; Lillie Dennis, guitar;
Marvin Igo, electric guitar; Curtis Allen and
Noah Crase, banjos; Markum, fiddle; Oscar
Woolum, bass. Pub. unknown. 2:24

s2/1 *Blackberry Blossom* (traditional). Billy Baker
[and Band]: Del McCoury, guitar; Buzz Busby,
mandolin; Bill Keith, banjo; Billy Baker, fiddle;
Jerry McCoury, bass. Pub. unknown. 2:24

225 (continued)

s2/2   *Hold Whatcha Got* (Jimmy Martin, C). Jimmy
Martin and the Sunny Mountain Boys: Jimmy
Martin, lead vocal and guitar; Paul Williams,
tenor vocal and mandolin; J. D. Crowe, banjo;
Chubby Wise, fiddle; Lightnin' Chance, bass.
Pub. unknown.   2:23

s2/3   *Diesel Train* (Jim McReynolds, Jesse
McReynolds, C). Jim and Jesse and the
Virginia Boys: Jim McReynolds, tenor vocal
and guitar; Jesse McReynolds, lead vocal and
mandolin; Allen Shelton, banjo; Vassar
Clements, fiddle; Don McHan, baritone vocal
and bass. Cedarwood Publishing, pub.   2:33

s2/4   *A Pathway of Teardrops* (Wayne P. Walker,
Webb Pierce, C). The Osborne Brothers;
Benny Birchfield, low tenor vocal and guitar;
Ray Eddington, guitar; Bobby Osborne, high
lead vocal and mandolin; Sonny Osborne,
baritone vocal and banjo; Lightnin' Chance,
bass, Willie Ackerman, drums. Cedarwood
Publishing, pub.   2:53

s2/5   *Hills and Home* (John Duffey, C). The
Country Gentlemen: Charlie Waller, lead vocal
and guitar; John Duffey, tenor vocal and
mandolin; Eddie Adcock, baritone vocal and
banjo; Jim Cox, bass. Fort Knox Music, pub.   2:24

s2/6   *Raise a Ruckus Tonight* (traditional). The
Lonesome River Valley Boys: John Kaparakis,
tenor vocal and guitar; Jack Tottle, lead vocal
and mandolin; Rick Churchill, baritone vocal
and banjo; James Buchanan, fiddle; Dick
Stowe, bass. Pub. unknown.   1:53

s2/7   *Fox on the Run* (Tony Hazzard, C). Emerson
and Waldron: Cliff Waldron, lead vocal and
guitar; Bill Emerson, tenor vocal and banjo;
Bill Poffinberger, fiddle; Mike Auldrich,
baritone vocal and dobro; Ed Ferris, bass.
Dick James Music, pub.   2:31

s2/8   *Body and Soul* (Virginia Stauffer, C). The
Newgrass Revival: Curtis Burch, vocal, guitar,
and dobro; Sam Bush, vocal and mandolin;
Cortney Johnson, vocal and banjo; Ebo
Walker, vocal and bass. Pub. unknown.   3:53

s2/9   *Dill Pickles Rag* (traditional). Bluegrass All-
Stars: Ray Edenten, guitar; Jesse McReynolds,
mandolin; Bobby Thompson, banjo; Benny
Martin, fiddle; Lloyd Green, dobro; Bob
Moore, bass. Pub. unknown.   2:09

226 *That's My Rabbit, My Dog Caught It*: Traditional
LP Southern Instrumental Styles
1910

Notes by Mark Wilson. Cover art: George Joseph Mess,
Living Better Without.

s1/1	*Groundhog.* Marion Reese, fife.	1:23
s1/2	*The Old Gray Horse.* Obed Pickard, jew's-harp.	3:15
s1/3	*My Pretty Little Pink.* I. D. Stamper, vocal and dulcimer.	1:38
s1/4	*Granny Went to Meeting with Her Old Shoes On.* Mr. and Mrs. Vernon Judd, banjos; Mrs. Judd, vocal.	:58
s1/5	*Spanish Fandango.* Pete Steele, banjo.	1:32
s1/6	*Run, Banjo.* Justis Begley, banjo.	1:30
s1/7	*Pearly Dew.* Lena Hughes, guitar.	2:09
s1/8	*Blues.* Hobart Smith, guitar.	2:53
s1/9	*Lights in the Valley.* Neriah and Kenneth Benfield, autoharps.	1:28
s1/10	*Lost Boy Blues.* Palmer McAbee, harmonica.	3:19
s1/11	*Fe Fe Ponchaux.* Joseph Falcon, accordion; Cleoma Breaux, guitar.	3:20
s1/12	*Kimball House.* Ezra "Ted" Hawkins, mandolin; Riley Puckett, guitar.	2:44
s2/1	*The Last of Sizemore.* Luther Strong, fiddle.	1:38
s2/2	*Hunky Dory.* Alva Greene, fiddle; Francis Gillum, straws.	:52
s2/3	*Bigfooted Nigger.* The Helton Brothers, fiddle and banjo.	2:01
s2/4	*That's My Rabbit, My Dog Caught It.* The Walter Family: Draper Walter, fiddle; jug, piano, guitar, washboard.	3:29
s2/5	*Rymer's Favorite.* Allen Sisson, fiddle; Jacob Burckhart, piano.	3:38
s2/6	*Le Rille Cajun.* Dennis McGee and Ernest Fruge, fiddles.	3:03
s2/7	*Lost Indian.* Louis H. Propps, fiddle; guitar.	1:43
s2/8	*Peacock Rag.* Arthur Smith and His Dixie-liners: Arthur Smith, fiddle; Alton and Rabon Delmore, guitars; bass.	2:36
s2/9	*Bibb County Hoedown.* Seven Foot Dilly and His Dill Pickles: A. A. Gray (?), fiddle; John Silleshaw, guitar; second fiddle, second guitar, washtub bass, banjo.	3:13
s2/10	*Jig.* Bill Boyd and His Cowboy Ramblers: Carroll Hubbard and Kenneth Pitts, fiddles; John "Knocky" Parker, piano; Marvin Montgomery, banjo; Bill Boyd and Curley Perrin, guitars; John Boyd, steel guitar; Jim Boyd, bass; clarinet, accordion.	2:18

227 The Mighty Wurlitzer: Music for Movie-Palace Organs

LP
1745

Notes by Warren Susman and Michael Moore. Producer: Michael Moore. Cover art: Joseph Stella, *Battle of Lights, Coney Island*. On all selections on Side 1: Ann Leaf, organ. On all selections on Side 2: Gaylord Carter, organ.

s1/1	*Strike Up the Band* (George Gershwin, C; Ira Gershwin, L). New World Music, pub.	1:57
s1/2	*You Do Something to Me*, from *Fifty Million Frenchmen* (Cole Porter, C/L). Harms, pub.	2:27
s1/3	*The Son of the Sheik* (arr. by Ann Leaf).	6:43
s1/4	*You Were Meant for Me*, from *The Broadway Melody* (Nacio Herb Brown, C; Arthur Freed, L). Robbins Music, pub.	2:49
s1/5	*Orphans of the Storm* (Louis F. Gottschalk, C; arr. by Ann Leaf).	7:33
s2/1	*Jeannine, I Dream of Lilac Time*, from *Lilac Time* (Nathaniel Shilkret, C; L. Wolfe Gilbert, L). Leo Feist, pub.	2:04
s2/2	*For Heaven's Sake* (arr. by Gaylord Carter). Fred Fisher Music/Robbins Music, pub.	5:04
s2/3	*My Romance*, from *Jumbo* (Richard Rogers, C; Lorenz Hart, L). T. B. Harms, pub.	1:58
s2/4	*Great Day* (Vincent Youmans, C; Billy Rose, Edward Eliscu, L). Miller Music/Anne-Rachel Music, pub.	1:24
s2/5	*Charmaine*, from *What Price Glory?* (Lew Pollack, Erno Rapee, C/L). Miller Music, pub.	2:10
s2/6	*Intolerance* (arr. by Gaylord Carter).	3:57
s2/7	*The Phantom of the Opera* (arr. by Gaylord Carter).	6:58

228 John Alden Carpenter, Henry F. Gilbert, Adolph Weiss, and John Powell

LP
1878

Notes by David Baker and R. D. Darrell. Producer: Andrew Raeburn. Cover art: Morgan Russell, *Abstraction*. On all selections: The Los Angeles Philharmonic Orchestra.

s1/1	*Krazy Kat* (John Alden Carpenter, C). Calvin Simmons, conductor. G. Schirmer, pub.	12:52
s1/2	*The Dance in Place Congo* (Henry F. Gilbert, C). Calvin Simmons, conductor. Belwin-Mills, pub.	11:23

228 (continued)

s2/1   *American Life* (Adolph Weiss, C). Lawrence
Foster, conductor. Copyright held by Weiss
estate.   5:07

s2/2   *Rhapsodie Nègre* (John Powell, C). Calvin
Simmons, conductor; Zita Carno, piano.
G. Schirmer, pub.   16:19

229   Songs of Samuel Barber and Ned Rorem

LP
1899

Notes by Phillip Ramey. Cover art: Leo Katz, *Pegasus*.
All selections on Side 2 accompanied by Ned Rorem.

s1/1   *Dover Beach*, Op. 3 (Samuel Barber, C;
Matthew Arnold, L). Samuel Barber, baritone; Curtis String Quartet: Jascha Brodsky,
violin; Charles Jaffe, violin; Max Aronoff,
viola; Orlando Cole, cello. G. Schirmer, pub.   7:48

s1/2-6   *Melodies Passagères*, Op. 27 (Samuel Barber,
C; Rainer Marie Rilke, L). Pierre Bernac,
baritone; Francis Poulenc, piano.
G. Schirmer, pub.
      Puisque tout passe   1:16
      Un Cygne   2:16
      Tombeau dans un parc   1:40
      Le Clocher chante   1:19
      Départ   1:39

s2/1   *Early in the Morning* (Ned Rorem, C;
Robert Hillyer, L). Donald Gramm, baritone.
Henmar Press, pub.   1:45

s2/2   *I am Rose* (Ned Rorem, C; Gertrude Stein,
L). Regina Sarfaty, mezzo-soprano. Henmar
Press, pub.   :17

s2/3   *To You* (Ned Rorem, C; Walt Whitman, L).
Donald Gramm, baritone. Elkan-Vogel, pub.   :36

s2/4   *Pippa's Song* (Ned Rorem, C; Robert
Browning, L). Gianna d'Angelo, soprano.
Henmar Press, pub.   1:53

s2/5   *Spring* (Ned Rorem, C; Gerard Manley
Hopkins, L). Phyllis Curtin, soprano.
Boosey & Hawkes, pub.   1:49

s2/6   *Spring and Fall* (Ned Rorem, C; Gerard
Manley Hopkins, L). Donald Gramm,
baritone. Mercury Music, pub.   1:53

229 (continued)

s2/7   Two songs from *Flight for Heaven* (Ned
        Rorem, C; Robert Herrick, L). Donald
        Gramm, baritone. Mercury Music, pub.
           Upon Julia's Clothes   :41
           To the Willow Tree   2:02

s2/8   *Lullaby of the Woman of the Mountain*
        (Ned Rorem, C; Padraic Pearse, L). Charles
        Bressler, tenor. Boosey & Hawkes, pub.   2:00

s2/9   *Snake* (Ned Rorem, C; Theodore Roethke, L).
        Gianna d'Angelo, soprano. Henmar Press, pub.   :51

s2/10   *Root Cellar* (Ned Rorem, C; Theodore
        Roethke, L). Donald Gramm, baritone.
        Henmar Press, pub.   2:08

s2/11   *My Papa's Waltz* (Ned Rorem, C; Theodore
        Roethke, L). Donald Gramm, baritone.
        Henmar Press, pub.   1:21

230 The Flowering of Vocal Music in America: Vol. 1
LP (Music of The Moravians and Heinrich)
1949–
1950

Notes by Edward A. Berlin. Produced by Elizabeth
Ostrow and Andrew Raeburn. Cover art: John Valentine
Haidt, *The First Fruits*. On all selections on Side 1: The
New World String Orchestra: Regis Iandiorio, first violin;
Ariana Bronne, William Henry, Benjamin Hudson,
Robert Rozek, Katsuko Esaki, Robin Bushman, violins;
Hugh Loughran, Janet Lyman Hill, Daniel Avshalomov,
violas; Lawrence Lenske, cello, John Vincent Carbone,
bass; Andrew Raeburn, conductor; Leonard Raver, organ.

s1/1   *Meine Seele erhebet dem Herrn* (Jeremiah
        Dencke, C). Cynthia Clarey, soprano. C. F.
        Peters, pub.   1:26

s1/2   *Mein Heiland geht ins Leiden* (Georg Gottfried
        Müller, C). Charles Bressler, tenor. C. F.
        Peters, pub.   4:05

s1/3   *Ich bin in meinem Geiste* (David Moritz
        Michael, C). Barbara Wallace, soprano.
        Boosey & Hawkes, pub.   3:03

s1/4   *Leite mich in Deiner Wahrheit* (Johann
        Friedrich Peter, C). Charles Bressler, tenor.
        C. F. Peters, pub.   2:23

s1/5   *Gehet in dem Geruch Seines Bräutigams-
        Namens* (Jeremiah Dencke, C). Barbara
        Wallace, soprano. C. F. Peters, pub.   3:45

230 (continued)

s1/6 *Abide in Me* (Johannes Herbst, C). Barbara
      Wallace, soprano. Boosey & Hawkes, pub.   2:59
s1/7 *See Him* (Johannes Herbst, C). Cynthia
      Clarey, soprano. Boosey & Hawkes, pub.   3:05
s1/8 *And Thou Shalt Know It* (Johannes Herbst,
      C). Charles Bressler, tenor. Boosey &
      Hawkes, pub.   3:07

s2/1 *How Greatly Doth My Soul Rejoice*
      (Johannes Herbst, C). Cynthia Clarey,
      soprano; Harriet Wingreen, piano. Moravian
      College, pub.   1:38
s2/2 *Thanks Be to Thee* (Johannes Herbst, C).
      Charles Bressler, tenor; Harriet Wingreen,
      piano. Moravian College, pub.   2:07
s2/3 *Philanthropy* (Anthony Philip Heinrich, C).
      Barbara Wallace, soprano; Evelyn Petros,
      mezzo-soprano; D'Anna Fortunato, mezzo-
      soprano; Richard Anderson, baritone;
      Joseph McKee, bass; Harriet Wingreen,
      piano; Andrew Raeburn, conductor.
      A-R Editions, pub.   17:12

**231 The Flowering of Vocal Music in America: Vol. 2
      (Music of Benjamin Carr, Oliver Shaw, George K.
      Jackson)**

LP
1950

      Notes by William Brooks. Producers: Andrew Raeburn,
      Elizabeth Ostrow. Cover art: Benjamin Tanner after
      John J. Barralet, *America Guided by Wisdom*.

s1/1-4 *The Lady of the Lake* (Benjamin Carr, C; Sir
        Walter Scott, L).
            Mary. Charles Bressler, tenor; Harriet
            Wingreen, fortepiano.   4:39
            Soldier, Rest. Cynthia Clarey, soprano;
            Harriet Wingreen, fortepiano.   3:10
            Hymn to the Virgin. Cynthia Clarey,
            soprano; Cynthia Otis, harp.   9:12
            Blanche of Devan. Barbara Wallace,
            soprano; Cynthia Otis, harp.   2:45

s2/1-2 *Alice Brand*. Cynthia Clarey, soprano;
        Charles Bressler, tenor; Richard Anderson,
        baritone; Harriet Wingreen, fortepiano.   8:53
        Coronach. Barbara Wallace, soprano;
        Harriet Wingreen, fortepiano.   3:43

231 (continued)

s2/3   *There's Nothing True But Heav'n* (Oliver
Shaw, C; Thomas Moore, L). Susan Belling,
soprano; Harriet Wingreen, fortepiano.   5:12

s2/4   *The Dying Christian to His Soul* (George K.
Jackson, C; Alexander Pope, L). Susan
Belling, soprano; Debra Vanderlinde, soprano;
James Tyeska, baritone; Regis Iandiorio,
violin; Harriet Wingreen, fortepiano.   7:02

232 **John Bray: *The Indian Princess* or *La Belle Sauvage*.
Raynor Taylor: *The Ethiop* or *The Child of the Desert***

LP
1951

Notes by Victor Fell Yellin. Producer of *The Indian
Princess*: Andrew Raeburn. Producer of *The Ethiop*: Max
Wilcox. Cover art: W. Strickland, Title-page design to
first edition of *The Ethiop*. The Federal Music Society
Opera Company, John Baldon, conductor; Alan G.
Moore, chorus-master.

The Indian Princess or *La Belle Sauvage* (John
Bray, C; J. N. Barker, L).

s1/1   *Chorus*. Judith Otten and chorus.   2:07
        Song: *Ever, Ever Cheery!* Judith Otten.   2:42

s1/2   Song: *Och! Hubbaboo! Gramachree! Hone!*
Joseph Porrello.   1:43
        Dialogue Quartetto. Richard Anderson,
Judith Otten, John Mack Ousley, Joseph
Porrello.   1:28
        Finale to the First Act. Chorus.   2:48

s1/3   *Incidental Music to Act II, Scene 2*.   2:40
        Song: *Fair Geraldine*. Michael Best.   3:12
        Glee: *Without a Penny of Money*. Joseph
Porrello, Richard Anderson, John Mack
Ousley.   1:19

s1/4   Song: *When the Midnight of Absence*.
Susan Belling.   4:31
        Song: *Careless Ned*. Debra Vanderlinde.   2:17

s1/5   Song: *Captain Smith*. John Mack Ousley.   2:35
        Finale. Soloists and chorus.   1:42

The Ethiop or *The Child of the Desert* (Raynor
Taylor, C; William Dimond, Jr., L; musical and
orchestral restoration by V. F. Yellin).

s2/1   *Overture*.   6:02
        Symphony: *While Cephania Comes on in
Her Barge*.   1:31

232 (continued)

	Chorus: *Queen of the East*.	:57
	Air: *The Camel's Bell*. Debra Vanderlinde.	1:27
	Trio: *Mighty Man! If I Surrender*. Debra Vanderlinde, R. Sebastian Russ, Charles Long.	2:05
	Duet: *How Boon Are the Hours*. Debra Vanderlinde, Charles Long.	1:09
s2/2	Chorus: *The Bezestein*.	1:02
	Musical Colloquy. R. Sebastian Russ, Charles Long, Debra Vanderlinde, and Chorus.	2:12
	Subterranean Chorus.	1:18
	Chorus: *Address of Conspirators to Orasmyn*.	1:09
	Accompanied Recitative: *Nourreddin at the Top of the Catacomb*. Charles Long.	:57
	Chorus: *Solo, Semi-Chorus, and Chorus of Conspirators*.	2:20
s2/3	*Pas Seul*. Orchestra.	3:39
	Song: *Corner Houses*. Charles Long.	1:08
	Air: *These Keys Can a Treasure Unfold*. Debra Vanderlinde.	1:39
	Finale. Chorus.	:36

233 *Come Josephine in My Flying Machine*: Inventions
$\frac{LP}{1746}$ and Topics in Popular Songs 1910–1929

Notes by Carl H. Scheele. Cover art: Joseph Pennell, *Hydroplanes at Rest*

s1/1	*Oceana Roll* (Lucien Denni, C; Roger Lewis, L). Eddie Morton, vocal. Jerry Vogel Music, pub.	2:46
s1/2	*The Girl on the Magazine Cover* (Irving Berlin, C/L). Harry Macdonough, vocal. Irving Berlin Music, pub.	3:17
s1/3	*He'd Have to Get Under, Get Out and Get Under (to Fix Up His Automobile)* (Maurice Abrahams, C; Grant Clarke, Edgar Leslie, L). Will Halley, vocal. Robbins Music, pub.	3:13
s1/4	*On the 5:15* (Henry I. Marshall, C; Stanley Murphy, L). American Quartet, vocals. Warner Bros. Music, pub.	2:49
s1/5	*Hello, Frisco* (Louis A. Hirsch, C; Gene Buck, L). Elida Morris and Sam Ash, vocals. Warner Bros. Music, pub.	3:02

233 (continued)

s1/6   *Come, Josephine, in My Flying Machine* (Fred Fisher, C; Alfred Bryan, L). Blanche Ring, vocal. Shapiro, Bernstein, pub.   2:37

s1/7   *Everybody Wants a Key to My Cellar* (Lew Pollack, C; Ed Rose, Billy Baskette, L). Bert Williams, vocal. Pub. unknown.   2:41

s1/8   *Take Your Girlie to the Movies* (Pete Wendling, C; Edgar Leslie, Bert Kalmar, L). Bill Murray, vocal. Mills Music/Edgar Leslie, pub.   2:36

s2/1   *The Argentines, the Portuguese and the Greeks* (Carey Morgan, Arthur M. Swanstrom, C). Nora Bayes, vocal. Edward B. Marks Music, pub.   2:57

s2/2   *Mr. Radio Man (Tell My Mammy to Come Back Home)* (Cliff Friend, C; Johnny White, L). Al Jolson, vocal; Isham Jones and His Orchestra. Leo Feist, pub.   3:13

s2/3   *Alabamy Bound* (Ray Henderson, C; G. B. DeSylva, Bud Green, L). Blossom Seeley, vocal. Shapiro, Bernstein/Anne-Rachel Music, pub.   2:48

s2/4   *All Alone* (Irving Berlin, C/L). Lewis James, vocal. Irving Berlin Music, pub.   3:06

s2/5   *The Little White House (At the End of Honeymoon Lane)* (James F. Hanley, C; Eddie Dowling, pseud. of Joseph Nelson Goucher, L). Frank Harris (pseud. of Irving Kaufman), vocal. Howard Lanin and His Orchestra. Shapiro, Bernstein, pub.   2:56

s2/6   *Lindbergh (The Eagle of the U.S.A.)* (Howard Johnson, Al Sherman, C). Vernon Dalhart, vocal. Shapiro, Bernstein, pub.   3:22

s2/7   *Henry's Made a Lady out of Lizzie* (Walter O'Keefe, C). The Happiness Boys, vocals. Chappell, pub.   3:02

s2/8   *If I Had a Talking Picture of You* (Ray Henderson, C; B. G. DeSylva, Lew Brown, L). Belle Baker, vocal. Chappell/Anne-Rachel Music, pub.   3:08

234 George F. Root: *The Haymakers*: An Operatic
Cantata, Part the Second

LP
1907

Notes by Dena J. Epstein and George F. Root. Producer:
Andrew Raeburn. Cover art: William Sidney Mount,
Farmers Nooning (or *The Haymakers*). On all selections:
North Texas State University Grand Chorus; Frank
McKinley, conductor; Erma Rose, piano.

s1/1   Full Chorus: *Good Morning*
Recitative: *How Pleasant Are Those Cheerful
Words*. Mark Myers, tenor.
Song: *Blithely Go We Forth*. Mark Myers,
tenor.
Chorus and Echo: *Light Hearted Are We*
Chorus: *How Like Some Tented Camp*
Recitative: *Joy!* Linda Brannon, mezzo-
soprano.
Song: *Scenes of Happiness*. Linda Brannon,
mezzo-soprano.
Recitative: *The Dew Now Is Off*. Gary
Petersen, bass.
Semi-Chorus. *Toss It Hither*
Double Semi-Chorus: *Hark to the Cheerful
Sound*
Quintette: *How Good Is He, the Giver*.
Carolyn Finley, soprano; Linda Brannon,
mezzo-soprano; Mark Myers, tenor; Chris
Hodges, baritone; Burr Phillips, bass   15:10

s1/2   Chorus: *How Sultry Is the Day*
Song: *How Hushed*. Mark Myers, tenor.
Chorus: *Yes! To the Work*   7:01

s2/1   Song: *Now Creaks the Heavy Wagon*. Gary
Petersen, bass.
Quartette and Chorus: *Shrouded Is the Sun*.
Patti Abasolo, soprano; Phyllis Bush, mezzo-
soprano; Marc Much, tenor; Mark Jones, bass.   8:20

s2/2   Duet: *Lo! The Clouds Are Breaking*. Phyllis
Bush, mezzo-soprano; Marc Much, tenor.
Chorus: *Rainbow, Hail to Thee*
Solo: *All Nature Now Rejoices*. Carolyn
Finley, soprano.
Recitative: *With Grateful Hearts*. Mark
Myers, tenor.
Finale–Full Chorus: *Harvest Home!*   9:47

235 *Maple Leaf Rag*: Ragtime in Rural America

LP
1536

Notes by Lawrence Cohn. Producer: Lawrence Cohn.
Cover by Elaine Sherer Cox.

s1/1	*Dallas Rag*. Dallas String Band: Coley Jones, mandolin; Sam Harris, guitar; Marco Williams, contrabass/cello.	2:46
s1/2	*Southern Rag*. Blind Blake.	2:47
s1/3	*Dew Drop Alley*. Sugar Underwood.	3:12
s1/4	*Piccolo Rag*. Blind Boy Fuller.	2:42
s1/5	*Atlanta Rag*. Cow Cow Davenport.	3:03
s1/6	*Kill It Kid*. Blind Willie McTell.	2:30
s1/7	*The Entertainer* (Scott Joplin, C). Bunk Johnson and His Band: Bunk Johnson, trumpet, Ed Cuffee, trombone; Garvin Bushell, clarinet; Don Kirkpatrick, piano; Danny Barker, guitar; Wellman Braud, bass; Alphonse Steele, drums.	2:54
s1/8	*Maple Leaf Rag* (Scott Joplin, C). Rev. Gary Davis.	2:53
s2/1	*Mexican Rag*. Jimmie Tarlton.	2:59
s2/2	*Hawkins Rag*. Gid Tanner and His Skillet Lickers.	2:49
s2/3	*Guitar Rag*. Roy Harvey and Jess Johnson.	3:12
s2/4	*Chinese Rag*. The Spooney Five.	3:15
s2/5	*Barn Dance Rag*. Bill Boyd and His Cowboy Ramblers: Bill Boyd, guitar; Art Davis, violin, mandolin; Walter Kirkes, banjo; Jim Boyd, bass; unidentified guitar and piano.	2:51
s2/6	*Sumter Rag/Steel Guitar Rag*. China Poplin.	1:57
s2/7	*Cannon Ball Rag/Bugle Call Rag*. Merle Travis.	4:21
s2/8	*Randy Lynn Rag*. Lester Flatt and Earl Scruggs and the Foggy Mountain Boys.	2:02

236 *Going Down the Valley*: Vocal and Instrumental Styles in Folk Music from the South

LP
1744

Notes by Norm Cohen. Cover art: Jackson Lee Nesbitt,
November Evening.

s1/1	*I Truly Understand, You Love Another Man*. Shortbuckle Roark and Family: George Roark, Sr., George Jr., Robert, and Oda Roark; banjo by George Sr.	2:45

236 (continued)

s1/2   *Old Joe Clark*. Ben Jarrell, accompanied by
DaCosta Woltz's Southern Broadcasters: vocal
solo with banjo and fiddle accompaniment.   2:41

s1/3   *Billy Grimes, the Rover*. Shelor Family: vocal
solo accompanied by piano, banjo, and
(possibly 2) fiddle(s).   2:43

s1/4   *George Washington*. Pope's Arkansas
Mountaineers: Chism Brothers, fiddle and
guitar; John Sparrow, guitar; Tip McKinnie,
banjo and vocal.   3:32

s1/5   *Little Maud*. Bela Lam and His Greene
County Singers: vocal quartet accompanied by
banjo and guitar.   2:44

s1/6   *Cotton-Eyed Joe*. Carter Brothers and Son:
George Carter, fiddle and vocal; Andrew
Carter, fiddle; Jimmie Carter, guitar.   2:38

s1/7   *Going Down the Valley*. Ernest V. Stoneman
and His Dixie Mountaineers: Stoneman,
vocal and guitar; Kahle Brewer, fiddle; Irma
Frost, organ; vocal chorus by Hattie Stoneman
and two or three others.   2:32

s1/8   *By the Cottage Door*. Perry County Music
Makers: Nonnie Smith Presson, vocal and
zither; Bulow Smith, vocal and guitar.   2:35

s1/9   *Carve that Possum*. Uncle Dave Macon and
His Fruit Jar Drinkers: Macon, lead vocal and
banjo; Sam McGee, guitar and vocal; Kirk
McGee, fiddle and vocal; Mazy Todd, fiddle.   2:54

s2/1   *Molly Put the Kettle On*. Gid Tanner and His
Skillet Lickers, with Riley Puckett and Clayton
McMichen: Puckett, lead vocal and guitar.   3:13

s2/2   *Milwaukee Blues*. Charlie Poole and the North
Carolina Ramblers: Poole, vocal and banjo;
Roy Harvey, guitar; Odell Smith, fiddle.   3:11

s2/3   *Corrina, Corrina*. Ashley and Abernathy:
probable personnel are Tom Ashley, lead vocal
and guitar; Will Abernathy, harmonica and
vocal; Gwen Foster, guitar and/or harmonica
and vocal; Clarence Greene, fiddle and vocal.   3:00

s2/4   *Katie Dear (Silver Dagger)*. Callahan Brothers:
Homer Callahan and Walter Callahan, vocal
duet and guitars.   2:56

s2/5   *A New Salty Dog*. Allen Brothers: Austin
Allen, vocal and tenor banjo; Lee Allen,
kazoo and guitar. Peer International, pub.   2:34

236 (continued)

s2/6   *Nancy Jane*. Fort Worth Doughboys: Milton
        Brown, lead vocal; Bob Wills, fiddle;
        Durwood Brown, guitar and vocal; C. H.
        "Sleepy" Johnson, tenor guitar. Unart
        Music, pub.   3:10

s2/7   *Sweet Rose of Heaven*. Taylor-Griggs
        Louisiana Melody Makers.   3:11

s2/8   *Banjo Pickin' Girl*. Coon Creek Girls: Lily
        May Ledford, vocal and banjo; Rosie Ledford,
        guitar; Violet Koehler, bass and vocal.   2:48

s2/9   *Little Maggie*. Wade Mainer, vocal and banjo;
        Zeke Morris, vocal and guitar; Steve Ledford,
        fiddle.   2:17

237 **Works by Paul Chihara, Chou Wen-Chung, Earl Kim,**
LP   **and Roger Reynolds**
1882

Notes by Tom Johnson. Producers: Andrew Raeburn
(Reynolds, Chihara); Elizabeth A. Ostrow (Chou, Kim).
Cover art: Anne Ryan, *XXXV*.

s1/1   *From Behind the Unreasoning Mask* (Roger
        Reynolds, C). Miles Anderson, trombone;
        Tom Raney, percussion; Roger Reynolds,
        assistant percussionist. C. F. Peters, pub.   17:10

s1/2   *Ceremony II ("Incantations")* (Paul Chihara,
        C). Paul Dunkel, flute; Timothy Eddy, cello;
        Fred Sherry, cello; Richard Fitz, percussion.
        C. F. Peters, pub.   6:32

s2/1   *Suite for Harp and Wind Quintet* (Chou Wen-
        Chung, C). Cynthia Otis, harp; Paul Dunkel,
        flute; Stephen Taylor, oboe; Virgil Blackwell,
        clarinet; Frank Morelli, bassoon; Stewart
        Rose, French horn. C. F. Peters, pub.   6:44

s2/2   *Earthlight* (Earl Kim, C; Samuel Beckett, L).
        Merja Sargon, soprano; Martha Potter, violin;
        Earl Kim, piano. Mobart Music, pub.   15:03

238 The Vintage Irving Berlin

L P
1743

Notes by George Oppenheimer. Cover art: William
Auerbach-Levy, *Irving Berlin*. All selections
published by Irving Berlin Music.

s1/1	*Oh, How I Hate to Get Up in the Morning*, from *Yip, Yip, Yaphank*. Irving Berlin, vocal; Milton Rosenstock, conductor, with male chorus.	3:15
s1/2	*Mandy*, from *Ziegfeld Follies of 1919*. Van and Schenck, vocal.	2:48
s1/3	*A Pretty Girl Is Like a Melody*, from *Ziegfeld Follies of 1919*. John Steele, vocal.	2:35
s1/4	*Rock-a-Bye Baby*, from *Music Box Revue*. Grace Moore, vocal; Rosario Bourdon, conductor.	3:26
s1/5	*Shaking the Blues Away*, from *Ziegfeld Follies of 1927*. Ruth Etting, vocal.	3:10
s1/6	*It All Belongs to Me*, from *Ziegfeld Follies of 1927*. Ruth Etting, vocal.	2:57
s1/7	*Where Is the Song of Songs for Me?* , from *Lady of the Pavements*. Lupe Velez, vocal.	2:46
s2/1	*Let Me Sing and I'm Happy*, from *Mammy*. Al Jolson, vocal.	2:46
s2/2	*Puttin' On the Ritz*, from *Puttin' On the Ritz*. Harry Richman, vocal; Earl Burtnett and His Los Angeles Biltmore Orchestra.	2:31
s2/3	*Not for All the Rice in China*, from *As Thousands Cheer*. Clifton Webb, vocal; Leo Reisman and His Orchestra.	3:30
s2/4	*How's Chances?* , from *As Thousands Cheer*. Clifton Webb, vocal; Leo Reisman and His Orchestra.	3:19
s2/5	*Heat Wave*, from *As Thousands Cheer*. Ethel Waters, vocal; Ben Selvin, conductor.	3:03
s2/6	*How Deep Is the Ocean?* Ethel Merman, vocal; Nathaniel Shilkret and His Orchestra.	3:29
s2/7	*Cheek to Cheek*, from *Top Hat*. Ginger Rogers, vocal; Victor Young and His Orchestra.	3:02
s2/8	*Louisiana Purchase*, from *Louisiana Purchase*. Carol Bruce, vocal.	3:01

239 *Brave Boys*: New England Traditions in Folk Music

LP
1847

Notes by Sandy Paton. Producer: Sandy Paton.
Cover art: Edward Hopper, *The Lighthouse*.

s1/1	*A Frog He Would A-Wooing Go* (traditional). Gail Stoddard Storm, vocal.	2:03
s1/2	*The Farmer's Curst Wife* (traditional). Lewis Lund, vocal.	2:55
s1/3	*The Two Brothers* (traditional). Ben Mandel, vocal.	1:28
s1/4	*My Man John* (traditional). Gail Stoddard Storm, vocal.	2:25
s1/5	*Ladies' Walpole Reel* (traditional). Newton F. Tolman, flute; Kay Gilbert, piano.	1:01
s1/6	*Brave Boys* (traditional). Gale Huntington, vocal.	1:44
s1/7	*Fair Fannie Moore* (traditional). Sara Cleveland, vocal.	3:21
s1/8	*The Jam on Gerry's Rock* (traditional). Lawrence Older, vocal.	4:22
s1/9	*And Now, Old Serpent, How Do You Feel? Who Will Bow and Bend Like a Willow?* (traditional). Mrs. Morris Austin, vocal.	1:45
s1/10	*A Medley of Scottish Fiddle Tunes* (traditional). Harvey Tolman, fiddle; Rose Tolman, piano.	4:10
s2/1	*The Flowers of Edinburgh* (traditional). Phil, Paul, and Sterl Van Arsdale, hammered dulcimers.	1:48
s2/2	*The Good Old State of Maine* (traditional, arr. Lawrence Gorman). James Brown, vocal.	5:32
s2/3	*The Dreadnaught* (traditional). Gale Huntington, vocal.	1:55
s2/4	*Three Men They Went A-Hunting* (traditional). Sara Cleveland, vocal.	1:06
s2/5	*Erin-Go-Bragh* (traditional). Edward Kirby, vocal.	1:23
s2/6	*Give an Honest Irish Lad a Chance* (traditional). Sara Cleveland, vocal.	4:17
s2/7	*Knit Stockings* (traditional). Wilfred Guillette, fiddle; Maurice Campbell, piano.	1:07
s2/8	*The Johnstown Flood* (traditional). Mack Moody, vocal.	2:12
s2/9	*The Good Old Days of Adam and Eve* (traditional). Rosalie Shaw, vocal.	:36

239 (continued)

    s2/10   *I'll Hit the Road Again, Boys* (traditional:
              Jehila "Pat" Edwards [?]). Grant Rogers, vocal.   2:27

    s2/11   *Cherish the Ladies* (traditional). Brendan
              Mulvihill, fiddle; Kevin Taylor, accordion;
              Seamus Logue, guitar.   4:11

240 *Where Have We Met Before?*: Forgotten Songs from Broadway, Hollywood, and Tin Pan Alley

L P
173

        Notes by Milton Babbitt; Cover art: Mark Tobey,
        Broadway.

    s1/1   *We'll Be the Same*, from *America's Sweetheart*
              (Richard Rogers, C; Lorenz Hart, L). Arden
              and Ohman Orchestra: Frank Luther, vocal.
              Warner Bros. Music, pub.   2:53

    s1/2   *You Forgot Your Gloves*, from *The Third Little
              Show* (Ned Lehac, C; Edward Eliscu, L). Fred
              Waring and His Pennsylvanians: Clare Hanlon,
              vocal. Robbins Music, pub.   2:54

    s1/3   *And So to Bed* (Harry Revel, C; Mack Gordon,
              L). George Olsen's Orchestra: Ethel Shutta
              and Paul Small, vocals. Miller Music, pub.   3:19

    s1/4   *How Do You Do It?* and *Riddle Me This*, from
              Ballyhoo of 1932 (Lewis Gensler, C; E. Y.
              Harburg, L). Leo Reisman's Orchestra: Frank
              Luther, vocal. Warner Bros. Music, pub.   3:00

    s1/5   *Where Have We Met Before?* from *Walk a Little
              Faster* (Vernon Duke, pseud. of Vladimir
              Dukelsky, C; E. Y. Harburg, L). Victor Young's
              Orchestra: Smith Ballew, vocal. Warner Bros.
              Music, pub.   2:52

    s1/6   *Let's Call It a Day*, from *Strike Me Pink* (Ray
              Henderson, C; Lew Brown, L). Arden and
              Ohman Orchestra: Frank Munn, vocal. Chappell,
              pub.   3:17

    s1/7   *Are You Making Any Money*, from *Moonlight
              and Pretzels*. (Herman Hupfeld, C). Paul
              Whiteman's Orchestra: Ramona, vocal. Warner
              Bros. Music, pub.   3:05

    s2/1   *Coffee in the Morning, Kisses in the Night*,
              from *Moulin Rouge* (Harry Warren, C; Al
              Dubin, L). Eddie Duchin's Orchestra: Lew
              Sherwood, vocal. Warner Bros. Music, pub.   3:31

240 (continued)

s2/2   *What Can You Say in a Love Song?* from *Life Begins at 8:40* (Harold Arlen, C; Ira Gershwin, E. Y. Harburg, L). Richard Himber's Orchestra: Joey Nash, vocal. New World Music, pub.   3:09

s2/3   *That Lucky Fellow*, from *Very Warm for May* (Jerome Kern, C; Oscar Hammerstein II, L). Tommy Dorsey's Orchestra: Jack Leonard, vocal. T. B. Harms, pub.   3:08

s2/4   *Boys and Girls Like You and Me* (Richard Rogers, C; Oscar Hammerstein II, L). George Stoll's Orchestra: Judy Garland, vocal. Williamson Music, pub.   3:09

s2/5   *Only Another Boy and Girl*, from *Seven Lively Arts* (Cole Porter, C/L). Benny Goodman's Quintet: Jane Harvey, vocal. Chappell, pub.   2:58

s2/6   *Nobody Else but Me*, from *Show Boat* (Jerome Kern, C; Oscar Hammerstein II, L). Jan Clayton, vocal. T. B. Harms, pub.   4:06

s2/7   *Can't You Just See Yourself*, from *High Button Shoes* (Jule Styne, C; Sammy Cahn, L). Orchestra directed by Milt Rosenstock: Lois Lee and Mark Dawson, vocals. Edwin H. Morris, pub.   3:15

241   Toward an American Opera (1911–1954)

LP
1963

   Notes by Patrick J. Smith. Cover art: Reginald Marsh, *Grand Tier at the Metropolitan*.

s1/1–2   From *Natoma* (Victor Herbert, C; Joseph D. Redding, L)
     I List the Trill. Alma Gluck, soprano; Victor Herbert, conductor. G. Schirmer, pub.   3:11
     No Country Can My Own Outvie. John McCormack, tenor; Victor Herbert, conductor. G. Schirmer, pub.   3:29

s1/3–4   From *The King's Henchman* (Deems Taylor, C; Edna St. Vincent Millay, L)
     Oh, Caesar, Great Wert Thou. Lawrence Tibbett, baritone; Metropolitan Opera Chorus and Orchestra, Guilio Setti, conductor. Belwin-Mills, pub.   4:05
     Nay, Maccus, Lay Him Down. Same as above.   4:32

241 (continued)

s1/5   *Standin' In the Need of Prayer*, from *The Emperor Jones* (Louis Gruenberg, C; Kathleen de Jaffa, L). Lawrence Tibbett, baritone; Metropolitan Opera Orchestra, Wilfred Pelletier, conductor. Copyright held by Mrs. Louis Gruenberg.   5:01

s1/6   *'Tis an Earth Defiled*, from *Merry Mount* (Howard Hanson, C; Richard Stokes, L). Lawrence Tibbett, baritone; Metropolitan Opera Orchestra, Wilfred Pelletier, conductor. Warner Bros. Music, pub.   4:46

s2/1   *Two Willow Hill*; *Sextet*; *Jeff's Song*; *Queenie's Song*, from *The Second Hurricane* (Aaron Copland, C; Edwin Denby, L). Soloists and Chorus of the High School of Music and Art; New York Philharmonic, Leonard Bernstein, conductor. Boosey & Hawkes, pub.   10:53

s2/2   *To This We've Come*, from *The Consul* (Gian Carlo Menotti, C/L). Patricia Neway, soprano. Lehman Engel, conductor. G. Schirmer, pub.   7:50

s2/3   *It Promises to Be a Fine Night*; *The Promise of Living*, from *The Tender Land* (Aaron Copland, C; Horace Everett, L). Joy Clements, soprano; Claramae Turner, mezzo-soprano; Richard Cassily, tenor; Richard Fredericks, baritone; Norman Treigle, bass; New York Philharmonic, Aaron Copland, conductor. Boosey & Hawkes, pub.   5:40

242 *Nica's Dream*: Small Jazz Groups of the 50s and Early 60s

LP
1846

Notes by Richard Seidel. Cover art: Lee Bontecou, *Untitled*.

s1/1   *Woody'n You* (Dizzy Gillespie, C). Modern Jazz Quartet: John Lewis, piano; Milt Jackson, vibraharp; Percy Heath, bass; Connie Kay, drums. Edwin H. Morris, pub.   4:25

s1/2   *Donna Lee* (Charlie Parker, C). Lee Konitz with Warne Marsh: Lee Konitz, alto saxophone; Warne Marsh, tenor saxophone; Sal Mosca, piano; Billy Bauer, guitar; Oscar Pettiford, bass; Kenny Clarke, drums. Atlantic Music, pub.   6:18

242 (continued)

s1/3   *Nica's Dream* (Horace Silver, C). The Jazz
          Messengers: Donald Byrd, trumpet; Hank
          Mobley, tenor saxophone; Horace Silver,
          piano; Doug Watkins, bass; Art Blakey,
          drums. Ecaroh Music, pub.   11:51

s2/1   *Blues March* (Benny Golson, C). Art
          Farmer–Benny Golson Jazztet: Art Farmer,
          trumpet; Curtis Fuller, trombone; Benny
          Golson, tenor saxophone; McCoy Tyner,
          piano; Addison Farmer, bass; Lex
          Humphries, drums. Andante Music, pub.   5:17

s2/2   *Now's the Time* (Charlie Parker, C). Sonny
          Rollins & Co.: Sonny Rollins, tenor saxo-
          phone; Herbie Hancock, piano; Ron Carter,
          bass; Roy McCurdy drums. Atlantic Music,
          pub.   4:01

s2/3   *War Gewessen* (David Baker, C). George
          Russell Sextet: Don Ellis, trumpet; David
          Baker, trombone; Dave Young, tenor saxo-
          phone; George Russell, piano; Chuck Israels,
          bass; Joe Hunt, drums. Russ-Hix Music, pub.   6:20

s2/4   *Original Faubus Fables* (Charles Mingus, C/L).
          Charles Mingus Jazz Workshop: Eric Dolphy,
          alto saxophone; Ted Curson, trumpet; Charles
          Mingus, bass and vocal; Dannie Richmond,
          drums and vocal. Jazz Workshop, pub.   9:11

243 But Yesterday Is Not Today

LP
1687

Notes by Ned Rorem. Producer: Andrew Raeburn.
Cover art: Philip Evergood, *Woman at Piano*. On Side 1:
Donald Gramm, baritone; Donald Hassard, piano. On
Side 2: Bethany Beardslee, soprano; Robert Helps, piano.

s1/1   *The Children*; *Once Upon a Time*; *The Rose*;
          Moo Is a Cow (Theodore Chanler, C; Leonard
          Feeney, L). G. Schirmer, pub.   8:26

s1/2   *Thomas Logge* (Theodore Chanler, C; Walter
          de la Mare, L). Boosey & Hawkes, pub.   1:23

s1/3   *Once a Lady Was Here* (Paul Bowles, C/L).
          G. Schirmer, pub.   2:33

s1/4   *Song of an Old Woman* (Paul Bowles, C; Jane
          Bowles, L). G. Schirmer, pub.   2:36

243 (continued)

s1/5 *Richard Cory* (John Duke, C; Edwin
Arlington Robinson, L). Carl Fischer, pub. 2:21

s1/6 *Luke Havergal* (John Duke, C; Edwin
Arlington Robinson, L). Carl Fischer, pub. 4:24

s1/7 *Miniver Cheevy* (John Duke, C; Edwin
Arlington Robinson, L). Carl Fischer, pub. 5:07

s2/1 Five Songs from *Chamber Music* (Israel
Citkowitz, C; James Joyce, L). Boosey &
Hawkes, pub. 8:23

s2/2 *Song* (Aaron Copland, C; E. E. Cummings, L).
Boosey & Hawkes, pub. 1:43

s2/3 *On the Beach at Fontana* (Roger Sessions, C;
James Joyce, L). Edward B. Marks Music, pub. 2:07

s2/4 *These, My Ophelia* (Theodore Chanler, C;
Archibald MacLeish, L). Boosey & Hawkes,
pub. 2:48

s2/5 *Sure on This Shining Night* (Samuel Barber, C;
James Agee, L). G. Schirmer, pub. 2:36

s2/6 *The Running Sun* (Robert Helps, C; James
Purdy, L). C. F. Peters, pub. 8:01

244 Caliente = Hot: Puerto Rican and Cuban Musical Expression in New York

LP
1845

Notes by Roberta Singer and Robert Friedman.
Producer: Rene Lopez. Cover art: Rafael Ferrér,
Grand Erg Occidental.

s1/1 *El Safacón de la 102nd St.* (Victor Montañez,
Sr., C). Victor Montañez y sus Pleneros de la
110th Street: Victor Montañez, Sr., lead vocal;
Victor Montañez, Jr., conga; Ismael Rivera,
pandereta (punto de clave) and chorus; Marcial
Reyes, *pandereta (requinto)* and chorus; Efraim
Ramos and Pedro Juan Dumas, *panderetas
(sequidoras)* and chorus; Francisco "Tan"
Martinez, harmonica and chorus; Jaime Flores,
güiro and chorus. Trina Jill Music, pub. 3:32

s1/2 *Bomba Calindé* (Anon.). Victor Montañez y
sus Pleneros de la 110th Street: Victor
Montañez, Sr., *bomba* drum and lead vocal;
Ismael Rivera, *pandereta (requinto)* and chorus;
Marcial Reyes, *cuá* and chorus; Jaime Flores,
maracas and chorus. 1:50

244 (continued)

s1/3   *Emi ra obini le wa* (Julito Collazo, C). Julito
       Collazo y su Grupo Afro-Cubano: Julito
       Collazo, lead vocal; Hector "Flaco" Hernandez,
       iya and chorus; Milton Cardona, *itótele* and
       chorus; Steve Berrios, *okónkolo* and chorus;
       Wilfredo "Moreno" Tejeda, *achere* (gourd
       rattle) and chorus; Augusto Lore, Virgilio Martí,
       and Osvaldo "Chihuahua" Martinez, chorus.
       Trina Jill Music, pub.   5:53

s1/4   *Loteria* (Julito Collazo, C). Julito Collazo y su
       Grupo Afro-Cubano: Julito Collazo, lead vocal;
       Hector "Flaco" Hernandez, *quinto* and chorus;
       Milton Cardona, *segundo* and chorus; Virgilio
       Martí, *tumba* and chorus; Steve Berrios, *cáscara*
       and chorus; Osvaldo "Chihuahua" Martinez
       and Wilfredo "Moreno" Tejeda, chorus. Trina
       Jill Music, pub.   5:31

s1/5   *Yo Quisiera Ser* (Hector Rivera, C). Hector
       Rivera y su Conjunto: Manny Ramos, lead
       vocal; Benjamin Cabrera and Brad Upton,
       trumpets; Hector Rivera, piano; Pablo Guzman,
       bass; Kike Perez, conga; Vitin Gonzales, bongos;
       Adalberto Santiago, maracas and chorus; José
       Garcia, chorus. Ki-Rey Music, pub.   8:43

s2/1   *Borinquen* (Israel Berrios, C). Sexteto Criollo
       Puertorriqueño: Israel Berrios, lead vocal and
       guitar; Tito Baez, guitar; Neri Orta and Nieves
       Quintero, *cuatros*; Jaime Flores, *güiro*. Trina
       Jill Music, pub.   3:08

s2/2-4 Sexteto Criollo Puertorriqueño: Cristobal
       "Tobita" Medina Colón, lead vocal; Israel
       Berrios and Tito Baez, guitars; Neri Orta and
       Nieves Quintero, *cuatros*; Jaime Flores, *güiro*.
       Trina Jill Music, pub.
           Las Mujeres de Borinquen (Cristobal
           "Tobita" Medina Colón, C)   4:26
           El Puertorriqueño (Cristobal "Tobita"
           Medina Colón, C)   3:55
           La Cuna de Mis Amores (Cristobal
           "Tobita" Medina Colón, C)   4:13

s2/5-6 Armando Sanchez y su Septeto Son de la Loma:
       Marcelino Morales, solo vocal; Marcelino
       Valendez, bongos; Teodoro Vanderpool, *tres*;
       Frankie Acevedo, first voice; Israel Berrios,
       guitar and second voice; Leo Fleming, bass;

244 (continued)

> Alfredo "Chocolate" Armenteros, trumpet;
> Armando Sanchez, conga; Vicentico Valdez,
> maracas. Trina Jill Music, pub.
>
>> *Amor a la Virtud* (Gerardo Martinez, C)   5:15
>> *Guajira del Mayoral* (Armando Sanchez, C)   4:52

245 *Oh My Little Darling*: Folk Song Types

LP
1695

> Notes by Jon Pankake. Cover art: Thomas Hart Benton,
> *I Got a Gal on Sourwood Mountain*. All selections on
> this album are traditional folk songs.

s1/1	*Chick-A-Li-Lee-Lo* (children's song). Almeda Riddle, vocal.	1:18
s1/2	*King William Was King George's Son* (play-party song). Mr. and Mrs. Crockett Ward, vocals.	:40
s1/3	*Sweet William* (child ballad). Fields Ward, vocal.	3:42
s1/4	*The Lexington Murder* (broadside ballad). Wesley Hargis, vocal and guitar.	3:34
s1/5	*Lily Schull* (native ballad). Mrs. Lena Bare Turbyfill and Mrs. Lloyd Bare Hagie, vocals.	3:17
s1/6	*The Farmer Is the Man that Feeds Them All* (agrarian song). Fiddlin' John Carson, vocal and fiddle.	3:01
s1/7	*Come All You Coal Miners* (labor song). Sarah Ogan, vocal.	2:12
s1/8	*Cotton Mill Blues* (labor song). Daddy John Love, vocal and guitar.	2:15
s1/9	*Whoopee-Ti-Yi-Yo* (cowboy song). John I. White, vocal; Roy Smeck, guitar and harmonica.	2:40
s1/10	*Mon Cherie Bebe Creole* (lyric song). Dennis McGee, vocal and fiddle; S. D. Courville, fiddle.	2:44
s2/1	*Oh My Little Darling* (banjo song). Thaddeus C. Willingham, vocal and banjo.	2:07
s2/2	*Been on the Job Too Long* (outlaw song). Wilmer Watts and the Lonely Eagles: Wilmer Watts, vocal; Charles Freshour and Palmer Rhyne, instrumentalists.	3:08
s2/3	*Dr. Ginger Blue* (minstrel song). Arthur Tanner and His Blue Ridge Corn Shuckers; Arthur Tanner, vocal.	3:00

245 (continued)

s2/4   *Crawling and Creeping* (bawdy song). Asa
          Martin, vocal and lead guitar; James Roberts,
          guitar.   2:40

s2/5   *Haunted Road Blues* (blues song). Tom
          Clarence Ashley, vocal and guitar; Guinn
          Foster, harmonica and guitar.   3:07

s2/6   *The Village School* (sentimental song).
          Nelstone's Hawaiians: Hubert Nelson and
          James Touchstone, vocals and guitars.   3:01

s2/7   *The Poor Drunkard's Dream* (homiletic song).
          Wade Mainer, vocal; Sons of the Mountaineers.   2:44

s2/8   *If the Light Has Gone Out in Your Soul*
          (Evangelical hymn). Ernest Phipps and His
          Holiness Singers: Minnie Phipps, Nora Byrley,
          and A. G. Baker, vocals; Ernest Phipps and
          R. N. Johnson, fiddles; Ethel Baker, piano;
          Eula Johnson, banjo; Shirley Jones, guitar;
          D. L. McVey, mandolin.   2:57

s2/9   *I'm a Long Time Traveling Away From Home*
          (hymn). J. T. Allison's Sacred Harp Singers.   2:52

246 Songs of Earth, Water, Fire and Sky: Music of the American Indian

L P
1537

Notes by Charlotte Heth. Producer: Charlotte Heth.
Cover art: Elaine Sherer Cox.

s1/1   *Butterfly Dance* (San Juan Pueblo). Singers:
          Herman Agoyo, Anthony S. Archuleta,
          Cipriano Garcia (bells), Jerry Garcia, Peter
          Garcia (drum), Steven Trujillo.   5:12

s1/2   *Alligator Dance* (Seneca). Singers: Leslie Bowen
          (leader), Herbert Dowdy, Sr., Avery Jimerson,
          Johnson Jimerson, Marty Jimerson, Richard
          Johnny-John; Dancers: Alvina C. Cooper, A.
          Eileen Jacobs, Fidelia Jimerson, Vera Jimerson,
          Cecil Johnny-John, Kevin Johnny-John, Lyford
          Johnny-John, Michael Johnny-John, Brian
          Mohr, Theresa R. Seltron.   3:04

s1/3   *Eagle Dance* (Northern Arapaho). The Los
          Angeles Northern Singers: Colin Bearstail,
          John Eagleshield, Stewart G. Headley (leader),
          Joseph Seaboy, Bill Vermillion, James Young.   2:32

s1/4   *Rabbit Dance* (Northern Plains). The Los
          Angeles Northern Singers; Colin Bearstail,
          leader.   3:16

246 (continued)

s1/5   *Gar Dance* (Creek). Singers: Jobie L. Fields, Van
Johnson, Archie Sam (leader), Eli Sam (drum),
Cedo Screechowl, Robert Sumpka, Luman
Wildcat, Squirrel Wildcat; Shell shakers: Sonja
Fields, Levana Harjo, Evelyn Screechowl, Eliza
Sumpka (leader), Leona Wildcat.   6:55

s2/1   *Women's Brush Dance* (Yurok). Singers: Loren
Bommelyn, Frank A. Douglas, Aileen Figueroa
(leader), Sam Lopez, Ella Vera Norris, Walter
Richards, Sr., Florence Shaughnessy, Hector
Simms, Oscar Taylor; Dancers: Carl James,
Carole Korb, Casbara Ruud, Frederick W. Scott,
Jr., Sheryl Steinruck, Lisa Sundberg.   2:37

s2/2   *Ribbon Dance* (Navajo). Singers: Frank Jishie,
Jr., Raymond K. Yazzie, Sam Yazzie, Jr.
(rattle), Sam Yazzie, Sr. (leader, basket drum).   2:38

s2/3   *Stomp Dance* (Cherokee). The singers and shell
shakers are the same as those in the *Gar Dance*
(s1/5); Eli Sam, drum; Leona Wildcat, lead shell
shaker; Luman Wildcat, leader.   7:06

s2/4   *Oklahoma Two-Step* (Southern Plains). Singers:
Jack Anquoe (lead singer for Two-Step), Henry
Collins, Bill Grass, James Kimble, Lionel Le
Clair, Ed Little Cook, Oliver Little Cook, Morris
Lookout, Adam Pratt (head singer), Joe Rush,
E. R. Satepauhoodle, Harvey Ware, Chris C.
White.   8:30

247 *When I Have Sung My Songs*: The American Art Song
  LP
 1538(1900–1940)

      Notes by Philip L. Miller. Producer: Max Wilcox.
      Cover art: Elaine Sherer Cox.

s1/1   *Long Ago, Sweetheart Mine*, Op. 56, No. 1
(Edward MacDowell, C/L).
A Maid Sings Light, Op. 56, No. 3 (Edward
MacDowell, C/L). Alma Gluck, soprano;
Rosario Bourdon, piano. Pub. unknown.   3:06

s1/2   *The Year's at the Spring*, Op. 44, No. 1 (Mrs.
H. H. A. Beach, C; Robert Browning, L).
Johanna Gadski, soprano; accompanist
unidentified.   :50

s1/3   *Love in May*, Op. 51, No. 1 (Horatio Parker, C;
Ella Higginson, L). Emma Eames, soprano; accompanist unidentified. Theodore Presser, pub.   1:20

247 (continued)

s1/4   *The Lark Now Leaves His Watery Nest*, Op. 47,
No. 6 (Horatio Parker, C; Sir William Davenant,
L). Emilio de Gogorza, baritone; accompanist
unidentified. Theodore Presser, pub.   1:43

s1/5   *Swans*, Op. 44, No. 4 (A. Walter Kramer, C;
Sara Teasdale, L). John McCormack, tenor;
Edwin Schneider, piano. Belwin-Mills, pub.   2:14

s1/6   *The Bitterness of Love* (James P. Dunn, C;
Shaemas O'Sheel, L). John McCormack, tenor;
Edwin Schneider, piano. Belwin-Mills, pub.   2:09

s1/7   *Danny Deever*, Op. 2, No. 7 (Walter Damrosch,
C; Rudyard Kipling, L). David Bispham, bari-
tone; accompanist unidentified. Theodore
Presser, pub.   3:35

s1/8   *Go Down, Moses (Let My People Go)* (arr. H.
T. Burleigh). Roland Hayes, tenor; Lawrence
Brown, piano. Belwin-Mills, pub.   2:14

s1/9   *Heav'n, Heav'n* (arr. H. T. Burleigh). Marian
Anderson, contralto; Kosti Vehanen, piano.
Belwin-Mills, pub.   1:51

s1/10 *Deep River* (arr. H. T. Burleigh). Paul Robeson,
baritone; Lawrence Brown, piano. Belwin-Mills,
pub.   2:20

s2/1   *At Dawning*, Op. 29, No. 1 (Charles Wakefield
Cadman, C; Nelle Richmond Eberhart, L).
Mary Garden, soprano; Jean H. Dansereau,
piano. Theodore Presser, pub.   3:05

s2/2   *By a Lonely Forest Pathway* (Charles
Tomlinson Griffes, C; Nikolaus Lenau, English
version by Henry G. Chapman, L). Eleanor
Steber, soprano; James Quillian, piano.
Schirmer, pub.   2:33

s2/3   *Do Not Go, My Love* (Richard Hageman, C;
Rabindranath Tagore, L). Rose Bampton, contralto; Wilfred Pelletier, piano. Schirmer, pub.   3:00

s2/4   *When I Bring You Coloured Toys*, from
Gitanjali, No. 1 (John Alden Carpenter, C;
Rabindranath Tagore, L). Rose Bampton, con-
tralto; accompanist unidentified. Schirmer, pub.   3:00

s2/5   *Light, My Light*, from *Gitanjali*, No. 6 (John
Alden Carpenter, C; Rabindranath Tagore, L).
Rose Bampton, contralto; accompanist
unidentified. Schirmer, pub.   2:14

s2/6   *Velvet Shoes* (Randall Thompson, C; Elinor
Wylie, L). Povla Frijsh, soprano; Celius
Dougherty, piano. E. C. Schirmer, pub.   3:35

247 (continued)

s2/7   *When I Have Sung My Songs* (Ernest Charles,
C/L). Kirsten Flagstad, soprano; Edwin
McArthur, piano. Schirmer, pub.   2:27

s2/8   *Lit'l Gal* (J. Rosamond Johnson, C; Paul
Lawrence Dunbar, L). Paul Robeson, baritone;
Lawrence Brown, piano. E. B. Marks, pub.   2:53

s2/9   *General William Booth Enters into Heaven*
(Charles Ives, C; Vachel Lindsay, L). Radiana
Pazmor, soprano; Genevieve Pitot, piano.
Theodore Presser, pub.   4:29

248   The Music Goes Round and Around: The Golden
   L P Years of Tin Pan Alley (1930–1939)
   1730

> Notes by Nat Shapiro. Cover art: Reginald Marsh,
> *Diana Dancing Academy.*

s1/1   *Stormy Weather*, from *Cotton Club Parade*
(Harold Arlen, C; Ted Koehler, C). Leo
Reisman and His Orchestra; Harold Arlen,
vocal. Arko Music, pub.   3:16

s1/2   *How Deep Is the Ocean?* (Irving Berlin, C/L).
Bing Crosby, vocal. Irving Berlin Music, pub.   3:11

s1/3   *Heartaches* (Al Hoffman, C; John Klenner, L).
Ted Weems and His Orchestra; Elmo Tanner,
whistling. MCA Music, pub.   2:32

s1/4   *All of Me*, from *Careless Lady* (Gerald Marks,
C; Seymour Simons, L). Russ Columbo, vocal.
Bourne/Marlong Music, pub.   3:07

s1/5   *Blue Moon* (Richard Rogers, C; Lorenz Hart, L).
Connee Boswell, vocal. Robbins Music, pub.   3:09

s1/6   *Ghost of a Chance* (Victor Young, C; Bing
Crosby, Ned Washington, L). John Kirby and
His Orchestra; Mildred Bailey, vocal. Mills
Music/Victor Young, pub.   3:08

s1/7   *Shoe Shine Boy* (Saul Chaplin, C; Sammy
Cahn, L). Louis Armstrong and His Orchestra.
Cahn Music/Dorsey Bros., pub.   3:17

s2/1   *The Music Goes Round and Round* (Ed Farley,
Mike Riley, C; Red Hodgson, L). Mike Riley-
Eddie Farley and Their Onyx Club Boys.
Anne-Rachel Music, pub.   2:54

248 (continued)

s2/2   *Until the Real Thing Comes Along*, from
Rhapsody in Black (Saul Chaplin, L. E.
Freeman, Alberta Nichols, C; Sammy Cahn,
Mann Holiner, L). Andy Kirk and His Twelve
Clouds of Joy; Pha Terrell, vocal. Chappell/
Anne-Rachel Music, pub.   3:00

s2/3   *When My Dreamboat Comes Home* (Cliff
Friend, C; Dave Franklin, L). Guy Lombardo
and His Royal Canadians; Lebert Lombardo,
vocal. Warner Bros. Music, pub.   3:12

s2/4   *Once in a While* (Michael Edwards, C; Bud
Green, L). Martha Raye, vocal. Miller Music,
pub.   2:26

s2/5   *Undecided* (Charles Shavers, C; Sid Robin, L).
Chick Webb and His Orchestra; Ella
Fitzgerald, vocal. MCA Music, pub.   3:15

s2/6   *Heart and Soul* (Hoagy Carmichael, C; Frank
Loesser, L). Larry Clinton and His Orchestra:
Bea Wain, vocal. Famous Music, pub.   3:07

s2/7   *'Tain't What You Do (It's the Way that Cha
Do It)* (Sy Oliver, James "Trummy" Young,
C). Jimmie Lunceford and His Orchestra;
Trummy Young, vocal. MCA Music, pub.   3:03

249 *Shake, Rattle & Roll*: Rock 'n' Roll in the 1950s

LP
1904   Notes by Gary Giddins. Cover art: Nicholas Krushenick,
Godzilla.

s1/1   *Shake, Rattle and Roll* (Charles E. Calhoun,
pseud. of Jesse Stone, C). Joe Turner, vocal.
Unichappell Music, pub.   2:59

s1/2   *The Clock* (David J. Mattis, C). Johnny Ace,
vocal and piano; the Beale Streeters, vocals.
Lion Music, pub.   2:55

s1/3   *Have Mercy, Baby* (Billy Ward, C). Billy Ward
and His Dominoes: Vocals: Clyde McPhatter,
lead tenor; James Van Loan, second tenor; Joe
Lamont, baritone; and Bill Brown, bass; Billy
Ward, piano. Billy Ward Music, pub.   2:23

s1/4   *Shake a Hand* (Joe Morris, C). Faye Adams,
vocal; Joe Morris and His Orchestra. Merrimac
Music, pub.   2:29

249 (continued)

s1/5	*See You Later, Alligator* (Robert Guidry, C). Bill Haley and the Comets: Bill Haley, vocal and guitar; Rudy Pompelli, tenor saxophone; John Grande, piano; Billy Williamson, steel guitar; Francis Beecher, guitar; Al Reed, bass; Don Raymond, drums. Arc Music, pub.	2:44
s1/6	*Maybellene* (Chuck Berry, Russ Fratto, Alan Freed, C). Chuck Berry, vocal and guitar; Johnny Johnson, piano; Willie Dixon, bass; Jasper Thomas, drums; Jerome Green, maracas. Arc Music, pub.	2:16
s1/7	*Mailman Blues* (Lloyd Price, C). Lloyd Price, vocal. Venice Music, pub.	2:09
s1/8	*I Can't Go On* (Fats Domino, Dave Bartholomew, C). Fats Domino, vocal and piano; Clarence Ford, alto saxophone; Lee Allen and Herb Hardesty, tenor saxophone; Ernest McLean, guitar; Frank Fields, bass; Cornelius Coleman, drums. Unart Music, pub.	2:12
s1/9	*Every Hour* (Richard Penniman, C). Little Richard, vocal; Willie Mays, trumpet; A. Dobbins, alto saxophone; Fred Jackson, tenor saxophone; J. Hudson, baritone saxophone; Julius Wimby, piano; Charles Holloway, bass; Donald Clark, drums. Copyright held by the composer.	2:55
s2/1	*Get a Job* (The Silhouettes, C). The Silhouettes, vocals: Earl Beal, Raymond Edwards, Billy Horton, and Richard Lewis. Dandelion Music, pub.	2:43
s2/2	*That'll Be the Day* (Jerry Allison, Norman Petty, Buddy Holly, C). Buddy Holly and the Crickets: Buddy Holly, vocal and guitar; Niki Sullivan, guitar; Larry Welborn, bass; Jerry Allison, drums. MPL Communications, pub.	2:16
s2/3	*Good Golly Miss Molly* (Robert A. Blackwell, John Marascalco, C/L). Jerry Lee Lewis, vocal and piano. Jondora Music, pub.	2:17
s2/4	*Reet Petite* (Tyran Carlo, Berry Gordy, Jr., C/L). Jackie Wilson, vocal; Dick Jacobs, arranger; Panama Francis (?), drums. Copyright held by the composers.	2:44
s2/5	*I Met Him on a Sunday* (The Shirelles, C). The Shirelles, vocals: Shirley Alston, Beverly Lee, Addie Harris, and Doris Kenner; Budd Johnson, tenor saxophone. Ludlow Music, pub.	2:19

249 (continued)

s2/6   *At My Front Door* (John C. Moore, Ewart G. Abner, Jr., C/L). Dee Clark, vocal. Conrad Music, pub.   1:49

s2/7   *I'm Movin' On* (Hank Snow, C). Ray Charles, vocal and piano; the Raelets, vocals; Marcus Belgrave and John Hunt, trumpets; David Newman, tenor saxophone; Hank Crawford, baritone saxophone; Edgar Willis, bass; Teagle Flemming, drums. Hill & Range Songs, pub.   2:17

s2/8   *What About Us?* (Jerry Leiber, Mike Stoller, C/L). The Coasters, vocals: Billy Guy, Carl Gardner, Cornell Gunter, and Will "Dub" Jones; King Curtis, tenor saxophone. Chappell Music, pub.   2:48

s2/9   *New Orleans* (Frank Guida, Joseph F. Royster, C/L). Gary U. S. Bonds, vocal. Rockmasters, pub.   2:47

250 Little Club Jazz: Small Groups in the 30s

L P
1670

Notes by Nat Hentoff. Producer: Michael Brooks. Cover art: Man Ray, *Jazz*.

s1/1   *My Honey's Loving Arms* (Joseph Meyer, C; Herman Ruby, L). Joe Venuti's Blue Four: Joe Venuti, violin; Jimmy Dorsey, baritone saxophone, clarinet, and trumpet; Rube Bloom, piano and vocal; Eddie Lang, guitar; Charlie Kegley, drums. Mills Music, pub.   3:08

s1/2   *Rocky Mountain Blues* (Bill Simmon, C). The Harlem Footwarmers: Arthur Whetsol, trumpet; Joe "Tricky Sam" Nanton, trombone; Barney Bigard, clarinet; Duke Ellington, piano, leader, and arranger; Fred Guy, banjo; Wellman Braud, string bass; Sonny Greer, drums. Southern Music Publishing, pub.   3:12

s1/3   *Hejre Kati* (Jeno Hubay, C). Eddie South and His International Orchestra: Clifford King (?), clarinet; Eddie South, violin and vocal; Antonia Spaulding, piano; Everett Barksdale, banjo and guitar; Jimmy Bertrand, drums. Normandy Music, pub.   2:47

250 (continued)

s1/4   [*I Wish That I Could Shimmy Like My*] *Sister Kate* (A. Piron, C). Henry Allen and Coleman Hawkins and Their Orchestra: Henry "Red" Allen, trumpet; Dickie Wells, trombone; Russell Procope, clarinet and alto saxophone; Coleman Hawkins, tenor saxophone; Don Kirkpatrick, piano; Bernard Addison, guitar; John Kirby, string bass; Walter Johnson, drums. Jerry Vogel Music, pub.   2:39

s1/5   *China Boy* (D. Winfree, P. Boutelje, C). Candy and Coco: Gene Austin, piano; Otto "Coco" Heimel, guitar; Candy Candido, string bass; Monk Hazel (?), drums and trumpet mouthpiece. Leo Feist, pub.   2:58

s1/6   *Squareface* (Gene Gifford, C). Gene Gifford and His Orchestra: Bunny Berigan, trumpet; Morey Samel, trombone; Matty Matlock, clarinet; Bud Freeman, tenor saxophone; Claude Thornhill, piano; Dick McDonough, guitar; Pete Peterson, string bass; Ray Bauduc, drums; Wingie Manone, vocal; Gene Gifford, arranger. Mayfair Music, pub.   3:22

s1/7   *I Got Rhythm* (George Gershwin, C; Ira Gershwin, L). Red Norvo and His Swing Sextet: Stew Pletcher, trumpet; Donald McCook, clarinet; Herbie Haymer, tenor saxophone; Howard Smith, piano; Red Norvo, xylophone; Dave Barbour, guitar; Pete Peterson, string bass; Maurice Purtill, drums. New World Music, pub.   2:47

s1/8   *Chasing Shadows* (A. Silver, C; B. Davis, L). Putney Dandridge and His Orchestra: Putney Dandridge, vocal; Roy Eldridge, trumpet; Leon "Chu" Berry, tenor saxophone; Harry Grey, piano; Hilton "Nappy" Lamare, guitar; Artie Bernstein, string bass; Bill Beason, drums. Pub. unknown.   2:43

s1/9   *Knock, Knock* (J. Morris, V. Lopez, W. Tyson-Davies, C/L). Stuff Smith and His Onyx Club Orchestra: Jonah Jones, trumpet; Hezekiah "Stuff" Smith, violin and vocal: James Sherman, piano; Bobby Bennett, guitar; Mack Walker, string bass; Cozy Cole, drums. Pub. unknown.   2:59

250 (continued)

s2/1   *In a Little Gypsy Tearoom* (J. Burke, C; E.
       Leslie, L). Louis Prima and His New Orleans
       Gang: Louis Prima, trumpet and vocal;
       Ellsworth "Pee Wee" Russell, clarinet; Frank
       Pinero, piano; Garry McAdams, guitar; Jack
       Ryan, string bass; Sam Weiss, drums. Fred
       Ahlert Music, pub.   2:49

s2/2   *Bugle Call Rag* (Jack Pettis, B. Meyers, E.
       Schoebel, C). Roly's Tap-Room Gang: Jonah
       Jones, trumpet; Sid Stoneburn, clarinet; Larry
       Binyon, tenor saxophone; Adrian Rollini, bass
       saxophone; Fulton McGrath, piano; Dick
       McDonough, guitar; George Hnida, string bass;
       Al Sidell, drums. Belwin Mills, pub.   2:58

s2/3   *Jungle Love* (R. Rainger, C; L. Robin, L).
       Teddy Wilson and His Orchestra: Bobby
       Hackett, cornet; Gene "Honey Bear" Sedric,
       clarinet; Johnny Hodges, alto saxophone;
       Teddy Wilson, piano; Alan Reuss (?), guitar;
       Al Hall (?), string bass; Johnny Blowers,
       drums. Paramount Music, pub.   2:45

s2/4   *What's the Use?* (I. Jones, C; C. Newman, L).
       Emilio Caceres Trio: Emilio Caceres, violin;
       Ernie Caceres, clarinet and baritone saxophone;
       Johnny Gomez, guitar. Leo Feist, pub.   3:20

s2/5   *Clarinet Marmalade* (H. Ragas, C; L. Shields, L).
       Joe Marsala's Chicagoans: Marty Marsala,
       trumpet; Joe Marsala, clarinet; Ray Biondi,
       violin; Adele Girard, harp; Joe Bushkin, piano;
       Eddie Condon, guitar; Artie Shapiro, string
       bass; Danny Alvin, drums. Leo Feist, pub.   3:04

s2/6   *Beale Street Mama* (J. R. Robinson, C; R. Turk,
       L). Bob Howard and His Orchestra: Bob
       Howard, vocal; Billy Kyle, piano; Teddy Bunn,
       guitar, Haig Stephens, string bass; O'Neill
       Spencer, drums. Fred Fisher Music, pub.   3:14

s2/7   *Tapioca* (W. Strayhorn, C). Barney Bigard and
       His Jazzopaters: Rex Stewart, cornet; Juan
       Tizol, valve trombone; Barney Bigard, clarinet;
       Harry Carney, baritone saxophone; Billy
       Strayhorn, piano; Jimmy Blanton, string bass;
       Sonny Greer, drums. American Academy of
       Music, pub.   2:29

250 (continued)

s2/8   *Blues in My Condition* (Cootie Williams, C).
Cootie Williams and His Orchestra: Charles
"Cootie" Williams, trumpet; Lou McGarity,
trombone; Les Robinson, alto saxophone;
Skippy Martin, baritone saxophone; Johnny
Guarnieri, piano; Artie Bernstein, string bass;
Jo Jones, drums. American Academy of Music,
pub.   2:51

s2/9   *Bugler's Dilemma* (Lou Singer, C). John Kirby
and His Orchestra: Charlie Shavers, trumpet;
Buster Bailey, clarinet; Russell Procope, alto
saxophone; Billy Kyle, piano; John Kirby,
string bass; O'Neill Spencer, drums; Lou
Singer, arranger. Pub. unknown.   2:52

251 *Where Home Is*: Life in Nineteenth-Century
Cincinnati/Crossroads of the East and West

1742

Notes by Kathryn Kish Sklar and Jon Newsom.
Producer: Horace Grenell. Cover art: Henry Mosler, Jr.,
Canal Market in 1860.

s1/1   *Where Home Is* (George F. Root, C). The
Harmoneion Singers, John Miner, conductor;
Peter Basquin, harmonium.   2:04

s1/2   *Sweet Home* (H. R. Bishop, C; J. H. Payne, L).
The Harmoneion Singers, John Miner, con-
ductor.   1:12

s1/3   *A Life in the West* (Henry Russell, C; G.
Morris, L). Clifford Jackson, baritone; Peter
Basquin, piano.   4:24

s1/4   *Old Rosin the Bow* (arr. William C. Peters).
Peter Basquin, piano.   6:01

s1/5   *Ho! For Kansas* (F. H. Pease, C; Lucy Larcom,
L). The Harmoneion Singers, John Miner, conductor.   2:23

s1/6   *The Old Canoe* (George F. Root, C; S. M.
Grannis, L). The Harmoneion Singers, John
Miner, conductor; Peter Basquin, harmonium.   3:53

s1/7   *You Never Miss the Water Till the Well Runs
Dry* (Rowland Howard, C). Clifford Jackson,
baritone; Peter Basquin, piano.   4:30

s1/8   *The Jovial Farmer Boy.* The Harmoneion
Singers, John Miner, conductor.   2:00

251 (continued)

s2/1	*Wake Up, Jake* (George Holman, C). Clifford Jackson, baritone; The Harmoneion Singers, John Miner, conductor; Peter Basquin, piano.	2:49
s2/2	*Sounds of the Singing School* (P. P. Bliss, C). The Harmoneion Singers, John Miner, conductor; Peter Basquin, piano.	3:53
s2/3	*Ohio* (Augustus Dameron Fillmore, C). The Harmoneion Singers, John Miner, conductor.	1:33
s2/4	*Ives* (Elam Oves, Jr., C/L). The Harmoneion Singers, John Miner, conductor.	1:59
s2/5	*Galop* (James R. Murray, C). Peter Basquin, piano.	2:13
s2/6	*Frankfort Belle* (attrib. William C. Peters). Peter Basquin, piano.	1:04
s2/7	*Louisville March & Quick-Step* (attrib. William C. Peters). Peter Basquin, piano.	2:18
s2/8	*The Blessed Bible* (Augustus D. Fillmore, C). The Harmoneion Singers, John Miner, conductor.	2:19
s2/9	*Henry* (Augustus D. Fillmore, C). The Harmoneion Singers, John Miner, conductor.	1:48
s2/10	*Who'll Buy (Temperance)* (James R. Murray, C/L). The Harmoneion Singers, John Miner, conductor.	1:14
s2/11	*Firmament* (Augustus D. Fillmore, C). John Aler, tenor; The Harmoneion Singers, John Miner, conductor.	4:06

252 Roots of the Blues

LP
1741

Notes by Alan Lomax. Producer: Alan Lomax.
Cover art: Prentiss Taylor, *Assembly Church*.

s1/1	*Louisiana*. Henry Ratcliff, vocal. *Field Song from Senegal*. Bakari-Badji, vocal.	2:45
s1/2	*Po' Boy Blues*. John Dudley, vocal.	2:36
s1/3	*Katie Left Memphis*. Tangle Eye, vocal.	3:00
s1/4	*Berta, Berta*. Leroy Miller and a group of prisoners, vocals.	2:53
s1/5	*Old Original Blues*. Fred McDowell, vocal and guitar; Miles Pratcher, rhythm guitar.	4:09
s1/6	*Jim and John*. Ed Young, home-made fife; Lonnie Young, vocal and bass drum.	2:10
s1/7	*Emmaline, Take Your Time*. Alec Askew, panpipes.	1:03

252 (continued)

s1/8	*Buttermilk*. Miles Pratcher, guitar and fiddle; Bob Pratcher, vocal, guitar, and fiddle.	3:17
s1/9	*Mama Lucy*. Leroy Gary, vocal.	:33
s1/10	*I'm Gonna Live Anyhow till I Die*. Miles Pratcher, guitar and fiddle; Bob Pratcher, vocal, guitar, and fiddle.	2:32
s2/1	*No More, My Lord*. Tangle Eye and a group of prisoners, vocals.	2:45
s2/2	*Lining Hymn and Prayer*. Rev. Crenshaw and the congregation of New Brown's Chapel, Memphis.	3:31
s2/3	*Death Comes A-Creepin' in My Room*. Fred McDowell, vocal and guitar.	3:12
s2/4	*Church-House Moan*. Congregation of New Brown's Chapel, Memphis.	1:50
s2/5	*Beggin' the Blues*. Bessie Jones, vocal.	2:05
s2/6	*Rolled and Tumbled*. Rose Hemphill, vocal; Fred McDowell, guitar.	2:52
s2/7	*Goin' Down to the Races*. Fred McDowell, vocal and guitar; Miles Pratcher, guitar; Fannie Davis, comb and paper.	4:13
s2/8	*You Gotta Cut That Out*. Forrest City Joe, vocal and harmonica; unidentified, guitar.	2:56

253 William Schuman: *Undertow*
Morton Gould: *Fall River Legend*

P
1952

Notes by Walter Terry. Cover art: Raymond Breinin, drop curtain for *Undertow*.

s1	*Undertow*. Ballet Theatre Orchestra, Joseph Levine, conductor. G. Schirmer, pub.	24:12
s2	*Fall River Legend*. The New York Philharmonic, Dimitri Mitropoulos, conductor. G. Schirmer, pub.	24:23

254 New Music for Virtuosos/2

LP
1909

Notes by Harvey Sollberger. Producer: Max Wilcox.
Cover art: Waldo Glover Kaufer, *Eye*.

s1/1	*Sunflowers* (Harvey Sollberger, C). Harvey Sollberger, flute; Claire Heldrich, vibraphone. McGinnis & Marx Music, pub.	9:37
s1/2	*Motet on Doo-Dah* (Robert Morris, C). Harvey Sollberger, flute; Donald Palma, double bass; Daniel Shulman, piano. Copyright held by the composer.	6:15
s1/3	*Inflections I* (Robert Hall Lewis, C). Bertram Turetzky, double bass. Seesaw Music, pub.	9:54
s2/1	*Configurations* (Ralph Shapey, C). Sophie Sollberger, flute; Robert Black, piano. Theodore Presser, pub.	13:45
s2/2	*Three Sketches* (Andrew Imbrie, C). Stuart Dempster, trombone; Kevin Aanerud, piano.	7:10
s2/3	*General Speech* (Robert Erickson, C). Stuart Dempster, trombone and recitation. Seesaw Music, pub.	5:00

255 Make a Joyful Noise: Mainstreams and Backwaters of American Psalmody (1770–1840)

LP
1953

Notes by Richard Crawford. Producer: Elizabeth Ostrow. Cover art: Benjamin West, *The Calling of Isaiah* and *Jeremiah*. On all selections: The Oregon State University Choir, Ron Jeffers, conductor.

s1/1	*An Anthem of Praise* (Supply Belcher, C).	3:43
s1/2	*Chesterfield* (William Billings, C).	2:26
s1/3	*Newburgh* (Amos Munson, C; Joseph Doll, L).	3:16
s1/4	*Crucifixion* (M. Keyes, C; Samuel Wesley, L).	3:12
s1/5	*Invitation* (Jacob Kimball, C; Isaac Watts, L).	1:12
s1/6	*Montague* (Timothy Swan, C; Philip Doddridge, L).	1:08
s1/7	*Providence* (Daniel Read, C).	2:38
s1/8	*New Jordan* (unknown, C; Samuel Stennet, L).	2:35
s1/9	*The Dying Christian's Last Farewell* (William Billings, C).	4:32
s2/1	*Washington* (William Billings, C; Isaac Watts, L).	2:12
s2/2	*Sunderland* (Joseph [?] Strong, C).	2:15

255 (continued)

s2/3	*Heroism* (Supply Belcher, C; Nathaniel Nyles, L).	3:07
s2/4	*Richmond* (William Billings, C; James Relly, L).	2:18
s2/5	*Macedonia* (Oliver Holden, C; Isaac Watts, L).	1:47
s2/6	*Ode on Martyrdom* (Oliver [?] King, C; Isaac Watts, L).	2:16
s2/7	*Summons* (Truman S. Wetmore, C).	2:56
s2/8	*Middletown* (Amos Bull, C; Charles Wesley, L).	2:41

256 *Sweet and Low Blues*: Big Bands and Territory Bands of the 20s

L P
1693

Notes by Frank Driggs. Cover art: Harold Altman, *Man*.

s1/1	*Static Strut* (Phil Wall, Paul Specht, C; Jack Yellen, L). Erskine Tate's Vendome Orchestra: Erskine Tate, leader and violin; James Tate and Louis Armstrong, trumpets; Fayette Williams, trombone; Alvin Fernandez, clarinet and alto saxophone; Paul "Stump" Evans, alto and baritone saxophone; Norval Morton, tenor saxophone; Teddy Weatherford, piano; Frank Ethridge, banjo and second piano; John Hare, tuba; Jimmy Bertrand, drums. Warner Bros. Music, pub.	2:49
s1/2	*Symphonic Raps* (Bert Stevens, Irwin Abrams, C). Carroll Dickerson and His Orchestra: Carroll Dickerson, leader and violin; Homer Hobson and Louis Armstrong, trumpets; Fred Robinson, trombone; Bert Curry and Crawford Wethington, alto saxophones; Jimmy Strong, clarinet and tenor saxophone; Earl Hines, piano; Mancy Carr, banjo; Peter Briggs, tuba; Zutty Singleton, drums. Paramount Music, pub.	3:13
s1/3	*The Boy in the Boat* (Charlie Johnson, C). Charlie Johnson and His Paradise Orchestra: Leonard Davis and Sidney DeParis, trumpets; Jimmy Harrison, trombone; Ben Whitted, clarinet and alto saxophone; Edgar Sampson, alto and baritone saxophone; Benny Waters, clarinet and tenor saxophone; Charlie Johnson, piano; Bobby Johnson, banjo; Cy St. Clair, tuba; George Stafford, drums. Peer International, pub.	3:36

256 (continued)

s1/4   *That's How I Feel Today* (Fats Waller, C). The Chocolate Dandies: Leonard Davis, trumpet; Rex Stewart, cornet; J. C. Higginbotham, trombone; Don Redman and Benny Carter, alto saxophones; Coleman Hawkins, tenor saxophone; Fats Waller, piano; unidentified, banjo; Cy St. Clair, tuba; George Staffore, drums. Pub. unknown.   2:59

s1/5   *Sweet and Low Blues* (Jabbo Smith, C). Jabbo Smith and His Rhythm Aces: Cladys "Jabbo" Smith, trumpet; Omer Simeon, clarinet and alto saxophone; Cassino Simpson, piano; Ikey Robinson, banjo; Hayes Alvis, tuba. Pub. unknown.   3:18

s1/6   *Till Times Get Better* (Jabbo Smith, C). Jabbo Smith and His Rhythm Aces: Cladys "Jabbo" Smith, vocal and trumpet; Willard Brown, clarinet and alto saxophone; Earl Frazer, piano; Ikey Robinson, banjo; Lawson Buford, tuba. Pub. unknown.   2:58

s1/7   *Willow Tree* (Fats Waller, C; Andy Razaf, L). The Louisiana Sugar Babes: Cladys "Jabbo" Smith, trumpet; Garvin Bushell, clarinet and alto saxophone; James P. Johnson, piano; Fats Waller, organ. Warner Bros. Music, pub.   3:23

s1/8   *What Is This Thing Called Love?* (Cole Porter, C). Leo Reisman and His Orchestra: Lew Conrad, vocal and violin; Lew Sherwood and James "Bubber" Miley, trumpets; Jess Smith, clarinet and alto saxophone; Eddie Duchin, piano; other players unidentified. Warner Bros. Music, pub.   3:19

s2/1   *Starvation Blues* (Jesse Stone, C). Jesse Stone's Blues Serenaders: Albert Hinton and Oliver "Slick" Jackson, trumpets; Druie Bess, trombone; Glenn Hughes and Jack Washington, alto saxophones; Elmer Burch, tenor saxophone; Jesse Stone, piano; Silas Cluke, banjo; Pete Harrison, tuba; Max Wilkinson, drums. Pub. unknown.   3:10

s2/2   *Blue Devil Blues* (Walter Page, C). Walter Page's Blue Devils: Jimmy Rushing, vocal; James Simpson, Oran "Hot Lips" Page, and James LuGrand, trumpets; Druie Bess, trombone; Buster Smith, clarinet and alto saxophone; Ted Manning, alto saxophone; Reuben Roddy, tenor saxophone; William "Count"

256 (continued)

Basie, piano; Reuben Lynch, guitar; Walter Page, baritone saxophone, tuba, and bass; Alvin Burroughs, drums. Northern Music, pub. 3:01

s2/3 *There's a Squabblin'* (Bill "Count" Basie, C). Same group as above. Pub. unknown. 2:45

s2/4 *Dreamland Blues I* (Troy Floyd, C). Troy Floyd and His Plaza Hotel Orchestra: Don Albert and Willie Long, trumpets; Benny Long, trombone; Si-Ki Collins and Troy Floyd, alto saxophones; Scott Bagby or Herschel Evans, tenor saxophone; Allen Van, piano; John H. Braggs, banjo; Charlie Dixon, trombone and tuba; John Humphries, drums. Pub. unknown. 2:28

s2/5 *Dreamland Blues II* (Troy Floyd, C). Same group as above. Pub. unknown. 2:51

s2/6 *Ruff Scuffling* (Jesse Stone, C). George E. Lee and His Kansas City Orchestra: Harold Knox and Sam Utterback, trumpets; Jimmy Jones, trombone; George Lee, Clarence Taylor, and Herman Walder, alto saxophones; Bud Johnson, tenor saxophone; Julia Lee, piano; Charles Rousseau, banjo; Clint Weaver, tuba; Pete Woods, drums. Pub. unknown. 2:44

s2/7 *Black and Blue Rhapsody* (Bingie Madison, C). Alphonso Trent and His Orchestra: Chester Clark and Herbert "Peanuts" Holland, trumpets; Leo "Snub" Mosley, trombone; James Jeter, alto saxophone; Hayes Pillars, tenor and baritone saxophone; Leroy "Stuff" Smith, violin; Alphonso Trent, piano; Eugene Crooke, banjo; Robert "Eppi" Jackson, tuba; A. G. Godley, drums. Denton & Haskins, pub. 2:51

s2/8 *After You've Gone* (Turner Layton, C; Henry Creamer, L). Alphonso Trent and His Orchestra: same group as the preceding, plus George Hudson, trumpet, and Charles Pillars, alto saxophone. Morley Music, pub. 3:26

s2/9 *I've Found a New Baby* (Spencer Williams, Jack Palmer, C/L). Alphonso Trent's Orchestra: Anderson Lacy, vocal and violin; Lee Hilliard, trumpet and alto saxophone; Herbert "Peanuts" Holland and Thierry "Red" Elston, trumpets; Leo "Snub" Mosley and Gus Wilson, trombones; James Jeter and Charles Pillars, alto saxophones; Hayes Pillars, tenor and baritone saxophone; Leslie Sheffield, piano; Gene Crooke, banjo; Lewis Pitts, bass; Robert "Eppi" Jackson, tuba; A. G. Godley, drums. MCA Music, pub. 3:34

257 *The Wind Demon* and Other Mid-Nineteenth-Century Piano Music

L P
1671

Notes by Robert Offergeld (with additions by Edward A. Berlin). Producer: Andrew Raeburn. Cover art: Frederick Edwin Church, *The Heart of the Andes*. On all selections: Ivan Davis, piano.

s1/1	*The Andes, Marche Di Bravoura* (George William Warren, C).	5:55
s1/2	*Dream Land*, Op. 59 (George F. Bristow, C).	6:58
s1/3	*United States Grand Waltz* (Charles Grobe, C).	2:16
s1/4	*A Pastoral Novellette* (William Mason, C).	3:56
s1/5	*In Memoriam L. M. G.* (Richard Hoffman, C).	4:45
s1/6	*Dixiana* (Richard Hoffman, C).	3:10
s2/1	*The Wind Demon, Rhapsodie Caracteristique* (C. Jerome Hopkins, C).	5:54
s2/2	*Laurel Waltz*, from *The Elssler Dances* (Anthony Philip Heinrich, C).	3:45
s2/3	*Romance* (Louis Moreau Gottschalk, C). Alexander Broude, pub.	4:13
s2/4	*Adieu* (William Henry Fry, C).	2:39
s2/5	*Grande Polka de Concert* (Homer N. Bartlett, C).	5:14
s2/6	*Silver Spring* (William Mason, C).	5:19

258 David Diamond, Symphony No. 4
Peter Mennin, Symphony No. 7, "Variation-Symphony"

L P
1672

Notes by Harvey E. Phillips. Producer of Diamond Symphony for Columbia: John McClure. Producer of Mennin Symphony for RCA: Howard Scott. Cover art: Ben Shahn, *Forest*.

s1/1-3	Symphony No. 4 (David Diamond, C). The New York Philharmonic, Leonard Bernstein, conductor.	
	Allegretto	5:46
	Adagio	6:18
	Allegro	6:42
s2	Symphony No. 7, "Variation-Symphony" (Peter Mennin, C). The Chicago Symphony Orchestra, Jean Martinon, conductor.	26:28

259 *Cuttin' the Boogie*: Piano Blues and Boogie Woogie (1926-1941)

Notes by Martin Williams. Cover art: Alexander Calder, *Horizontal Spines*.

s1/1	*Chicago Stomp* (Jimmy Blythe, C). Jimmy Blythe, piano. Pub. unknown.	2:56
s1/2	*Mr. Freddie Blues* (J. H. Shayne, C). Jimmy Blythe, piano. MCA Music, pub.	3:07
s1/3	*Suitcase Blues* (Hersal Thomas, C). Hersal Thomas, piano. Pub. unknown.	2:31
s1/4	*Pinetop's Boogie Woogie* (Clarence "Pinetop" Smith, C). Clarence "Pinetop" Smith, piano. MCA Music, pub.	3:22
s1/5	*Jump Steady Blues* (Clarence "Pinetop" Smith, C). Clarence "Pinetop" Smith, piano. MCA Music, pub.	3:00
s1/6	*Honky Tonk Train* (Meade "Lux" Lewis, C). Meade "Lux" Lewis, piano. Shapiro, Bernstein, pub.	2:48
s1/7	*Yancey Special* (Meade "Lux" Lewis, C). Meade "Lux" Lewis, piano. Shapiro, Bernstein, pub.	3:13
s1/8	*Mr. Freddie Blues* (J. H. Shayne, C). Meade "Lux" Lewis, piano. MCA Music, pub.	2:57
s2/1	*Boogie Woogie Stomp* (Albert Ammons, C). Albert Ammons and His Rhythm Kings: Albert Ammons, piano; Guy Kelly, trumpet; Dalbert Bright, clarinet and alto saxophone; Ike Perkins, guitar; Israel Crosby, bass; Jimmy Hoskins, drums. Leeds Music, pub.	2:56
s2/2	*Bass Goin' Crazy* (Albert Ammons, C). Albert Ammons, piano. Leeds Music, pub.	3:36
s2/3	*The Mellow Blues* (Jimmy Yancey, C). Jimmy Yancey, piano. MCA Music, pub.	2:39
s2/4	*Tell 'Em about Me* (Jimmy Yancey, C). Jimmy Yancey, piano. MCA Music, pub.	2:45
s2/5	*Climbin' and Screamin'* (Pete Johnson, C). Pete Johnson, piano. MCA Music, pub.	3:19
s2/6	*Blues on the Downbeat* (Pete Johnson, C). Pete Johnson, piano. MCA Music, pub.	3:11
s2/7	*Kaycee on My Mind* (Dave Dexter, C; Pete Johnson, L). Pete Johnson, piano. MCA Music, pub.	2:53
s2/8	*Cuttin' the Boogie* (Albert Ammons, Pete Johnson, C). Albert Ammons and Pete Johnson, pianos; James Hoskins, drums. MCA Music, pub.	2:22

260 Sissle & Blake's *Shuffle Along*

LP
1539

Notes by Robert Kimball. Producer: Robert Kimball.
Cover by Elaine Sherer Cox. All selections published by
Warner Bros. Music, except Side 2/4-5. Unless otherwise
noted: Eubie Blake, C; Noble Sissle, L.

s1/1	*Bandana Days: I'm Just Wild About Harry*. Eubie Blake and the Shuffle Along Orchestra.	3:14
s1/2	*In Honeysuckle Time*. Noble Sissle and His Sizzling Syncopators.	2:28
s1/3	*Love Will Find a Way*. Noble Sissle, vocal; Eubie Blake, piano.	3:00
s1/4	*Bandana Days*. Noble Sissle, vocal; Eubie Blake, piano.	2:36
s1/5	*Daddy, Won't You Please Come Home*. Gertrude Saunders, vocal; Tim Brymm and His Black Devil Orchestra.	3:03
s1/6	*Baltimore Buzz; In Honeysuckle Time*. Eubie Blake, solo piano.	2:27
s1/7	*Gypsy Blues*. Paul Whiteman and His Orchestra.	3:23
s2/1	*I'm Craving For That Kind of Love*. Gertrude Saunders, vocal; Tim Brymm and His Black Devil Orchestra.	3:19
s2/2	*The Flight* (Dialogue) (Flournoy Miller, Aubrey Lyles, L). Flournoy Miller and Aubrey Lyles.	2:40
s2/3	*Gee, I'm Glad That I'm From Dixie*. Noble Sissle and Orchestra.	2:59
s2/4	*Mirandy* (James Reese Europe, Noble Sissle, Eubie Blake, C/L). Noble Sissle, vocal; Lt. Jim Europe's 369th U. S. Infantry ("Hell Fighters") Band. Joseph W. Stern, pub.	2:48
s2/5	*How Ya' Gonna Keep 'Em Down on the Farm* (Walter Donaldson, C; Sam M. Lewis, Joe Young, L). Same group as above. Belwin-Mills, pub.	1:21
s2/6	*On Patrol In No Man's Land* (James R. Europe, Noble Sissle, Eubie Blake, C/L). Same group as above.	2:27
s2/7	*Baltimore Buzz*. Noble Sissle, vocal, and His Sizzling Syncopators.	2:18

261 *Straighten Up and Fly Right*: Rhythm & Blues from
LP the Close of the Swing Era to the dawn of
1850 Rock 'n' Roll

Notes by Don Heckman. Cover art: Harold Krisel,
Untitled.

s1/1   *Flying Home* (Benny Goodman, Lionel
Hampton, C; Sid Robin, L). Lionel Hampton
and His Orchestra: Karl George, Ernest Royal,
and Joe Newman, trumpets; Fred Beckett,
Sonny Craven, and Harry Sloan, trombones;
Jack McVea, baritone saxophone; Milton
Buckner, piano; Irving Ashby, guitar; Wendell
Marshall, bass; George Jenkins, drums; Lionel
Hampton, vibraphone. Regent Music, pub.   3:10

s1/2   *Roll 'Em, Pete* (Pete Johnson, Joe Turner,
C/L). Joe Turner, vocal; Pete Johnson, piano.
Leeds Music, pub.   2:48

s1/3   *The Sun Didn't Shine* (Roosevelt Fennoy, C).
The Golden Gate Quartet: Henry Owens and
William Landford, tenors; Willie Johnson and
Arlandus Wilson, basses. Berwick Music, pub.   2:08

s1/4   *Straighten Up and Fly Right* (Nat "King" Cole,
Irving Mills, C/L). Nat "King" Cole, piano and
vocal; Oscar Moore, guitar; Johnny Miller, bass.
American Academy of Music, pub.   2:23

s1/5   *I Wonder* (Private Cecil Gant, Raymond
Leveen, C/L). Cecil Gant, vocal and piano.
Leeds Music, pub.   2:37

s1/6   *Choo Choo Ch'Boogie* (Vaughn Horton, Denver
Darling, Milton Gabler, C/L). Louis Jordan,
vocal and alto saxophone; Aaron Izenhall,
trumpet; Josh Jackson, tenor saxophone; Bill
Davis, piano; Carl Hogan, guitar; Po Simpkins,
bass; Eddie Byrd, drums. Rytvoc, pub.   2:46

s1/7   *Call It Stormy Monday* (Aaron Walker, C).
T-Bone Walker, vocal and guitar; Teddy
Buckner, trumpet; Bump Meyers, tenor saxo-
phone; Lloyd Glenn, piano; Arthur Edwards,
bass; Oscar Lee Bradley, drums. Gregmark
Music, pub.   2:59

s1/8   *Good Rockin' Tonight* (Roy Brown, C).
Wynonie "Blues" Harris, vocal; Hot Lips Page,
trumpet; Joe Britton, trombone; Vincent
Blair-Bey, alto saxophone; Hal Singer and Tom
Archia, tenor saxophones; Joe Knight, piano;
Carl "Flat Top" Wilson, bass; Clarence
Donaldson, drums. Fort Knox Music, pub.   2:26

261 (continued)

s1/9   *Give Me a Simple Prayer* (J. Kohen, C). The
        Ravens. Pub. unknown.   2:35

s2/1   *Well, Oh Well* (Tiny Bradshaw, Henry Bernard,
        C; Lois Mann, L). Tiny Bradshaw and His
        Orchestra: Tiny Bradshaw, vocal; Leslie Ayres,
        trumpet; Rufus Gore, tenor saxophone;
        Orrington Hall, alto and baritone saxophone;
        Jimmy Robinson, piano; Leroy Harris, guitar;
        Clarence Mack, bass; Calvin "Eagle Eyes"
        Shields, drums. Fort Knox Music, pub   2:41

s2/2   *Hello, Central* (Sam Hopkins, C). Lightnin'
        Hopkins, vocal and guitar; Donald Cooks, bass.
        Sam Hopkins, pub.   2:54

s2/3   *One Mint Julep* (Rudolph Toombs, C). The
        Clovers, Charlie White, lead singer. Unichappell
        Music/Regent Music, pub.   2:28

s2/4   *Hound Dog* (Jerry Leiber, Mike Stoller, C/L).
        Willie Mae "Big Mama" Thornton, vocal;
        Devonia Williams, piano; Pete Lewis, guitar;
        Albert Winston, bass; Leard Bell, drums. Elvis
        Presley Music/Lion Publishing, pub.   2:48

s2/5   *Mama, He Treats Your Daughter Mean* (Johnny
        Wallace, Herbert J. Lance, Charles Singleton,
        C/L). Ruth Brown, vocal. Marvin Music, pub.   2:53

s2/6   *Crying in the Chapel* (Artie Glenn, C). The
        Orioles, Sonny Til, lead singer. Unichappell
        Music, pub.   1:48

s2/7   *Hoochie Coochie Man* (Muddy Waters, pseud.
        of Morganfield McKinley, C). Muddy Waters,
        vocal and guitar; Little Walter, harmonica; Otis
        Spann, piano; Jimmie Rodgers, guitar; Fred
        Bellow, drums; Big Crawford, bass. Pub.
        unknown.   2:49

262/63 John Knowles Paine: *Mass in D*

LP
1900 –
1901

Notes by Peter Eliot Stone, Andrew Raeburn, and Gunther Schuller. Producer: Andrew Raeburn. Cover art: Albert Bierstadt, *Sunset in the Yosemite Valley*. Gunther Schuller conducting The Saint Louis Symphony Orchestra; The Saint Louis Symphony Chorus, Thomas Peck, director.

s1/1	*Kyrie*. Chorus.	7:13
s1/2	*Gloria*. Chorus and quartet: Carmen Balthrop, soprano; Joy Blackett, contralto; Vinson Cole, tenor; John Cheek, bass.	5:47
s1/3	*Qui tollis*. Joy Blackett, contralto; John Korman, solo violin; John Sant'Ambrogio, solo cello.	8:07
s1/4	*Quoniam*. Vinson Cole, tenor solo.	7:39
s2/1	*Cum Sancto Spiritu*. Chorus.	8:08
s2/2	*Credo*. Chorus. *Et incarnatus*. Carmen Balthrop, soprano solo *Crucifixus*. Chorus.	17:41
s3/1	*Et resurrexit*. Chorus.	3:52
s3/2	*Et in Spiritum Sanctum*. John Cheek, bass solo. *Confiteor*. Chorus, a capella. *Et vitam venturi*. Chorus.	11:50
s3/3	*Sanctus*. Chorus; Joanna Lange, organ. *Pleni sunt*. Chorus. *Osanna*. Chorus.	9:00
s4/1	*Benedictus*. Chorus and quartet: Carmen Balthrop, soprano; Joy Blackett, contralto; Vinson Cole, tenor; John Cheek, bass; John Korman, solo violin.	10:33
s4/2	*Agnus Dei*. Carmen Balthrop, soprano; Joy Blackett, contralto; chorus. *Dona nobis*. Chorus.	10:52

264 Old-Country Music in a New Land: Folk Music of Immigrants from Europe and the Near East

LP
1876

Notes by Oscar Handlin and Richard Spottswood.
Cover art: Ida Abelman, *My Father Reminisces*.

s1/1	*Sedliacky Zabavny Czardaš* (The Farmer's Diversion Czardaš). Mike Lapčak Slovensky Hudba.	3:25
s1/2	*Malenky Barabanshtchik* (The Little Drummer-Boy). Krestyanskyj Orkestr, Konstantin Sadovnik, leader.	3:14
s1/3	*Kasakka Polka: Tchornyj Ostrov* (Cossack Polka: Black Island). Aili and Lyyli Wainikainen, violin and accordion.	2:54
s1/4	*Zalim Te Momce* (I Saw You, Lad). Braca Kapugi Tamburica Orchestra: Martin and Adam Kapugi, *tamburitzas*; G. Douckick, violin; Louis Kapugi, string bass; B. Bialog, instrument unknown.	2:42
s1/5	*Stack-o-Barley*. Patrick Killoran and His Pride of Erin Orchestra: Patrick Killoran and Patrick Sweeney, violins; E. Tucker, piano.	2:53
s1/6	*The Tailor's Thimble; The Red-Haired Lass*. Morrison and McKenna: James Morrison, violin; John McKenna, flute.	3:05
s1/7	*El Coco-Cancion* (The Coconut Song). Lydia Mendoza y Familia: Lydia Mendoza, violin; Maria Mendoza, mandolin; Leonor Mendoza, guitar; Francisco Mendoza, triangle.	3:04
s1/8	*La Piedrera*. Santiago Jimenez y Sus Valedores: Santiago Jimenez, accordion; (?) Caballero, guitar; I. Gonzales, string bass.	2:40
s2/1	*I Tickled 'Em*. New Arkansas Travelers: A. Bishop, vocal.	2:58
s2/2	*Jeuns Gens Campagnard* (Young Men from the Country). Dennis McGee, vocal and violin; Ernest Fruge, violin.	2:43
s2/3	*La Valse de Bon Baurche (Valse du Bambocheur)* (The Drunkard's Sorrow Waltz). Elise Deshotel and the Louisiana Rhythmaires: Dewey Balfa, vocal and violin; Atlas Fruge, steel guitar; Elise Deshotel, rhythm guitar; Esther Deshotel, drums.	4:11
s2/4	*Pastorale. Zampogna* (bagpipe), *ciarmella* (reed pipe).	3:41

264 (continued)

s2/5   *Yar Ounenal* (I Love You) (Reuben Sarkisian, C). Vart Sarkisian, vocal; Reuben Sarkisian, violin; J. Berberian, *oud*; H. Parigian, banjo; P. Gamoian, *dembeg* (drum).   3:05

s2/6   *Sayf Lahziq* (Your Sword Has Pierced Me). Nahem Simon, vocal.   5:53

s2/7   *Siteiako* (Dance of Siteia). Harilaos Piperakis, vocal and lyra.   2:51

s2/8   *Kuomet Šokis* (When You Dance). Mahanojaus Lietviška Maineru Orkestra (Mahanoy City Lithuanian Miners Band), Fr. Yotko, leader; A. Saukevičius, vocal.   3:22

265 Don't Give the Name a Bad Place: Types & Stereotypes in American Musical Theater (1870–1900)

L P
1908

Notes by Richard M. Sudhalter. Producer: Sam Parkins. Cover art: Charles Witham, scene from *The Leather Patch*: "Grand View of Baxter Street," Act II, Scene III.

s1/1–5   (David Braham, C; Edward Harrigan, L). Max Morath, tenor solo; Dick Hyman, piano and conductor; Lois Winter, soprano; Rose Marie Jun, alto; Phil Olson, tenor; Charles Magruder, bass.

        The babies on Our Block, from *The Mulligan Guard Ball*   3:12

        Maggie Murphy's Home, from *Reilly and the 400*   3:37

        John Riley's Always Dry, from *Mulligan's Silver Wedding*   3:51

        Paddy Duffy's Cart, from *Squatter Sovereignity*   3:55

        Hang the Mulligan Banner Up, from *The Mulligan Guard Nominee*   2:23

s1/6   *Stay in Your Own Backyard* (Lyn Udall, C; Karl Kennett, L). Danny Barker, baritone; Dick Hyman, piano.   3:07

s1/7   *De Golden Wedding* (James A. Bland, C). Danny Barker, baritone solo; Dick Hyman, piano and conductor; Boddy Floyd, first tenor; Ralph Fields, second tenor; Bernard Knee, baritone; Charles Magruder, bass.   3:02

265 (continued)

s2/1	*My Gal Is a High-Born Lady* (Barney Fagan, C). Danny Barker, baritone; Dick Hyman, piano.	2:39
s2/2	*Darktown Is Out Tonight* (Will Marion Cook, C). Danny Barker, baritone solo; Dick Hyman, piano and conductor; Bobby Floyd, first tenor; Ralph Fields, second tenor; Bernard Knee, baritone; Charles Magruder, bass.	4:24
s2/3	*Tell 'Em I'll Be There* (James A. Bland, C). Bobby Floyd, tenor solo; Dick hyman, piano and conductor; Ralph Fields, tenor; Bernard Knee, baritone; Charles Magruder, bass.	3:00
s2/4	*The German 5th* (Gus Williams, C). Clifford Jackson, tenor solo; Dick Hyman, piano and conductor; Alan Sokoloff, first tenor; Ralph Fields, second tenor; Bernard Knee, baritone; Charles Magruder, bass.	2:46
s2/5	*Cat Song* or *Can Any One Tell Vere Dot Cat Is Gone?* (Gus Williams, C). Same as above.	2:38
s2/6	*Rip Van Winkle Was a Lucky Man* (Jean Schwartz, C; William Jerome, L). Clifford Jackson, tenor; Dick Hyman, piano.	4:02
s2/7	*Don't Give De Name a Bad Blace* (Gus Williams, C). Clifford Jackson, tenor solo; Dick Hyman, piano and conductor; Alan Sokoloff, first tenor; Ralph Fields, second tenor; Bernard Knee, baritone; Charles Magruder, bass.	3:49

266 *The Pride of America*: The Golden Age of the
LP American March
1540

Notes by Richard Franko Goldman. Producer: Andrew Raeburn. Cover by Elaine Sherer Cox. On all selections: The Goldman Band.

s1/1	*The Governor's Own* (Alton A. Adams, C). R. F. Goldman, conductor. Carl Fisher, pub.	2:22
s1/2	*Boston Commandery* (Thomas M. Carter, C). R. F. Goldman, conductor.	2:01
s1/3	*The Pathfinder of Panama* (John Philip Sousa, C). Ainslee Cox, conductor. Theodore Presser, pub.	3:18
s1/4	*Gate City* (A. F. Weldon, C). Ainslee Cox, conductor.	2:07

266 (continued)

s1/5	*His Excellency* (Henry Fillmore, C). R. F. Goldman, conductor. Carl Fisher, pub.	2:11
s1/6	*The Chimes of Liberty* (Edwin Franko Goldman, C). R. F. Goldman, conductor. Leo Feist, pub.	3:11
s1/7	*Bonnie Annie Laurie* (John Philip Sousa, C). R. F. Goldman, conductor.	2:29
s1/8	*The President's March* (Victor Herbert, C). R. F. Goldman, conductor. Carl Fisher, pub.	2:58
s1/9	*Our Director* (Frederick Bigelow, C). Ainslee Cox, conductor.	2:12
s2/1	*The Pride of America* (Edwin Franko Goldman, C). R. F. Goldman, conductor. Carl Fischer, pub.	2:18
s2/2	*Tabasco* (George Chadwick, C). Ainslee Cox, conductor.	2:42
s2/3	*Revival March* (John Philip Sousa, C). R. F. Goldman, conductor.	2:57
s2/4	*Grandioso* (Roland F. Seitz, C). Ainslee Cox, conductor. Southern Music, pub.	2:23
s2/5	*My Maryland* (W. S. Mygrant, C). Ainslee Cox, conductor.	2:07
s2/6	*On Jersey Shore* (Arthur Pryor, C). Ainslee Cox, conductor. Carl Fischer, pub.	2:23
s2/7	*Gardes du Corps* (R. B. Hall, C). R. F. Goldman, conductor.	2:30
s2/8	*The Serenade* (Victor Herbert, C). R. F. Goldman, conductor. Carl Fischer, pub.	2:45
s2/9	*Sesquicentennial March* (John Philip Sousa, C). R. F. Goldman, conductor. Sam Fox, pub.	3:47

267 *The Hand That Holds the Bread*: Progress and Protest
LP in the Gilded Age (Songs from the Civil War to the
1912 Columbian Exposition)

> Notes by William Brooks. Producer: Andrew Raeburn.
> Cover art: Edward Laning, *Passage to India*. Cincinnati's
> University Singers; Earl Rivers, director; with Thomas
> Bankston; Bonnie Wollpert, piano; Earl Rivers,
> harmonium; Chuck Riehle, percussion.

s1/1	*The Hand That Holds the Bread* (George F. Root, C). Chorus.	1:25
	The Anti-Monopoly War Song (R. J. Harrison [?], C). Michael Van Engen, bass.	2:15
	The Pacific Railroad (George F. Root, C). Chorus.	2:15
	The Song of the Red Man (Henry C. Work, C). Thomas Mariner, bass; with Kimberly Johns, alto; Janice Conrads, alto; Samuel Watts, tenor; Jeffrey Lewis, bass.	2:54
	The Future America (traditional; H. C. Dodge, L). Chorus.	1:37
s1/2	*Drill, Ye Tarriers, Drill* (Thomas F. Casey [?], C). Bruno Kazenas, tenor; with Richard Perry, tenor; Philip Yutzy, bass.	2:53
	A Laborer You See, and I Love Liberty (George W. Loyd, C). Philip Yutzy, bass.	1:03
	Out of Work (Alice Hawthorne, pseud. of Septimus Winner, C). Thomas Mariner, bass.	2:59
	Eight Hours (Jesse H. Jones, C; I. G. Blanchard, L). Philip Yutzy, bass.	2:29
s1/3	*The Chinese, the Chinese, You Know* (W. S. Mullally, C; John E. Donnelly, L). Richard Perry, tenor.	1:16
	Little Ah Sid (Joseph P. Skelly, C). Richard Perry, tenor.	2:24
	No Irish Need Apply (O'Reilly [?], C). Kate Scharre, alto.	2:35
	Uncle Sam's Farm (E. P. Christy, Jesse Hutchinson, C). Douglas Pennington, tenor; with Carol Sweeney-Sparrow, soprano; Janice Conrads, alto; Michael van Engen, bass.	2:15

267 (continued)

s2/1 *Jim Fisk*, or *He Never Went Back on the Poor* (William J. Scanlan [?], C). Ronald Campbell, bass; with Carol Sweeney-Sparrow, soprano; Janice Conrads, alto; Douglas Pennington, tenor; Michael van Engen, bass.   3:54
Kick Him When He's Down (T. Martin Towne, C). Marianne Specht, soprano; Kimberly Johns, alto; Samuel Watts, tenor; Jeffrey Lewis, bass.   1:57
We Never Speak as We Pass By (Anon. and Frank Egerton [?], C). Douglas Pennington, tenor; with Carol Sweeney-Sparrow, soprano; Janice Conrads, alto; Michael van Engen, bass.   2:49

s2/2 *When the Girls Can Vote* (M. H. Evans, C; Emma Pow Smith [Bauder], L). Chorus.   1:14
The Fatherhood of God and the Brotherhood of Man (John Hutchinson, C; arr. H. H. Hawley). Carol Penterman, soprano.   3:11

s2/3 *Ma! Ma! Where's My Pa?* (H. R. Monroe, pseud. of Monroe H. Rosenfeld, C). Joel Imbody, bass; with Vera Grujin and Marianne Specht, sopranos.   4:27
Little Brown Jug (Eastburn [Joseph Eastburn Winner], C). Richard Perry, tenor.   1:26
Father's A Drunkard, and Mother Is Dead (Mrs. E. A. Parkhurst, C; "Stella" of Washington [Nellie H. Bradley], L). Faith Prince, alto.   4:13
Crooked Whiskey (Anon., C; "Sour Mash," L). Richard Perry, tenor.   2:07

s2/4 *After the Fair* (Otto Bonnell, Charles K. Harris, C). Thomas Bankston, vocal.   2:44
Ta-Ra-Ra Boom-De-Ay (Angelo A. Asher, arr.; Richard Morton, L; earlier version arr. Henry J. Sayers). Kim Criswell, soprano.   1:54

268 Mrs. H. H. A. Beach: **Sonata in A Minor for Piano and Violin, Op. 34**

L P

1737 Arthur Foote: **Sonata in G Minor for Piano and Violin, Op. 20**

Notes by Herbert A. Kenny. Producer: Andrew Raeburn. Cover art: John Singer Sargent, *Astarte* (portion of a sketch for mural in the Boston Public Library). On both selections: Joseph Silverstein, violin; Gilbert Kalish, piano.

s1/1-4   Sonata in A Minor for Piano and Violin, Op. 34 (Mrs. H. H. A. Beach, C).

Allegro moderato	9:04
Scherzo: Molto vivace	4:08
Largo con dolore	7:57
Allegro con fuoco	7:16

s2/1-4   Sonata in G Minor for Piano and Violin, Op. 20 (Arthur Foote, C).

Allegro appassionato	5:09
Andantino grazioso: Alla siciliano	4:22
Adagio	7:30
Allegro molto	8:06

269 *Steppin' on the Gas*: **Rags to Jazz (1913–1927)**

L P

1692

Notes by Lawrence Gushee. Cover art: Billy Morrow Jackson, *The Offering*.

s1/1   *Castle House Rag* (James Reese Europe, C). Europe's Society Orchestra: Cricket Smith, cornet; Edgar Campbell, clarinet; Tracy Cooper, George Smith, and Walker Scott, violins; Chandler Ford, cello; Leonard Smith and Ford Dabney, pianos; Buddy Gilmore, drums. Edward B. Marks Music, pub.   3:33

s1/2   *Castle Walk* (James Reese Europe, Ford T. Dabney, C). Same group as above. Edward B. Marks Music, pub.   3:17

s1/3   *Memphis Blues* (W. C. Handy, C; W. George Norton, L). Lieutenant Jim Europe's 369th Infantry ("Hell Fighters") Band. Jerry Vogel Music, pub.   2:54

s1/4   *Clarinet Marmalade* (H. Ragas, C; L. Shields, L). Same group as above. Leo Feist, pub.   2:52

269 (continued)

s1/5   *Down Home Rag* (Wilbur Sweatman, C; Roger Lewis, Lew Brown, L). The Six Brown Brothers: Tom Brown, soprano and alto saxophone; Harry Cook, baritone saxophone; Harry Finkelstein, bass saxophone. Shapiro Bernstein, pub.   2:43

s1/6   *Stock Yard Strut* (Anon., C). Freddie Keppard's Jazz Cardinals: Freddie Keppard, cornet; Eddie Vincent, trombone; Johnny Dodds, clarinet; Arthur Campbell, piano; Jasper Taylor, washboard. Pub. unknown.   2:28

s1/7   *Ory's Creole Trombone* (Edward "Kid" Ory, C). Ory's Sunshine Orchestra: Mutt Carey, cornet; Kid Ory, trombone; Dink Johnson, clarinet; Fred Washington, piano; Ed Garland, string bass; Ben Borders, drums. Edwin H. Morris, pub.   3:31

s1/8   *Society Blues* (Anon., C). Same group as above. Pub. unknown.   3:02

s2/1   *Bogulousa Strut* (Sam Morgan, C). Sam Morgan's Jazz Band: Sam Morgan and Ike Morgan, cornets; Jim Robinson, trombone; Andrew Morgan, clarinet and tenor saxophone; Earl Fouché, alto saxophone; O. C. Blancher, piano; Johnny Davis, banjo; Sidney Brown, string bass; Roy Evans, drums. Pub. unknown.   3:02

s2/2   *Steppin' on the Gas* (Sam Morgan, C). Same group as above, except Tink Baptiste, piano, and Nolan Williams, drums. Pub. unknown.   2:46

s2/3   *West Indies Blues* (Clarence Williams, Spencer Williams, Edgar Dowell, C/L). Piron's New Orleans Orchestra: Peter Bocage, cornet; John Lindsay, trombone; Lorenzo Tio, Jr., clarinet and tenor saxophone; Louis Warnecke, alto saxophone; Armand J. Piron, violin; Steve Lewis, piano; Charles Bocage, banjo; Charles Seguirre, brass bass; Louis Cottrell, drums. MCA Music, pub.   3:34

s2/4   *She's Cryin' for Me* (Santo Pecora, C). New Orleans Rhythm Kings: Paul Mares, cornet; Santo Pecora, trombone; Charlies Cordilla, clarinet; Red Long, piano; Bill Eastwood, banjo; Chink Martin, brass bass; Leo Adde, drums. Pub. unknown.   2:46

269 (continued)

s2/5 *Bugle Blues* (Robert Kelly, C). Johnny Dunn's Original Jazz Hounds: Johnny Dunn, cornet; Herb Flemming, trombone; Herschel Brassfield, clarinet and alto saxophone; Ernest Elliott, clarinet and tenor saxophone; Dan Wilson, piano; John Mitchell, banjo; Harry Hull, brass bass. MCA Music, pub. 2:51

s2/6 *Dunn's Cornet Blues* (Johnny Dunn, C). Johnny Dunn and His Jazz Band: Johnny Dunn, cornet; Leroy Tibbs, piano; Samuel Speed, banjo. Pub. unknown. 3:09

s2/7 *Old Fashion Love* (James P. Johnson, C). Clarence Williams' Blue Five: Thomas Morris, cornet; John Masefield (or Mayfield), trombone; Sidney Bechet, soprano saxophone; Clarence Williams, piano; Buddy Christian, banjo. Warner Bros. Music, pub. 3:04

s2/8 *I Ain't Gonna Play No Second Fiddle* (Perry Bradford, C). Perry Bradford's Jazz Phools: Perry Bradford, vocal; Louis Armstrong, cornet; Charlie Green, trombone; Buster Bailey, clarinet; Don Redman, alto saxophone; James P. Johnson, piano; Sam Speed (?), banjo; Kaiser Marshall, drums. Pub. unknown. 2:35

270 *Brother, Can You Spare a Dime?* American Song During The Great Depression

LP
1740

Notes by Charles Hamm. Cover art: James Naumburg Rosenberg, *Dies Irae*.

s1/1 *Brother, Can You Spare a Dime?* from *Americana* (Jay Gorney, C; E. Y. Harburg, L). Bing Crosby, vocal; with Lennie Hayton and His Orchestra. Warner Bros. Music, pub. 3:14

s1/2 *The Boulevard of Broken Dreams*, from *Moulin Rouge* (Harry Warren, C; Al Dubin, L). Deane Janis, vocal; with Hal Kemp's Orchestra. Warner Bros. Music, pub. 3:10

s1/3 *Life Is Just a Bowl of Cherries*, from *George White's Scandals of 1931* (Ray Henderson, C; Lew Brown, L). Rudy Vallee, vocal; and His Connecticut Yankees. Chappell, pub. 3:12

s1/4 *In the Still of the Night*, from *Rosalie* (Hoagy Carmichael, C; "Trent," L). Glen Gray, vocal; the Casa Loma Orchestra. Chappell, pub. 3:14

270 (continued)

s1/5   *Love Walked In*, from *Goldwyn Follies* (George
Gershwin, C; Ira Gershwin, L). Kenny Baker,
vocal; orchestra conducted by Harry Sosnik.
Gershwin Publishing/Chappell, pub.   2:41

s1/6   *On the Good Ship Lollypop*, from *Bright Eyes*
(Richard A. Whiting, C; Sidney Clare, C/L).
Shirley Temple, vocal. Movietone Music, pub.   2:25

s1/7   *Unemployment Stomp* (Anon., C). Big Bill
Broonzy (William Lee Conley Broonzy), vocal.
Pub. unknown.   2:36

s1/8   *The Gold Diggers' Song (We're in the Money)*,
from *Gold Diggers of 1933* (Harry Warren, C;
Al Dubin, L). Dick Powell, vocal. Warner Bros.
Music, pub.   3:13

s2/1   *All in Down and Out Blues* (David Harrison
Macon, C). Uncle Dave Macon (D. H. Macon),
vocal and banjo. Pub. unknown.   2:30

s2/2   *Fifteen Miles from Birmingham* (Alton
Delmore, C). The Delmore Brothers. Vidor
Publications, pub.   2:45

s2/3   *The Coal Loading Machine* (George Korson, C).
The Evening Breezes Sextet. Pub. unknown.   2:42

s2/4   *NRA Blues* (Bill Cox, C). Bill Cox, vocal.
Pub. unknown.   2:52

s2/5   *I Ain't Got No Home in This World Anymore*
(Woody Guthrie, C). Woody Guthrie, vocal,
harmonica, guitar (?). Pub. unknown.   2:46

s2/6   *The Death of Mother Jones* (Anon., C). Gene
Autry, vocal. Pub. unknown.   2:40

s2/7   *All I Want* (Millard Lampell, *et al.*, L). The
Almanac Singers and Pete Seeger, vocals.
Pub. unknown.   3:00

s2/8   *The White Cliffs of Dover* (Walter Kent, C;
Nat Burton, L). Ray Eberle, vocal; Glenn
Miller and His Orchestra. Shapiro, Bernstein,
pub.   2:54

271 Bebop

LP
1541

Notes by Dan Morgenstern. Producer: Michael Brooks.
Cover by Elaine Sherer Cox.

s1/1   *Congo Blues* (Red Norvo, C). Red Norvo and
          His Selected Sextet: Dizzy Gillespie, trumpet;
          Charlie Parker, alto saxophone; Flip Phillips,
          tenor saxophone; Teddy Wilson, piano; Red
          Norvo, vibraharp; Slam Stewart, bass; J. C.
          Heard, drums. Edwin H. Morris, pub.   3:52
s1/2   *You're Not the Kind* (Will Hudson, arr.;
          Irving Mills, C/L). Sarah Vaughan with Tadd
          Dameron's Orchestra: Freddie Webster, trum-
          pet; Leroy Harris, alto saxophone and flute;
          Leo Parker, baritone saxophone; Bud Powell,
          piano; Ted Sturgis, bass; Kenny Clarke,
          drums. Belwin-Mills, pub.   2:43
s1/3   *Shaw 'Nuff* (Dizzy Gillespie, Charlie Parker,
          C/L). Dizzy Gillespie All Star Quintet: Dizzy
          Gillespie, trumpet; Charlie Parker, alto saxo-
          phone; Al Haig, piano; Curly Russell, bass;
          Sid Catlett, drums. Music Sales, pub.   2:57
s1/4   *Parker's Mood* (Charlie Parker, C). Charlie
          Parker All Stars: Charlie Parker, alto saxo-
          phone; John Lewis, piano; Curly Russell,
          bass; Max Roach, drums. Screen-Gems
          Columbia Music, pub.   3:02
s1/5   *Things to Come* (Dizzy Gillespie, Walter
          Fuller, C). Dizzy Gillespie and His Orchestra:
          Dizzy Gillespie, Dave Burns, Raymond Orr,
          Talib Daawud, and John Lynch, trumpets;
          Gordon Thomas, Alton Moore, and Leon
          Comegys, trombones; Howard Johnson and
          John Brown, alto saxophones; Ray Abrams
          and Warren Luckey, tenor saxophones; Pee
          Wee Moore, baritone saxophone; John Lewis,
          piano; Milt Jackson, vibraharp, Ray Brown,
          bass; Kenny Clarke, drums. Music Sales, pub.   2:42
s1/6   *Relaxin' at Camarillo* (Charlie Parker, C).
          Charlie Parker's New Stars: Howard McGhee,
          trumpet; Charlie Parker, alto saxophone;
          Wardell Gray, tenor saxophone; Dodo
          Marmarosa, piano; Barney Kessel, guitar; Red
          Callender, bass; Don Lamond, drums. Duchess
          Music, pub.   2:51

271 (continued)

s1/7   *Embraceable You* (George Gershwin, C; Ira Gershwin, L). Charlie Parker Quintet: Miles Davis, trumpet; Charlie Parker, alto saxophone; Duke Jordan, piano; Tommy Potter, bass; Max Roach, drums. Warner Bros. Music, pub.   3:39

s1/8   *Ko-Ko* (Charlie Parker, C). Charlie Parker's Reboppers: Dizzy Gillespie, trumpet and piano; Charlie Parker, alto saxophone; Curly Russell, bass; Max Roach, drums. Criterion Music, pub.   2:54

s2/1   *Lemon Drop* (George Washington [Giorgio Figlio], C). Woody Herman and His Orchestra: Ernie Royal, Bernie Glow, Stan Fischelson, Red Rodney, and Shorty Rogers, trumpets; Ollie Wilson, Earl Swope, Bill Harris, and Bob Swift, trombones; Sam Marowitz, alto saxophone; Woody Herman, clarinet; Al Cohn, Zoot Sims, and Stan Getz, tenor saxophones; Serge Chaloff, baritone saxophone; Lou Levy, piano; Terry Gibbs, vibraharp; Chubby Jackson, bass; Don Lamond, drums; Jackson, Rogers, and Gibbs, vocals. Belwin-Mills, pub.   2:51

s2/2   *Un Poco Loco* (Bud Powell, C). Bud Powell Trio: Bud Powell, piano; Curly Russell, bass; Max Roach, drums.   4:44

s2/3   *Jahbero* (Tadd Dameron, Fats Navarro, C). Tadd Dameron Septet: Fats Navarro, trumpet; Allen Eager and Wardell Gray, tenor saxophones; Tadd Dameron, piano; Curly Russell, bass; Kenny Clarke, drums. Chino Pozo, bongo drums.   2:50

s2/4   *Misterioso* (Thelonious Monk, C). Thelonious Monk Quartet: Thelonious Monk, piano; Milt Jackson, vibraharp; John Simmons, bass; Shadow Wilson, drums.   3:18

s2/5   *What Is This Thing Called Love?* (Cole Porter, C). Clifford Brown-Max Roach Quintet: Clifford Brown, trumpet; Sonny Rollins, tenor saxophone; Richie Powell, piano; George Morrow, bass; Max Roach, drums. Warner Bros. Music, pub.   7:31

s2/6   *Stop Time* (Horace Silver, C). Horace Silver Quintet: Kenny Dorham, trumpet; Hank Mobley, tenor saxophone; Horace Silver, piano; Doug Watkins, bass; Art Blakey, drums.   4:05

272 . . . and then we wrote . . . (American Composers and
Lyricists Sing, Play, and Conduct Their Own Songs)

LP
1849

Notes by Nat Shapiro. Cover art: William Charles
McNulty, *Times Square*.

s1/1   *The Enchantress*, from *The Enchantress* (Victor
Herbert, C). Victor Herbert and His Orchestra.
Warner Bros. Music, pub.   4:13

s1/2   *Hello! Ma Baby* (Joe Howard, C; Ida Emerson,
L). Joe Howard, vocal; Gene Kardos and His
Orchestra.   3:22

s1/3   *Loveless Love* (W. C. Handy, C). W. C. Handy's
Orchestra: W. C. Handy, cornet and vocal;
J. C. Higgenbotham, trombone; Edmond Hall,
clarinet; Bingie Madison, tenor saxophone; Luis
Russell, piano; "Pops" Foster, bass; Sidney
Catlett, drums. Handy Bros. Music, pub.   3:15

s1/4   *Like He Loves Me*, from *Oh, Please!* (Vincent
Youmans, C; Anne Caldwell, L). Beatrice Lillie,
vocal; Vincent Youmans, piano. Warner Bros.
Music, pub.   3:11

s1/5   *Someone to Watch Over Me*, from *Oh, Kay!*
(George Gershwin, C; Ira Gershwin, L). George
Gershwin, piano. New World Music, pub.   3:10

s1/6   *Star Dust* (Hoagy Carmichael, C; Mitchell
Parish, L). Hoagy Carmichael, vocal, whistling,
and piano; Artie Bernstein, bass; Spike Jones,
drums. Mills Music, pub.   2:29

s1/7   *Honeysuckle Rose*, from *As Thousands Cheer*
(Thomas Fats Waller, C; Andy Razaf, L). Fats
Waller, piano. Anne-Rachel Music, pub.   3:07

s2/1   *Mood Indigo* (Duke Ellington, Albany Bigard,
Irving Mills, C/L). The Jungle Band: Duke
Ellington, piano; Arthur Whetsol, trumpet; Joe
Nanton, trombone; Albany "Barney" Bigard,
clarinet; Fred Guy, banjo; Wellman Braud,
bass; Sonny Greer, drums. Mills Music, pub.   2:56

s2/2   *Anything Goes*, from *Anything Goes* (Cole
Porter, C/L). Cole Porter, vocal and piano.
Warner Bros. Music, pub.   3:09

s2/3   *Strip Polka (Take It Off! Take It Off!)*
(Johnny Mercer, C/L). Johnny Mercer, vocal;
Pied Pipers, backup vocals; Paul Weston and
His Orchestra. Edwin H. Morris, pub.   2:57

s2/4   *Sunday in the Park*, from *Pins and Needles*
(Harold Rome, C). Harold Rome, vocal and
piano. Florence Music, pub.   1:41

272 (continued)

s2/5   *You Are Never Away*, from *Allegro* (Richard
Rogers, C; Oscar Hammerstein II, L). Mary
Martin, vocal; Richard Rogers, piano;
orchestra conducted by John Lesko.
Williamson Music, pub.   3:44

s2/6   *A Sleepin' Bee*, from *House of Flowers*
(Harold Arlen, C; Truman Capote, L). Harold
Arlen, vocal; orchestra arranged and con-
ducted by Peter Matz. Harwin Music, pub.   4:44

s2/7   *Anyone Can Whistle*, from *Anyone Can Whistle*
(Stephen Sondheim, C). Stephen Sondheim,
vocal and piano. Burthen Music, pub.   1:47

s2/8   *If My Friends Could See Me Now*, from *Sweet
Charity* (Cy Coleman, C; Dorothy Fields, L).
Cy Coleman, vocal, with orchestra. Notable
Music/Lida Enterprises, pub.   2:42

273   Charles Tomlinson Griffes

L P
1 542

Notes by Donna K. Anderson, Producer: Andrew
Raeburn. Cover by Elaine Sherer Cox.

s1/1   *An den Wind* (Nikolaus Lenau, L). Sherrill
Milnes, baritone; Jon Spong, piano. C. F.
Peters, pub.   1:39

s1/2   *Am Kreuzweg wird begraben* (Heinrich Heine,
L). Same as above. C. F. Peters, pub.   1:29

s1/3   *Meeres Stille* (J. W. von Goethe, L). Same as
above. C. F. Peters, pub.   1:40

s1/4   *Auf geheimem Waldespfade* (N. Lenau, L).
Same as above. Schirmer, pub.   2:01

s1/5-8   *Four Impressions* (Oscar Wilde, L). Olivia
Stapp, mezzo-soprano; Diane Richardson,
piano. C. F. Peters, pub.
     Le Jardin   2:20
     Impression du Matin   3:07
     La Mer   2:26
     Le Réveillon   2:56

s1/9   *Song of the Dagger*. Sherrill Milnes, baritone;
Jon Spong, piano. Copyright held by A.
Marguerite Griffes.   4:38

s2/1   *The Pleasure-Dome of Kubla Khan*. The
Boston Symphony Orchestra, Seiji Ozawa,
conductor. Schirmer, pub.   10:32

273 (continued)

s2/2-4   *Three Poems of Fiona MacLeod*, Op. 11. Phyllis
         Bryn-Julson, soprano; The Boston Symphony
         Orchestra, Seiji Ozawa, conductor. Schirmer, pub.
                 The Lament of Ian the Proud   4:17
                 Thy Dark Eyes to Mine   2:57
                 The Rose of the Night   4:07
s2/5   *Three Tone-Pictures*, Op. 5: *The Lake at
         Evening*; *The Vale of Dreams*; *The Night Winds*.
         New World Chamber Ensemble: Gilbert Kalish,
         piano; Felix Galimir and Isidore Cohen, violin;
         John Graham, viola; Timothy Eddy, cello; Alvin
         Brehm, bass; Thomas Nyfenger, flute; Ronald
         Roseman, oboe; David Glazer, clarinet; William
         Purvis, French horn; Donald MacCourt, bassoon.
         Schirmer, pub.   9:13

274 *Jive at Five*: The Stylemakers of Jazz (1920s-1940s)

LP
1673

Notes by Frank Driggs. Producer: Sam Parkins. Cover
art: Abraham Rattner, *Frightened Faces*.

s1/1   *Every Tub* (Count Basie, C). Count Basie
         Orchestra: Ed Lewis, Buck Clayton, and Harry
         Edison, trumpets; Dan Minor, Eddie Durham,
         and Benny Morton, trombones; Earl Warren,
         alto saxophone; Lester Young and Herschel
         Evans, tenor saxophones; Jack Washington, alto
         and baritone saxophones; Count Basie, piano;
         Freddie Green, guitar; Walter Page, bass; Jo
         Jones, drums. Breyman, Vocco, and Conn, pub.   3:14
s1/2   *Melancholy* (Marty Bloom, Walter Melrose,
         C/L). Johnny Dodd's Black Bottom Stompers:
         Louis Armstrong, trumpet; Gerald Reeves,
         trombone; Johnny Dodds, clarinet; Barney
         Bigard, tenor saxophone; Earl "Fatha" Hines,
         piano; Bud Scott, banjo; Baby Dodds, drums.
         Melrose Music, pub.   3:07
s1/3   *What Is This Thing Called Love?* (Cole Porter,
         C). James P. Johnson, piano. Harms, pub.   3:02
s1/4   *What Is This Thing Called Love?* (Cole Porter,
         C). Sidney Bechet, soprano saxophone; Charlie
         Shavers, trumpet; Willie "The Lion" Smith,
         piano; Everett Barksdale, guitar; Wellman
         Braud, bass; Sidney Catlett, drums. Harms, pub. 3:32

274 (continued)

s1/5   *Pardon Me, Pretty Baby* (Vincent Rose, C; Ray
Klages, Jack Meskill, L). Benny Carter and His
Orchestra: Benny Carter (arr.), trumpet and
alto saxophone; George Chisholm, trombone;
Coleman Hawkins, tenor saxophone; Jimmy
Williams, clarinet and tenor saxophone; Freddy
Johnson, piano; Ray Webb, guitar; Len
Harrison, bass; Robert Montmarche, drums.
Mills Music, pub.   2:57

s1/6   *I Know That You Know* (Vincent Youmans,
C; Anne Caldwell, L). Jimmie Noone's Apex
Club Orchestra: Jimmie Noone, clarinet; Joe
Poston, alto saxophone and clarinet; Earl
"Fatha" Hines, piano; Bud Scott, banjo and
guitar; Johnny Wells, drums. Harms, pub.   2:55

s1/7   *I've Found a New Baby* (Clarence Williams,
C; Jack Palmer, L). Benny Goodman Sextet:
Benny Goodman, clarinet; Cootie Williams,
trumpet; Georgie Auld, tenor saxophone;
Count Basie, piano; Charlie Christian, guitar;
Artie Bernstein, bass; Jo Jones, drums.
MCA Music, pub.   3:03

s1/8   *Body and Soul* (Johnny Green, C; Edward
Heyman, Robert Sour, Frank Eyton, L).
Coleman Hawkins and His Orchestra:
Coleman Hawkins, tenor saxophone; Tommy
Linday and Joe Guy, trumpets; Earl Hardy,
trombone; Jackie Fields and Eustis Moore,
alto and baritone saxophones; Gene Rodgers,
piano; William Oscar Smith, bass; Arthur
Herbert, drums. Harms, pub.   3:00

s2/1   *I Double Dare You* (Jimmy Eaton, C; Terry
Shand, L). Louis Armstrong and His Orchestra:
Louis Armstrong, trumpet and vocal; Shelton
Hemphill, Louis Bacon, and Red Allen, trum-
pets; Wilbur DeParis, George Washington, and
J. C. Higginbotham, trombones; Pete Clark
and Charlie Holmes, alto saxophones; Bingie
Madison and Albert Nicholas, tenor saxo-
phones; Luis Russell, piano; Lee Blair, guitar;
Pops Foster, bass; Paul Barbarin, drums.
Shapiro, Bernstein, pub.   2:58

274 (continued)

s2/2   *Passion Flower* (Billy Strayhorn, C). Johnny
Hodges and His Orchestra: Ray Nance, cornet;
Lawrence Brown, trombone; Johnny Hodges,
alto saxophone; Harry Carney, baritone saxophone; Duke Ellington, piano; Jimmy Blanton,
bass; Sonny Greer, drums. Tempo Music, pub.   3:07

s2/3   *Three Blind Mice* (Frankie Trumbauer, C;
Chauncey Morehouse, L). The Chicago
Loopers: Bix Beiderbecke, cornet; Don Murray,
clarinet; Frankie Trumbauer, C-melody saxophone; Frank Signorelli, piano; Eddie Lang,
banjo; Vic Berton, drums. Robbins Music, pub.   2:56

s2/4   *Love Me Tonight* (Bing Crosby, Victor Young,
C; Ned Washington, L). Earl "Fatha" Hines,
piano. Robbins Music, pub.   2:39

s2/5   *Bugle Call Rag* (Jack Pettis, Billy Meyers,
Elmer Schoebel, C). The Chocolate Dandies:
Benny Carter (leader), alto saxophone, and
clarinet; Bobby Stark, trumpet; Jimmy
Harrison, trombone; Coleman Hawkins, tenor
saxophone; Horace Henderson (arr.), piano;
Benny Jackson, guitar; John Kirby, tuba.
Mills Music, pub.   2:48

s2/6   *Wolverine Blues* (Jelly Roll Morton, C). Baby
Dodds Trio: Albert Nicholas, clarinet; Don
Ewell, piano; Baby Dodds, drums. Melrose
Music, pub.   2:55

s2/7   *Slippin' Around* (Miff Mole, C). Red and
Miff's Stompers: Red Nichols, cornet; Miff
Mole, trombone; Fud Livingston, clarinet;
Arthur Schutt, piano; Dick McDonough,
banjo; Jack Hansen, tuba; Vic Berton, drums.
Robbins Music, pub.   2:48

s2/8   *Pitter Panther Patter* (Duke Ellington, C).
Duke Ellington, piano; Jimmy Blanton, bass.
Robbins Music, pub.   3:02

s2/9   *Jive at Five* (Harry Edison, C). Count Basie
Orchestra: Ed Lewis, Buck Clayton, Shad
Collins, and Harry Edison, trumpets; Dickie
Wells and Eddie Durham, trombones; Lester
Young, tenor saxophone; Jack Washington,
baritone saxophone; Count Basie, piano;
Freddie Green, guitar; Walter Page, bass;
Jo Jones, drums. Bregman, Vocco, and Conn,
pub.   2:44

275 Introspection: Neglected Jazz Figures of the 1950s
LP and Early 1960s
1875

>   Notes by Bob Blumenthal. Cover art: Kevin O'Callahan,
>   *Stern Timbers*.

s1/1	*'S Wonderful* (George Gershwin, C; Ira Gershwin, L). Herbie Nichols Quartet: Herbie Nichols, piano; Chocolate Williams, bass; Shadow Wilson, drums. New World Music, pub.	2:45
s1/2	*Into the Orbit* (Elmo Hope, C). Curtis Counce Quintet: Rolf Ericson, trumpet; Harold Land, tenor saxophone; Elmo Hope, piano; Curtis Counce, bass; Frank Butler, drums. Dootsie Williams, pub.	4:42
s1/3	*Race for Space* (Elmo Hope, C). Same as above. Dootsie Williams, pub.	4:30
s1/4	*II, V, I* (Jaki Byard, C). Jaki Byard, piano. Pub. unknown.	2:35
s1/5	*Diane's Melody* (Jaki Byard, C). Jaki Byard, piano. Pub. unknown.	5:02
s1/6	*Body and Soul* (Johnny Green, C; Edward Heyman, Robert Sour, Frank Eyton, L). Serge Chaloff Sextet: Herb Pomeroy, trumpet; Boots Mussulli, alto saxophone; Serge Chaloff, baritone saxophone; Ray Santisi, piano; Everett Evans, bass; Jimmy Zitano, drums. Warner Bros. Music, pub.	3:50
s2/1	*Louise* (Cecil Taylor, C). Steve Lacy Quartet: Steve Lacy, soprano saxophone; Charles Davis, baritone saxophone; John Ore, bass; Roy Haynes, drums. Unit Core, pub.	5:21
s2/2	*Introspection* (Thelonious Monk, C). Same as above. Embassy Music, pub.	5:28
s2/3	*We Speak* (Booker Little, C). Booker Little Sextet: Booker Little, trumpet; Julian Priester, trombone; Eric Dolphy, alto saxophone; Don Friedman, piano; Art Davis, bass; Max Roach, drums and timpani. Pub. unknown.	6:41
s2/4	*Strength and Sanity* (Booker Little, C). Same as above, except Ron Carter, bass. Pub. unknown.	6:13

276 The Birth of Liberty: Music of the American
Revolution

LP
1543

Notes by Richard Crawford. Producer: Andrew Raeburn.
Cover by Elaine Sherer Cox.

s1/1	*The Brickmaker March* (traditional). American Fife Ensemble: John Benoit, John Ciaglia, Barlow Healy, Edward Jesinkey, Craig Stopka, fifes; Daniel Mullen, snare drum.	:57
	Lamentation Over Boston (William Billings, C). The Continental Harmony Singers, conducted by Thomas Pyle. C. T. Wagner, pub.	5:04
	March for the 3rd Regt. of Foot, Lord Amherst's (General John Reid, C). The Liberty Tree Wind Players: Ronald Roseman, first oboe; Virginia Brewer, second oboe; Donald MacCourt, bassoon; A. Robert Johnson and William Purvis, French horns.	(?)
s1/2	*British Grenadiers* (traditional). American Fife Ensemble.	1:10
	Song on Liberty (traditional, C; attrib. to Joseph Warren, L). Sherrill Milnes, baritone; Jon Spong, harpsichord.	2:50
s1/3	*General Scott's March* (traditional). The Liberty Tree Wind Players.	:59
	Junto Song (attrib. to Thomas Arne, C). Seth McCoy, tenor; James Richman, harpsichord.	2:12
	Lovely Nancy, from *The Jovial Crew* (James Oswald, C; harmonization by John Ciaglia). American Fife Ensemble.	1:13
s1/4	*American Vicar of Bray* (traditional). Sherrill Milnes, baritone.	4:26
s1/5	*Independence* (William Billings, C/L). The Continental Harmony Singers, Neely Bruce, conductor.	6:59
s2/1	*March of the 35th Regiment* (traditional). The Liberty Tree Wind Players.	1:51
	Liberty Song (William Boyce, C; John Dickinson, L). Sherrill Milnes, baritone; Jon Spong, harpsichord.	3:33
	Lady Hope's Reel (traditional). American Fife Ensemble.	1:16
s2/2	*Parody upon a Well-known Liberty Song* (Anon.). Seth McCoy, tenor; James Richman, harpsichord.	3:09
	March for the 76th Regt. (General John Reid, C). The Liberty Tree Wind Players.	1:19

276 (continued)

s2/3   *Warren* (Abraham Wood, C). The Continental
Harmony Singers, Neely Bruce, conductor.   4:10
Stone Grinds All (traditional). American Fife
Ensemble.   1:03

s2/4   *The King's Own Regulars* (attrib. Benjamin
Franklin, L). Seth McCoy, tenor; James
Richman, harpsichord.   4:33
Washington's March (traditional). The Liberty
Tree Wind Players.   1:24

s2/5   *A Hymn on Peace* (Abraham Wood, C). The
Continental Harmony Singers, Neely Bruce,
conductor.   4:41

277 Aaron Copland: Works for Piano (1926–1948)

LP
1674

Notes by David Hamilton. Cover art: Charles Sheeler,
Delmonico Building. All works published by Boosey &
Hawkes.

s1/1-3   Piano Sonata. Leonard Bernstein, piano.
     Molto Moderato   7:47
     Vivace   4:35
     Andante sostenuto   8:29

s2/1   *Piano Variations*. Aaron Copland, piano.   10:46
s2/2   *Danzón Cubano*. Aaron Copland and Leo
Smit, pianos.   6:51
s2/3   *Four Piano Blues/ Freely Poetic; Soft and
Languid; Muted and Sensuous; With Bounce.*
Aaron Copland, piano.   8:28

278 Georgia Sea Island Songs

LP
1848

Notes by Alan Lomax. Producer: Alan Lomax. Cover art: Jean MacKay, *Peter Ring dem Bells*.
Performers: Group A: Joe Armstrong, Jerome Davis, John Davis, Peter Davis, Bessie Jones, Henry Morrison, Willis Proctor, Ben Ramsey. Group B: John Davis, Peter Davis, Bessie Jones, Henry Morrison, Willis Proctor. Group C: John Davis, Bessie Jones, Henry Morrison, Nat Rahmings (drums), Alberta Ramsey, Emma Ramsey, Hobart Smith (banjo and guitar), Ed Young (fife).

s1/1	*Moses*. John Davis, leader; Group B.	4:10
s1/2	*Kneebone*. Joe Armstrong, leader; Group A.	2:07
s1/3	*Sheep, Sheep, Don't You Know the Road.* Bessie Jones, leader; Group B.	2:18
s1/4	*Live Humble*. John Davis, leader; Group A.	3:44
s1/5	*Daniel*. Willis Proctor, leader; Group A.	2:08
s1/6	*O Death*. Bessie Jones, leader; Group A.	2:45
s1/7	*Read 'Em, John*. John Davis, leader; Group A.	2:01
s1/8	*Beulah Land*. John Davis, leader; Group C.	4:15
s2/1	*The Buzzard Lope*. Bessie Jones, leader; Group A.	1:58
s2/2	*Raggy Levy*. John Davis, leader; Group B.	1:05
s2/3	*Ain't I Right*. Henry Morrison, leader; Group A.	1:33
s2/4	*See Aunt Dinah*. Bessie Jones, leader; Group C.	3:01
s2/5	*Walk, Billy Abbot*. Willis Proctor, leader; Group A.	:54
s2/6	*Reg'lar, Reg'lar, Rollin' Under*. Bessie Jones, leader; Group C.	2:16
s2/7	*Pay Me*. Joe Armstrong, leader; Group A.	1:23
s2/8	*Carrie Belle*. John Davis, leader; Group A.	3:29
s2/9	*Laz'rus*. Henry Morrison, leader; Group B.	1:36
s2/10	*The Titanic*. Bessie Jones, leader; Group C.	3:30

279 *Yes Sir, That's My Baby*: **The Golden Years of Tin Pan Alley (1920-1929)**

LP
1735

Notes by Nat Shapiro. Cover art: Reginald Marsh, *Chop Suey Dancers No. 2.*

s1/1	*Whispering* (John Schonberger, Vincent Rose, C; Richard Coburn, L). Paul Whiteman and His Ambassador Orchestra. Fisher Music/Miller Music, pub.	2:49
s1/2	*April Showers* (Louis Silvers, C; B. G. DeSylva, L). Guy Lombardo and His Royal Canadians. Warner Bros. Music, pub.	3:00
s1/3	*Collegiate* (Moe Jaffe, C; Nat Bonx, L). Fred Waring and His Pennsylvanians. Shapiro, Bernstein, pub.	3:00
s1/4	*Dinah* (Harry Akst, C; Sam Lewis, Joe Young, L). Ethel Waters, vocal. Mills Music and Morley Music, pub.	3:16
s1/5	*A Good Man Is Hard To Find* (Eddie Green, C). Ted Lewis and His Band. Mayfair Music, pub.	2:45
s1/6	*Gimme a Little Kiss, Will Ya Huh?* (Roy Turk, Jack Smith, Maceo Pinkard, C/L). Jack Smith, vocal and piano. Bourne Co./Cromwell Music, pub.	3:10
s1/7	*'Deed I Do* (Walter Hirsch, Fred Rose, C/L). Ruth Etting, vocal. The Times Square Music Publications Co., pub.	2:46
s2/1	*There'll Be Some Changes Made* (W. Benton Overstreet, C; Billy Higgins, L). Sophie Tucker, vocal; Ted Shapiro, piano. Edward B. Marks, pub.	2:58
s2/2	*Sunday* (Ned Miller, Chester Conn, Jule Styne, Bennie Kreuger, C/L). Cliff ("Ukulele Ike") Edwards and His Hot Combination: Red Nichols, cornet; Miff Mole, trombone; Jimmy Dorsey, alto saxophone and clarinet; Arthur Schutt, piano; Dick McDonough, banjo; Vic Berton, drums. Leo Feist, pub.	2:57
s2/3	*Yes Sir, That's My Baby* (Walter Donaldson, C; Gus Kahn, L). Blossom Seeley, vocal; Charlie Bourne and Phil Ellis, pianos. Bourne Co./Donaldson Publishing, pub.	2:34
s2/4	*Mississippi Mud* (Harry Barris, C; James Cavanaugh, L). Paul Whiteman and His Orchestra; The Rhythm Boys, vocal. Shapiro, Bernstein, pub.	3:34

279 (continued)

s2/5   *My Blue Heaven* (Walter Donaldson, C;
George Whiting, L). Gene Austin, vocal. Leo
Feist, pub.   3:32

s2/6   *Deep Night* (Charlie Henderson, C; Rudy
Vallee, L). Rudy Vallee and His Connecticut
Yankees. Warner Bros. Music, pub.   3:20

s2/7   *Ain't Misbehavin'* (*Connie's Hot Chocolates*)
(Thomas "Fats" Waller, Harry Brooks, C;
Andy Razaf, L). Louis Armstrong and His
Orchestra. Mills Music/Anne-Rachel Music,
pub.   3:22

280 Fugues, Fantasia, & Variations: Nineteenth-Century American Concert Organ Music

LP
1544

Notes by Barbara Owen. Producer: Andrew Raeburn.
Cover art by Elaine Sherer Cox. On all selections:
Richard Morris, organ.

s1/1-4   Grand Sonata in E Flat, Op. 22 (Dudley
Buck, C).
    Allegro con brio   8:33
    Andante espressivo   4:27
    Scherzo: vivace non troppo   3:55
    Allegro maestoso   4:45

s2/1   *Variations on the Russian National Hymn*,
Op. 12 (W. Eugene Thayer, C).   8:28

s2/2   Fugue in C Minor, Op. 36, No. 3 (Horatio
Parker, C).   3:36

s2/3   *Fantasie über "Ein' feste Burg,"* Op. 13
(John Knowles Paine, C).   7:27

s2/4   *Postlude*, Op. 53 (George E. Whiting, C).   3:16

281 Chamber Music by Lou Harrison, Ben Weber, Lukas Foss, Ingolf Dahl

LP
1666

Notes by Carter Harman. Cover art: Paul Cadmus, *Mobile.*

s1/1   *Suite for Cello and Harp* (Lou Harrison, C).
Chorale; Pastoral; Interlude; Aria; Chorale.
Seymour Barab, cello; Lucile Lawrence, harp.
Peer International, pub.   10:54

281 (continued)

s1/2 *Sonata da Camera* (Ben Weber, C). Lento, con
gran eleganza; Moderato; Allegro con spirito.
Alexander Schneider, violin; Mieczyslaw
Horszowski, piano. Boosey & Hawkes, pub.   10:40

s2/1 *Capriccio for Cello and Piano* (Lukas Foss, C).
Gregor Piatigorsky, cello; Lukas Foss, piano.
Carl Fischer, pub.   5:58

s2/2 *Concertino a Tre* (Ingolf Dahl, C). Mitchell
Lurie, clarinet; Eudice Shapiro, violin; Victor
Gottlieb, cello. Joseph Boonin, pub.   18:15

282 The Sousa and Pryor Bands: Original Recordings (1901–1926)

LP
1665

Notes by James R. Smart. Producer: James R. Smart.
Cover art: Joseph Pennell, *Hail America*. Side 1: The
Sousa Band; Side 2: The Pryor Band, conducted by
Arthur Pryor.

s1/1 *Federal March* (John Philip Sousa, C). Edwin
G. Clarke, conductor. Theodore Presser, pub.   2:21

s1/2 *Creole Belles* (J. Bodewalt Lampe, C). Arthur
Pryor, conductor.   2:30

s1/3 *At a Georgia Camp Meeting* (Frederick A.
"Kerry" Mills, C). Walter B. Rogers,
conductor.   2:35

s1/4 *The Patriot* (Arthur Pryor, C). Conductor
unknown; Arthur Pryor, trombone.   2:56

s1/5 *Pasquinade* (Louis Moreau Gottschalk, C).
Arthur Pryor, conductor.   2:14

s1/6 *Glory of the Yankee Navy* (John Philip Sousa,
C). Walter B. Rogers, conductor. Theodore
Presser, pub.   2:56

s1/7 *Trombone Sneeze* (Arthur Pryor, C). Arthur
Pryor, conductor.   2:05

s1/8 *A Musical Joke on "Bedelia"* (Herman
Bellstedt, C). Herbert L. Clarke, conductor.   3:37

s1/9 *The Ben-Hur Chariot Race March* (Edward
T. Paull, C). Arthur Pryor, conductor   2:56

s2/1 *General Pershing March* (Carl D. Vandersloot,
C). Belwin Mills, pub.   2:31

s2/2 *General Mixup, U.S.A.* (Anon., C).   2:23

s2/3 *March Shannon* (Alvin Willis, arr.).   2:28

282 (continued)

s2/4	*Battleship Connecticut March* (James E. Fulton, C). Oliver Ditson, pub.	2:14
s2/5	*Alagazam March* (Abe Holzman, C).	1:31
s2/6	*Yankee Shuffle* (Fred L. Moreland, C).	2:33
s2/7	*The Teddy Bear's Picnic* (John W. Bratton, C). Warner Bros. Music, pub.	2:24
s2/8	*Down the Field March* (Stanleigh P. Friedman, C).	2:10
s2/9	*Falcon March* (W. Paris Chambers, C).	2:16
s2/10	*Repasz Band March* (Charles C. Sweeley, C).	2:38

283 *'Spiew Juchasa/Song of the Shepherd*: Songs of the
LP   Slavic Americans
1874

> Notes by Andrzej Kaminski and Richard Spottswood.
> Cover art: Arshile Gorky, *The Artist's Mother*.

s1/1	*Oberek Puławiak* (Oberek from Puławy). J. Baczkowskiego Orkiestra.	3:07
s1/2	*Zawzięta Dziewczyna* (Stubborn Girl). Orkiestra Dukli: Jan Kapalka, vocal; Franciszek Dukla, violin.	2:47
s1/3	*Wspomnienia Sabaly* (Reminiscences of Sabala). Orkiestra Karol Stoch: Stanisław Janik, Antonina Blazończyk, and Andrew Wróbel, vocals; Karol Stoch, violin; Joe Pat, accordion with Solo-Vox attachment; Andrew Bernas and Jan Krzysiak, second violins; Frank Kwak, string bass.	2:56
s1/4	*"Na Obi Nogi" Polka* ("On Two Feet" Polka). Bruno Rudziński, vocal and concertina.	3:10
s1/5	*Pieśń Zbójników* (Song of the Bandits). Sichelski i Bachleda i Karola Stocha Oryginalna Góralska Muzyka: Mr. and Mrs. Stanisław Bachleda and members of the band, vocals; Karol Stoch, violin; Józef Nówobielski and Franciszek Chowaniec, second violins; Stanisław Tatar, cello.	3:01
s1/6	*Nie Będę Się Żynił* (I Will Not Marry). Same as above, except Jan (?) Sichelski, vocal, replaces Mrs. Bachleda.	3:06
s1/7	*'Spiew Juchasa* (Song of the Shepherd). Same as above, with Mrs. Bachleda.	2:56
s1/8	*Zakopiańska Picsnka* (Song from Zakopane). Same as above, without Mrs. Bachleda.	3:00

283 (continued)

s1/9   *Dye Se Dołu Białką* (Down the Bialka Valley).
Same as above.   3:09

s2/1   *Kozak Zawydija* (Fast Kozak). Ukrainska
Orchestra Pawla Humeniuka: Pawlo Humeniuk,
violin.   3:04

s2/2   *Bohacki Zaruczyny* (Engagement Ceremony
among the Rich). Ukrainska Orchestra i Chor
Pawla Humeniuka: Ewgen Żukowsky, Nasza
Roza Krasnowska, and unknown male, vocals
and dialogue; Pawlo Humeniuk, violin.   2:58

s2/3   *Na Wesiliu pid Chatoju* (At a Wedding under
the Eaves). Ukrainska Orchestra Pawla
Humeniuka: Ewgen Żukowsky, spoken intro-
duction; Pawlo Humeniuk, violin.   2:59

s2/4   *Ukrainskyj Trisak* (Ukrainian Trisak).
Ukrainska Selska Orchestra.   3:17

s2/5   *Sztajer z Góry Baraniej* (Dance from the
Sheep Mountains). Wiejska Czwórka
"Bracia Kuziany."   2:57

s2/6   *Hutzulka w Semereczyni* (Hutzulka from
Semereczyn). Ukrainska Orchestra Michala
Thomasa: Michal Thomas, violin.   3:04

s2/7   *Poprawyny* (Second-Day Wedding Feast).
Zlozyw i Widohraw Solo Skrypkowe Pawlo
Humeniuk: Ewgen Żukowsky and Nasza Roza
Krasnowska, vocals; Pawlo Humeniuk, violin.   6:14

s2/8   *Wiwczar Na Supylci* (Shepherd Playing the
Flute). Zlozyw i Widohraw Solo Skrypkowe
Pawlo Humeniuk: Ewgen Żukowsky, vocal
and animal imitations; Pawlo Humeniuk, violin.   3:05

284 **Jazz in Revolution: The Big Bands in the 1940s**

LP
1237

    Notes by Burt Korall. Cover art: Henry Pearson,
Ethical Movement.

s1/1   *A-La-Bridges* (arr. Tadd Dameron). Harlan
Leonard and His Rockets: Edward Johnson,
William H. "Smitty" Smith, and James Ross,
trumpets; Fred Beckett and Richmond
Henderson, trombones; Darwin Jones, Ben
Kynard, Harlan Leonard, Henry Bridges, and
James Keith, saxophones; William S. Smith,
piano; Stan Morgan, guitar; Billy Hadnott,
bass; Jesse Price, drums. Bregman, Vocco, &
Conn, pub.   3:20

284 (continued)

s1/2   *Dameron Stomp* (arr. Tadd Dameron). Same
as above, except Walter Monroe replaces Fred
Beckett, and Winston Williams replaces Billy
Hadnott. Bregman, Vocco, & Conn, pub.   3:02

s1/3   *The Saint* (Gerald Wilson, C; Snooky Young,
L; arr. Gerald Wilson). Gerald Wilson and His
Orchestra; Al Killian, James Anderson, Joe
"Red" Kelly, and Hobart Dodson, trumpets;
Melba Liston, Henry Coker, Robert Huerta,
and Vic Dickenson, trombones; Floyd Turner,
Maurice Simon, Eddie "Lockjaw" Davis,
Vernon Slater, and Gus Evans, saxophones;
Vivian Fears, piano; Irving Ashby, guitar; Red
Callender, bass; Henry Green, drums. Pub.
unknown.   3:08

s1/4   *Elevation* (arr. Elliot Lawrence). Elliot
Lawrence and His Orchestra: Joe Techner,
Johnny Dee, and Jimmy Padget, trumpets;
Sy Berger, Vince Forrest, and Chuck Harris,
trombones; Bill Danzien, trumpet and French
horn; Joe Soldo, Louis Giamo, Phil Urso,
Bruno Rondelli, and Merle Bredwell, saxophones; Elliot Lawrence and Bob Karch,
pianos; Tommy O'Neill, bass; Howie Mann,
drums. Elliot Music, pub.   2:35

s1/5   *Five O'Clock Shadow* (arr. Elliot Lawrence).
Elliot Lawrence and His Orchestra: Alec Fila,
Johnny Dee, and Ralph Clemson, trumpets;
Frank Rodowicz, Joe Verrechico, and Tony
Lala, trombones; Ernie Angelucci, French
horn; Mitch Miller, oboe; Harold Goldozer,
bassoon; Ernie Cantonucci, Mike Giamo, Jerry
Fields, Andy Pino, and Mike Donic, saxo-
phones; Elliot Lawrence and Mike D'Aquilla,
pianos; Hy White, guitar; Andy Riccardi, bass;
Max Spector, drums. Elliot Music, pub.   3:18

s1/6   *Good Jelly Blues*. Billy Eckstine and His
Orchestra: Dizzy Gillespie, Freddie Webster,
Shorty McConnell, and Al Killian, trumpets;
Trummy Young, Claude Jones, and Howard
Scott, trombones; Jimmy Powell, Budd
Johnson, Wardell Gray, Thomas Crump, and
Rudy Rutherford, saxophones; Clyde Hart,
piano; Connie Wainwright, guitar; Oscar
Pettiford, bass; Shadow Wilson, drums. Pub.
unknown.   2:52

284 (continued)

s1/7   *Mingus Fingers* (Charles Mingus, C). Lionel
Hampton and His Orchestra: Wendell Culley,
Duke Garrett, Walter Williams, Teddy
Buckner, and Leo Sheppard, trumpets; James
Robinson, Andrew Penn, Jimmy Wormick,
and Britt Woodman, trombones; Jack Kelson,
Bobby Plater, Ben Kynard, Morris Lane,
Johnny Sparrow, and Charles Fowkes, reeds;
Lionel Hampton, vibraharp; Milt Buckner,
piano; Billy Mackell, guitar; Joe Comfort and
Charles Mingus, basses; Earl Walker, drums.
Jazz Workshop, pub.   3:08

s1/8   *Donna Lee* (Charlie Parker, C; arr. Gil Evans).
Claude Thornhill and His Orchestra: Louis
Mucci, Red Rodney, and Eddie Zandy, trum-
pets; Allan Langstaff and Tak Takvorian,
trombones; Sandy Siegestein and Fred
Schmidt, French horns; Bill Barber, tuba;
Danny Polo, Lee Konitz, Mickey Folus, Mario
Rollo, and Bill Bushey, reeds; Claude Thornhill,
piano; Barry Galbraith, guitar; Joe Shulman,
bass; Billy Exiner, drums. Pub. unknown.   3:02

s2/1   *Perdido* (Juan Tizol, C). Ben Webster Quartet:
Ben Webster, tenor saxophone; Marlowe
Morris, piano; John Simmons, bass; Sid
Cartlett, drums. Tempo Music, pub.   2:59

s2/2   *Zonky* (Thomas "Fats" Waller, C; Andy
Razaf, L; arr. Gil Evans). Six Men and a Girl:
Earl Thompson, trumpet; Buddy Miller,
clarinet; Dick Wilson, tenor saxophone; Mary
Lou Williams, piano; Floyd Smith, guitar;
Booker Collins, bass; Ben Thigpen, drums.
Chappell, pub.   2:57

s2/3   *Tea for Two* (Vincent Youmans, C; Irving
Caesar, L; arr. Gil Evans). Joe Mooney Quartet:
Joe Mooney, vocal and accordion; Andy
Fitzgerald, clarinet; Jack Hotop, guitar; Gate
Frega, bass. Warner Bros. Music, pub.   2:44

s2/4   *I Can't Get Up the Nerve* (George Weiss,
Bennie Benjamin, C). Same as above.
Chappell, pub.   3:17

s2/5   *Mellow Mood* (Dodo Marmarosa, C). Dodo
Marmarosa Trio: Dodo Marmarosa, piano;
Ray Brown, bass; Jackie Mills, drums. Pub.
unknown.   3:12

284 (continued)

s2/6   *Royal Roost* (Kenny Clarke, C; arr. Walter
        "Gil" Fuller). Kenny Clarke and His 52nd
        Street Boys: Fats Navarro and Kenny
        Dorham, trumpets; Ray Abramson, Eddy
        DeVertevill, and Sonny Stitt, saxophones;
        Bud Powell, piano; John Collins, guitar; Al
        Hall, bass; Kenny Clarke, drums. J. J.
        Robbins & Sons, pub.   2:57

s2/7   *The Chase (parts I and II)* (Dexter Gordon,
        C). Dexter Gordon–Wardell Gray Quintet:
        Dexter Gordon and Wardell Gray, tenor
        saxophones; Jimmy Bunn, piano; Red
        Callender, bass; Chuck Thompson, drums.
        American Academy of Music, pub.   6:31

285 Works by Henry Cowell, Wallingford Riegger,
LP   **John J. Becker, and Ruth Crawford Seeger**

1905
        Notes by Alfred Frankenstein. Producer: Horace Grenell.
        Cover art: Man Ray, *Aerograph*.

s1/1   *Quartet Romantic* (Henry Cowell, C). Paul
        Dunkel, flute; Susan Palma, flute; Rolf
        Schulte, violin; John Graham, viola. C. F.
        Peters, pub.   17:06

s1/2   Wind Quintet (Wallingford Riegger, C). Paul
        Dunkel, flute; Stephen Taylor, oboe; Virgil
        Blackwell, clarinet; Frank Morelli, bassoon;
        Stewart Rose, horn. Ars Viva Verlag, pub.   6:40

s2/1   *The Abongo* (John J. Becker, C). New Jersey
        Percussion Ensemble at William Paterson
        College, Raymond DesRoches, Director.
        Philharmusica, pub.   9:40

s2/2-4 Three Songs (Ruth Crawford Seeger, C; Carl
        Sandburg, L). Beverly Morgan, mezzo-
        soprano; Members of Speculum Musicae, Paul
        Dunkel conducting. Theodore Presser, pub.
            Rat Riddles   3:25
            Prayers of Steel   1:50
            In Tall Grass   4:05

286 Walter Piston: Symphony No. 6
LP Leon Kirchner: Piano Concerto No. 1
1690

Notes by Bruce Archibald. Cover art: Paul Landacre, *The Press*.

s1/1-4 Symphony No. 6 (Walter Piston, C). The
Boston Symphony Orchestra, Charles Munch,
conductor; Samuel Mayes, cello. Associated
Music, pub.

Fluendo espressivo	6:39
Leggerissimo vivace	3:22
Adagio sereno	9:35
Allegro energico	4:22

s2/1-3 Piano Concerto No. 1 (Leon Kirchner, C).
The New York Philharmonic Orchestra,
Dimitri Mitropoulos, conductor; Leon
Kirchner, piano. Associated Music, pub.

Allegro	10:45
Adagio	10:01
Rondo	9:21

287 Country Music: South and West
LP 1696

Notes by Douglas B. Green. Producer: William Ivey.
Cover art: Grant Wood, *March*.

s1/1 *Georgia Wildcat Breakdown* (Clayton
McMichen, C). Clayton McMichen and His
Georgia Wildcats: Clayton McMichen and
Bert Layne, fiddles; Hoyt "Slim" Bryant,
Pat Perryman, and Jack Dunigan, guitars;
Perry Becktel, banjo. Pub. unknown. 3:02

s1/2 *Blue Yodel No. 11* (Jimmie Rodgers, C).
Jimmie Rodgers, vocal and guitar; Billy
Burke, guitar. Peer International, pub. 2:57

s1/3 *Sweet Fern* (A. P. Carter, C). The Carter
Family: Sara Carter, lead vocal and rhythm
guitar; Maybelle Carter, vocal harmony and
steel guitar; A. P. Carter, vocal harmony.
Peer International, pub. 3:04

s1/4 *Dreaming with Tears in My Eyes* (Jimmie
Rodgers, Waldo O'Neal, C/L). Jimmie
Rodgers, vocal and guitar. Peer Interna-
tional, pub. 2:56

287 (continued)

s1/5   *Gospel Ship* (A. P. Carter, C). The Carter
       Family: Sara Carter, lead vocal and rhythm
       guitar; Maybelle Carter, vocal harmony and
       lead guitar; A. P. Carter, vocal harmony.
       Peer International, pub.   2:55

s1/6   *Fais Pas Ça* (Don't Do That) (Richard M.
       Jones, C). The Hackberry Ramblers: Probable
       personnel: Luderin Darbonne, leader and fiddle;
       Lennis Sonnier, vocal and guitar; Edwin Duhon,
       mandolin; Joe Werner and Lonnie Rainwater,
       guitars; Floyd Rainwater, bass. Pub. unknown.   2:29

s1/7   *The Last Roundup* (Billy Hill, C). Gene Autry,
       vocal; Tex Atchison (?), fiddle; Charles Sargent
       (?), guitar. Shapiro, Bernstein, pub.   3:17

s1/8   *Forgotten Soldier Boy* (Bert Layne, C). The
       Monroe Brothers: Charlie Monroe, lead vocal
       and guitar; Bill Monroe, vocal and mandolin.
       Pub. unknown.   2:40

s1/9   *Ida, Sweet as Apple Cider* (Eddie Leonard, C).
       Milton Brown and His Brownies: Milton Brown,
       vocal; Cliff Bruner and Cecil Brower, fiddles;
       Bob Dunn, steel guitar; Durwood Brown,
       rhythm guitar; Ocie Stockard, banjo; Fred
       "Papa" Calhoun, piano; Wanna Coffman, bass.   2:57

s1/10 *There'll Come a Time* (Charles K. Harris, C).
       The Blue Sky Boys: Earl Bolick, lead vocal and
       guitar; Bill Bolick, vocal and mandolin. ABC/
       Dunhill Music, pub.   3:02

s2/1   *I Wanna Be a Cowboy's Sweetheart* (Patsy
       Montana, pseud. of Rubye Blevins, C). Patsy
       Montana and the Prairie Ramblers: Patsy
       Montana, vocal and guitar; Willie Thawl,
       clarinet; Tex Atchison, fiddle; Chick Hurt,
       mandolin; Salty Holmes, guitar; John Brown,
       piano; Jack Taylor, bass. MCA Music, pub.   3:04

s2/2   *The Rescue from Moose River Gold Mine*
       (Wilf Carter, [Montana Slim], C). Wilf Carter,
       vocal and guitar. Gordon V. Thompson, pub.   2:22

s2/3   *Railroad Boomer* (Carson J. Robison, C). Roy
       Acuff and His Smoky Mountain Boys: Roy
       Acuff, vocal and fiddle; Beecher Kirby
       ("Bashful Brother Oswald"), dobro; Lonnie
       Wilson, guitar; Jess Easterday, bass. Peer
       International, pub.   2:33

287 (continued)

s2/4   *Born To Lose* (Ted Daffan, C). Ted Daffan's
       Texans: Ted Daffan, steel guitar; Leon Seago,
       vocal and fiddle; Buddy Buller, lead guitar;
       Chuck Keeshan, rhythm guitar; Ralph Smith,
       piano; Freddy Courtney, accordion; Johnny
       Johnson, bass; Spike Jones, drums. Peer
       International, pub.   2:40

s2/5   *It Won't Be Long* (traditional). Harry Choates,
       vocal and fiddle.   2:17

s2/6   *Chant of the Wanderer* (Bob Nolan, C). The
       Sons of the Pioneers: Bob Nolan, Tim Spencer,
       Lloyd Perryman, Ken Carson, and Pat Brady,
       vocals; Hugh Farr, vocal and fiddle; Karl Farr,
       vocal and guitar; Country Washburn's Orches-
       tra: J. H. "Country" Washburn, leader; P.
       Shuken, flute; M. Friedman, saxophone; C.
       Hunt, M. Russell, and W. Callies, violins; D.
       Sterkin, viola; L. Roundtree, guitar; E. LePique,
       piano; A. Shapiro, bass; O. Downes, drums.
       Unichappell Music and Elvis Presley Music, pub. 3:00

s2/7   *Dark as a Dungeon* (Merle Travis, C). Merle
       Travis, vocal and guitar. Elvis Presley Music,
       Unichappell Music, for Hill & Range and
       Norma Music, pub.   2:47

s2/8   *Cotton Eyed Joe* (Bob Wills, Tommy Duncan,
       arr.). Bob Wills and His Texas Playboys:
       Tommy Duncan, vocal; Alex Brashear, trumpet;
       Bob Wills, Jesse Ashlock, Joe Holley, and Louis
       Tierney, fiddles; Lester Barnard, Jr., lead guitar;
       Les Anderson, steel guitar; Harley Huggins,
       rhythm guitar; Bill Mounce, banjo; Millard
       Kelso, piano; Billy Jack Wills, bass; Johnny
       Edwards, drums. Unichappell Music for Hill &
       Range, pub.   2:36

s2/9   *Fat Boy Rag* (Bob Wills, Lester Barnard, Jr.,
       C). Johnny Gimble, fiddle; Bill Joor, trumpet;
       Buddy Emmons, steel guitar; Eldon Shamblin,
       guitar; Tiny Moore, mandolin; Bob Moore,
       bass; Monte Mountjoy, drums. Unichappel
       Music, pub.   5:06

288/89   *The Mother of Us All*: an Opera. Music by
LP   Virgil Thomson; Text by Gertrude Stein
1688-
1689   Notes by Robert Marx. Producer: Andrew Raeburn.
             Cover design: Robert Indiana. The Santa Fe Opera,
             Raymond Leppard, conductor. Cast: Mignon Dunn,
             Batyah Godfrey, Aviva Orvath, Gene Ives, Philip
             Booth, James Atherton, Joseph McKee, Linn Maxwell,
             Ashley Putnam, Billie Nash, Ronald Raines, David W.
             Fuller, William Lewis, Douglas Perry, Helen Vanni,
             James McKeel, Sondra Stowe, Karen Beck, Jimmie Lu
             Null, Steven Loewengart, Paul Mabrey, Thomas Parker,
             Marla McDaniels, D'Artagnan Petty, Stephen Bryant.

s1/1	A Political Meeting	3:10
s1/2	Act I, Scene 1	6:41
s1/3	Act I, Scene 2	17:08
s2/1	Interlude: Cold Weather—Act I, Scene 3	9:28
s2/2	Act I, Scene 4	10:19
s2/3	Act I, Scene 5 (first part)	4:19
s3/1	Act I, Scene 5 (conclusion)	9:34
s3/2	Act II, Scene 1—Last Intermezzo	12:03
s3/3	Act II, Scene 2 (first part)	6:31
s4/1	Act II, Scene 2 (conclusion)	7:29
s4/2	Act II, Scene 3	19:56

290 *Let's Get Loose*: Folk and Popular Blues Styles from
LP   the Beginnings to the Early 1940s
1913
             Notes by David Evans. Cover art: J. J. Lankes, *Spring
             Twilight.*

s1/1	*Peach Tree Blues* (Yank Rachell, C). Yank Rachell, vocal and guitar; Sonny Boy Williamson, harmonica; Alfred Elkins, washtub bass; Washboard Sam, washboard. Duchess Music, pub.	2:44
s1/2	*Brownskin Woman*. Pillie Bolling, vocal and guitar.	3:19
s1/3	*Violin Blues*. The Johnson Boys: T. C. Johnson, guitar; Nap Hayes, vocal and violin; Matthew Prater, mandolin.	3:16
s1/4	*What's the Matter Now?* Monarch Jazz Quartet of Norfolk. MCA Music, pub.	3:12

290 (continued)

s1/5   *Yodeling Blues*. Buck Mountain Band: Earl
       Edwards (?), vocal and guitar; Van Edwards,
       fiddle; Wade Ward, banjo. MCA Music, pub.   2:56

s1/6   *Doggone My Good Luck Soul*. Hattie Hudson,
       vocal; Willie Tyson, piano.   3:06

s1/7   *Let's Get Loose* (Gray, C). Clara Smith, vocal;
       Ed Allen, cornet.   2:40

s1/8   *Nigger Blues* (Leroy "Lasses" White, C).
       George O'Connor, vocal.   2:54

s2/1   *Dad's Ole Mule* (Charles and Effie Tyus, C).
       Tyus and Tyus, vocals.   3:14

s2/2   *Keep It Clean*. Rufus and Ben Quillian; Rufus
       Quillian, vocal and piano; Ben Quillian, vocal;
       James McCrary, vocal and guitar.   3:24

s2/3   *Blue Night Blues* (Leroy Carr, C). Leroy Carr,
       vocal and piano; Francis "Scrapper" Blackwell,
       guitar.   2:53

s2/4   *House Lady Blues*. Walter Roland, vocal and
       piano.   2:53

s2/5   *I'm Cuttin' Out* (Wilbur "Joe" McCoy, Herb
       Morland, C). Harlem Hamfats: Wilbur "Joe"
       McCoy, vocal; Herb Morand, trumpet; Odell
       Rand, clarinet; Horace Malcolm, piano; John
       Lindsay, string bass; Fred Flynn or Pearlis
       Williams, drums.   2:36

s2/6   *Deep Blue Sea Blues* (Tommy McClennan, C).
       Tommy McClennan, vocal and guitar.   2:57

s2/7   *Love Me, Baby* (John Lee "Sonny Boy"
       Williamson, C). John Lee "Sonny Boy"
       Williamson, vocal and harmonica; Big Bill
       Broonzy, guitar; Blind John Davis, piano;
       Alfred Elkins, one-string bass.   3:20

s2/8   *My Buddy Blues* (Eugene Gilmore, C). The
       Five Breezes: Gene Gilmore, lead vocal;
       Leonard "Baby Doo" Caston, vocal and
       guitar; Joseph Bell and Willie Hawthorne,
       vocals; Willie Dixon, one-string bass.   2:46

291 *Old Mother Hippletoe*: Rural and Urban Children's Songs

Notes by Kate Rinzler. Cover art: Mabel McKibbin Farmer, *Story Hour*.

s1/1	*Frog Went A-Courtin'*. Almeda Riddle, vocal.	2:46
	Old Mother Hippletoe. J. D. Dillingham, vocal.	2:12
	Robin Hood and the Peddler. Carrie Grover, vocal.	2:44
	Bobby Halsey. E. C. Ball (?), vocal and fiddle.	2:15
s1/2	*Round to Maryanne's*. Kenneth Atwood, vocal.	3:04
	Diez Perritos. Arseño Rodriguez, vocal and guitar.	1:52
	Little Sally Water. Captain Pearl R. Nye, vocal.	2:14
	Je Me Suis Mis-t-à Courir. Sabry Guidry, vocal.	1:32
	Jim Crack Corn. Uncle Alec Dunforn, vocal.	1:23
s1/3	*Little Rooster*. Almeda Riddle, vocal.	
	Oh, Blue. Thelma Beatrice, and Irene Scruggs, vocals.	1:41
	The Gray Goose. Washington (Lightin'), vocal.	3:14
s2/1	Untitled Fife Tune with Clapping Accompaniment. Ed Young, cane fife; Bessie Jones and Georgia Sea Islanders, clapping.	1:32
	Apple Tree Song. Lonnie Pitchford, vocal and one-string "guitar."	2:20
	Catfish. Joe Patterson, vocal and panpipe.	1:19
s2/2	*Sally Died*; *Ronald McDonald*; *George Washington*; *Bump, Bump, Bump*; *Salome*; *Zoodiac*; *Zing-Zing-Zing*. Schoolchildren from Washington, D.C., vocals.	4:07
s2/3	*Think*; *Your Left*; *Cheering Is My Game*; *Hollywood Now Swingin'/Dynomite*. Barbara Borum and other schoolgirls from Washington, D.C., vocals.	2:28
s2/4	*All Hid*. Bessie Jones, vocal.	1:44
	I'm Runnin' on the River. Group of girls, vocals.	:30
	La Puerta esta Quebrada. Govita Gonzales and group, vocals.	:30
	Ojibwa War Dance Song. Albert, Vernon, and James Kingbird, vocals.	:37
	Chariot. Group of girls, vocals.	:47
s2/5	*Dos y Dos Son Cuatro* (Mexican counting song). Alicia Gonzalez, vocal.	:25
	B-A-Bay (spelling song). Mrs. A. P. Wilson, vocal.	:19

291 (continued)

	Today Is Monday (days-of-the-week song). Mississippi schoolchildren, vocals.	1:20
s2/6	*Mister Rabbit.* Susie Miller and two boys, vocals.	1:25
	Old John the Rabbit. Four girls, vocals.	:47
	Rabbit. Four girls, vocals.	:56
s2/7	*Rabbit in the Pea Patch.* Angie Clark, vocal.	:47
	Old Grandpaw Yet. Mrs. Nell Hampton, vocal.	:47
	Roxie Anne. Samuel Clay Dixon, vocal.	:35
s2/8	*Go to Sleep, Little Baby.* Lester Powell, vocal.	:36
	Dors, Dors, 'tit Bebe. Barry Ancelet, vocal.	:32
	Come Up, Horsey. Vera Hall, vocal. TRO-Ludlow Music, pub.	1:03

292 Dark and Light in Spanish New Mexico: Music of the Alabados from Cerro, New Mexico; Music of the Bailes from El Rancho, New Mexico

LP
1914

Notes by Richard B. Stark. Cover art: Charles Merrick Capps, *Mission at Trampas.* All selections on Side 2 are played by Melitón Roybal, violin.

s1	Alabados	
s1/1	*Al Pie de Este Santo Altar.* Luis Montoya, vocal; Vicente Padilla, *pito* (flute).	4:00
s1/2	*Considera, Alma Perdida.* Luis Montoya, vocal.	1:56
s1/3	*Venir, Almas Devotas.* Luis Montoya, vocal.	2:35
s1/4	*Dividido el Corazón.* Ricardo Archuleta and Luis Montoya, vocals; Vicente Padilla, *pito* (flute).	4:26
s1/5	*Tened Piedad, Dios Mío.* Luis Montoya and Ricardo Archuleta, vocals.	1:52
s1/6	*Buenos Días, Paloma Blanca.* Ricardo Archuleta, vocal.	2:12
s1/7	*Dulce Esposo de Mi Alma.* Luis Montoya and Ricardo Archuleta, vocals.	1:44
s2	Bailes	
s2/1	*El Valse (in G)*	1:50
s2/2	*El Cutilio (in G and C)*	1:15
s2/3	*El Cutilio (in G)*	1:16
s2/4	*El Cutilio (in D)*	:59
s2/5	*El Cutilio (in D)*	1:24
s2/6	*Turkey in the Straw*	1:19
s2/7	*The Arkansas Traveler*	1:41

292 (continued)

s2/8	*Listen to the Mockingbird*	4:00
s2/9	*La Tercera de Noviembre (El Valse)*	1:16
s2/10	*El Valse (in A)*	1:52
s2/11	*La Polca (in G and D)*	1:49
s2/12	*La Indita*	1:44
s2/13	*El Chotis*	1:30

293 Come and Trip It: Instrumental Dance Music 1780–1920s

LP
1955

Notes by Thornton Hagert. Producer of Side 1: Max Wilcox. Producer of Side 2: Sam Parkins. Cover art: John Sloan, *Night on the Boardwalk*. All selections are in the public domain unless otherwise noted.

s1/1	*Prima Donna Waltz* (G. Jullien, C). Judith Plant, keyed bugle; Federal Music Society, John Baldon, conductor. Primary players: Mary Barto, flute; Joanne Tanner, principal violin; Richard Wagner, clarinet. The Ensemble: Kathy Seplow, Diane Volpe, Carol Zeavin, Nancy Diggs, violins; Julie Tanner, cello; Frederick Selch, contrabass.	1:44
s1/2	*Jenny Lind Polka* (arr. Allen Dodworth). Ellen Farren, pianoforte.	1:00
s1/3	*Minuet and Gavotte* (Alexander Reinagle, C). Same as above.	2:55
s1/4	*County Fiddle Music: College Hornpipe*; *La Belle Catherine*; *Hunt the Squirrel*; *Down Went McGinty to the Bottom of the Sea*; *Ashley's Ride*; *Fisher's Hornpipe*. Rodney Miller, fiddle.	6:57
s1/5	*Natalie Polka-Mazurka* (Charles Grobe, C). Ellen Farren, pianoforte.	2:54
s1/6	*Flying Cloud Schottische* (Charles d'Albert, C). Same group as s1/1.	1:16
s1/7	*Victoria Galop* (Francis Johnson, C). Same group as s1/1 with Alan Moore, pianoforte.	1:06
s1/8	*The Flirt Polka* (arr. Charles Grobe). Ellen Farren and Alan Moore, pianofortes.	3:10
s1/9	*La Sonnambula Quadrille Number Two* (Francis Johnson, C). Same group as s1/1.	4:30

293 (continued)

s2/1   *Eliza Jane McCue* (arr. L. O. deWitt). Gerard
       Schwarz and His Dance Orchestra: Gerard
       Schwarz, cornet and conductor; Miles
       Anderson, trombone; John Beal, bass; Harvey
       Estrin, flute and piccolo; Mark Gould, cornet;
       Herb Harris, drums and percussion; John
       Moses, clarinet; Tony Mottola, guitar; Eugene
       Moye, cello; Max Pollikoff, violin; Charles
       Russo, clarinet.
       Blaze-Away! (Abe Holzman, C). Leo Feist, pub.   4:45
s2/2   *Ma Ragtime Baby* (Fred S. Stone, C). Same
       group as above.
       Hiawatha (Neil Moret, C).   6:01
s2/3   *Chinatown, My Chinatown* (Jean Schwartz, C).
       Warner Bros. Music, pub.
       El Irresistible (L. Logatti, C). Same group as
       above. G. Schirmer, pub.   4:00
s2/4   *At the Mississippi Cabaret* (Albert Gumble, C).
       Dick Hyman and His Dance Orchestra: Dick
       Hyman, piano and conductor; John Beal, bass;
       Phil Bodner, piccolo, flute, clarinet, saxophone;
       Ray Crisara, cornet; Jack Gale, trombone; Al
       Gallodoro, clarinet and saxophone; Don
       Hammond, piccolo, flute, clarinet, saxophone;
       Phil Kraus, drums and percussion; Tony
       Mottola, guitar and banjo; Max Pollikoff, violin;
       Richard Sudhalter, cornet; Sarner Bros. Music,
       pub.
       Valse de Ma Coeur (M. K. Jerome, C). Same
       group as above. Mills Music, pub.   4:50
s2/5   *Kansas City Blues* (E. L. Bowman, C). Same
       group as above. Shapiro, Bernstein, pub.
       Hold Me (Art Hickman, C; Ben Black, L). Same
       group as above. Warner Bros., pub.   3:45
s2/6   *Waltzing the Blues* (Clarence Gaskill, C). Same
       group as above. Warner Bros. Music, pub.
       Sweet Man (Maceo Pinkard, C; Roy Turk, L).
       Same group as above. Leo Feist, pub.   4:49

294 The Gospel Ship: Baptist Hymns & White Spirituals from the Southern Mountains

LP
1938

Notes by Alan Lomax. Producer: Alan Lomax.
Cover art: Charles Burchfield, *Country Church*.

s1/1	*Guide Me, O Thou Great Jehovah*. Ike Caudill leading the congregation of the Mount Olivet Regular Baptist Church, Blackey, Kentucky.	5:41
s1/2	*Testimony on Pioneer Religion*. D. N. Asher, speaker. *Amazing Grace*. Howard Adams leading the congregation of the Mount Olivet Regular Baptist Church.	4:40
s1/3	*Poor Pilgrim of Sorrow*. Testimony by Rev. I. D. Beck. Congregation of the Mount Olivet Regular Baptist Church.	3:09
s1/4	*Testimony*. George Spangler, speaker. *Why Must I Wear This Shroud*. Congregation of the Thornton Regular Baptist Church.	4:58
s1/5	*Testimony*. Rev. I. D. Beck, speaker. *When Jesus Christ Was Here on Earth*. Rev. I. D. Beck leading the congregation of the Mount Olivet Regular Baptist Church.	6:50
s2/1	*The Old Gospel Ship*. Ruby Vass, vocal and guitar.	2:53
s2/2	*When the Stars Begin to Fall* (Hobart Smith, C). Hobart Smith and Preston Smith, vocals and guitars; Texas Gladden, vocal.	4:17
s2/3	*Hicks' Farewell* (William Walker, C). Texas Gladden, vocal.	2:07
s2/4	*See That My Grave Is Kept Clean* (Blind Lemon Jefferson, C). Hobart Smith, vocal and guitar.	3:17
s2/5	*I Am a Poor Wayfaring Stranger*. Almeda Riddle, vocal.	2:57
s2/6	*The Little Family*. Ollie Gilbert, vocal.	1:40
s2/7	*Jim and Me* (Garner Brothers, C). Hobart Smith and Preston Smith, vocals and guitars; Texas Gladden, vocal. Garner Brothers, pub.	2:30
s2/8	*The Airplane Ride* (Nell Hampton, C). Nell Hampton, vocal.	1:36
s2/9	*My Lord Keeps a Record*. The Mountain Ramblers: James Lindsay, vocal, guitar, and mandolin; Cullen Galyen and Charles Hawes, vocals amd banjos; Eldridge Montgomery, vocal and guitar; Thurman Pugh, vocal and bass.	3:19

295 *When Malindy Sings*: Jazz Vocalists 1938-1961

LP
1873

Notes by Peter Keepnews. Cover art: Yasuo Kuniyoshi, *Juggler*.

s1/1   *I Can't Get Started* (Vernon Duke, C: Ira
Gershwin, L). Billie Holiday and Her Orchestra:
Billie Holiday, vocal; Buck Clayton, trumpet;
Lester Young, tenor saxophone; Margaret
"Queenie" Johnson, piano; Freddie Green,
guitar; Walter Page, bass; Jo Jones, drums.
Chappell Music, pub.   2:48

s1/2   *I Left My Baby* (Count Basie, James Rushing,
C; Andy Gibson, L). Jimmy Rushing, vocal;
Count Basie and His Orchestra: Buck Clayton,
Ed Lewis, Harry Edison, and Shad Collins,
trumpets; Dickie Wells, Bennie Morton, and Dan
Minor, trombones; Earle Warren, alto saxophone; Jack Washington, alto and baritone saxophones; Buddy Tate and Lester Young, tenor
saxophones; Count Basie, piano; Freddie Green,
guitar; Walter Page, bass; Jo Jones, drums.
Bregman, Vocco, & Conn, pub.   3:13

s1/3   *Piney Brown Blues* (Joe Turner, Peter Johnson,
C/L). Joe Turner and His Fly Cats: Joe Turner,
vocal; Hot Lips Page, trumpet; Pete Johnson,
piano; John Collins, guitar; Abe Bolar, bass; A.
G. Godley, drums. Leeds Music, pub.   2:55

s1/4   *Careless Love* (Anon.). Joe Turner, vocal:
Willie "The Lion" Smith, piano.   2:50

s1/5   *Ja-Da* (Bob Carleton, C). Leo Watson and His
Orchestra: Leo Watson, vocal; Johnny McGee
and Ralph Muzillo, trumpets; Paul Ricci,
clarinet and tenor saxophone; Gene de Paul,
piano; Frank Victor, guitar; O'Neal Spencer,
drums. Leo Feist, pub.   2:41

s1/6   *It's the Tune That Counts* (Jan Savitt, C; Don
Raye, L). Same group as above. MCA Music,
pub.   2:38

s1/7   *Robbins Nest* (Sir Charles Thompson, Illinois
Jacquet, C). Ella Fitzgerald, vocal; Hank Jones,
piano; Hy White, guitar; John Simmons, bass;
J. C. Heard, drums. Atlantic Music, pub.   2:33

s1/8   *Blowtop Blues* (Leonard Feather, C; Jane
Feather, L). Dinah Washington, vocal; Lionel
Hampton and His Septet: Wendell Culley, trum-
pet; Herbie Fields, alto saxophone; Arnett Cobb,
tenor saxophone; Lionel Hampton, vibraharp;
John Mehegan, piano; Billy Mackell, guitar;
Charles Harris, bass; George Jones, drums.
Model Music, pub.   3:31

295 (continued)

s2/1	*Key Largo* (Benny Carter, C; Karl Suessdorf, Leah Worth, L). Sarah Vaughan, vocal; Barney Kessel, guitar; Joe Comfort, bass. Granson Music, pub.	3:30
s2/2	*Moonlight in Vermont* (John Blackburn, C; Karl Suessdorf, L). Betty Carter, vocal; Ray Bryant, piano; Wendell Marshall, bass; Jo Jones, drums. Michael H. Goldsen, pub.	3:24
s2/3	*Thou Swell* (Richard Rogers, C; Lorenz Hart, L). Same group as above. Warner Bros. Music, pub.	1:40
s2/4	*Can't We Be Friends?* (Kay Swift, C; Paul James, L). Same group as above. Warner Bros. Music, pub.	2:28
s2/5	*Misty* (Erroll Garner, C; Johnny Burke, L). Chris Connor, vocal; Bill Rubenstein, piano; Kenny Burrell, guitar; Eddie de Haas, bass; Lex Humphries, drums. Vernon Music, by arrangement with Octave Music, pub.	3:14
s2/6	*Love* (Hugh Martin, Ralph Blane, C/L). Chris Connor, vocal; Danny Stiles and Burt Collins, trumpets; Willie Dennis, trombone; Phil Woods, alto saxophone; Ronnie Ball, piano; George Duvivier, bass; Ed Shaughnessy, drums. Leo Feist, pub.	2:46
s2/7	*When Malindy Sings* (Oscar Brown, Jr., C; Paul Lawrence Dunbar, L). Abbey Lincoln, vocal; Booker Little, trumpet; Julian Priester, trombone; Eric Dolphy, alto saxophone, bass clarinet, and flute; Walter Benton and Coleman Hawkins, tenor saxophones; Mal Waldron, piano; Art Davis, bass; Max Roach, drums. Pub. unknown.	4:02
s2/8	*The End of a Love Affair* (Edward C. Redding, C). Billie Holiday, vocal; Ray Ellis and His Orchestra: Urbie Green, Tom Mitchell, and J. J. Johnson, trombones; Ed Powell, Tom Parshley, Romeo Penque, and Phil Bodner, reeds; Bradley Spinney, xylophone; Janet Putman, harp; Mal Waldron, piano; Barry Galbraith, guitar; Milt Hinton, bass; Don Lamond, drums. Duchess Music, pub.	4:52

296 *When Lilacs Last in the Dooryard Bloom'd.* Music by
LP Roger Sessions; Text by Walt Whitman
1844

> Notes by Michael Steinberg and Justin Kaplan.
> Producer: Andrew Raeburn. Cover art: Larry Rivers,
> *Dying and Dead Veteran*. On all selections: The Boston
> Symphony Orchestra, Seiji Ozawa, conductor; Tangle-
> wood Festival Chorus, John Oliver, conductor.
> Vocalists: Esther Hinds, soprano; Florence Quivar,
> mezzo-soprano; Dominic Cossa, baritone. Theodore
> Presser Co., publisher.

s1/1	Part One	5:35
s1/2	Part Two	16:09
s2	Part Three	20:25

297 Songs of Love, Luck, Animals, and Magic: Music of
LP the Yurok and Tolowa Indians
1734

> Notes by Charlotte Heth. Producer: Charlotte Heth.
> Cover art: Tolowa dance apron. Beads, olivella and
> abalone shells and white deerskin (photograph by
> Maria LaVigna). Karok, Yurok, and Hupa elk-antler
> spoons.

s1	Yurok	
s1/1	*Love Song.* Frank A. Douglas, vocal.	1:01
s1/2	*Grizzly Bear War Song.* Same as above.	:22
s1/3	*Rabbit Song.* Same as above.	:18
s1/4	*Gambling Song.* Same as above.	1:17
s1/5	*Love Song.* Aileen Figueroa, vocal.	:47
s1/6	*Basket Song.* Same as above.	1:06
s1/7	*Brush Dance Song (Don't Make Fun of My Sweetheart).* Same as above.	:36
s1/8	*Brush Dance Song (Grandpa Natt's Song).* Same as above.	:38
s1/9	*Love Song.* Ella Norris, vocal.	1:11
s1/10	*Seagull Song.* Same as above.	:22
s1/11	*Song To Stop the Rain.* Same as above.	:18
s1/12	*Hunting Song.* Florence Shaughnessy, vocal.	:28
s1/13	*Brush Dance (Hobo Song).* Frank A. Douglas, leader.	2:28
s1/14	*Brush Dance.* Hector Simms, leader.	3:42

297 (continued)

s2   Tolowa
s2/1   *Gambling Songs*. Sam Lopez, leader, and
Lauren Bommelyn, second.   5:35
s2/2   *Pelican Song*. Loren Bommelyn, vocal.   :15
s2/3   *Gambling Songs*. Loren Bommelyn, leader;
Frederick W. Scott, Jr., Carl James, and Walter
Richards, Sr., seconds.   2:56
s2/4   *Gambling Songs*. Walter Richards, Sr., leader;
Lauren Bommelyn and Sam Lopez, leaders.   2:56
s2/5   *Ceremonial Dance*. Loren Bommelyn, Walter
Richards, Sr., and Sam Lopez, leaders.   8:25
s2/6   *Ending Ceremonial Dance*. Same as above.   :59

298 *It Had To Be You*: Popular Keyboard from the Days
[LP 851] of the Speakeasy to the Television Era

Notes by Mort Goode. Cover art: Peggy Bacon,
The Social Graces.

s1/1   *Mine, All Mine (Mia-todo Mia)* (Sammy Stept,
C; Herman Ruby, Ruby Cowan, L). Lee
Simms, piano. Bourne, pub.   2:42
s1/2   *Canadian Capers* (Gus Chandler, Bert White,
Henry Cohen, C/L). Phil Ohman & Victor
Arden, pianos. Warner Bros. Music, pub.   3:13
s1/3   *Kitten on the Keys* (Zez Confrey, C). Zez
Confrey and His Orchestra. Mills Music, pub.   3:13
s1/4   *I'm Always Chasing Rainbows* (Harry Carroll,
C; Joseph McCarthy, L). Walter Gross, piano.
Robbins Music/Venus Music, pub.   2:57
s1/5   *Enlloro* (Voodoo Moon) (Obdulio Morales,
Julio Blanco, Marion Sunshine, C/L). Carmen
Cavallaro and His Orchestra. MCA Music, pub.   7:37
s1/6   *Aquellos Ojos Verdes* (Green Eyes) (Nilo
Menendez, C). Nat Brandwynne, piano. Peer
International, pub.   3:01
s1/7   *It Had To Be You* (Isham Jones, C; Gus
Kahn, L). Eddy Duchin, piano. Warner
Bros.-Seven Arts, pub.   1:21

s2/1   *A Lover's Lullaby* (Frankie Carle, Larry
Wagner, C; Andy Razaf, L). Frankie Carle,
piano.
A Sunrise Serenade (Frankie Carle, C; Jack
Lawrence, L). Frankie Carle, piano. Dorsey
Bros. Music/Edwin H. Morris & Co., pub.   2:40

298 (continued)

s2/2	*Happy Talk* (Richard Rogers, C; Oscar Hammerstein II, L). Cy Walter, piano. Williamson Music, pub.	1:50
s2/3	*Begin the Beguine* (Cole Porter, C/L). Eddie Heywood, Jr., piano. Harms, pub.	3:19
s2/4	*Carioca* (Vincent Youmans, C; Gus Kahn, Edward Eliscu, L). Liberace, piano. T. B. Harms, pub.	2:17
s2/5	*Autumn in New York* (Vernon Duke, C/L). Buddy Weed, piano. Harms, pub.	3:03
s2/6	*La Vie en Rose* (Louiguy, C; Edith Piaf, Mack David, L). George Feyer, piano. Harms, pub.	1:51
s2/7	*The Most Beautiful Girl in the World* (Richard Rogers, C; Lorenz Hart, L). Fairchild and Carroll, pianos. T. B. Harms, pub.	3:26
s2/8	*Autumn Leaves* (Joseph Kosma, C; Johnny Mercer, Jacques Prévert, L). Roger Williams, piano. Morley Music, pub.	3:03

299 Music of the Federal Era

LP
1906

Notes by Richard Crawford and Cynthia Adams Hoover. Producer: Max Wilcox. Cover art: Cover from James Hewitt's *Fourth of July Sonata*. Performers are members of the Federal Music Society, John Baldon, conductor.

s1/1	*Quintetto* (Samuel Holyoke (?), C). Richard Wagner and Gerhardt Koch, clarinets; Randall Ulmer and Anne Slayden, horns; Eugene Scholtens, bassoon.	5:27
s1/2	*The Silver Rain* (Raynor Taylor, C). Cindy Lynn Ralph, Judith Otten, and Cynthia Richards Hewes, sopranos; Alan G. Moore, pianoforte.	1:48
s1/3	*Alknomook, or the Death Song of the Cherokee Indians* (Anon., Anne Home Hunter, L). John D. Broome, tenor; Alan G. Moore, pianoforte.	2:08
s1/4	*Six Imitations* (Benjamin Carr, C). Ellen Farren, pianoforte.	4:35
s1/5	*The Cypress Wreath* (Charles Gilfert, C; Sir Walter Scott, L). John D. Broome, tenor; Alan G. Moore, pianoforte.	4:22

299 (continued)

s1/6	Sonata for the Piano Forte with an Accompaniment for a Violin (Raynor Taylor, C). Ellen Farren, pianoforte; Joanne Tanner, violin.	5:33
s2/1	*When Brazen Trumpets from Afar* (Col. Simond's March) (Anon.). Chorus and orchestra.	2:15
s2/2	*Turkish Quickstep*, from *The Battle of Prague* (Franz Kotzwara, C). Linda Comparone and Susan Deaver, flutes; Richard Wagner and Gerhardt Koch, clarinets; Eugene Scholtens and Dennis Godburn, bassoons; Randall Ulmer and Anne Slayden, horns; Robert Vacca, drum.	:52
s2/3	*Kennebec March* (Anon.). Linda Comparone and Susan Deaver, flutes; Richard Wagner and Gerhardt Koch, clarinets; Eugene Scholtens and Dennis Godburn, bassoons; Alan G. Moore, serpent; Randall Ulmer and Anne Slayden, horns; Douglas Hedwig, trumpet; Robert Vacca, drum.	2:45
s2/4	*March and Chorus "She is Condemned,"* from *The Voice of Nature* (Victor Pelissier, C; William Dunlap, L). Cindy Lynn Ralph, soprano; chorus and orchestra.	4:41
s2/5	*Gov. Arnold's March* (Oliver Shaw, C; arr. John Baldon). Linda Comparone and Susan Deaver, flutes; Richard Wagner and Gerhardt Koch, clarinets; Eugene Scholtens and Dennis Godburn, bassoons; Alan G. Moore, serpent; Randall Ulmer and Anne Slayden, horns; Robert Vacca, drum.	3:18
s2/6	*Air* (Oliver Shaw, C). Linda Comparone, flute; Richard Wagner and Gerhardt Koch, clarinets; Alan G. Moore, serpent.	1:30
s2/7	*First Grand March* and *First Grand Minuet* (Samuel Holyoke (?), C). Orchestra.	3:30
s2/8	*Jolley's March* (Joseph Herrick, C). Richard Wagner and Gerhardt Koch, clarinets; Eugene Scholtens, bassoon.	1:37
s2/9	*The President's March (Hail, Columbia)* (Philip Phile, C). Linda Comparone and Susan Deaver, flutes; Richard Wagner and Gerhardt Koch, clarinets; Eugene Scholtens and Dennis Godburn, bassoons; Randall Ulmer and Anne Slayden, horns; Robert Vacca, drum.	1:51

300 Songs of Charles Ives, Theodore Chanler, Norman
LP Dello Joio, Irving Fine, Robert Ward
1898

Notes by George Gelles. Producer: Andrew Raeburn.
Cover art: Thomas Hart Benton, *Wheat*. On all
selections: William Parker, baritone; Dalton Baldwin,
piano. Side 1: All selections composed by Charles Ives.

s1/1	*At the River* (Robert Lowry, L). Merion Music, pub.	1:18
s1/2	*His Exaltation* (Robert Robinson, L). Peer International, pub.	2:09
s1/3	*Watchman!* (John Bowring, L). Peer International, pub.	1:51
s1/4	*The Camp Meeting* (Charlotte Elliott, L). Peer International, pub.	4:13
s1/5	*Sunrise* (Charles Ives, L). With Ani Kavafian, violin. C. F. Peters, pub.	5:50
s1/6	*Chanson de Florian* (J. P. Claris de Florian, L). Mercury Music, pub.	1:55
s1/7	*Rosamunde* (Helmine von Chezy, translated Belanger). Peer International, pub.	2:03
s1/8	*Qu'il m'irait bien* (Anon.). Peer International, pub.	1:06
s1/9	*Elégie* (Gallet, L). Peer International, pub.	4:01
s2/1	*Four Rhymes* from *"Peacock Pie"* (Theodore Chanler, C; Walter de la Mare, L). Associated Music, pub.	
	The Ship of Rio	1:17
	Old Shellover	1:21
	Cake and Sack	1:07
	Tillie	2:31
s2/2	*Ballad*, from *Pantaloon—He Who Gets Slapped* (Robert Ward, C; Bernard Stambler, L). Highgate Press, pub.	4:56
s2/3	*The Listeners* (Norman Dello Joio, C; Walter de la Mare, L). Carl Fischer, pub.	4:46
s2/4	*Four Songs*, from *"Childhood Fables for Grownups"* (Irving Fine, C; Gertrude Norman, L). Boosey & Hawkes, pub.	
	Two Worms	3:42
	The Duck and the Yak	3:02
	Lenny the Leopard	3:04
	Tigeroo	1:16

Index to Recorded Material

This index contains the titles of all recorded works and the names of all persons connected with the performances. The latter are identified by the following codes: C (composer), L (lyricist), P (performer), arr. (arranger). Only the record number is provided, and the reader is referred back to the Master Index for all information, except in the case of multiple recordings for a single composer, where titles are provided as well. Titles appear as they are found on the recording. Excerpt titles are followed by the name of the larger work in parentheses: e.g., *Standin' in the Need of Prayer (Emperor Jones)*. On the other hand, the entry for the larger work appears in the following format: *Emperor Jones: Standin' in the Need of Prayer*.

Aanerud, Kevin, (P) 254:s2/2
Abasolo, Patti, (P) 234:s2/1
Abernathy, Will (P) 236:s2/3
Abide in Me, 230:s1/6
Abner, Ewart G., Jr., (C,L) 249:s2/6
Abongo, The, 285:s2/1
Abrahams, Maurice, (C) 233:s1/3
Abrams, Irwin, (C) 256:s1/2
Abrams, Ray, (P) 271:s1/5
Abramson, Ray, (P) 284:s2/6
Ace, Johnny, (P) 249:s1/2
Acevedo, Frankie, (P) 244:s2/5-6
Acuff, Roy, (P) 287:s2/3
Adams, Alton A., (C) 266:s1/1
Adams, Faye, (P) 249:s1/4
Adams, Howard, (P) 294:s1/2
Adams, Sarah Flower, (L) 224:s2/7
Adcock, Eddie, (P) 225:s2/5
Adde, Leo, (P) 269:s2/4
Addison, Bernard, (P) 250:s1/4
Adieu, 257:s2/4
Aeolian Harp, 203:s1/2
Aerolinos, 204:s2/3
After the Fair, 267:s2/4
After You've Gone, 256:s2/8
Agee, James, (L) 243:s2/5
Agoyo, Herman, (P) 246:s1/1
Ain't I Right, 278:s2/3
Ain't Misbehavin' (Connie's Hot Chocolates), 279:s2/7
Air, 299:s2/6
Airplane Ride, The, 294:s2/8
Akst, Harry, (C) 279:s1/4
Alabamy Bound, 233:s2/3
A-La-Bridges, 284:s1/1
Alagazam March, 282:s2/5
Albert, Don, (P) 256:s2/4-5
Aldrich, Thomas B., (L) 236:s1/5
Aler, John, (P) 202:s1/2, 6, s2/2; 251:s2/11
Alexander, Jr., John Marshall, *see* Ace, Johnny

Alice Brand, 231:s2/1
Alknomook, or the Death Song of the Cherokee Indians (The Contrast), 299:s1/3
All Alone, 233:s2/4
Allegro: You Are Never Away, 272:s2/5
Allen, Austin, (P) 236:s2/5
Allen, Charlie, (P) 217:s1/4
Allen, Ed, (P) 290:s1/7
Allen, Fulton, *see* Fuller, Blind Boy
Allen, Lee, (P) 236:s2/5
Allen, Lee, (P) 249:s1/8
Allen, "Red" (Henry), (P) 250:s1/4; 274:s2/1
All Hid, 291:s2/4
Alligator Dance, 246:s1/2
All I Love Is You, 207:s2/6
All in Down and Out Blues, 270:s2/1
Allison, J. T., (P) 245:s2/9
Allison, Jerry, (C,P) 249:s2/2
All I Want, 270:s2/7
All of Me, 248:s1/4
All Quiet Along the Potomac Tonight, 202:s1/2
Almanac Singers, (P) 270:s2/7
Almeida, Laurindo, (P) 216:s1/4
Alonge, Ray, (P) 216:s2/4
Alston, Shirley, (P) 249:s2/5
Alvarez, Chico, (P) 216:s1/4
Alvin, Danny, (P) 250:s2/5
Amazing Grace, 294:s1/2
Amazons' March (Black Crook), 221:s1/1
Ambassador Orchestra, (P) 279:s1/1
Ameen, Ramsey, (P) 201
Americana: Brother, Can You Spare a Dime, 270:s1/1
Americana: May Every Tongue; The Staff Necromancer; God's Bottles; The Sublime Process of Law Enforcement; Loveli-Lines, 219:s1/1-5
American Fife Ensemble, (P) 276:s1/1-3, s2/1, 3

American Indian Rhapsody, 213:s1/2

American Life, 228:s2/1

American Mercury, 219:s1/1-5

American Quartet, (P) 222:s1/3, 233:s1/4

American Vicar of Bray, 276:s1/4

America's Sweetheart: We'll Be the Same, 240:s1/1

Am Kreuzweg wird begraben, 273:s1/2

Ammons, Albert, (C) 259:s2/1-2, 8 (P) 259:s2/8

Amor a la Virtud, 244:s2/5

Amsterdam, 205:s2/4

Anatole of Paris (*Straw Hat Revue*), 215:s2/5

Ancelet, Barry, (P) 291:s2/8

An den Wind, 273:s1/1

Anderson, Charles, (P) 217:s2/2

Anderson, Charlie, (P) 217:s2/8

Anderson, Gary, *see* Bonds, Gary U. S.

Anderson, James, (P) 284:s1/3

Anderson, Lee, (P) 287:s2/8

Anderson, Marian, (P) 247:s1/9

Anderson, Miles, (P) 237:s1/1

Anderson, Richard, (P) 230:s2/3; 231:s2/1; 232:s1/1-3, 5

Andes, Marche di Bravoura, The, 257:s1/1

And Now, Old Serpent, How Do You Feel, 239:s1/9

And So to Bed, 240:s1/3

And Thou Shalt Know It, 230:s1/8

Angels' Visits, 220:s2/1

Angelucci, Ernie, (P) 284:s1/5

Anquoe, Jack, (P) 246:s2/4

Anthem of Praise, An, 255:s1/1

Anti-Monopoly War Song, The, 267:s1/1

Anyone Can Whistle, 272:s2/7

Anything Goes, 272:s2/2

Apex Club Orchestra, (P) 274:s1/6

Apple Tree Song, 291:s2/1

April Showers, 279:s1/2

Aquellos Ojos Verdes, 298:s1/6

Arapaho Indians, Northern, *see* Northern Arapaho Indians

Archia, Tom, (P) 261:s1/8

Archuleta, Anthony S., (P) 246:s1/1

Archuleta, Ricardo, (P) 292:s1/4-7

Arden, Victor, (P) 240:s1/1, 6; 298:s1/2

Arden and Ohman Orchestra, (P) 240:s1/1, 6

Are You Havin' Any Fun (*Scandals of 1939*), 215:s2/6

Are You Making Any Money (*Moonlight and Pretzels*), 240:s1/7

Argentines, the Portuguese and the Greeks, The, 233:s2/1

Arkansas Traveler, The, 292:s2/7

Arlen, Harold, (C) *What Can You Say in a Love Song*, 240:s2/2; *Stormy Weather*, 248:s1/1; *A Sleepin' Bee*, 272:s2/6 (P) 248:s1/1; 272:s2/6

Armenteros, Alfredo "Chocolate," (P) 244:s2/5-6

Armstrong, Joe, (P) 278:s1/2, 4-7, s2/1, 3, 5, 7-8

Armstrong, Louis, (P) 248:s1/7; 256:s1/1-2; 269:s2/8; 274:s1/2, s2/1; 279:s2/7

Arnold, Eddy, (P) 207:s1/1

Arnold, Harold, (P) 217:s1/8, s2/3

Arnold, Matthew, (L) 229:s1/1

Aronoff, Max, (P) 229:s1/1

Art Farmer-Benny Golson Jazztet, (P) 242:s2/1

Ash, Sam, (P) 233:s1/5

Ashby, Irving, (P) 261:s1/1; 284:s1/3

Asher, Angelo A., (arr.) 267:s2/4

Asher, D. N., (P) 294:s1/2

Asher, Mrs. William, (P) 224:s2/6

Ashley, B. W., (P) 205:s2/6

Ashley, Tom Clarence, (P)
236:s2/3; 245:s2/5

Ashley's Ride, 293: s1/4

Ashlock, Jesse, (P) 287:s2/8

Askew, Alec, (P) 252:s1/7

Astaire, Adele, (P) 215:s2/3

Astaire, Fred, (P) 215:s2/3

*As Thousands Cheer: Heat Wave;
How's Chances; Not for All
the Rice in China*, 238:s2/3-5;
Honeysuckle Rose, 272:s1/7

At a Georgia Camp Meeting,
282:s1/3

At a Wedding under the Eaves,
283:s2/3

Atchison, Tex, (P) 287:s1/7,
s2/1

At Dawning, 247:s2/1

Atherton, James, (P) 288/89

At Home Abroad: Paree,
215:s2/4

Atkins, Boyd, (C) 217:s1/5

Atkins, Chet, (P) 207:s1/8

Atlanta Low Down, 217:s2/5

Atlanta Rag, 235:s1/5

At My Front Door, 249:s2/6

At the Mississippi Cabaret,
293:s2/4

At the River, 300:s1/1

Atwood, Kenneth, (P) 291:s1/2

Auburn Avenue Stomp, 217:s2/6

Auf geheimem Waldespfade,
273:s1/4

Auld, Georgie, (P) 274:s1/7

Austin, Gene, (P) 250:s1/5;
279:s2/5

Austin, Mrs. Morris, (P) 239:s1/9

Autry, Gene, (P) 270:s2/6;
287:s1/7

Autumn in New York (*Thumbs
Up*), 298:s2/5

Autumn Leaves, 298:s2/8

Ayres, Jim, (P) 205:s2/3

Ayres, Leslie, (P) 261:s2/1

B-A-Bay, 291:s2/5

Babbitt, Milton, (C) 209:s1/1-2,
4, s2/2

Babe of Bethlehem, The,
220:s2/6

*Babes In Toyland: I Can't Do
the Sum*, 221:s2/8

Babies on Our Block, The (*The
Mulligan Guard Ball*), 265:s1/1

Bachleda, Stanisław, (P)
283:s1/5, 9

Bachleda, Mrs. Stanisław, (P)
283:s1/5, 7

Bacon, Louis, (P) 217:s1/5;
274:s2/1

Baczkowskiego Orkiestra, (P)
283:s1/1

Baez, Tito, (P) 244:s2/1-4

Bagby, Scott, (P) 256:s 2/4-5

Bagley, Don, (P) 216:s1/4, s2/1

Bailey, Buster, (P) 250:s2/9;
269:s2/8

Bailey, Mildred, (P) 248:s1/6

Bakari-Badji, (P) 252:s1/1

Baker, Alan, (P) 201:s1/3;
202:s1/1, s2/4-6

Baker, Belle, (P) 233:s2/8

Baker, Billy, (P) 225:s2/1

Baker, David, (P) 216:s2/4;
242:s2/3

Baker, Harold, (P) 216:s1/2

Baker, Kenny, (P) 222:s2/5;
270:s1/5

Baldon, John, (P) 232; 293:s1/1,
6, 9; 299:s2/1, 7

Baldwin, Dalton, (P) 300

Balfa, Dewey, (P) 264:s2/3

Baline, Israel, *see* Berlin, Irving

Ball, E. C., (P) 291:s1/1

Ball, Ronnie, (P) 295:s2/6

*Ballad (Pantaloon—He Who Gets
Slapped)*, 300:s2/2

Ballet Theatre Orchestra, (P)
253:s1

Ballew Smith, (P) 240:s1/5

*Ballyhoo of 1932: How Do You
Do It; Riddle Me This*,
240:s1/4

Balthrop, Carmen, (P)
262/63:s1/2, s2/2, s4/1-2

Baltimore Buzz (*Shuffle Along*), 260:s1/6, s2/7

Bampton, Rose, (P) 247:s2/3-5

Bandana Days (*Shuffle Along*), 260:s1/1, 4

Band Wagon, The: Hoops, 215:s2/3

Banjo Pickin' Girl, 236:s2/8

Bank, Danny, (P) 216:s1/5

Bankston, Thomas, (P) 221:s2/4; 267:s2/4

Banshee, The, 203:s1/1

Baptismal Anthem, 205:s2/3

Baptiste, Tink, (P) 269:s2/2

Barab, Seymour, (P) 281:s1/1

Barbara Allen, 223:s1/5

Barbarin, Paul, (P) 274:s2/1

Barber, Bill, (P) 284:s1/8

Barber, Samuel, (C) 229:s1; 243:s2/5

Barbour, Dave, (P) 250:s1/7

Barefield, Eddie, (C,P) 217:s2/1

Barker, Danny, (P) 217:s1/6-8; 235:s1/7

Barker, Danny, (P) 265:s1/6-7; s2/1-2

Barker, James Nelson, (L) 232:s1

Barksdale, Everett, (P) 250:s1/3; 274:s1/4

Barnard, Lester, Jr., (C) 287:s2/9 (P) 287:s2/8

Barn Dance Rag, 235:s2/5

Barr, Alex, (P) 223:s2/1

Barrett, Delores, (P) 224:s1/5

Barris, Harry, (C) 279:s2/4

Barrows, John, (P) 216:s2/4

Bartholomew, Dave, (C,P) 249:s1/8

Bartlett, Homer N., (C) 257:s2/5

Basie, "Count" William, (C) *There's a Squabblin'*, 256:s2/3; *Every Tub*, 274:s1/1; *I Left My Baby*, 295:s1/2 (P) 217:s2/1; 256:s2/2-3; 274:s1/1, 7, s2/9; 295:s1/2

Basket Song, 297:s1/6

Baskette, Billy, (L) 233:s1/7

Basquin, Peter, (P) 213:s1/2, s2/2; 251:s1/1, 3-4, 6-7, s2/1-2, 5-7

Bassett, Leslie, (C) 209:s2/1

Bass Goin' Crazy, 259:s2/2

Bassoon Variations (C. Wuorinen), 209:s2/3

Battle, Edgar, (P) 217:s1/3

Battle, Kathleen, (P) 220:s1/6, s2/1

Battle of Prague, The, 229:s2/2

Battleship Connecticut March, 282:s2/4

Bauduc, Ray, (P) 250:s1/6

Bauer, Billy, (P) 216:s1/3; 242:s1/2

Baugham, Stanley, (P) 222:s1/8

Bauza, Mario, (P) 217:s1/6-7

Baxter, J. R. ("Pap"), (C) 223:s2/8

Bayes, Nora, (C) 215:s2/1 (P) 222:s1/4; 233:s2/1

Beach, Mrs. H. H. A., (C) 247:s1/2; 268:s1

Beal, Earl, (P) 249:s2/1

Beale Streeters, The, (P) 249:s1/2

Beale Street Mama, 250:s2/6

Beardslee, Bethany, (P) 243:s2

Bearstail, Colin, (P) 246:s1/3-4

Beason, Bill, (P) 250:s1/8

Beauregard's Retreat From Shiloh, 202:s2/1

Bechet, Sidney, (P) 269:s2/7; 274:s1/4

Beck, I. D., (P) 294:s1/3, 5

Beck, Karen, (P) 288/89

Becker, John J., (C) 285:s2/1

Beckett, Fred, (P) 261:s1/1; 284:s1/1

Beckett, Samuel, (L) 237:s2/2

Becktel, Perry, (P) 287:s1/1

Beecher, Francis, (P) 249:s1/5

Been a Long Time Traveling Here Below, 223:s2/6

Beener, Oliver, (P) 204

Been on the Job Too Long, 245:s2/2

Before the Cask of Wine (Li Po Songs), 214:s1/7
Beggin' the Blues, 252:s2/5
Begin the Beguine, 298:s2/3
Begley, Justis, (P) 226:s1/6
Beiderbecke, "Bix" (Leon), (P) 274:s2/3
Belcher, Supply, (C) 255:s1/1, s2/3
Belgrave, Marcus, (P) 249:s2/7
Bell, Joseph, (P) 290:s2/8
Bell, Leard, (P) 261:s2/4
Belle Catherine, La, 293:s1/4
Belling, Susan, (P) 231:s2/3-4; 232:s1/4
Bellow, Fred, (P) 261:s2/7
Bellstedt, Herman, (C) 282:s1/8
Bemko, Gregory, (P) 216:s1/4
Benfield, Kenneth, (P) 226:s1/9
Benfield, Neriah, (P) 226:s1/9
Ben-Hur Chariot Race March, The, 282:s1/9
Benjamin, Bennie, (C) 284:s2/4
Benjamin, Joe, (P) 216:s2/3
Bennett, Robert Russell, (C) 211:s2/3-5
Bennett, Sanford Fillmore, (L) 220:s1/1
Benoit, John, (P) 276:s1/3, s2/1, 3
Benton, Walter, (P) 295:s2/7
Benton, William, (P) 217:s2/7-8
Berberian, J., (P) 264:s2/5
Berger, Sy, (P) 284:s1/4
Berigan, Bunny, (P) 250:s1/6
Berlin, Irving, (C) *The Girl on the Magazine Cover*, 233:s1/2; *All Alone*, 233:s2/4; Songs, 238; *How Deep Is the Ocean*, 248:s1/2
(P) 238:s1/1
Berman, Sonny, (P) 216:s1/1
Bernac, Pierre, (P) 229:s1/2-6
Bernard, Henry, (C,P) 261:s2/1
Bernas, Andrew, (P) 283:s1/3
Bernhardt, Clyde, (P) 217:s1/1
Bernhart, Milt, (P) 216:s1/4

Bernstein, Artie, (P) 250:s1/8, s2/8; 272:s1/6; 274:s1/7
Bernstein, Leonard, (P) 241:s2/1; 258:s1; 277:s1
Berrios, Israel, (C) 244:s2/1 (P) 244:s2
Berrios, Steve, (P) 244:s1/3-4
Berry, "Chu" (Leon), (P) 217:s1/6-7; 250:s1/8
Berry, Chuck (Charles Edward), (C,P) 249:s1/6
Berry, Leroy, (P) 217:s2/1
Berta, Berta, 252:s1/4
Berton, Vic, (P) 274:s2/3, 7; 279:s2/2
Bertram, H. A., (P) 205:s1/8
Bertrand, Jimmy, (P) 250:s1/3; 256:s1/1
Bess, Druie, (P) 256:s2/1-3
Best, Michael, (P) 232:s1/3
Betts, Harry, (P) 216:s1/4
Beulah Land, 278:s1/8
Bialog, B., (P) 264:s1/4
Bibb County Hoedown, 226:s2/9
Bigard, "Barney" (Albany), (C) 272:s2/1 (L) 272:s2/1 (P) 250:s1/2, s2/7; 272:s2/1; 274:s1/2
Big Crawford, (P) 261:s2/7
Bigelow, Frederick, (C) 266:s1/9
Bigfooted Nigger, 226:s2/3
Billings, William, (C) 205:s1/2; 255:s1/2, 9, s2/1, 4; 276:s1/1, 5
Billy Graham's Australian Crusade Choir, (P) 224:s2/4, 9
Billy Grimes, the Rover, 236:s1/3
Binyon, Larry, (P) 250:s2/2
Biondi, Ray, (P) 250:s2/5
Bishop, A., (P) 264:s2/1
Bishop, H. R., (C) 251:s1/2
Bishop, Wallace, (P) 217:s1/4
Bispham, David, (P) 247:s1/7
Bitterness of Love, The, 247:s1/6
Bjornson, Katherine, (P) 214:s1/9
Black, Ben, (L) 293:s2/5

Black, Robert, (P) 254:s2/1
Black and Blue Rhapsody, 256:s2/7
Blackberry Blossom, 225:s2/1
Blackbirds of 1928: Doin' the New Low-down, 215:s1/6
Black Bottom Stompers, (P) 274:s1/2
Blackburn, John, (C) 295:s2/2
Black Crook, The: Amazons' March, 221:s1/1; *The Broadway, Opera and Bowery Crawl*, 221:s2/4
Black Devil Orchestra, (P) 260:s1/5, s2/1
Black Devils, (P) 217:s2/4
Blackett, Joy, (P) 262/63:s1/2-3, s4/1-2
Black Island Polka, 264:s1/3
Blackman, Martin, (P) 205:s2/8
Black Sheep, The, 223:s2/3
Blackwell, Francis "Scrapper," (P) 290:s2/3
Blackwell, Robert A., (C,L) 249:s2/3
Blackwell, Virgil, (P) 237:s2/1; 285:s1/2
Blair, Lee, (P) 274:s2/1
Blair-Bey, Vincent, (P) 261:s1/8
Blake, Blind, (P) 235:s1/2
Blake, Eubie (James Hubert), (C) 260:s1, s2/1-4, 6-7 (P) 260:s1/1, 3-4, 6
Blake, Jerry, (P) 217:s1/6-7
Blake, Ran, (P) 216:s2/5
Blakey, Art, (P) 242:s1/3; 271:s2/6
Blanchard, I. G., (L) 267:s1/2
Blanche of Devan, 231:s1/4
Blancher, O. C., (P) 269:s2/1
Blanco, Julio, (C,L) 298:s1/5
Bland, James A., (C) 265:s1/7, s2/3
Blane, Ralph, (C,L) 295:s2/6
Blanton, Jimmy, (P) 250:s2/7; 274:s2/2, 8
Blaze-Away, 293:s2/1

Blazończyk, Antonina, (P) 283:s1/3
Blessed Bible, The, 251:s2/8
Blevins, Rubye, *see* Montana, Patsy
Bliss, Phillip P., (C) 251:s2/2
Bloom, Marty, (C,L) 274:s1/2
Bloom, Rube, (P) 250:s1/1
Blowers, Johnny, (P) 250:s2/3
Blowtop Blues, 295:s1/8
Blue Devil Blues, 256:s2/2
Blue Devils, (P) 256:s2/2-3
Blue Five, (P) 269:s2/7
Blue Four, (P) 250:s1/1
Bluegrass All-Stars, (P) 255:s2/9
Blue Grass Boys, (P) 225:s1/1
Blue Jay Singers, The Famous, *see* Famous Blue Jay Singers, The
Blue Moon, 248:s1/5
Blue Night Blues, 290:s2/3
Blue Ridge Cabin Home, 225:s1/2
Blue Ridge Cornshuckers, (P) 245:s2/3
Blues, 226:s1/8
Blues in My Condition, 250:s2/8
Blue Sky Boys, The, (P) 287:s1/10
Blues March, 242:s2/1
Blues of Avalon, 217:s2/2
Blues on the Downbeat, 259:s2/6
Blues Peru, 204:s1/3
Blues Serenaders, (P) 256:s2/1
Bluette (Twelve Virtuoso Studies), 206:s2/8
Blue Yodel No. 11, 287:s1/2
Blythe, Jimmy, (C) 259:s1/1 (P) 259:s1/1-2
Bobby Halsey, 291:s1/1
Bocage, Peter, (P) 269:s2/3
Bock, Zachary, (P) 216:s1/4
Bodner, Phil, (P) 295:s2/8
Body and Soul, 225:s2/8
Body and Soul, 274:s1/8; 275:s1/6
Bogulousa Strut, 269:s2/1

Bohacki Zaruczyny (Engagement Ceremony among the Rich), 283:s2/2

Bold McCarthy or The City of Baltimore, 223:s1/4

Bolick, Bill, (P) 287:s1/10

Bolick, Earl, (P) 287:s1/10

Bolling, Pillie, (P) 290:s1/2

Bomba Calindé, 244:s1/2

Bommelyn, Lauren, (P) 297:s2/1, 4

Bommelyn, Loren, (P) 246:s2/1; 297:s2/2-3, 5-6

Bonds, Gary U. S., (P) 249:s2/9

Bonnell, Otto, (C) 267:s2/4

Bonney, Betty, (P) 222:s2/2

Bonnie Annie Laurie, 266:s1/7

Bonx, Nat, (L) 279:s1/3

Boogie Woogie Stomp, 259:s2/1

Booth, Philip, (P) 288/89

Boots and His Buddies, (P) 217:s2/2

Borders, Ben, (P) 269:s1/7-8

Borinquen, 244:s2/1

Born to Lose, 287:s2/4

Borum, Barbara, (P) 291:s2/3

Boston Commandery, 266:s1/2

Boston Symphony Orchestra, (P) 273:s2/1-4; 286:s1; 296

Boswell, Connee, (P) 248:s1/5

Boulevard of Broken Dreams, The (*Moulin Rouge*), 270:s1/2

Bouquet of Roses, 207:s1/1

Bourdon, Rosario, (P) 238:s1/4; 247:s1/1

Bourne, Charlie, (P) 279:s2/3

Bouteljie, P., (C) 250:s1/5

Bowen, Leslie, (P) 246:s1/2

Bowers, Robert Hood, (C) 215:s1/1

Bowers, Teresa, (P) 221:s1/8

Bowery, The, 221:s2/7

Bowles, Jane, (L) 243:s1/4

Bowles, Paul, (C) 243:s1/3-4 (L) 243:s1/3

Bowman, E. L., (C) 293:s2/5

Bowring, John, (L) 300:s1/3

Boyd, Bill, (P) 226:s2/10; 235:s2/5

Boyd, Jim, (P) 226:s2/10; 235:s2/5

Boyd, John, (P) 226:s2/10

Boyd, Roger, (P) 217:s1/1

Boy in the Boat, The, 256:s1/3

Boys and Girls Like You and Me, 240:s2/4

Braca Kapugi, (C,P) 264:s1/4

Bracia Kuziany, (P) 283:s2/5

Bradbury, William Batchelder, (C) 224:s2/9

Bradford, Perry, (C,P) 269:s2/8

Bradley, Carey, (P) 224:s1/1

Bradley, Nellie H., (L) 267:s2/3

Bradley, Oscar Lee, (P) 261:s1/7

Bradshaw, Tiny, (C,P) 261:s2/1

Brady, Floyd, (P) 217:s2/7-8

Brady, Pat, (P) 287:s2/6

Braggs, John H., (P) 256:s2/4-5

Braham, David, (C) 265:s1/1-5

Braham, John, (C) 221:s1/4

Brandeis Jazz Festival Ensemble, (P) 216:s2/3

Brandwynne, Nat, (P) 298:s1/6

Brannon, Linda, (P) 234:s1/1

Brant, Henry Dreyfuss, (C) 211:s1/3

Brashear, Alex, (P) 287:s2/8

Brassfield, Herschel, (P) 269:s2/5

Bratton, John W., (C) 282:s2/7

Braud, Wellman, (P) 235:s1/7; 250:s1/2; 272:s2/1; 274:s1/4

Brave Boys, 239:s1/6

Bray, John, (C) 232:s1

Breaux, Cleoma, (P) 226:s1/11

Bredwell, Merle, (P) 284:s1/4

Bressler, Charles, (P) 229:s2/8; 230:s1/2, 4, 8, s2/2; 231:s1/1, s2/1

Breuer, Ernest, (C) 222:s1/6

Brewer, Kahle, (P) 236:s1/7

Brewer, Virginia, (P) 276:s1/1, 3, s2/2, 4

Brice, Fanny, (P) 215:s1/2

Brickmaker March, The, 276:s1/1

Bridges, Charlie, (P) 224:s1/2

Bridges, Henry, (P) 284:s1/1-2

Briggs, Peter, (P) 256:s1/2

Bright, Dalbert, (P) 259:s2/1

Bright and Morning Star, 223:s2/2

Brighten the Corner Where You Are, 224:s2/5

Bright Eyes: On the Good Ship Lollypop, 270:s1/6

Briglia, Tony, (P) 217:s1/2

Bristow, George F., (C) 257:s1/2

British Grenadiers, 276:s1/2

Britton, Joe, (P) 217:s1/1; 261:s1/8

Broadway, Opera and Bowery Crawl, The (Black Crook), 221:s2/4

Broadway Brevities of 1920: The Moon Shines on the Moonshine, 215:s1/1

Broadway Melody: You Were Meant for Me, 227:s1/4

Brodeur, Arthur, (P) 223:s2/1

Brodsky, Jascha, (P) 229:s1/1

Brooks, Alva, (P) 217:s2/2

Brooks, Harry, (C) 279:s2/7

Broome, John D., (P) 299:s1/3, 5

Broonzy, "Big Bill," (P) 270:s1/7; 290:s2/7

Brother, Can You Spare a Dime (Americana), 270:s1/1

Brower, Cecil, (P) 287:s1/9

Brown, (P) 217:s2/5-6

Brown, Andrew, (P) 217:s1/6-7

Brown, Bill, (P) 249:s1/3

Brown, Clifford, (P) 271:s2/5

Brown, Durwood, (P) 236:s2/6; 287:s1/9

Brown, James, (P) 239:s2/2

Brown, Jesse H., (L) 236:s1/7

Brown, John, (P) 271:s1/5

Brown, John, (P) 287:s2/1

Brown, Lawrence, (P) 247:s1/8, 10, s2/8

Brown, Lawrence, (P) 274:s2/2

Brown, Les, (P) 222:s2/2

Brown, Lew, (L) 233:s2/8; 240:s1/6; 269:s1/5; 270:s1/3

Brown, Milton, (P) 236:s2/6; 287:s1/9

Brown, Nacio Herb, (C) 227:s1/4

Brown, Oscar, Jr., (C) 295:s2/7

Brown, Ray, (P) 271:s1/5; 284:s2/5

Browning, Robert, (L) 229:s2/4; 247:s1/2

Brown, Roy, (C) 261:s1/8

Brown, Ruth, (P) 261:s2/5

Brown, Sidney, (P) 269:s2/1-2

Brown, Tom, (P) 269:s1/5

Brown, Willard, (P) 217:s2/4; 256:s1/6

Brownies, (P) 287:s1/9

Brownskin Woman, 290:s1/2

Bruce, Carol, (P) 238:s2/8

Bruce, Neeley, (P) 220:s1/1-3, 5-7. s2/2-6; 276:s1/5, s2/3, 5

Bruner, Cliff, (P) 287:s1/9

Brush Dance, 297:s1/14

Brush Dance, Hobo Song, 297:s1/13

Brush Dance Song, *Don't Make Fun of My Sweetheart*, 297:s1/7

Brush Dance Song, *Grandpa Natt's Song*, 297:s1/8

Bryan, Alfred, (L) 222:s1/2, 6; 233:s1/6

Bryan, Vincent, (L) 221:s1/5

Bryant, Hoyt "Slim," (P) 287:s1/1

Bryant, Ray, (P) 295:s2/2-4

Bryant, Stephen, (P) 288/89

Brymm, Tim, (P) 260:s1/5, s2/1

Bryn-Julson, Phyllis, (P) 273:s2/2-4

Buchanan, Jack, (P) 215:s1/5

Buck, Dudley, (C) 220:s1/7; 280:s1/1-4

Buck, Gene, (L) 233:s1/5

Buckets of Gore (Corsair), 221:s1/4

Buckley, R. Bishop, (C) 202:s2/4

Buck Mountain Band, (P) 290:s1/5

Buckner, Milton, (P) 261:s1/1; 284:s1/7

Buckner, Teddy, (P) 261:s1/7; 284:s1/7

Buenos Dias, Paloma Blanca, 292:s1/6

Buffington, Jimmy, (P) 216:s2/3

Buford, Lawson, (P) 256:s1/6

Bugle Blues, 269:s2/5

Bugle Call Rag, 235:s2/7; 250:s2/2

Bugler's Dilemma, 250:s2/9

Bull, Amos, (C) 255:s2/8

Buller, Buddy, (P) 287:s2/4

Bully Song, The (Widow Jones), 221:s1/8

Bump, Bump, Bump, 291:s2/2

Bunn, Jimmy, (P) 284:s2/7

Bunn, Teddy, (P) 250:s2/6

Burch, Curtis, (P) 225:s2/8

Burch, Elmer, (P) 256:s2/1

Burckhart, Jacob, (P) 226:s2/5

Burgess, Dave, (C) 207:s2/1

Burke, Bill, (P) 287:s1/2

Burke, J., (C) 250:s2/1

Burke, Johnny, (L) 295:s2/5

Burleigh, Harry T., (arr.) 247:s1/8-10

Burlesque (Twelve Virtuoso Studies), 206:s2/7

Burns, Dave, (P) 271:s1/5

Burns, Karl, (P) 217:s2/5-6

Burns, Ralph, (C,P) 216:s1/1

Burr, Henry, (P) 222:s1/8

Burroughs, Alvin, (P) 256:s2/2-3

Burtnett, Earl, (P) 238:s2/2

Burton, Nat, (L) 270:s2/8

Bush, Percy, (P) 217:s2/2

Bush, Phyllis, (P) 235:s2

Bushell, Garvin, (P) 235:s1/7; 256:s1/7

Bushey, Bill, (P) 284:s1/8

Bushkin, Joe, (P) 250:s2/5

Butler, Frank, (P) 275:s1/2

Butterfly Dance, 246:s1/1

Buttermilk, 252:s1/8

Buzzard Lope, The, 278:s2/1

By a Lonely Forest Pathway, 247:s2/2

Byard, Jaki (John Arthur, Jr.), (C,P) 275:s1/4-5

Byrd, Donald, (P) 242:s1/3

Byrd, Eddie, (P) 261:s1/6

Byrnside, Ron, (P) 221

By the Cottage Door, 236:s1/8

Cabrera, Benjamin, (P) 244:s1/5

Caceres, Emilio, (P) 250:s2/4

Caceres, Ernie (Ernesto), (P) 250:s2/4

Cadman, Charles Wakefield, (C) 213:s2/3; 247:s2/1

Caesar, Irving, (L) 284:s2/3

Cage, John, (C) 203:s1/4-8; 214:s2

Cagle, A. Marcus, (C) 205:s1/4

Cahn, Sammy, (L) 240:s2/7; 248:s2/2; 298:s1/7

Caine, Eddie, (P) 216:s1/5

Cake and Sack (Peacock Pie), 300:s2/1

Caldwell, Anne, (L) 272:s1/4; 274:s1/6

Caldwell, Lola, (P) 223:s2/2

Caldwell, Walter, (P) 223:s2/2

Calhoun, Charles E., *see* Stone, Jessie

Calhoun, Fred "Papa," (P) 287:s1/9

Callahan, Homer, (P) 236:s2/4

Callahan, Walter, (P) 236:s2/4

Callahan Brothers, (P) 236:s2/4

Callender, Red, (P) 271:s1/6; 284:s1/3, s2/7

Callies, W., (P) 287:s2/6

Call It Stormy Monday, 261:s1/7

Calloway, Cab, (P) 217:s1/6-7

Campbell, Arthur, (P) 269:s1/6

Campbell, Edgar, (P) 269:s1/1

Campbell, Maurice, (P) 239:s2/7

Campbell, Ronald, (P) 221:s1/6; 267:s2/1

Camp Meeting, The, 300:s1/4

Canaan Land, 224:s1/2

Canadian Capers, 298:s1/2
Candido, Candy, (P) 250:s1/5
Candoli, Pete, (P) 216:s1/1
Candy and Coco, (P) 250:s1/5
Cannon Ball Rag, 235:s2/7
Cantonucci, Ernie, (P) 284:s1/5
Can't We Be Friends, 295:s2/4
Can't You Just See Yourself
   (High Button Shoes), 240:s2/7
Capote, Truman, (L) 272:s2/6
Capriccio for Cello and Piano,
   281:s2/1
Caravan, 217:s1/1
Cardarell, Bart, (P) 216:s1/4
Cardone, Milton, (P) 244:s1/3-4
Careless Love, 295:s1/4
Carey, Mutt, (P) 269:s1/7-8
Carioca, 298:s2/4
Carle, Frankie, (C,P) 298:s2/1
Carleton, Bob, (C) 295:s1/5
Carlo, Tyran (C,L) 249:s2/4
Carmichael, Hoagy,
   (C) 248:s2/6; 270:s1/4;
   272:s1/6
   (P) 272:s1/6
Carney, Harry, (P) 216:s1/2;
   250:s2/7; 274:s2/2
Carno, Zita, (P) 228:s2/2
Carpenter, John Alden, (C)
   228:s1/1; 247:s2/4-5
Carr, Benjamin, (C) 231:s1,
   s2/1-2; 299:s1/4
Carr, Leroy, (C,P) 290:s2/3
Carr, Mancy, (P) 256:s1/2
Carrie Belle, 278:s2/8
Carroll, Adam, (P) 298:s2/7
Carroll, Harry, (C) 298:s1/4
Carson, Fiddlin' John, (P)
   245:s1/6
Carson, Ken, (P) 287:s2/6
Carter, A. P., (C,P) 287:s1/3, 5
Carter, Andres, (P) 236:s1/6
Carter, Benny, (C) 295:s2/1
   (P) 217:s1/5; 256:s1/4;
   274:s1/5, s2/5
Carter, Betty, (P) 295:s2/2-4
Carter, Elliot, (C) 219:s1/6
Carter, Gaylord, (P) 227:s2

Carter, George, (P) 236:s1/6
Carter, Jimmie, (P) 236:s1/6
Carter, Maybelle, (P) 287:s1/3, 5
Carter, Ron, (P) 242:s2/2;
   275:s2/4
Carter, Sara, (P) 287:s1/3, 5
Carter, Thomas M., (C) 266:s1/1
Carter, Wilf, (C,P) 287:s2/2
Carter Family, (P) 287:s1/3, 5
Caruso, Ron, (P) 214:s1/9
Carve That Possum, 236:s1/9
Casa Loma Orchestra, (P)
   217:s1/2; 270:s1/4
Casa Loma Stomp, 217:s1/2
Casey, T. F., (C) 267:s1/2
Cash, Johnny, (P) 207:s2/4
Cassily, Richard, (P) 241:s2/3
Castle House Rag, 269:s1/1
Castle Walk, 269:s1/2
Caston, Leonard, ("Baby Doo"),
   (P) 290:s2/8
Catfish, 291:s2/1
Cathcart, Jim, (P) 216:s1/4
Catlett, Sidney, (P) 271:s1/3;
   272:s1/3; 274:s1/4; 284:s2/1
Cat Song or Can Anyone Tell
   Vere Dot Cat Is Gone,
   265:s2/5
Caudill, Ike, (P) 294:s1/1
Cavallero, Carmen, (P) 298:s1/5
Cavanaugh, James, (L) 279:s2/4
Cennick, John, (L) 205:s2/6
Ceremonial Dance, 297:s2/5-6
Ceremony II ("Incantations"),
   237:s1/2
Certain, Louise, (C) 225:s1/2
Chadwick, George Whitefield,
   (C) 266:s2/2
Chaloff, Serge, (P) 271:s2/1;
   275:s1/6
Chamber Music, 243:s2/1
Chambers, W. Paris, (C) 282:s2/9
Chance, Lightnin', (P) 225:s2/2, 4
Chandler, Gus, (C,L) 298:s1/2
Chanler, Theodore, (C)
   243:s1/1-2, s2/4; 300:s2/1
Chanson de Florian, 300:s1/6
Chant of the Wanderer, 287:s2/6

Chaplin, Saul, (C) 248:s1/7, s2/2
Chariot, 291:s2/4
Charles, Ernest, (C) 247:s2/7
Charles, Ray, (P) 249:s2/7
Charles, Teddy, (P) 216:s2/3
Charles Mingus Jazz Workshop, (P) 242:s2/4
Charlie Mingus Octet, (P) 216:s1/5
Charlot's Revue of 1926: A Cup of Coffee, a Sandwich and You, 215:s1/5
Charmaine, 227:s2/5
Chase, Parts I and II, The, 284:s2/7
Chasing Shadows, 250:s1/8
Cheek, John, (P) 262/63:s1/2, s2/1-2, 4
Cheek to Cheek (Top Hat), 238:s2/7
Cheering Is My Game, 291:s2/3
Cherish the Ladies, 239:s2/11
Cherokee Indians, (C,P) 246:s2/3
Chesterfield, 255:s1/2
Chezy, Helmine von, (L) 300: s1/7
Chicagoans, (P) 250:s2/5
Chicago Loopers, The, (P) 274:s2/3
Chicago Stomp, 259:s1/1
Chicago Symphony Orchestra, (P) 258:s2
Chick-A-Li-Lee-Lo, 245:s1/1
Chihara, Paul, (C) 237:s1/2
Childers, Buddy, (P) 216:s1/4, s2/1
Childhood Fables for Grownups: The Duck and the Yak; Lenny the Leopard; Tigeroo; Two Worms, 300:s2/4-7
Children: The Children; Moo Is a Cow; Once Upon a Time; The Rose, 243:s1/1
Chimes of Liberty, The, 266:s1/6
China Boy, 250:s1/5

Chinatown, My Chinatown, 293:s2/3
Chinese, the Chinese, You Know, The, 267:s1/3
Chinese Rag, 235:s2/4
Chisholm, George, (P) 274:s1/5
Chism Brothers, (P) 236:s1/4
Chittison, Herman, (P) 217:s2/7-8
Choates, Harry, (P) 287:s2/5
Chocolate Beau Brummels, (P) 217:s2/7-8
Chocolate Dandies, The, (P) 256:s1/4; 274:s2/5
Choo Choo Ch'Boogie, 261:s1/6
Chotis, El, 292:s2/13
Chou Wen-Chung, (C) 237:s2/1
Chowaniec, Franciszek, (P) 283:s1/5-9
Christian, Buddy, (P) 269:s2/7
Christian, Charlie, (P) 274:s1/7
Christy, E. P., (C) 267:s1/3
Church-House Moan, 252:s2/4
Ciaglia, John, (P) 276:s1/1, 3, s2/3
Ciavardone, Joe, (P) 216:s2/1
Cicchetti, Mike, (P) 216:s2/1
Cincinnati's University Singers, (P) 221; 267
Cincinnati's University Theater Orchestra, (P) 221
Citkowitz, Israel, (C) 243:s2/1
City Slickers, (P) 222:s2/1
Clare, Sidney, (C,L) 270:s1/6
Clarey, Cynthia, (P) 230:s1/1, 7, s2/1; 231:s1/2-3, s2/1
Clarinet Marmalade, 250:s2/5; 269:s1/4
Claris de Florian, Jean Pierre, (L) 300:s1/6
Clark, Angie, (P) 291:s2/7
Clark, Chester, (P) 256:s2/7-8
Clark, Dee "Delectus," (P) 249:s2/6
Clark, Donald, (P) 249:s1/9
Clark, Pete, (P) 274:s2/1
Clarke, Edwin G., (P) 282:1/1

Clarke, Grant, (L) 215:s1/2; 233:s1/3

Clarke, Herbert L., (P) 282:s1/8

Clarke, Kenny, (C) 284:s2/6 (P) 216:s1/5; 217:s1/1; 242:s1/2; 271:s1/2, 5, s2/3; 284:s2/6

Clayton, Buck, (P) 274:s1/1, s2/9; 295:s1/1, s2/2

Clayton, Jan, (P) 240:s2/6

Clayton, Paul, (C) 225:s1/8

Clear, Lindy ("Cousin Mort"), (P) 223:s1/1

Clements, Joy, (P) 241:s2/3

Clements, Vassar, (P) 225:s2/3

Clements, Zeke, (C) 207:s1/5

Clemson, Ralph, (P) 284:s1/5

Clephane, Elizabeth Cecilia, (L) 224:s2/3

Cleveland, Sara, (P) 239:s1/7, s2/4, 6

Clifton, Bill, (C,P) 225:s1/8

Climbin' and Screamin', 259:s2/5

Clinch Mountain Boys, (P) 225:s1/3

Cline, Patsy, (P) 207:s1/7

Clinton, Larry, (P) 248:s2/6

Clocher change, Le (Melodies Passagères), 229:s1/5

Clock, The, 249:s1/2

Clorindy, the Origin of the Cake-walk: Darktown Is Out Tonight, 265:s2/2

Clothed Woman, The, 216:s1/2

Clouds of Joy, Twelve, *see* Twelve Clouds of Joy

Clovers, The, (P) 261:s2/3

Cluke, Silas, (P) 256:s2/1

Coal Loading Machine, The, 270:s2/3

Coasters, The, (P) 249:s2/8

Coat of Many Colors, 207:s2/8

Cobb, Arnett, (P) 295:s1/8

Cobbs, Alfred, (P) 217:s1/8

Coburn, Richard, (L) 279:s1/1

Coco-Cancion, El (The Coconut Song), 264:s1/7

Coconut Song, The, 264:s1/7

Coffee in the Morning, Kisses in the Night (Moulin Rouge), 240:s2/1

Coffman, Wanna, (P) 287:s1/9

Cohan, George M., (C) 221:s1/2; 222:s1/4

Cohen, Henry, (C,L) 298:s1/2

Cohn, Al, (P) 271:s2/1

Coker, Henry, (P) 284:s1/3

Cole, Cozy, (P) 217:s1/6-7; 250:s1/9

Cole, Nat "King," (C,L,P) 261:s1/4

Cole, Orlando, (P) 229:s1/1

Cole, Vinson, (P) 262/63:s1/2, 4, s4/1

Coleman, Cornelius, (P) 249:s1/8

Coleman, Cy, (C,P) 272:s2/8

Collazo, Julito, (C,P) 244:s1/3-4

College Hornpipe, 293:s1/4

Collegiate, 279:s1/3

Collins, Booker, (P) 284:s2/2

Collins, Burt, (P) 295:s2/6

Collins, Henry, (P) 246:s2/4

Collins, John, (P) 284:s2/6; 295:s1/3

Collins, Shad, (P) 274:s2/9; 295:s1/2

Collins, Si-Ki, (P) 256:s2/4-5

Colnot, Clifford, (P) 211:s1/3

Coltrane, John, (C) 204:s2/2

Columbo, Russ, (P) 248:s1/4

Come, Josephine, in My Flying Machine, 233:s1/6

Come All You Coal Miners, 245:s1/7

Comegys, Leon, (P) 271:s1/5

Comets, (P) 249:s1/5

Come Up, Horsey, 291:s2/8

Comfort, Joe, (P) 284:s1/7; 295:s2/1

Comparone, Linda, (P) 299:s2/2-3, 5-6, 9

Concertino a Tre, (Dahl, C) 281:s2/2

Concerto for Alto Saxophone and Orchestra of Wind Instruments, (Finney, C) 211:s2/1

Concerto for Billy the Kid, 216:s2/2

Condon, Eddie, (P) 250:s2/5

Configurations, 254:s2/1

Confrey, Zez (Edward E.), (C,P) 298:s1/3

Congo Blues, 271:s1/1

Conley, William Lee, *see* Broonzy, "Big Bill"

Conn, Chester, (C,L) 279:s2/2

Connecticut Yankees, (P) 270:s1/3; 279:s2/6

Connie's Hot Chocolates: Ain't Misbehavin', 279:s2/7

Connor, Chris, (P) 295:s2/5-6

Conrad, Lew, (P) 256:s1/8

Conrads, Janice, (P) 267:s1/1, 3, s2/1

Considera, Alma Perdida, 292:s1/2

Consul, The: To This We've Come, 241:s2/2

Continental Harmony Singers, The, (P) 276:s1/1, 5, s2/3, 5

Contrast, The: The Death Song of the Cherokee Indians, 299:s1/3

Cook, Ed Little, *see* Little Cook, Ed

Cook, Harry, (P) 269:s1/5

Cook, Oliver Little, *see* Little Cook, Oliver

Cook, Will Marion, (C) 265:s2/2

Cooks, Donald, (P) 261:s2/2

Coon Creek Girls, (P) 236:s2/8

Cooper, Bob, (P) 216:s1/4

Cooper, George, (L) 202:s2/2

Cooper, Gwendolyn, (P) 224:s1/7

Cooper, Tracy, (P) 269:s1/1

Coots, J. Fred, (C) 207:s1/7; 222:s2/6

Copland, Aaron, (C) *The Second Hurricane*: Excerpts, 242:s2/1; *The Tender Land*: Excerpts, 242:s2/3; *Song*, 243:s2/2; Piano works, 277 (P) 277:s1, s2/2-3

Cordilla, Charlie, (P) 269:s2/4

Corley, George, (P) 217:s2/2

Cornwell, Earl, (P) 216:s1/4

Coronach (Lady of the Lake), 231:s2/2

Corrina, Corrina, 236:s2/3

Corsair, The: Buckets of Gore, 221:s1/4

Cossa, Dominic, (P) 296

Cossack Polka, 264:s1/3

Cotton Club Parade: Stormy Weather, 248:s1/1

Cotton-Eyed Joe, 236:s1/6; 287:s2/8

Cotton Mill Blues, 245:s1/8

Cottrelle, Louis, (P) 269:s2/3

Counce, Curtis, (P) 275:s1/2-3

Country Boys, (P) 225:s1/5

Country Gentlemen, (P) 225:s2/5

Courtney, Freddy, (P) 287:s2/4

Courville, Sady D., (P) 245:s1/10

Cowan, Ruby, (L) 298:s1/1

Cowans, Herbert, (P) 224:s1/6

Cowboy Ramblers, (P) 226:s2/10; 235:s2/5

Cowell, Henry, (C) *The Banshee, Aeolian Harp, Piano Piece (Paris 1924)*, 203:s1/1-3; *Quartet Euphometric*, 218:s2/1; *Quartet Romantic*, 285:s1/1

Cox, Ainslee, (P) 266:s1/3-4, 9, s2/2, 4-6, 9

Cox, Bill, (C,P) 270:s2/4

Crain, S. R., (P) 224:s1/3

Cramp, Bill, (P) 223:s1/4

Crandall, George, (C) 217:s2/4

Craven, Sonny, (P) 261:s1/1

Crawford, Hank, (P) 249:s2/7

Crawling and Creeping, 245:s2/4

Creamer, Henry, (C) 256:s2/8

Creek Indians, (C,P) 246:s1/5

Crenshaw, Reverend, (P) 252:s2/2

Creoles Belles, 282:s1/2

Crickets, The, (P) 249:s2/2

Criswell, Kim, (P) 221:s1/7, s2/8; 267:s2/4

Crook, Howard, (P) 220:s2/2

Crooke, Eugene, (P) 256:s2/7-9
Crooked Whiskey, 267:s2/3
Crosby, "Bing" (Harry Lillis),
  (L) 248:s1/6; 274:s2/4
  (P) 248:s1/2; 270:s1/1
Crosby, Fanny Jane, (L)
  224:s2/4, 8
Crosby, Israel, (P) 259:s2/1
Crosier, Michael, (P) 214:s1/9
Crowden, Mrs. Leslie, (P)
  205:s1/4
Crowe, J. D., (P) 225:s2/2
Crucifixion, 255:s1/4
Crumbley, Elmer, (P) 217:s2/3-4
Crump, Thomas, (P) 284:s1/6
Crutcher, Renee, (P) 221:s1/5
Crying in the Chapel, 261:s2/6
Cuffee, Ed, (P) 235:s1/7
Cull, Augustus, (L) 220:s1/5
Culley, Wendell, (P) 284:s1/7;
  295:s1/8
Cummings, E. E., (L) 243:s2/2
Cuna de Mis Amores, La,
  244:s2/4
*Cup of Coffee, a Sandwich and
  You, A* (*Charlot's Revue of
  1926*), 215:s1/5
Curry, Bert, (P) 256:s1/2
Curson, Ted, (P) 242:s2/4
Curtin, Phyllis, (P) 229:s2/5
Curtis, King, (P) 249:s2/8
Curtis String Quartet, (P)
  229:s1/1
Cusseta, 205:s2/8
Cutilio, El, 292:s2/2-5
Cuttin' the Boogie, 259:s2/8
Cygne, Un (*Melodies Passagères*),
  229:s1/3
Cypress Wreath, The, 299:s1/5

Daawud, Talib, (P) 271:s1/5
Dabney, Ford T., (C) 269:s1/2
  (P) 269:s1/1-2
*Daddy, Won't You Please Come
  Home* (*Shuffle Along*),
  260:s1/5
Dadmun, John William, (C)
  220:s2/6

Dad's Ole Mule, 290:s2/1
Daffan, Ted, (C,P) 287:s2/4
Dahl, Ingolf, (C) 281:s2/2
d'Albert, Charles, (C) 298:s1/6
Dalhart, Vernon, *see* Slaughter,
  Marion T.
Dallas Blues, 217:s1/3
Dallas Rag, 235:s1/1
Dallas String Band, (P) 235:s1/1
Dameron, Tadd, (C) 271:s2/3
  (P) 271:s1/2, s2/3
  (arr.) 284:s1/1-2
Dameron Stomp. 284:s1/2
Damrosch, Walter, (C) 247:s1/7
Dana, Mary Stanley Bruce, (L)
  220:s1/4
Dance in Place Congo, The,
  228:s1/2
Dance from the Sheep Mountains,
  283:s2/5
Dance of Siteia, 264:s2/7
Dandridge, Putney, (P) 250:s1/8
d'Angelo, Gianna, (P) 229:s2/4, 9
Daniel, 278:s1/5
Daniel in the Lion's Den,
  224:s1/6
Daniel Prayed, 225:s1/3
Danny Deever, 247:s1/7
Dansereau, Jean H., (P) 247:s2/1
Danzin, Bill, (P) 284:s1/4
Danzon Cubano, 277:s2/2
Darby, Tom, (P) 223:s2/3
Darbonne, Luderin, (P) 287:s1/6
Dark as a Dungeon, 287:s2/7
Darktown Is Out Tonight
  (*Clorindy, the Origin of the
  Cakewalk*), 265:s2/2
Darling, Denver, (C,L) 261:s1/6
Davenant, William, (L) 247:s1/4
Davenport, "Cow Cow" (Charles),
  (P) 235:s1/5
David, Mack, (L) 298:s2/6
David's Lamentation, 205:s1/2
Davis, Art, (P) 235:s2/5;
  274:s2/3; 295:s2/7
Davis, B., (L) 250:s1/8
Davis, Bill, (P) 261:s1/6
Davis, Blind John, (P) 290:s2/7

Davis, Charles, (P) 275:s2/1-2
Davis, Eddie ("Lockjaw"), (P)
    284:s1/3
Davis, Fannie, (P) 252:s2/7
Davis, Gary, (P) 235:s1/8⁻
Davis, Ivan, (P) 257
Davis, Jerome, (P) 278:s1/2, 4-7,
    s2/1, 3, 5, 7-8
Davis, John, (P) 278
Davis, Johnny, (P) 269:s2/1-2
Davis, Leonard, (P) 217:s1/1;
    256:s1/3-4
Davis, Miles, (P) 271:s1/7
Davis, Pat, (P) 217:s1/2
Davis, Peter, (P) 278:s1/1-7,
    s2/1-3, 5, 7-9
Davis, Richard, (P) 204
Dawson, Mark, (P) 240:s2/7
Day Is No More, The (Triptych),
    218:s2/3
*Death Comes A-Creepin' in My
    Room*, 252:s2/3
Death of Mother Jones, The,
    270:s2/6
Deaver, Susan, (P) 229:s2/2-3,
    5, 9
Dee, Johnny, (P) 284:s1/4-5
'Deed I Do, 279:s1/7
Deep Blue Sea Blues, 290:s2/6
Deep Night, 279:s2/6
Deep River, 247:s1/10
De Koven, Reginald, (C)
    221:s2/5
Dello Joio, Norman, (C)
    300:s2/3
Delmore, Alton, (C) 223:s2/4;
    270:s2/2
    (P) 223:s2/4; 226:s2/8;
    270:s2/2
Delmore, Rabon, (C) 223:s2/4
    (P) 223:s2/4; 226:s2/8;
    270:s2/2
Dempster, Stuart, (P) 254:s2/2-3
Denby, Edwin, (L) 241:s2/1
Dencke, Jeremiah, (C)
    230:s1/1, 5
Denni, Lucien, (C) 233:s1/1
Dennis, Stanley, (P) 217:s1/2

Dennis, Willie, (P) 216:s1/5;
    295:s2/6
Denoon, Ray R., (P) 223:s1/3
Denson, Howard, (C) 205:s2/11
Denson, S. M., (C) 205:s1/7
Denson Quartet, (P) 223:s2/7
DeParis, Sidney, (P) 256:s1/3
DeParis, Wilbur, (P) 217:s1/8;
    274:s2/1
Départ (Melodies Passagères),
    229:s1/6
Derigotte, George, (P) 217:s2/5-6
Deshotel, Elise, (P) 264:s2/3
Deshotel, Esther, (P) 264:s2/3
DesRoches, Raymond, (P)
    285:s2/1
DeSylva, G. B. (Buddy), (L)
    215:s1/4; 233:s2/3, 8;
    279:s1/2
De Vertevill, Eddy, (P) 284:s2/6
Dew Drop Alley, 235:s1/3
De Witt, Francis, (L) 215:s1/1
Dexter, 204:s1/4
Dexter, Dave, (C) 259:s2/7
Diamond, David, (C) 258:s1
Diane's Melody, 275:s1/5
Dickenson, Vic, (P) 284:s1/3
Dickerson, Carroll, (P) 256:s1/2
Dickinson, John, (L) 276:s2/1
DiDomenica, Robert, (P)
    216:s2/3
Diesel Train, 225:s2/3
Dietz, Howard, (L) 215:s1/7,
    s2/3-4
Diez Perritos, 291:s1/2
Dillingham, J. D., (P) 291:s1/1
Dill Pickles, (P) 226:s2/9
Dill Pickles Rag, 225:s2/9
Dimond, William, Jr., (L) 232:s2
Dinah, 279:s1/4
Dirvin, William, (P) 217:s1/3
Dividido el Corazon, 292:s1/4
Dixey, Henry E., (L) 221:s1/4
Dixiana, 257:s1/6
Dixieliners, (P) 226:s2/8
Dixie Mountain Boys, (P)
    225:s1/8
Dixie Mountaineers, (P) 236:s1/7

Dixon, Charlie, (P) 256:s2/4-5
Dixon, George, (P) 217:s1/4
Dixon, Lawrence, (P) 217:s1/4
Dixon, Samuel Clay, (P) 291:s2/7
Dixon, Willie, (P) 249:s1/6; 290:s2/8
Doane, William Howard, (C) 224:s2/4
Dobbins, A., (P) 249:s1/9
Dr. Ginger Blues, 245:s2/3
Doddridge, Philip, (L) 255:s1/6
Dodds, "Baby" (Warren), (P) 274:s1/2, s2/6
Dodds, Johnny, (P) 269:s1/6; 274:s1/2
Dodge, J. C., (L) 267:s1/1
Dodson, Hobart, (P) 284:s1/3
Dodworth, Allen, (arr.) 293:s1/2
Doggone My Good Luck Soul, 290:s1/6
Doin' the New Low-Down (Blackbirds of 1928), 215:s1/6
Dolphy, Eric, (P) 242:s2/4; 275:s2/3-4; 295:s2/7
Domino, Fats (Antoine), (C,P) 249:s1/8
Dominoes, (P) 249:s1/3
Donaldson, Clarence, (P) 261:s1/8
Donaldson, Walter, (C) 260:s2/5; 279:s2/3, 5
Donic, Mike, (P) 284:s1/5
Donna Lee, 242:s1/2; 284:s1/8
Donnelly, John E., (L) 267:s1/3
Do Not Go, My Love, 247:s2/3
Don't Give de Name a Bad Blace, 265:s2/7
Don't Let Her Know, 207:s2/5
Don't Put Off Salvation Too Long, 223:s2/5
Dorham, Kenny, (P) 271:s2/6; 284:s2/6
Doria, Anthony, (P) 216:s1/4
Dorn, Jonathan, (P) 204:s1/2, s2/2
Dors, Dors, 'tit Bebe, 291:s2/8

Dorsey, Jimmy, (P) 250:s1/1; 279:s2/2
Dorsey, Tommy, (P) 240:s2/3
Dos y Dos Son Cuatro, 291:s2/5
Douckick, G., (P) 264:s1/4
Dougherty, Celius, (P) 247:s2/6
Douglas, Boots (Clifford), (P) 217:s2/2
Douglas, Frank A., (P) 246:s2/1; 297:s1/1-4, 13
Dover Beach, 229:s1/1
Dowdy, Herbert, Sr., (P) 246:s1/2
Dowell, Edgar, (C,L) 269:s2/3
Dowling, Eddie, *see* Goucher, Joseph Nelson
Downes, O., (P) 287:s2/6
Down Home Rag, 269:s1/5
Down the Bialka Valley, 283:s1/9
Down the Field March, 282:s2/8
Down Went McGinty to the Bottom of the Sea, 293:s1/4
Dreadnaught, The, 239:s2/3
Dreamer That Remains, The, 214:s1/9
Dreaming With Tears in My Eyes, 287:s1/4
Dream Land, 257:s1/2
Dreamland Blues I, 256:s2/4-5
Drill, Ye Tarriers, Drill, 267:s1/2
Drucker, Eugene, (P) 212; 218
Drummer Boy of Shiloh, The, 202:s1/6
Drunkard's Sorrow Waltz, The, 264:s2/3
Dubin, Al, (L) 215:s1/5, s2/7; 222:s1/8; 240:s2/1; 270:s1/2, 8
Duchin, Eddie (Edwin Frank), (P) 240:s2/1; 256:s1/8; 298:s1/7
Duck and the Yak, The (Childhood Fables for Grownups), 300:s2/5
Dudley, John, (P) 252:s1/2
Duffey, John, (C,P) 225:s2/5
Dugan, Patti, (P) 222:s2/7
Duhon, Edwin, (P) 287:s1/6
Duke, John, (C) 243:s1/5-7

Duke, Vernon, (C) *Where Have We Met Before*, 240:s1/5; *I Can't Get Started*, 295:s1/1; *Autumn in New York*, 298:s2/5

Dukelsky, Vladimir, *see* Duke, Vernon

Dukla, Franciszek (Frank), (P) 283:s1/2

Dulce Esposo de mi Alma, 292:s1/7

Dumas, Pedro Juan, (P) 244:s1/1

Dunbar, Paul Laurence, (L) 247:s2/8; 295:s2/7

Duncan, Tommy, (arr.) 287:s2/8

Dunforn, Uncle Alec, (P) 291:s1/2

Dunigan, Jack, (P) 287:s1/1

Dunkel, Paul, (P) 237:s1/2, s2/1; 285:s1, s2/2-4

Dunlap, William, (L) 299:s2/4

Dunn, Bob, (P) 287:s1/9

Dunn, David, (P) 214:s1/9

Dunn, Dennis, (P) 214:s1/9

Dunn, James P., (C) 247:s1/6

Dunn, Johnny, (C) 269:s2/6 (P) 269:s2/5-6

Dunn, Mignon, (P) 288/89

Dunn's Cornet Blues, 269:s2/6

Durham, Alden, (P) 217:s1/3

Durham, Eddie, (P) 217:s2/1; 274:s1/1, s2/9

Dutton, Lawrence, (P) 212

Duvivier, George, (P) 216:s2/4; 295:s2/6

Dye Se Dołu Białką, Down the Bialka Valley, 283:s1/9

Dying Christian's Last Farewell, The, 255:s1/9

Dying Christian to His Soul, The, 231:s2/4

Eager, Allen, (P) 271:s2/3

Eagle Dance, 246:s1/3

Eagleshield, John, (P) 246:s1/3

Eames, Emma, (P) 247:s1/3

Eanes, Jim, (C) 225:s1/5-6 (P) 225:s1/6

Earl and the Girl, The: *How'd You Like to Spoon With Me*, 221:s1/7

Early in the Morning, 229:s2/1

Earthlight, 237:s2/2

Eastburn (Joseph Eastburn Winner), (C) 267:s2/3

Easterday, Jess, (P) 287:s2/3

Eastwood, Bill, (P) 269:s2/4

Eaton, Jimmy, (C) 274:s2/1

Eberhart, Nelle Richmond, (L) 213:s2/3; 247:s2/1

Eberle, Ray, (P) 217:s1/2; 270:s2/8

Ebony Silhouette, 217:s1/7

Ebron, J. Norman, (P) 217:s2/4

Eckstine, Billy, (P) 284:s1/6

Eclipse, 216:s1/5

Eddington, Ray, (P) 225:s2/4

Eddy, Timothy, (P) 237:s1/2

Edenten, Ray, (P) 225:s2/9

Edison, Harry, (C) 274:s2/9 (P) 217:s1/8; 274:s1/1; 295:s1/2

Edwards, Arthur, (P) 261:s1/7

Edwards, Cliff ("Ukelele Ike"), (P) 279:s2/2

Edwards, Earl, (P) 290:s1/5

Edwards, Joe, (P) 217:s2/3

Edwards, Johnny, (P) 287:s2/8

Edwards, Michael, (C) 248:s2/4

Edwards, Raymond, (P) 249:s2/1

Edwards, Van, (P) 290:s1/5

Eephing, 223:s1/1

Egdon Heath, 216:s2/1

Egerton, Frank, (L) 267:s2/1

Eight Hours, 267:s1/2

Eldridge, Roy, (P) 250:s1/8

Elégie, 300:s1/9

Elevation, 284:s1/4

Eleven Intrusions: The Rose; The Street; The Waterfall; The Wind, 214:s1/1-2, 8

Elfin Dance (Twelve Virtuoso Studies), 206:s2/5

Elias, Lew, (P) 216:s1/4

Eliscu, Edward, (L) 227:s2/4; 240:s1/2; 298:s2/4

Eliza Jane McCue, 293:s2/1

Elkins, Alfred, (P) 290:s1/1, s2/7

Ellington, Duke (Edward K.), (C) *The Clothed Woman*, 216:s1/2; *Caravan*, 217:s1/1; *Mood Indigo*, 272:s2/1; *Pitter Panther Patter*, 274:s2/8
(L) 272:s2/1
(P) 216:s1/2; 250:s1/2; 272:s2/1; 274:s2/2, 8

Elliott, Charlotte, (L) 224:s2/9; 300:s1/4

Elliott, Ernest, (P) 269:s2/5

Ellis, David, (P) 217:s2/2

Ellis, Don, (P) 242:s2/3

Ellis, Phil, (P) 279:s2/3

Ellis, Ray, (P) 295:s2/8

Elssler Dances, 257:s2/2

Elston, Thierry "Red," (P) 256:s2/9

Emanuel, Leonard, (P) 223:s1/1

Embraceable You, 271:s1/7

Emerson, Bill, (P) 225:s2/7

Emerson, Ida, (L) 272:s1/2

Emerson, Luther O., (C) 202:s1/3

Emerson String Quartet, (P) 212; 218

Emi ra obini le wa, 244:s1/3

Emmaline, Take Your Time, 252:s1/7

Emmet, Joseph K., (C) 221:s2/6

Emmett, Dan D., (C) 202:s1/1

Emmons, Buddy, (P) 287:s2/9

Emperor Jones: Standin' in the Need of Prayer, 241:s1/5

Enchantress, The, 272:s1/1

End of a Love Affair, The, 295:s2/8

Engagement Ceremony among the Rich, 283:s2/2

Engel, Lehman, (P) 241:s2/2

Engen, Michael van, (P) 221:s2/1, 5, s2/1; 267:s1/1, 3, s2/1

Englander, Ludwig, (C) 221:s2/1

Englund, Gene, (P) 216:s1/4

Enlloro, 298:s1/5

Entertainer, The, 235:s1/7

Erickson, Robert, (C) 254:s2/3

Ericson, Rolf, (P) 275:s1/2-3

Erin-Go-Bragh, 239:s2/5

Estes, "Red" Buck, (P) 223:s1/1

Eternitie (Seven Pious Pieces), 210:s2/3

Ethiop, The or *The Child of the Desert*, 232:s2

Ethridge, Frank, (P) 256:s1/1

Etting, Ruth, (P) 215:s2/1; 238:s1/5-6; 279:s1/7

Etude in Form of a Scherzo, 206:s1/1

Europe, Lt. Jim (James Reese), (C) 260:s2/4, 6; 269:s1/1
(P) 260:s2/4-6; 269:s1/2-3

Evangeline, or The Bell of Acadia, 221:s1/3

Evans, Bill, (P) 216:s2/2-3

Evans, Everett, (P) 275:s1/6

Evans, Gil, (arr.) 284:s1/2, s2/2-3

Evans, Gus, (P) 284:s1/3

Evans, Herschel, (P) 256:s2/4-5; 274:s1/1

Evans, M. H., (C) 267:s2/2

Evans, Paul "Stump," (P) 256:s1/1

Evans, Redd, (C) 222:s2/2

Evening Breezes Sextet, The, (P) 270:s2/3

Everett, Horace, (L) 241:s2/3

Everidge, Charlie, (P) 223:s1/3

Everybody Wants a Key to My Cellar, 233:s1/7

Every Hour, 249:s1/9

Every Tub, 274:s1/1

Ewell, Don, (P) 274:s2/6

Exiner, Billy, (P) 284:s1/8

Expansions, 211:s1/2

Eyton, Frank, (L) 274:s1/8; 275:s1/6

Fagan, Barney, (C) 265:s2/1

Fain, Sammy, (C) 215:s2/6

Fairchild, Edgar, *see* Suskind, Milton

Fair Fannie Moore, 239:s1/7

Fairfield Four, The, (P) 224:s1/4

Fais Pas Ça, Don't Do That, 287:s1/6

Falcon, Joseph, (P) 226:s1/11

Falcon March, 282:s2/9

Fall River Legend, 253:s2

Famous Blue Jay Singers, The, (P) 224:s1/2

Fancies for Clarinet Alone, 209:s1/3

Fantaisie über "Ein feste Burg," 237:s2/3

Farley, Eddie, (C,P) 248:s2/1

Farley, J. J., (P) 224:s1/3

Farmer, Addison, (P) 242:s2/1

Farmer, Art, (P) 216:s2/2; 242:s2/1

Farmer Is the Man That Feeds Them All, The, 245:s1/6

Farmer's Curst Wife, The, 239:s1/2

Farmer's Diversion Czardaš, The, 264:s1/1

Farningham, Marianne, (L) 220:s2/5

Far Off I Hear a Lover's Flute (Four American Indian Songs), 213:s2/3

Farr, Hugh, (P) 287:s2/6

Farr, Karl, (P) 287:s2/6

Farren, Ellen, (P) 293:s1/2–3, 5, 8; 229:s1/4, 6

Farwell, Arthur, (C) 213:s1/1, 3, s2/2–3

Fast Kozak, 283:s2/1

Fat Boy Rag, 287:s2/9

Fatherhood of God and the Brotherhood of Man, The, 267:s2/2

Father's a Drunkard, and Mother Is Dead, 267:s2/3

Fears, Vivian, (P) 284:s1/3

Feather, Jane, (L) 295:s1/8

Feather, Leonard, (C) 295:s1/8

Federal March, 282:s1/1

Federal Music Society Opera Company, (P) 232

Federal Music Society Orchestra, (P) 293:s1/1, 6, 9; 299:s2/1, 4, 7

Feeney, Leonard, (L) 243:s1/1

Fe Fe Ponchaux, 226:s1/11

Fennoy, Roosevelt, (C) 261:s1/3

Ferguson, Maynard, (P) 216:s1/4

Ferina, Tony, (P) 216:s2/1

Fernandez, Alvin, (P) 256:s1/1

Ferraro, Gina, (P) 221:s2/3

Feyer, George, (P) 298:s2/6

Fields, Dorothy, (L) 215:s1/6, s2/2, 8

Fields, Frank, (P) 249:s1/8

Fields, Herbie, (P) 295:s1/8

Fields, Jackie, (P) 274:s1/8

Fields, Jerry, (P) 284:s1/5

Fields, Jobie, L., (P) 246:s1/5, s2/3

Fields, Ralph, (P) 265:s1/7, s2/2–5, 7

Fifteen Miles From Birmingham, 270:s2/2

Fifty Million Frenchmen, 227:s1/2

52nd Street Boys, (P) 284:s2/6

Fight, The (Shuffle Along), 260:s2/2

Figueroa, Aileen, (P) 246:s2/1; 297:s1/5–8

Fila, Alec, (P) 284:s1/5

Fillmore, Augustus Dameron, (C) 251:s2/3, 9, 11

Fillmore, Henry, (C) 266:s1/5

Fillmore, J. H., (C) 236:s1/7

Fine, Irving, (C) 300:s2/4–7

Fine, Sylvia, (C,L) 215:s2/5

Finkelstein, Harry, (P) 269:s1/5

Finley, Carolyn, (P) 234:s1/1, s2/2

Finney, Ross Lee, (C) 211:s2/1–2

Firmament, 251:s2/11

First Grand March, 299:s2/7

First Grand Minuet, 299:s2/7

Fischelson, Stan, (P) 271:s2/1

Fischer, William G., (C) 220:s2/4

Fisher, Fred, (C) 233:s1/6
Fisher's Hornpipe, 293:s1/4
Fishkin, Arnold, (L) 216:s1/3
Fitz, Richard, (P) 237:s1/2
Fitzgerald, Andy, (P) 284:s2/3-4
Fitzgerald, Ella, (P) 248:s2/5;
  295:s1/7
Fitzpatrick, Bob, (P) 216:s1/4,
  s2/1
Five Breezes, The, (P) 290:s2/8
Five O'Clock Shadow, 284:s1/5
Flagstad, Kirsten, (P) 247:s2/7
Flatt, Lester, (C) 225:s1/1
  (P) 225:s1/2; 235:s2/8
Flee as a Bird, 220:s1/4
Fleming, Leo, (P) 244:s2/5-6
Flemming, Herb, (P) 269:s2/5
Flemming, Teagle, (P) 249:s2/7
Flight for Heaven, 229:s2/7
Flirt Polka, The, 293:s1/8
Flood, Bernie, (P) 217:s1/1
Flood, Harold, (P) 217:s2/4
Flores, Jaime, (P) 244:s1/1-2;
  s2/1-4
Flowers of Edinburgh, 239:s2/1
Floyd, Bobby, (P) 265:s1/7,
  s2/2-3
Floyd, Harold, *see* Flood, Harold
Floyd, Horace ("Noble"), (P)
  217:s2/3
Floyd, Reuben, (C) 217:s2/3
Floyd, Troy, (C) 256:s2/4-5
  (P) 256:s2/5
Fly Cats, (P) 295:s1/3
Flying Cloud Schottische,
  293:s1/6
Flying Home, 261:s1/1
Flynn, Fred, (P) 290:s2/5
Foerster, Adolph Martin, (C)
  206:s1/6
Foggy Mountain Boys, (P)
  225:s1/2; 235:s2/8
Folus, Mickey, (P) 216:s1/1;
  284:s1/8
Foote, Arthur, (C) 268:s2
Ford, Chandler, (P) 269:s1/1
Ford, Clarence, (P) 249:s1/8

Ford, Ricky, (C) 204:s1, s2/3
  (P) 204
Forgotten Solder Boy, The,
  287:s1/8
For Heaven's Sake, 227:s2/2
Forrest, Helen, (P) 222:s2/9
Forrest, Vince, (P), 284:s1/4
Forrest City Joe, (P) 252:s2/8
Fortunato, D' Anna, (P) 230:s2/3
Fort Worth Doughboys, (P)
  236:s2/6
Foss, Lukas, (C,P) 281:s2/1
Foster, Guinn, *see* Foster, Gwen
Foster, Gwen, (P) 236:s2/3;
  245:s2/5
Foster, Lawrence, (P) 228:s2/1
Foster "Pops" (George), (P)
  272:s1/3; 274:s2/1
Fouche, Earl, (P) 269:s2/1-2
Four American Indian Songs,
  213:s2/3
*Four Impressions: Impression du
  Matin; Le Jardin; La Mer;
  Le Réveillon*, 273:s1/5-8
Four Piano Blues, 277:s2/3
Fowkes, Charles, (P) 284:s1/7
Fox on the Run, 225:s2/7
Frager, Malcolm, (P) 206
Françoix, Jean-Charles, (P)
  214:s1/9
Frank, Ted, (P) 217:s2/3
Frankfort Belle, 251:s2/6
Franklin, Dave, (L) 248:s2/3
Franklin, Mozelle, (P) 224:s1/3
Franklin, William, (P) 217:s1/4
Fratto, Russ, (C) 249:s1/6
Frazer, Earl, (P) 256:s1/6
Fredericks, Richard, (P) 241:s2/3
Freed, Alan, (C) 249:s1/6
Freed, Arthur, (L) 227:s1/4
Freeman, Bud, (P) 250:s1/6
Freeman, Dicky, (P) 224:s1/4
Freeman, L. E., (C) 248:s2/2
Freeman, Lawrence, (P) 217:s1/3
Frega, Gate, (P) 284:s2/3-4
Freshour, Charles, (P) 245:s2/2
Friedman, Don, (P) 275:s2/3-4

Friedman, M., (P) 287:s2/6

Friedman, Stanleigh P., (C) 282:s2/8

Friend, Cliff, (C) *We Did It Before and We Can Do It Again*, 222:s2/4; *Mr. Radio Man*, 233:s2/2; *When My Dreamboat Comes Home*, 248:s2/3

Frijsh, Povla, (P) 247:s2/6

Fritz, Our Cousin German, 221:s2/6

Frizzel, Lefty, (P) 207:s1/2

Frog He Would A-Wooing Go, A, 239:s1/1

Frog Went A-Courtin', 291:s1/1

From Behind the Unreasoning Mask, 237:s1/1

From the Land of the Sky-Blue Water (*Four American Indian Songs*), 213:s2/3

Frost, Irma, (P) 236:s1/7

Fruge, Atlas, (P) 264:s2/3

Fruge, Ernest, (P) 226:s2/6; 264:s2/2

Fruit Jar Drinkers, (P) 236:s1/9

Fry, William Henry, (C) 257:s2/4

Fuehrer's Face, Der, 222:s2/1

Fuga Giocosa, 206:s1/3

Fugue in C Minor (A. Parker), 280:s2/2

Fuller, Blind Boy, (P) 235:s1/4

Fuller, Curtis, (P) 242:s2/1

Fuller David W., (P) 288/89

Fuller, Walter ("Gil"),
    (C) 271:s1/5
    (P) 217:s1/4
    (arr.) 284:s2/6

Fulton, James E., (C) 282:s2/4

Future America, The, 267:s2/1

Gabbard, Rusty, (C) 207:s1/3

Gabler, Milton, (C,L) 261:s1/6

Gabriel, Charles H., (C) 224:s2/5

Gadski, Johanna, (P) 247:s1/2

Galbraith, Barry, (P) 216:s2/2; 284:s1/8; 295:s2/8

Gallagher, Ed, (C,P) 215:s1/3

Gallet, (L) 300:s1/9

Galop, 251:s2/5

Gambling Song, 297:s1/4, s2/3-4

Gamoian, P., (P) 264:s2/5

Gant, Cecil, (C,L,P) 261:s1/5

Garcia, Cipriano, (P) 246:s1/1

Garcia, Jerry, (P) 246:s1/1

Garcia, Jose, (P) 244:s1/5

Garcia, Peter, (P) 246:s1/1

Gar Dance, 246:s1/5

Garden, Mary, (P) 247:s1, s2/1

Gardes du Corps, 266:s2/7

Gardner, Carl, (P) 249:s2/8

Garland, Ed, (P) 269:s1/7-8

Garland, Joe, (P) 217:s1/1

Garland, Judy, (P) 240:s2/4

Garner, Erroll, (C) 295:s2/5

Garner Brothers, (P) 294:s2/7

Garrett, Duke, (P) 284:s1/7

Garrett, Lloyd, (C,L) 217:s1/3

Gary, Leroy, (P) 252:s1/9

Gaskill, Clarence, (C) 293:s2/6

Gate City, 266:s1/4

Gaunt, Percy, (C) 221:s2/3, 7

Gee, I'm Glad That I'm From Dixie (*Shuffle Along*), 260:s2/3

Gehet in dem Geruch Seines Bräutigams-Namen, 230:s1/5

General Mixup U.S.A., 282:s2/2

General Pershing March, 282:s2/1

General Scott's March, 276:s1/3

General Speech, 254:s2/3

General William Booth Enters into Heaven, 247:s2/9

Gensler, Lewis, (C) 240:s1/4

George, Karl, (P) 261:s1/1

George Russell and His Smalltet, (P) 216:s2/2

George Washington, 236:s1/4

George Washington, 291:s2/2

Georgia Sea Islanders, (P) 291:s2/1

Georgia Wildcat Breakdown, 287:s1/1

Georgia Wildcats, (P) 287:s1/1

German 5th, The, 265:s2/4

Gershwin, George, (C) *I'll Build a Stairway to Paradise*, 215:s1/4; *Strike Up the Band*, 227:s1/1; *I Got Rhythm*, ·250:s1/7; *Love Walked In*, 270:s1/5; *Embraceable You*, 271:s1/7; *'S Wonderful*, 275:s1/1 (P) 272:s1/5

Gershwin, Ira, (L) 215:s1/4; 227:s1/1; 240:s2/2; 250:s1/7; 270:s1/5; 271:s1/7; 272:s1/5; 275:s1/1; 295:s1/1

Get a Job, 249:s2/1

Getz, Stan, (P) 271:s2/1

Ghost of a Chance, 248:s1/6

Giamo, Louis, (P) 284:s1/4

Giamo, Mike, (P) 284:s1/5

Gibbons, John Sloan, (L) 202:s1/3

Gibbs, Terry, (P) 271:s2/1

Gibson, Andy, (arr.) 217:s1/7 (L) 295:s1/2

Gifford, Gene, (C) 271:s1/2; 250:s1/6 (P) 250:s1/6

Gilbert, Henry F., (C) 206:s1/5; 228:s1/2

Gilbert, Key, (P) 239:s1/5

Gilbert, L. Wolfe, (L) 227:s2/1

Gilbert, Ollie, (P) 294:s2/6

Gilfert, Charles, (C) 299:s1/5

Gillespie, Dizzy (John Birks), (C) *Pickin' the Cabbage*, 217:s1/6; *Woody'n You*, 242:s1/1; *Shaw 'Nuff*, 271:s1/3; *Things to Come*, 271:s1/5 (L) 271:s1/3 (P) 217:s1/6, 7; 271:s1/1, 3, 5, 8; 282:s1/6

Gillum, Francis, (P) 226:s2/2

Gillum, Ted, (P) 217:s2/5-6

Gilmore, Buddy, (P) 269:s1/1

Gilmore, Eugene, (C,P) 290:s2/8

Gilmore, Patrick Sarsfield, (C) 202:s2/5

Gimble, Johnny, (P) 287:s2/9

Gimme a Little Kiss, Will Ya Huh, 279:s1/6

Gioga, Bob, (P) 216:s1/4

Girard, Adele, (P) 250:s2/5

Girl on the Magazine Cover, The, 233:s1/2

Gitanjali: Light, My Light; *When I Bring You Coloured Toys*, 247:s2/4

Give an Honest Irish Lad a Chance, 239:s2/6

Give Me a Simple Prayer, 261:s1/9

Give Me Wings, 224:s1/7

Gladden, Texas, (P) 294:s2/2-3, 7

Glasier, Jonathan, (P) 214:s1/9

Glattly, Alexis, (P) 214:s1/9

Glenn, Artie, (C) 261:s2/6

Glenn, Lloyd, (P) 261:s1/7

Glenn, Tyree, (P) 217:s1/6-7

Glenn, Wilfred, (P) 222:s1/6

Glory of the Yankee Navy, 282:s1/6

Glow, Bernie, (P) 216:s2/4; 271:s2/1

Gluck, Alma, (P) 241:s1/1; 247:s1/1

Godburn, Dennis, (P) 299:s2/2-3, 5, 9

Godfrey, Batyah, (P) 288/89

Godley, A. G., (P) 256:s2/7-9; 295:s1/3

Go Down Moses, 247:s1/8

God's Bottles (Americana), 219:s1/3

God Shall Wipe All Tears Away, 224:s1/1

Goethe, Wolfgang von, (L) 273:s1/3

Gogorza, Emilio de, (P) 247:s1/4

Goin' Down to the Races, 252:s2/7

Going Down the Valley, 236:s1/7

Gold, Milt, (P) 216:s2/1

Gold Diggers of 1933, 270:s1/8

Golden, Jack, (P) 215:s2/2

Golden Gate Quartet, The, (P) 222:s2/3; 261:s1/3

Golden Wedding, De, 265:s1/7

Goldman, Edwin Franko, (C) 266:s1/6, s2/1

Goldman, Richard Franko, (P) 266:s1/2-3, 5-8, s2/1, 3, 7-8

Goldman Band, (P) 266

Goldozer, Harold, (P) 284:s1/5

Goldwyn Follies: Love Walked In, 270:s1/5

Golson, Benny, (C,P) 242:s2/1

Gomez, Johnny, (P) 250:s2/4

Gonzalez, Alicia, (P) 291:s2/5

Gonzalez, Govita, (P) 291:s2/4

Gonzales, I., (P) 264:s1/8

Gonzales, Vitin, (P) 244:s1/5

Goodbye, Mama, 222:s2/6

Good Feelin' Blues, 217:s2/8

Good Golly Miss Molly, 249:s2/3

Good Jelly Blues, 284:s1/6

Goodman, Benny, (C) 261:s1/1 (P) 240:s2/5; 274:s1/7

Good Man Is Hard to Find, A, 279:s1/5

Good Old Days of Adam and Eve, The, 239:s2/9

Good Old State of Maine, The, 239:s2/2

Good Rockin' Tonight, 261:s1/8

Goodwin, Henry, (P) 217:s1/1

Goodwin, J. Cheever, (L) 221:s1/3, s2/2

Gordon, Dexter, (C,P) 284:s2/7

Gordon, Mack, (L) 240:s1/3

Gordy, Barry, Jr., (C,L) 249:s2/4

Gore, Rufus, (P) 261:s2/1

Gorman, Lawrence, (arr.) 239:s2/2

Gorney, Jay, (C) 270:s1/1

Gospel Ship, 287:s1/5

Go to Sleep, Little Baby, 291:s2/8

Gottlieb, Gordon, (P) 209:s2/3

Gottlieb, Victor, (P) 281:s2/2

Gottschalk, Louis Ferdinand, (C) 227:s1/5

Gottschalk, Louis Moreau, (C) *Night in the Tropics*, 208:s2; *Romance*, 257:s2/3; *Pasquinade*, 282:s1/5

Goucher, Joseph Nelson, (L) 233:s2/5

Gould, Morton, (C) 253:s2

Governor Arnold's March, 299:s2/5

Governor's Own, The, 266:s1/1

Gozzo, Conrad, (P) 216:s1/1

Graas, John, (P) 216:s1/4

Graham, Billy, (P) 224:s2/4, 9

Graham, John, (P) 285:s1/1

Gramm, Donald, (P) 229:s2/1, 3, 6-7, 10-11; 243:s1

Grande, John, (P) 249:s1/5

Grande Polka de Concert, 257:s2/5

Grandioso, 266:s2/4

Grandpa Isom Ritchie's Church Congregation, (P) 223:s2/6

Grand Sonata in E Flat, 280:s1/1-4

Grannis, S. M., (L) 251:s1/6

Granny Went to Meeting with Her Old Shoes On, 226:s1/4

Granowsky, Harold, (P) 216:s1/3

Grass, Bill, (P) 246:s2/4

Graves, Buck ("Uncle Josh"), (P) 225:s1/2

Gray, (C) 290:s1/7

Gray, A. A., (P) 226:s2/9

Gray, Glen (Knoblauch), (P) 217:s1/2; 270:s1/4

Gray, Wardell, (P) 271:s1/6, s2/3; 284:s1/6, s2/7

Gray Goose, The, 291:s1/3

Great Day, 227:s2/4

Green, Bud, (L) 233:s2/3; 248:s2/4

Green, Charlie, (P) 269:s2/8

Green, Eddie, (C) 279:s1/5

Green, Freddie, (P) 274:s1/1, s2/9; 292:s1/1-2

Green, Henry, (P) 284:s1/3

Green, Jerome, (P) 249:s1/6

Green, Johnny, (C) 274:s1/8; 275:s1/6
Green, Lloyd, (P) 225:s2/9
Green, Urbie, (P) 295:s2/8
Greene, Alva, (P) 226:s2/2
Greene, Clarence, (P) 236:s2/3
Greene County Players, (P) 236:s1/5
Greenwich, 205:s2/1
Greer, Sonny, (P) 216:s1/2; 250:s1/2, s2/7; 272:s2/1; 274:s2/2
Grey, Harry, (P) 250:s1/8
Griffes, Charles Tomlinson, (C) 247:s2/1; 273
Grizzly Bear War Song, 297:s1/2
Grobe, Charles, (C) 257:s1/3; 293:s1/5
   (arr.) 293:s1/8
Gross, Walter, (P) 298:s1/4
Groundhog, 226:s1/1
Grover, Carrie, (P) 291:s1/1
Gruenberg, Louis, (C) 241:s1/5
Grujin, Vera, (P) 267:s2/3
Guajira del Mayoral, 244:s2/6
Guarnieri, Johnny, (P) 250:s2/8
Guida, Frank, (C,L) 249:s2/9
Guide Me, O Thou Great Jehovah, 294:s1/1
Guidry, Robert, (C) 249:s1/5
Guidry, Sabry, (P) 291:s1/2
Guillette, Wilfred, (P) 239:s2/7
Guitar Rag, 235:s2/3
Gumble, Albert, (C) 293:s2/4
Gunter, Cornell, (P) 249:s2/8
Guthrie, Woody, (C,P) 270:s2/5
Guy, Billy, (P) 249:s2/8
Guy, Fred, (P) 250:s1/2; 272:s2/1
Guy, Joe, (P) 274:s1/8
Guzman, Pablo, (P) 244:s1/5
Gypsy Blues (*Shuffle Along*), 260:s1/7

Haas, Eddie de, (P) 295:s2/5
Hackberry Ramblers, The, (P) 287:s1/6
Hackett, Bobby, (P) 250:s2/3

Hadnott, Billy, (P) 284:s1/1
Hageman, Richard, (C) 247:s2/3
Haggard, Merle, (P) 207:s2/7
Hagie, Mrs. Lloyd Bare, (P) 245:s1/5
Haig, Al, (P) 271:s1/3
Hail, Columbia, The President's March, 299:s2/9
Haley, Bill, (P) 249:s1/5
Hall, Al, (P) 250:s2/3; 284:s2/6
Hall, Edmond, (P) 272:s1/3
Hall, Joe, (P) 217:s1/2
Hall, Orrington, (P) 261:s2/1
Hall, Robert Browne, (C) 266:s2/7
Hall, Vera, (P) 291:s2/8
Hallelujah, 205:s1/9
Halley, Will, (P) 233:s1/3
Hamilton, Bonnie, (P) 202:s1/4, s2/3, 5
Hamilton, Mrs. Goldie, (P) 233:s1/4
Hammerstein, Oscar II, (L) 240:s2/3-4, 6; 272:s2/5; 298:s2/2
Hampton, Artie, (P) 217:s2/2
Hampton, Lionel, (C) 261:s1/1 (P) 261:s1/1; 284:s1/7; 295:s1/8
Hampton, Nell, (C,P) 291:s2/7; 294:s2/8
Hancock, Herbie, (P) 242:s2/2
Hand That Holds the Bread, The, 267:s1/1
Handy, William Christopher, (C) 269:s1/3; 272:s1/3
Hanging Johnny, 223:s2/1
Hang the Mulligan Banner Up (*The Mulligan Guard Nominee*), 265:s1/5
Hankey, Kate, (L) 220:s2/4
Hanley, James F., (C) 215:s1/2; 233:s2/5
Hanlon, Clare, (P) 240:s1/2
Hannah, Herbert, *see* Hannas, Herbert
Hannas, Herbert, (P) 217:s2/3

Hansen, Jack, (P) 274:s2/7
Hanson, Howard, (C) 241:s1/6
Happiness Boys, The, (P) 233:s2/7
Happy Talk, 298:s2/2
Harbach, Otto, (L) 216:s1/3
Harburg, E. Y. ("Yip"), (L) 240:s1/4-5, s2/2; 270:s1/1
Hardesty, Herb, (P) 249:s1/8
Hardy, D. B., (C) 224:s1/7
Hare, John, (P) 256:s1/1
Hargis, Wesley, (P) 245:s1/4
Harlem Hamfats, (P) 290:s2/5
Harlem Footwarmers, The, (P) 250:s1/2
Harmoneion Singers, The, (P) 202:s1/1, 3, 5, s2/1, 3, 5-6; 220:s1/1-3, 5-7, s2/2-6; 251:s1/1-2, 5-6, 8, s2/1-4, 8-11
Harrigan, Edward ("Ned"), (L) 265:s1/1-5
Harrington, John, (P) 217:s1/3
Harris, Addie, (P) 249:s2/5
Harris, Bill, (P) 216:s1/1; 271:s2/1
Harris, Charles, (P) 295:s1/8
Harris, Charles K., (C) 267:s2/4; 287:s1/10
Harris, Chuck, (P) 284:s1/4
Harris, Frank, *see* Kaufman, Irving
Harris, L. D., (P) 217:s2/2
Harris, Leroy, (P) 261:s2/1
Harris, Leroy, (P) 271:s1/2
Harris, R. H., (C,P) 224:s1/3
Harris, Roy, (C) 218:s1
Harris, Sam, (P) 235:s1/1
Harris, Stan, (P) 216:s1/4
Harris, Wynonie ("Blues"), (P) 261:s1/8
Harrison, Jimmy, (P) 217:s1/5; 256:s1/3; 274:s2/5
Harrison, Len, (P) 274:s1/5
Harrison, Lou, (C) 281:s1/1
Harrison, Pete, (P) 256:s2/1
Harrison, R. J., (C) 267:s1/1
Hart, Charles, (P) 222:s1/6
Hart, Clyde, (P) 284:s1/6

Hart, Lorenz, (L) 204:s2/1; 227:s2/3; 240:s1/1; 248:s1/5; 295:s2/3; 298:s2/7
Harvey, Jane, (P) 240:s2/5
Harvey, Morton, (P) 222:s1/2
Harvey, Roy, (P) 235:s2/3; 236:s2/2
Haskell, Antonio, (C) 224:s1/1
Hassard, Donald, (P) 243:s1
Haunted Road Blues, 245:s2/5
Have Mercy, Baby, 249:s1/3
Hawkins, Coleman, (P) 250:s1/4; 256:s1/4; 274:s1/5, 8, s2/5; 295:s2/7
Hawkins, Ezra ("Ted"), (P) 226:s1/12
Hawkins Rag, 235:s2/2
Hawthorne, Alice, *see* Winner, Septimus
Hawthorne, Willie, (P) 290:s2/8
Hayes, Roland, (P) 247:s1/8
Haymakers, The, 234
Haymer, Herbie, (P) 250:s1/7
Haynes, Roy, (P) 275:s2/1-2
Hays, William Shakespeare, (C) 202:s1/6
Hayton, Lennie, (P) 270:s1/1
Hazel, Monk, (P) 250:s1/5
Hazzard, Tony, (C) 225:s2/7
Headley, Stewart G., (P) 246:s1/3
Healy, Barlow, (P) 276:s1/3, s2/1, 3
Heard, J. C., (P) 271:s1/1; 295:s1/7
Heartaches, 248:s1/3
Heart and Soul, 248:s2/6
Heath, Percy, (P) 242:s1/1
Heat Wave (As Thousands Cheer), 238:s2/5
Heav'n, Heav'n, 247:s1/9
He'd Have to Get Under, Get Out and Get Under, 233:s1/3
Hedwig, Douglas, (P) 299:s2/3
Heebie Jeebies, 217:s1/5
Heidelberg Stein Song, The (Prince of Pilsen), 221:s1/6
Heimel, Otto ("Coco"), (P) 250:s1/5

Heine, Heinrich, (L) 273:s1/2

Heinrich, Anthony Philip, (C) *The Ornithological Combat of Kings*, 208:s1; *Philanthropy*, 230:s2/3; *Laurel Waltz*, 257:s2/2

He It Is (Triptych), 218:s2/2

Hejre Kati, 250:s1/3

Heldrich, Claire, (P) 254:s1/1

Hello, Central, 261:s2/2

Hello, Central! Give Me No Man's Land (Sinbad), 222:s1/5

Hello, Frisco, 233:s1/5

Hello! Ma Baby, 272:s1/2

Help Me Make It Through the Night, 207:s2/9

Helps, Robert, (C) 243:s2/6 (P) 243:s2

Helton Brothers, (P) 226:s2/3

Hemke, Frederick L., (P) 211:s2/1-2

Hemphill, Rose, (P) 252:s2/6

Hemphill, Shelton, (P) 217:s1/5; 274:s2/1

Henderson, Charles, (C) 279:s2/6

Henderson, Horace, (P) 274:s2/5

Henderson, Ray, (C) *Alabamy Bound*, 233:s2/3; *If I Had a Talking Picture of You*, 233:s2/8; *Let's Call It a Day*, 240:s1/6; *Life Is Just a Bowl of Cherries*, 270:s1/3

Henderson, Richmond, (P) 284:s1/2

Henry, 251:s2/9

Henry's Made a Lady Out of Lizzie, 233:s2/7

Herbert, Victor, (C) *I Can't Do the Sum*, 221:s2/8; *Natoma*: Excerpts, 241:s1/1-2; *The President's March*, 266:s1/8; *The Serenade*, 266:s2/8; *The Enchantress*, 272:s1/1 (P) 241:s1/1-2; 272:s1/1

Herbst, Arthur, (P) 274:s1/8

Herbst, Johannes, (C) 230:s1/6-8, s2/1-2

Herman, Woody, (P) 216:s1/1; 271:s2/1

Hernandez, Hector ("Flaco"), (P) 244:s1/3-4

Heroism, 255:s2/3

Herrick, Joseph, (C) 299:s2/8

Herrick, Robert, (L) 210:s2/3; 219:s1/6

He's 1-A in the Army and He's A-1 in My Heart, 222:s2/2

Hewitt, John Hill, (C) 202:s1/2

Hey Hey, I'm Memphis Bound, 223:s2/4

Heyman, Edward, (L) 274:s1/8; 275:s1/6

Heywood, Eddie, Jr., (P) 298:s2/3

Hiawatha, 293:s2/2

Hickman, Art, (C) 293:s2/5

Hicks, J. W., (C) 220:s2/5

Hicks, Rev. B., (C) 294:s2/3

Hicks' Farewell, 294:s2/3

Higginbotham, Jay C., (P) 265:s1/4; 272:s1/3; 274:s2/1

Higgins, Billy, (L) 279:s2/1

Higginson, Ella, (L) 247:s1/2

High Button Shoes: *Can't You Just See Yourself*, 240:s2/7

High School of Music and Art Chorus, (P) 241:s2/1

Hilbish, Thomas, (P) 219

Hill, Billy, (C) 287:s1/7

Hilliard, B., (C) 207:s1/1

Hilliard, Lee, (P) 256:s2/7-9

Hills and Home, 225:s2/5

Hillyer, Robert, (L) 229:s2/1

Himber, Richard, (P) 240:s2/2

Hindermyer, Harvey, (P) 222:s1/6

Hinds, Esther, (P) 296

Hines, Earl ("Fatha"), (C) 217:s1/4 (P) 217:s1/4; 256:s1/2; 274:s1/2, 6, s2/4

Hinton, Albert, (P) 256:s2/1

Hinton, Milton, (C) 217:s1/6-7 (P) 217:s1/7

Hirsch, Louis A., (C) 233:s1/5

Hirsch, Walter, (C,L) 279:s1/7

His Ejaculation to God (Seven Pious Pieces), 210:s2/3

His Exaltation, 300:s1/2

His Excellency, 266:s1/5

Hixon, Dick, (P) 216:s2/4

Hnida, George, (P) 250:s2/2

Hobson, Homer, (P) 256:s1/2

Hodges, Chris, (P) 234:s1/1

Hodges, Johnny, (P) 216:s1/2; 250:s2/3; 274:s2/2

Hodgson, "Red," (L) 248:s2/1

Hoffman, Al, (C) 248:s1/3

Hoffman, Mark, (P) 214:s1/9

Hoffman, Randy, (P) 214:s1/9

Hoffman, Richard, (C) 257:s1/5-6

Ho! for Kansas, 251:s1/5

Hogan, Carl, (P) 261:s1/6

Holden, Oliver, (C) 255:s2/5

Hold Me, 293:s1/5

Hold Whatcha Got, 255:s2/2

Holiday, Billie, (P) 295:s1/1, s2/8

Holiday en Masque, 201:s2/1

Holiner, Mann, (L) 248:s2/2

Holiness Singers, (P) 245:s2/8

Holland, Herbert ("Peanuts"), (P) 256:s2/7-9

Hollerin', 223:s1/1

Holley, Buddy (Charles Hardin), (C,P) 249:s2/2

Holley, Joe, (P) 287:s2/8

Hollingsworth, James, (P) 224:s1/2

Holloway, Charles, (P) 249:s1/9

Hollywood Now Swingin'/ Dynomite, 291:s2/3

Holman, George, (C) 251:s2/1

Holman, Libby, (P) 215:s1/7

Holmes, Charlie, (P) 274:s2/1

Holmes, Jim, (P) 216:s1/4

Holmes, Sally, (P) 287:s2/1

Holyoke, Samuel, (C?) 299:s1/1, s2/7

Holzman, Abe, (C) 282:s2/5; 293:s2/1

Homeward Bound, 215:s2/11

Honeymoon Lane: The Little White House, 233:s2/5

Honeysuckle Rose (As Thousands Cheer), 272:s1/7

Honky Tonk Train, 259:s1/6

Hoochie Coochie Man, 261:s2/7

Hooley, William F., (P) 222:s1/3

Hoops (The Band Wagon), 215:s2/3

Hope, Elmo, (C,P) 275:s1/2-3

Hopkins, Charles Jerome, (C) 257:s2/1

Hopkins, Gerard Manley, (L) 229:s2/5-6

Hopkins, Sam ("Lightnin'"), (C,P) 261:s2/2

Horszowski, Mieczyslaw, (P) 281:s1/2

Horton, Billy, (P) 249:s2/1

Horton, Robert, (P) 217:s1/1

Horton, Vaughn, (C,L) 261:s1/6

Hoskins, James, (P) 259:s2/1, 8

Hostetter, Joe, (P) 217:s1/2

Hot Combination, (P) 279:s2/2

Hotop, Jack, (P) 284:s2/3-4

Hound Dog, 261:s2/4

House Lady Blues, 290:s2/4

House of Flowers: A Sleepin' Bee, 272:s2/6

Howard, Bob, (P) 250:s2/6

Howard, Darnell, (P) 217:s1/4

Howard, Joseph, E., (C,P) 272:s1/2

Howard, Rowland, (C) 251:s1/7

Howard, Thomas, (P) 217:s2/4

How Deep Is the Ocean, 248:s1/2, s2/6

How Do You Do It (Ballyhoo of 1932), 240:s1/4

How'd You Like to Spoon With Me (Earl and the Girl), 221:s1/7

How Greatly Doth My Soul Rejoice, 230:s2/1

How's Chances (As Thousands Cheer), 238:s2/4

How Ya' Gonna Keep 'Em Down on the Farm (*Shuffle Along*), 260:s2/5

Hoyt, Charles H., (L) 221:s2/3, 7

Hubay, Jeno, (C) 250:s1/3

Hubbard, Carroll, (P) 226:s2/10

Huckaby, William, (P) 213:s1/1, s2/3

Hudson, George, (P) 256:s1/8

Hudson, Hattie, (P) 290:s1/6

Hudson, J., (P) 249:s1/9

Hudson, Robert, (P) 284:s1/3

Hudson, Will, (arr.) 271:s1/2

Huerta, Robert, (P) 284:s1/3

Huggins, Harley, (P) 287:s2/8

Hughes, Glenn, (P) 256:s2/1

Hughes, Lena, (P) 226:s1/7

Hughes, Rosie, (P) 205:s2/13

Hull, Harry, (P) 269:s2/5

Humeniuk, Pawlo, (P) 283:s2/1-3, 7-8

Humphries, John, (P) 256:s2/4-5

Humphries, Lex, (P) 242:s2/1; 295:s2/5

Hunky Dory, 226:s2/2

Hunt, C., (P) 287:s2/6

Hunt, Joe, (P) 242:s2/3

Hunt, John, (P) 249:s2/7

Hunt, Louis, (P) 217:s1/5

Hunt, Walter "Pee Wee," (P) 217:s1/2

Hunter, Anne Home, (L) 299:s1/3

Hunter, Lloyd, (P) 217:s2/3

Hunting Song, 297:s1/12

Huntington, Gale, (P) 239:s1/6, s2/3

Hunt the Squirrel, 293:s1/4

Hupfeld, Herman, (C) 240:s1/7

Hurt, Chick, (P) 287:s2/1

Huss, Henry Holden, (C) 206:s1/2

Hutchinson, Jesse, (C) 267:s1/3

Hutchinson, John, (C) 267:s2/2

Hutzulka w Semereczyni (Hutzulka from Semereczyn), 283:s2/6

Hyman, Dick, (P) 265; 293:s2/4-6

Hymn on Peace, A, 276:s2/5

Hymn to the Virgin (*Lady of the Lake*), 231:s1/3

I Ain't Gonna Play No Second Fiddle, 269:s2/8

I Ain't Got No Home in This World Anymore, 270:s2/5

I Am a Peach Tree (*Li Po Songs*), 214:s1/5

I Am a Poor Wayfaring Stranger, 294:s2/5

I Am O'ershadowed by Love, 223:s2/8

I Am Rose, 229:s2/2

Iandiorio, Regis, (P) 231:s2/4

I Can't Do the Sum (*Babes in Toyland*), 221:s2/8

I Can't Get Started, 295:s1/1

I Can't Get Up the Nerve, 284:s2/4

I Can't Go On, 249:s1/8

Ida, Sweet as Apple Cider, 287:s1/9

I Didn't Raise My Boy to Be a Soldier, 222:s1/2

I Double Dare You, 274:s2/1

Idut, 201:s1/1

If I Had a Talking Picture of You, 233:s2/8

If My Friends Could See Me Now (*Sweet Charity*), 272:s2/8

If the Light Has Gone Out in Your Soul, 245:s2/8

I Got Rhythm, 250:s1/7

I Know That You Know, 274:s1/6

I Left My Baby, 295:s1/2

I Left My Heart at the Stage Door Canteen (*This Is the Army*), 222:s2/5

I List the Trill (*Natoma*), 241:s1/1

I'll Build a Stairway to Paradise (*Scandals of 1922*), 215:s1/4

I'll Hit the Road Again, Boys, 239:s2/10

I Love to Tell the Story, 220:s2/4

I Love You, 264:s2/5

I'm a Good Old Rebel, 202:s2/4

I'm a Honky-Tonk Girl, 207:s2/3

I'm a Long Time Traveling Away From Home, 245:s2/9

I'm Always Chasing Rainbows, 298:s1/4

Imbody, Joel, (P) 221:s1/7; 267:s2/3

Imbrie, Andrew, (C) 212:s1; 254:s2/2

I'm Craving for That Kind of Love (Shuffle Along), 260:s2/1

I'm Cuttin' Out, 290:s2/5

I Met Him on a Sunday, 249:s2/5

I'm Gonna Live Anyhow till I Die, 252:s1/10

I'm Just Wild About Harry (Shuffle Along), 260:s1/1

I'm Movin' On, 249:s2/7

I'm on My Journey Home, 223:s2/7

Impression du Matin (Four Impressions), 273:s1/6

Impromptu (Twelve Virtuoso Studies), 206:s2/11

Improvisation (Twelve Virtuoso Studies), 206:s2/4

I'm Runnin' on the River, 291:s2/4

In a Little Gypsy Tearoom, 250:s2/1

In Dahomey: I Wants to Be a Actor Lady, 221:s1/5

Independence, 276:s1/5

Indian Princess, The, or La Belle Sauvage, 232:s1

Indita, La, 292:s2/12

Ineluctable Modality Chorus, The, (P) 210:s1, s2/1-2

Inflections I, 254:s1/3

Ingalls, Jeremiah, (C) 205:s2/13

In Honeysuckle Time (Shuffle Along), 260:s1/2, 6

Inketunga's Thunder Song (Three Indian Songs), 213:s1/1

In Memoriam L. M. G., 257:s1/5

In Tall Grass, 285:s2/4

International Orchestra, (P) 250:s1/3

International Revue, The: On the Sunny Side of the Street, 215:s2/2

In the Garden, 224:s2/6

In the Still of the Night (Rosalie), 270:s1/4

Intolerance, 227:s2/6

Into the Orbit, 275:s1/2

Introspection, 275:s2/2

Intruder, The (Li Po Songs), 214:s1/4

Invitation, 255:s1/5

Irresistible, El, 293:s2/3

Irwin, Cecil, (P) 217:s1/4

I Saw You, Lad, 264:s1/4

Israels, Chuck, (P) 242:s2/3

It All Belongs to Me (Ziegfeld Follies of 1927), 238:s1/6

It Had To Be You, 298:s1/7

I Tickled 'Em, 264:s2/1

It Promises to Be a Fine Night (The Tender Land), 241:s2/3

I Truly Understand, You Love Another Man, 236:s1/1

It's the Tune That Counts, 295:s1/6

It Won't Be Long, 287:s2/5

I've Found a New Baby, 256:s2/9; 274:s1/7

I've Got My Captain Working for Me Now (Ziegfeld Follies of 1919), 222:s1/7

Ives, 251:s2/4

Ives, Charles Edward, (C) 300:s1 (L) 300:s1/5

Ives, Elam, Jr., (C) 251:s2/4

Ives, Gene, (P) 288/89

I Wanna Be a Cowboy's Sweetheart, 287:s2/1

I Wants to Be a Actor Lady (In Dahomey), 221:s1/5
I Will Not Marry, 283:s1/6
I Wish I Was in Dixie's Land, 202:s1/1
I Wish that I Could Shimmy Like My Sister Kate, 250:s1/4
I Wonder, 261:s1/5
Izenhall, Aaron, (P) 261:s1/1

Jackson, Andy, (P) 217:s1/1
Jackson, Bennie, (P) 274:s2/5
Jackson, Chubby, (P) 271:s2/1
Jackson, Clifford, (P) 251:s1/3, 7, s2/1; 265:s2/4-7
Jackson, Fred, (P) 217:s2/8; 249:s1/9
Jackson, George K., (C) 231:s2/4
Jackson, Josh, (P) 261:s1/6
Jackson, Milt, (P) 242:s1/1; 271:s1/5, s2/4
Jackson, Oliver ("Slick"), (P) 256:s2/1
Jackson, Quentin, (P) 217:s1/6-7
Jackson, Robert ("Eppi"), (P) 256:s2/7-9
Jackson, Ronald Shannon, (P) 201
Jacobs, Dick, (arr.) 249:s2/4
Jacquet, Illinois, (C) 295:s1/7
Ja-Da, 295:s1/5
Jaffe, Moe, (C) 279:s1/3
Jahbero, 271:s2/3
James, Carl, (P) 297:s2/3
James, J. S., (C) 205:s1/7
James, Lewis, (P) 222:s1/6; 233:s2/4
James, Paul, (L) 295:s2/4
Jammin' for the Jackpot, 217:s1/8
Jam on Gerry's Rock, The, 239:s1/8
Jam Session Band, (P) 287:s2/9
Janik, Stanisław, (P) 283:s1/3
Janis, Deane, (P) 270:s1/2

Jardin, Le *(Four Impressions)*, 273:s1/5
Jarrell, Ben, (P) 236:s1/2
Jazz Cardinals, (P) 269:s1/6
Jazz Messengers, The, (P) 242:s1/3
Jazzopaters, (P) 250:s2/7
Jazz Phools, (P) 269:s2/8
Jeannine, I Dream of Lilac Time (Lilac Time), 227:s2/1
Jean's Song, 207:s1/8
Jeffers, Ron, (P) 255
Jefferson, Blind Lemon, (C) 294:s2/4
Jefferson, Hilton, (P) 217:s1/5-7
Jeff in Petticoats, 202:s2/2
Jeffrey, Paul, (arr.) 204:s1/2, s2/2
Jeff's Song (The Second Hurricane), 241:s2/1
Je me suis mis-t-à courir, 291:s1/2
Jenkins, Frank, (P) 236:s1/2
Jenkins, George, (P) 261:s1/1
Jenny Lind Polka, 293:s1/2
Jerome, M. K., (C) 293:s2/4
Jerome, William, (L) 265:s2/6
Jesinskey, Edward, (P) 276:s1/1, 3, s2/1, 3
Jesus Is All the World to Me, 224:s2/2
Jeter, James, (P) 256:s2/7-9
Jeuns Gens Campagnard (Young Men from the Country), 264:s2/2
Jig, 226:s2/10
Jim and John, 252:s1/6
Jim and Me, 294:s2/7
Jim Crack Corn, 291:s1/2
Jimenez, Santiago, (P) 264:s1/8
Jimerson, Avery, (P) 246:s1/2
Jimerson, Johnson, (P) 246:s1/2
Jimerson, Marty, (P) 246:s1/2
Jim Fisk, or He Never Went Back on the Poor, 267:s2/1
Jimmy Martinez, 207:s2/2
Jishie, Frank Jr., (P) 246:s2/2
Jive at Five, 274:s2/9

Johnnyjohn, Richard, (P) 246:s1/2

John Oliver Chorale, (P) 210:s2/3

John Riley's Always Dry (Mulligan's Silver Wedding), 265:s1/3

Johns, Kimberly, (P) 267:s1/1, s2/1

Johnson, A. J., (P) 217:s2/2

Johnson, A. Robert, (P) 276:s1/3-4, s2/2, 4

Johnson, Bobby, (P) 256:s1/3

Johnson, Bud, (P) 249:s2/5; 256:s2/6; 284:s1/6

Johnson, Bunk, (P) 235:s1/7

Johnson, C. H. ("Sleepy"), (P) 236:s2/6

Johnson, Charlie, (C,P) 256:s1/3

Johnson, Cortney, (P) 225:s2/8

Johnson, Dink, (P) 269:s1/7-8

Johnson, Edward, (P) 284:s1/1-2

Johnson, Francis, (C) 293:s1/7, 9

Johnson, Freddy, (P) 274:s1/5

Johnson, Howard, (C) 233:s2/6

Johnson, Howard, (P) 271:s1/5

Johnson, J. J., (P) 295:s2/8

Johnson, James P., (C) 269:s2/7 (P) 256:s1/7; 269:s2/8; 274:s1/3

Johnson, Jess, (P) 235:s2/3

Johnson, Johnny, (P) 249:s1/6

Johnson, Johnny, (P) 287:s2/4

Johnson, John Rosamond, (C) 247:s2/8

Johnson, Keg, (P) 217:s1/6-7

Johnson, Margaret ("Queenie"), (P) 295:s1/1

Johnson, Pete, (C) *Climbin' and Screamin',* 259:s2/5; *Blues on the Downbeat,* 259:s2/6; *Old Fashion Love,* 269:s2/7; *Piney Brown Blues,* 295:s1/3 (L) 259:s2/7; 295:s1/3 (P) 259:s2/5-8; 269:s2/8

Johnson, T. C., (P) 290:s1/3

Johnson, Van, (P) 246:s1/3, 5, s2/3

Johnson, Walter, (P) 250:s1/4

Johnson, Willie, (C) 222:s2/3; 261:s1/3

Johnson Boys, The, (P) 290:s1/3

Johnston, Ben, (C) 203:s2/1-4 (P) 214:s1/1-3, 8

Johnston Flood, The, 239:s2/8

Jolles, Susan, (P) 209:s2/3

Jolley's March, 299:s2/8

Jolson, Al, (P) 222:s1/5, 7; 233:s2/2; 238:s2/1

Jones, Bessie, (P) 252:s2/5; 278; 291:s2/1, 4

Jones, Bobby, (P) 217:s1/2

Jones, C. H., (P) 217:s2/2

Jones, Claude, (P) 284:s1/6

Jones, Coley, (P) 235:s1/1

Jones, Darwin, (P) 284:s1/1-2

Jones, George, (P) 295:s1/8

Jones, Hank, (P) 295:s1/7

Jones, I., (C) 250:s2/4

Jones, Isham, (C) 298:s1/7 (P) 233:s2/2

Jones, Jesse, (C) 267:s1/2

Jones, Jimmy, (P) 256:s2/6

Jones, Jo (Jonathan), (P) 217:s2/3-4; 250:s2/8; 274:s1/1, 7, s2/9; 295:s1/1-2, s2/2-4

Jones, Jonah, (P) 250:s1/9, s2/2

Jones, Mark, (P) 234:s2/1

Jones, Richard M., (C) 287:s1/6

Jones, "Spike" (Lindley Armstrong), (P) 222:s2/1; 272:s1/6; 287:s2/4

Jones, Will ("Dub"), (P) 249:s2/8

Joor, Bill, (P) 287:s2/9

Joplin, Scott, (C) 235:s1/7-8

Jordan, Duke, (P) 271:s1/7

Jordan, Joe, (C) 217:s2/4

Jordan, Louis, (P) 261:s1/6

Jovial Crew, The, 276:s1/3

Jovial Farmer Boy, The, 251:s1/8

Joyce, James, (L) 243:s2/1, 3

Judd, Mr. and Mrs. Vernon, (P) 226:s1/4

Jullien, G., (C) 293:s1/1
Jumbo: My Romance, 204:s2/1;
227:s2/3
Jump Steady Blues, 259:s1/5
Jun, Rose Marie, (P) 265:s1/1-5
Jungle Band, The, (P) 272:s2/1
Jungle Love, 250:s2/3
Junto Song, 276:s1/3
Just as I Am, Without One Plea,
224:s2/9

Kahn, Gus, (C) 298:s1/7, s2/4
(L) 279:s2/3
Kalish, Gilbert, (P) 268
Kalish, Sonia, *see* Tucker, Sophie
Kalmar, Bert, (L) 233:s1/8
Kansas City Blues, 293:s2/5
Kansas City Orchestra, (P)
217:s2/1; 256:s2/6
Kapalka, Jan, (P) 283:s1/2
Kapugi, Adam, (C,P) 264:s1/4
Kapugi, Louis, (C,P) 264:s1/4
Kapugi, Martin, (C,P) 264:s1/4
Kapugi Brothers Tamburica
Orchestra, (P) 264:s1/4
Karch, Bob, (P) 284:s1/4
Kardos, Gene, (P) 272:s1/2
Kasakka Polka, 264:s1/3
Kast, George, (P) 216:s1/4
Katie Dear (Silver Dagger),
236:s2/4
Katie Left Memphis, 252:s1/3
Kaufman, Irving (Frank Harris),
(P) 233:s2/5
Kavafian, Ani, (P) 300:s1/5
Kawasaki, Masao, (P) 218
Kay, Connie, (P) 216:s2/4;
242:s1/1
Kaycee on My Mind, 259:s2/7
Kaye, Danny, (P) 215:s2/5
Kazenas, Bruno, (P) 267:s1/2
Keene, Christopher, (P) 208:s1
Keep It Clean, 290:s2/2
Keeshan, Chuck, (P) 287:s2/4
Kegley, Charlie, (P) 250:s1/1
Keith, Bill, (P) 225:s2/1
Keith, Earl, (P) 217:s2/4
Keith, James, (P) 284:s1/1-2

Kelley, Frank, (P) 221:s2/6
Kelly, Guy, (P) 259:s2/1
Kelly, Robert, (C) 269:s2/5
Kelso, Millard, (P) 287:s2/8
Kelson, Jack, (P) 284:s1/7
Kemp, Hal, (P) 270:s1/2
Kennebec March, 299:s2/3
Kenner, Doris, (P) 249:s2/5
Kennett, Karl, (L) 265:s1/6
Kenny, Charles, (C) 207:s1/7
Kenny, Nick, (C) 207:s1/7
Kent, Walter, (C) 270:s2/8
Kenton, Stan, (P) 216:s1/4, s2/1
Kentucky Mountain Boys, (P)
225:s1/9
Keppard, Freddie, (P) 269:s1/6
Kern, Jerome, (C) *Yesterdays*,
216:s1/3; *How'd You Like to
Spoon With Me*, 221:s1/7;
That Lucky Fellow, 240:s2/3;
Nobody Else but Me, 240:s2/6
Kessel, Barney, (P) 271:s1/6;
295:s2/1
Keyes, Joe, (P) 217:s2/1
Key Largo, 295:s2/1
Kick Him When He's Down,
267:s2/1
Kiefer, Ed, (P) 216:s1/1
Kiger, Al, (P) 216:s2/4
Killian, Al, (P) 284:s1/3, 6
Kill It Kid, 235:s2/6
Killoran, Patrick, (P) 264:s1/5
Kim, Earl, (C,P) 237:s2/2
Kimball, Jacob, (C) 255:s1/5
Kimball House, 226:s1/12
Kimble, James, (P) 246:s2/4
King, Clifford, (P) 250:s1/3
King, Oliver, (C) 255:s2/6
Kingbird, Albert, (P) 291:s2/4
Kingbird, James, (P) 291:s2/4
Kingbird, Vernon, (P) 291:s2/4
*King's Henchman, The: Nay,
Maccus, Lay Him Down*,
241:s1/4; *Oh, Caesar, Great
Wert Thou*, 241:s1/3
Kings of Harmony, The, (P)
224:s1/1

King's Own Regulars, The, 276:s2/4

King William Was King George's Son, 245:s1/2

Kipling, Rudyard, (L) 247:s1/7

Kirby, Beecher ("Bashful Brother Oswald"), (P) 287:s2/3

Kirby, Edward, (P) 239:s2/5

Kirby, John, (P) 248:s1/6; 250:s1/4, s2/9; 274:s2/5

Kirchner, Leon, (C,P) 286:s2

Kirk, Andy, (P) 217:s1/3; 248:s2/2

Kirkes, Walter, (P) 235:s2/5

Kirkpatrick, Don, (P) 217:s1/5; 235:s1/7; 250:s1/4

Kitten on the Keys, 298:s1/3

Kittredge, Walter, (C) 202:s1/5

Klages, Ray, (L) 274:s1/5

Klenner, John, (L) 248:s1/3

Knee, Bernard, (P) 265:s1/7, s2/2-5, 7

Kneebone, 278:s1/2

Knepper, Jimmy, (P) 216:s2/3

Knight, Joe, (P) 261:s1/8

Knit Stockings, 239:s2/7

Knock, Knock, 250:s1/9

Knox, Harold, (P) 256:s2/6

Koch, Gerhardt, (P) 299:s1/1, s2/2-3, 5-6, 8-9

Koehler, Ted, (L) 248:s1/1

Koehler, Violet, (P) 236:s2/8

Kohen, J., (C) 261:s1/9

Ko-Ko, 271:s1/8

Konitz, Lee, (P) 216:s2/1; 242:s1/2; 284:s1/8

Korman, John, (P) 262/63: s1/3, s4/1

Korson, George, (C) 270:s2/3

Kosma, Joseph, (C) 298:s2/8

Kotzwara, Franz, (C) 299:s2/2

Kozak Zawydija (Fast Kozak), 283:s2/1

Kramer, A. Walter, (C) 247:s1/5

Krasnowska, Nasza Roza, (P) 283:s2/2, 7

Krazy Kat, 228:s1/1

Krestyanskyj Orkestr, (P) 264:s1/2

Kristofferson, Kris, (C,P) 207:s2/9

Kruger, Bennie, (C,L) 279:s2/2

Krzysiak, Jan, (P) 283:s1/3

Kuderna, Jerry, (P) 209:s1/1

Kunkel, Charles, (C) 220:s2/1

Kuomet Šokis (When You Dance), 264:s2/8

Kuziany Brothers, (P) 283:s2/5

Kwak, Frank, (P) 283:s1/3

Kyes, M., (C) 255:s1/4

Kyle, Billy, (P) 217:s1/8; 250:s2/6, 9

Kynard, Ben, (P) 284:s1/1-2, 7

Kyser, Kay, (P) 222:s2/8

Laborer You See, and I Love Liberty, A, 267:s1/2

Lacy, Anderson, (P) 256:s2/9

Lacy, Reba Dell, (P) 205:s2/2

Lacy, Steve, (P) 275:s2/1-2

Ladies' Walpole Reel, 239:s1/5

Lady Hope's Reel, 276:s2/1

Lady of the Lake, The: Alice Brand; Blanche of Devan; Coronach; Hymn to the Virgin; Mary; Soldier, Rest, 231

Lady of the Pavements: Where Is the Song of Songs for Me, 238:s1/7

Lake at Evening, The (*Three Tone Pictures*), 273:s2/5

Lala, Tony, (P) 284:s1/5

Lam, Bela, (P) 236:s1/5

Lamare, "Nappy" (Hilton), (P) 250:s1/8

Lambert, Louis, *see* Gilmore, Patrick S.

Lamentation Over Boston, 276:s1/1

Lament of Ian the Proud, The (*Three Poems of Fiona MacLeod*), 273:s2/2

Laminack, Uncle Will, (P) 205:s1/3

Lamond, Don, (P) 216:s1/1;
271:s1/6, s2/1; 295:s2/8
Lamont, Joe, (P) 249:s1/3
Lampe, J. Bodewalt, (C)
282:s1/2
Lampell, Millard, (L) 270:s2/7
Lancaster, M. L. A., (C)
205:s1/8
Lancaster, Sarah, (C) 205:s2/9
Lance, Herbert J., (C,L)
261:s2/5
Land, Harold, (P) 275:s1/2-3
Landford, William, (P) 261:s1/3
Lane, Morris, (P) 284:s1/7
Lang, Eddie, (P) 250:s1/1;
274:s2/3
Lange, Joanna, (P) 262/63:s3/3
Langstaff, Allan, (P) 284:s1/8
Lanin, Howard, (P) 233:s2/5
Lapčak, Mike, (P) 264:s1/1
La Porta, John, (P) 216:s1/1,
s2/3
Larcom, Lucy, (L) 251:s1/5
*Lark Now Leaves His Watery
Nest, The*, 247:s1/4
LaRocca, D. J. (Nick), (C)
217:s2/4
Laska, Edward, (L) 221:s1/7
Last Hymn, The, 220:s2/5
Last of Sizemore, The, 226:s2/1
Last Roundup, The, 287:s1/7
Last Words of Copernicus, The,
205:s2/9
Late One Evening, 223:s1/6
Latimore, Walter, (P) 224:s1/1
Laura, 216:s2/5
Laurel Waltz (Elssler Dances),
257:s2/2
Law, Alex, (P) 216:s1/4
Lawrence, Elliot, (P) 284:s1/4-5
Lawrence, Gertrude, (P)
215:s1/5
Lawrence, Jack, (L) 298:s2/1
Lawrence, Lucile, (P) 281:s1/1
Lawson, Harry, (P) 217:s1/3
Layne, Bert, (C) 287:s1/8
(P) 287:s1/1
Layton, Turner, (C) 256:s2/8

Laz'rus, 278:s2/9
Leaf, Ann, (P) 227:s1
LeClair, Lionel, (P) 246:s2/4
Ledford, Lily May, (P) 236:s2/8
Ledford, Rosie, (P) 236:s2/8
Ledford, Steve, (P) 236:s2/9
Lee, Beverly, (P) 249:s2/5
Lee, George E., (P) 256:s2/6
Lee, Jeanne, (P) 216:s2/5
Lee, Julia, (P) 256:s2/6
Lee, Lois, (P) 240:s2/7
Lehac, Ned, (C) 240:s1/2
Leiber, Jerry, (C,L) 249:s2/8;
261:s2/4
Leite mich in Deiner Wahrheit,
230:s1/4
Lemon Drop, 271:s2/1
Lenau, Nikolaus, (L) 247:s2/2;
273:s1/1, 4
Lennie Tristano Quartet, (P)
216:s1/3
*Lenny the Leopard (Childhood
Fables for Grownups)*,
300:s2/6
Leonard, Eddie, (C) 287:s1/9
Leonard, Harlan, (P) 284:s1/1-2
Leonard, Jack, (P) 240:s2/3
LePique, E., (P) 287:s2/6
Leppard, Raymond, (P) 288/89
Lesher, Bob, (P) 216:s2/1
Lesko, John, (P) 272:s2/5
Leslie, Edgar, (L) 222:s1/3;
233:s1/3, 8; 250:s2/1
*Let Me Sing and I'm Happy
(Mammy)*, 238:s2/1
Let's All Be Americans Now,
222:s1/3
*Let's Call It a Day (Strike Me
Pink)*, 240:s1/6
Let's Get Loose, 290:s1/7
Leveen, Raymond, (C,L)
261:s1/5
Levey, Stan, (P) 216:s2/1
Levine, Joseph, (P) 253:s1
Levy, Lou, (P) 271:s2/1
Lewis, Cappy, (P) 216:s1/1
Lewis, Dick, (P) 217:s2/3

Lewis, Ed, (P) 274:s1/1, s2/9;
    295:s1/2
Lewis, Jeffrey, (P) 267:s1/1,
    s2/1
Lewis, Jerry Lee, (P) 249:s2/3
Lewis, John, (C) 216:s2/4
    (P) 216:s1/5; 242:s1/1;
    271:s1/4-5
Lewis, Meade ("Lux"),
    (C) 259:s1/6-7
    (P) 259:s1/6-8
Lewis, Pete, (P) 261:s2/4
Lewis, Richard, (P) 249:s2/1
Lewis, Robert Hall, (C) 254:s1/3
Lewis, Roger, (L) 233:s1/1;
    269:s1/5
Lewis, Sam M., (L) 222:s1/5;
    260:s2/5; 279:s1/4
Lewis, Steve, (P) 269:s2/3
Lewis, Ted (Theodore
    (Friedman), (P) 279:s1/5
Lewis, William, (P) 288/89
Lewis, Willie, (P) 224:s1/4
Lexington Murder, The,
    245:s1/4
Liberace, Wladziu Valentino, (P)
    298:s2/4
Liberty Song, 276:s2/1
Liberty Tree Wind Players, The,
    (P) 276:s1/1, 3, s2/1-2, 4
*Life Begins at 8:40: What Can
    You Say in a Love Song*,
    240:s2/2
Life in the West, 251:s1/3
*Life Is Just a Bowl of Cherries
    (Scandals of 1931)*, 270:s1/3
Light, My Light (Gitanjali),
    247:s2/5
Light, My Light (Triptych),
    218:s2/4
Lights in the Valley, 226:s1/9
Like He Loves Me (Oh, Please),
    272:s1/4
*Lilac Time: Jeannine, I Dream
    of Lilac Time*, 227:s2/1
Lillie, Beatrice, (P) 215:s2/4;
    272:s1/4
Lily Schull, 245:s1/5

*Lindbergh (The Eagle of the
    U. S. A.)*, 233:s2/6
Lincoln, Abbey, (P) 295:s2/7
Linday, Tommy, (P) 274:s1/8
Lindsay, John, (P) 269:s2/3
Lindsay, John, (P) 290:s2/5
Lindsay, Vachel, (L) 247:s2/9
Lining Hymn and Prayer,
    252:s2/2
*Li Po Songs: Before the Cask of
    Wine; I Am a Peach Tree; The
    Intruder; A Midnight Farewell*,
    214:s1/4-7
Listeners, The, 300:s2/3
Listen to the Mockingbird,
    292:s2/8
Liston, Melba, (P) 284:s1/3
Lit'l Gal, 247:s2/8
Little, Booker, (C,P) 275:s2/4-5
    (P) 295:s2/7
Little Ah Sid, 267:s1/3
Little Brown Jug, 267:s2/3
Little Cook, Ed, (P) 246:s2/4
Little Cook, Oliver, (P) 246:s2/4
Little Drummer Boy, The,
    264:s1/2
Little Family, The, 294:s2/6
*Little Johnny Jones: Yankee
    Doodle Boy*, 221:s1/2
Little Maggie, 236:s2/9
Little Maud, 236:s1/5
Little Ole You, 207:s2/1
Little Richard (Penniman), (C,P)
    249:s1/9
Little Rooster, 291:s1/3
Little Sally Water, 291:s1/2
*Little Show, The First: Moanin'
    Low*, 215:s1/7
*Little Show, The Third: You
    Forgot Your Gloves*, 240:s1/2
Little Walter, (P) 261:s2/7
*Little White House (Honeymoon
    Lane)*, 233:s2/5
Live Humble, 278:s1/4
Livingston, Joseph ("Fud"), (P)
    274:s2/7
Loan, James Van, *see* Van Loan,
    James

Loesser, Frank, (C) 222:s2/8
(L) 248:s2/6
Loewengart, Steven, (P) 288/89
Logan, Ella, (P) 215:s2/6
Logan, Jack, (P) 214:s1/9
Logatti, L., (C) 293:s2/3
Logue, Seamus, (P) 239:s2/11
Lombardo, Guy, (P) 248:s2/3;
279:s1/2
Lombardo, Lebert, (P) 248:s2/3
London, Edwin, (P) 210:s1,
s2/1-2
Lonely Eagles, The, (P) 245:s2/2
Lonesome Pine Fiddlers, (P)
225:s1/7
Lonesome River Boys, The, (P)
225:s2/6
Long, Benny, (P) 256:s2/4-5
Long, Charles, (P) 232:s2
Long, Johnny, (P) 222:s2/7
Long, Red, (P) 269:s2/4
Long, Willie, (P) 256:s2/4-5
Long Ago, Sweetheart Mine,
247:s1/1
Lookout, Morris, (P) 246:s2/4
Lopez, Sam, (P) 246:s2/1;
297:s2/1, 4-6
Lopez, Vincent, (C,L) 250:s1/9
Lore, Augusto, (P) 244:s1/3
Lorena, 207:s2/4
Los Angeles Biltmore Orchestra,
(P) 238:s2/2
Los Angeles Northern Singers,
The, (P) 246:s1/3-4
Los Angeles Philharmonic
Orchestra, (P) 228
Lost Boy Blues, 226:s1/10
Lost Indian, 226:s2/7
Loteria, 244:s1/4
Lott, George, (P) 217:s2/3
Louiguy, (C) 298:s2/6
Louise, 275:s2/1
Louisiana, 252:s1/1
Louisiana Purchase, 238:s2/8
Louisiana Rhythmaires, (P)
264:s2/3
Louisiana Sugar Babes, (P)
256:s1/7

Louisville March and Quickstep,
251:s2/7
Love, 295:s2/6
Love, Daddy John, (P) 245:s1/8
Love in May, 247:s1/3
Loveless Love, 272:s1/3
Love Letters in the Sand,
207:s1/7
Loveli-Lines (Americana),
219:s1/5
Lovely Nancy (The Jovial Crew),
276:s1/3
Love Me, Baby, 290:s2/7
Love Me Tonight, 274:s2/4
Love Please Come Home,
225:s1/4
Lover's Lullaby, A, 298:s2/1
Love Song, 297:s1/1, 5, 9
*Love Walked In (Goldwyn
Follies),* 270:s1/5
*Love Will Find a Way (Shuffle
Along),* 260:s1/3
Loving Jesus, 205:s1/11
Lowry, Robert,
(C) 220:s1/5; 224:s2/1
(L) 300:s1/1
Loxodonta Africana, 204:s1/2
Loyd, George W., (C) 267:s1/2
Lucas, Sam, (C) 236:s1/9
Luckey, Warren, (P) 271:s1/5
Luders, Gustav, (C) 221:s1/6
LuGrand, James, (P) 256:s2/2-3
Luke Havergal, 243:s1/6
*Lullaby (Fritz, Our Cousin
German),* 221:s2/6
*Lullaby of the Woman of the
Mountain,* 229:s2/8
Lunceford, Jimmie, (P) 248:s2/7
Lund, Lewis, (P) 239:s1/2
Lurie, Mitchell, (P) 281:s2/2
Luther, Frank, (P) 240:s1/1, 4
Lyles, Aubrey, (L,P) 260:s2/2
Lynch, John, (P) 271:s1/5
Lynch, Reuben, (P) 256:s2/2-3
Lynn, Loretta, (C,P) 207:s2/3
Lyons, Jimmy, (P) 201

Mabrey, Paul, (P) 288/89
McAbee, Palmer, (P) 226:s1/10
McAdams, Garry, (P) 250:s2/1
McArthur, Edwin, (P) 247:s2/7
McCarron, Charles, (L) 222:s1/1
McCarthy, Joseph, (L) 298:s1/4
McClennan, Tommy, (C,P) 290:s2/6
McConnell, Shorty, (P) 284:s1/6
McCook, Donald, (P) 250:s1/7
McCormack, John, (P) 241:s1/2; 247:s1/5-6
MacCourt, Donald, (P) 209:s2/3; 276:s1/1, 3, s2/2, 4
McCoy, Seth, (P) 276:s1/3, s2/2, 4
McCoy, Wilber ("Joe"), (C,P) 290:s2/5
McCrary, James, (P) 290:s2/2
McCrary, Sam, (P) 224:s1/4
McCurdy, Roy, (P) 242:s2/2
McDaniels, Marla, (P) 288/89
McDonough, Dick, (P) 250:s1/6, s2/2; 274:s2/7; 279:s2/2
MacDonough, Glen, (L) 221:s2/8
Macdonough, Harry, (P) 233:s1/2
MacDowell, Edward A., (C) 206:s2; 247:s1/1-2
McDowell, Fred, (P) 252:s1/5, s2/3, 6-7
Macedonia, 255:s2/5
Macero, Teo, (P) 216:s1/5
McGarity, Lou, (P) 250:s2/8
McGee, Dennis, (P) 226:s2/6; 245:s1/10; 264:s2/2
McGee, Johnny, (P) 295:s1/5-6
McGee, Kirk, (P) 236:s1/9
McGee, Sam, (P) 236:s1/9
McGhee, Howard, (P) 271:s1/6
McGrath, Fulton, (P) 250:s2/2
McHenry, Walter, (P) 217:s2/2
McHugh, Jimmy, (C) 215:s1/6, s2/2, 7; 222:s1/8
Mack, Clarence, (P) 261:s2/1
McKee, Joseph, (P) 230:s2/3; 288/89

McKeel, James, (P) 288/89
Mackell, Billy, (P) 284:s1/7; 295:s1/8
McKenna, John, (P) 264:s1/6
McKenzie, Leighton, (P) 223:s2/1
McKinley, Frank, (P) 234
McKinley, Ray, (L) 222:s2/9
McKinnie, Tip, (P) 236:s1/4
McKissick, Norsalus, (P) 224:s1/5
McKusick, Hal, (P) 216:s2/2-3
McLean, Ernest, (P) 249:s1/8
MacLeish, Archibald, (L) 243:s2/4
MacLeod, Fiona, *see* Sharp, William
McMichen, Clayton, (C) 287:s1/1 (P) 236:s2/1; 287:s1/1
McNeil, Edward, (P) 217:s1/3
Macon, Uncle Dave (David Harrison), (C) 270:s2/1 (P) 236:s1/9; 270:s2/1
McPhatter, Clyde, (P) 249:s1/3
McReynolds, Jesse, (C) 225:s2/3 (P) 225:s2/3, 9
McReynolds, Jim, (C,P) 225:s2/3
McTell, Blind Willie, (P) 235:s1/6
McVea, Jack, (P) 261:s1/1
McWashington, Willie, (P) 217:s2/1
McWilliams, E., (L) 207:s1/2
Madhouse, 217:s1/4
Madison, Bingie, (C) 256:s2/7 (P) 272:s1/3; 274:s2/1
Madison, George, (P) 217:s2/3
Maggie Murphy's Home (*Reilly and the 400*), 265:s1/2
Magruder, Charles, (P) 265:s1/1-5, 7, s2/2-5, 7
Mahanojaus Lietviška Maineru Orkestra (Mahanoy City Lithuanian Miners Band), (P) 264:s2/8
Maid Sings Light, A, 247:s1/1
Mailman Blues, 249:s1/7
Mainer, Wade, (P) 236:s2/9; 245:s2/7
Malcolm, Horace, (P) 290:s2/5

Malenky Barabanshtchik (The
  Little Drummer Boy),
  264:s1/2
Malik, Ralph, (P) 201
Ma! Ma! Where's My Pa?
  267:s2/3
*Mama, He Treats Your Daughter
  Mean*, 261:s2/5
Mama Lucy, 252:s1/9
Mammy (*Let Me Sing and I'm
  Happy*), 238:s2/1
Mandel, Ben, (P) 239:s1/3
Mandy (*Ziegfeld Follies 1919*),
  238:s1/2
Mann, Howie, (P) 284:s1/4
Mann, Lois, (L) 261:s2/1
Manne, Shelly, (P) 216:s1/4
Manning, Ted, (P) 256:s2/2-3
Manone, Wingie, (P) 250:s1/6
Maple Leaf Rag, 235:s1/8
Ma Ragtime Baby, 293:s2/2
Marascalco, John, (C,L)
  249:s2/3
March for the 76th Regt.,
  276:s2/2
*March for the 3rd Regt. of Foot,
  Lord Amherst's*, 276:s1/1
March of the 35th Regiment,
  276:s2/1
March Shannon, 282:s2/3
March Wind (*Twelve Virtuoso
  Studies*), 206:s2/10
Mare, Walter de la, (L) 243:s1/2;
  300:s2/1, 3
Mares, Paul, (P) 269:s2/4
Mariano, Charlie, (P) 216:s2/1
Mariner, Thomas, (P) 221:s2/2;
  267:s1/1-2
Marks, G., (C) 248:s1/4
Marlor, I. N. (Nick), (P)
  223:s1/5
Marmarosa, Dodo, (C) 284:s2/5
  (P) 271:s1/6; 284:s2/5
Marowitz, Sam, (P) 216:s1/1;
  271:s2/1
Marsala, Joe, (C) 250:s2/5
Marsala, Marty, (P) 250:s2/5
Marsh, Warne, (P) 242:s1/2

Marshall, Henry I., (C) 233:s1/4
Marshall, Kaiser, (P) 269:s2/8
Marshall, Wendell, (P) 261:s1/1;
  295:s2/2-4
Marti, Virgilio, (P) 244:s1/3-4
Martin, Asa, (P) 245:s2/4
Martin, Benny, (P) 225:s2/9
Martin, Bill, (P) 217:s2/4
Martin, Chink, (P) 269:s2/4
Martin, Hugh, (C,L) 295:s2/6
Martin, Jimmy, (C,P) 225:s2/2
Martin, Mary, (P) 272:s2/5
Martin, Roberta, (P) 224:s1/5
Martin, Skippy, (P) 250:s2/8
Martiñez, Francisco ("Tan"), (P)
  244:s1/1
Martinez, Frank, (P) 217:s1/2
Martinez, Gerardo, (C) 244:s2/5
Martinez, Osvaldo ("Chihuahua"),
  (P) 244:s1/3-4
Martino, Donald, (C) 210:s2/3
Martinon, Jean, (P) 258:s2
Martirano, Salvatore, (C) 210:s1,
  s2/1-2
Mary (*Lady of the Lake*),
  231:s1/1
Masefield, John, (P) 269:s2/7
Mason, Henry, (C,P) 217:s2/5-6
Mason, Lowell, (C) 224:s2/7
Mason, William, (C) 257:s1/4,
  s2/6
Mass, 210:s1, s2/1-2
Massengale, John, (C) 205:s2/8
Massey, Billy, (P) 217:s1/3
Mass in D, 262/63
Mathieu, Carl, (P) 222:s1/8
Matlock, Matty, (P) 250:s1/6
Mattis, David J., (C) 249:s1/2
Matz, Peter, (P) 272:s2/6
Maxwell, Linn, (P) 288/89
Maybellene, 249:s1/6
Mayes, Samuel, (P) 286:s1
May Every Tongue (*Americana*),
  219:s1/1
Mayfield, John, *see* Masefield,
  John
May Irwin's "Bully" Song
  (*Widow Jones*), 221:s1/8

Mays, Willie, (P) 249:s1/9
Mazurka, 206:s1/5
Meadows, J. Paul, (P) 236:s1/5
Means, Alexander, (L) 205:s1/6
Medina Colón, Cristobel
   ("Tobita") (C,P) 244:s2/2-4
*Medley of Scottish Fiddle
   Tunes, A*, 239:s1/10
Meeres Stille, 273:s1/3
Mehegan, John, (P) 295:s1/8
Meine Seele erhebet dem Herrn,
   230:s1/1
Mein Heiland geht ins Leiden,
   230:s1/2
Melancholy, 274:s1/2
Melancholy Day, 205:s1/3
Mellow Blues, The, 259:s2/3
Mellow Mood, 284:s2/5
Melnotte, Claude, *see* Kunkel,
   Charles
*Mélodies Passagères: Le Clocher
   chante*; *Un Cygne*; *Départ*;
   Puisque tout passe; *Tombeau
   dans un parc*, 229:s1/2-6
Melrose, Walter, (C,L) 274:s1/2
Memphis Blues, 269:s1/3
Mendoza, Francisco, (P)
   264:s1/7
Mendoza, Leonor, (P) 264:s1/7
Mendoza, Lydia, (P) 264:s1/7
Mendoza, Maria, (P) 264:s1/7
Menendez, Nilo, (C) 298:s1/6
Mennin, Peter, (C) 258:s2
Menotti, Gian Carlo, (C)
   241:s2/2
Mer, La (*Four Impressions*),
   273:s1/7
Mercer, Johnny, (C) 272:s2/3
   (L) 216:s2/5; 272:s2/3;
   298:s2/8
   (P) 272:s2/3
Mercy and Love (*Seven Pious
   Pieces*), 210:s2/3
Merman, Ethel, (P) 238:s2/6
*Merry Mount: 'Tis an Earth
   Defiled*, 241:s2/6
Meskill, Jack, (L) 274:s1/5

Metropolitan Opera Chorus, (P)
   241:s1/3-4, 6
Metropolitan Opera Orchestra,
   (P) 241:s1/3-6
Mexican Rag, 235:s2/1
Meyer, George W., (C) 222:s1/3
Meyer, Joseph, (C) 215:s1/5;
   250:s1/1
Meyers, Billy, (C,L) 250:s2/2;
   274:s2/5
Meyers, Bump, (P) 261:s1/7
Michael, David Moritz, (C)
   230:s1/3
Middletown, 255:s2/8
Midnight Farewell, A (*Li Po
   Songs*), 214:s1/6
Miles, C. Austin, (C) 224:s2/6
Miley, James "Bubber," (P)
   256:s1/8
Milford, 205:s2/2
Millay, Edna St. Vincent, (L)
   241:s1/3
Miller, Bob, (C) 225:s1/7
Miller, Buddy, (P) 284:s2/2
Miller, Flournoy E., (L,P)
   260:s2/2
Miller, Glenn, (P) 270:s2/8
Miller, Johnny, (P) 261:s1/4
Miller, Leroy, (P) 252:s1/4
Miller, Mitch, (P) 284:s1/5
Miller, Ned, (C,L) 279:s2/2
Miller, Robert, (P) 203:s1,
   s2/1-4; 209:s1/2
Miller, Rodney, (P) 293:s1/4
Miller, Roger, (C,P) 207:s2/6
Miller, Susie, (P) 291:s2/6
Millian, Baker, (P) 217:s2/2
Millinder, Lucky (Lucius), (P)
   217:s1/8
Mills, Frederick A. ("Kerry"),
   (C) 282:s1/3
Mills, Irving, (C) *Caravan*,
   217:s1/1; *Straighten Up and
   Fly Right*, 261:s1/4; *You're
   Not the Kind*, 271:s1/2;
   Mood Indigo, 272:s2/1
   (L) 261:s1/4; 272:s2/1

Mills, Jackie, (P) 284:s2/5

Mills Blue Rhythm Band, (P)
    217:s1/6

Milnes, Sherrill, (P) 273:s1/1-4,
    9; 276:s1/2, 4, s2/1

Milwaukee Blues, 236:s2/2

Mine, All Mine, 298:s1/1

Miner, John, (P) 213:s1/3, s2/1;
    251

Mingus, Charles, (C,P) *Eclipse*,
    216:s1/5; *Original Faubus
    Fables*, 242:s2/4; *Mingus
    Fingers*, 284:s1/7

Mingus Fingers, 284:s1/7

Minichiello, Vic, (P) 216:s2/1

Miniver Cheevy, 243:s1/7

Minor, Dan, (P) 217:s2/1;
    274:s1/1; 295:s1/2

Minuet and Gavotte, 293:s1/3

Mirage, 216:s1/4

Miranda, Carmen, (P) 215:s2/7

Mirandy (*Shuffle Along*),
    260:s2/4

Mississippi Mud, 279:s2/4

Mr. Freddie Blues, 259:s1/2, 8

*Mister Gallagher and Mister
    Shean* (*Ziegfeld Follies of
    1922*), 215:s1/3

Misterioso, 271:s2/4

Mister Rabbit, 291:s2/6

Mr. Radio Man, 233:s2/2

Misty, 295:s2/5

Mitchell, Danlee, (P) 214:s1/9

Mitchell, John, (P) 269:s2/5

Mitchell, S. N., (L) 220:s2/3

Mitchell, Tom, (P) 295:s2/8

Mitropoulos, Dimitri, (P)
    253:s2; 286:s2

Moanin' Low (*The Little Show*),
    215:s1/7

Mobley, Hank, (P) 242:s1/3;
    271:s2/6

Modern Jazz Quartet, (P)
    242:s1/1

Mole, "Miff" (Irving Milfred),
    (C,P) 274:s2/7; 279:s2/2

Molly Put the Kettle On,
    236:s2/1

Monarch Jazz Quartet of Norfolk,
    (P) 290:s1/4

Mon Cherie Bebe Creole,
    245:s1/10

Mondragon, Joe, (P) 216:s1/1

Monk, Thelonious, (C) 271:s2/4;
    275:s2/2

Monnot, Marguerite, (C) 207:s1/8

Monroe, Bill, (C) 225:s1/1
    (P) 225:s1/1; 287:s1/8

Monroe, Charlie, (P) 287:s1/8

Monroe, H. R., *see* Rosenfeld,
    Monroe H.

Monroe, Walter, (P) 284:s1/2

Montague, 255:s1/6

Montana, Patsy, (C,P) 287:s2/1

Montana Slim, *see* Carter, Wilf

Montañez, Victor, Jr., (P)
    244:s1/1

Montañez, Victor, Sr.,
    (C) 244:s1/1
    (P) 244:s1/1-2

Montgomery, 205:s2/5

Montgomery, J. Neal, (P)
    217:s2/5-6

Montgomery, Marvin, (P)
    226:s2/10

Montmarche, Robert, (P)
    274:s1/5

Montoya, Luis, (P) 292:s1/1-5, 7

Mood Indigo, 272:s2/1

Moody, Mack, (P) 239:s2/8

Moo Is a Cow (*The Children*),
    243:s1/1

Moon Drops Low, The (*Four
    American Indian Songs*),
    213:s2/3

Mooney, Joe, (P) 284:s2/3-4

Moonlight and Pretzels (*Are You
    Making Any Money?*),
    240:s1/7

Moonlight in Vermont, 295:s2/2

*Moon Shines on the Moonshine,
    The* (*Broadway Brevities of
    1920*), 215:s1/1

Moore, Alan G., (P) 232;
    293:s1/7-8; 299:s1/2-3, 5,
    s2/3, 5-6

Moore, Alton, (P) 271:s1/5
Moore, Bob, (P) 225:s2/9; 287:s2/9
Moore, Eustis, (P) 274:s1/8
Moore, Grace, (P) 238:s1/4
Moore, Grant, (P) 217:s2/4
Moore, John C., (C,L) 249:s2/6
Moore, Oscar, (P) 261:s1/4
Moore, Pee Wee, (P) 271:s1/5
Moore, Thomas, (L) 231:s2/3
Moore, Tiny, (P) 287:s2/9
Morales, Marcelino, (P) 244:s2/5-6
Morales, Obdulio, (C,L) 298:s1/5
Morand, Herb, (C,P) 290:s2/5
Morath, Max, (P) 265:s1/1-5
Morehouse, Chauncey, (L) 274:s2/3
Moreland, Fred L., (C) 282:s2/6
Morelli, Frank, (P) 237:s2/1; 285:s1/2
Moret, Neil, (C) 293:s2/2
Morgan, Andrew, (P) 269:s2/1-2
Morgan, Beverly, (P) 285:s2/2-4
Morgan, Bill, (P) 224:s1/1
Morgan, Carey, (C) 233:s2/1
Morgan, David, (C) 205:s2/5
Morgan, Ike, (P) 269:s2/1-2
Morgan, Sam, (C,P) 269:s2/1-2
Morgan, Stan, (P) 284:s1/1-2
Morning Trumpet, The, 205:s2/10
Morris, Elida, (P) 233:s1/5
Morris, George Pope, (L) 251:s1/3
Morris, J., (C,L) 250:s1/9
Morris, Joe, (C,P) 249:s1/4
Morris, Marlowe, (P) 284:s2/1
Morris, Neil, (P) 223:s1/3
Morris, Richard, (P) 280
Morris, Robert, (C) 254:s1/2
Morris, Thomas, (P) 269:s2/7
Morris, Zeke, (P) 236:s2/9
Morrison, Henry, (P) 278
Morrison, James, (P) 264:s1/6
Morrison, Montgomery, (P) 217:s2/7-8

Morrow, George, (P) 271:s2/5
Morse, Woolson, (C) 221:s2/2
Morton, Benny, (P) 274:s1/1; 295:s1/2
Morton, Eddie, (P) 233:s1/1
Morton, "Jelly Roll" (Ferdinand), (C) 274:s2/6
Morton, Norval, (P) 256:s1/1
Morton, Richard, (L) 267:s2/4
Mosca, Sal, (P) 242:s1/2
Moses, 278:s1/1
Mosley, Leo "Snub," (P) 256:s2/7-9
Most Beautiful Girl in the World, The, 298:s2/7
Moten, Bennie, (P) 217:s2/1
Moten, Buster, (C) 217:s2/1
Motet on Doo-Dah, 254:s1/2
Mother, Is the Battle Over?, 202:s1/4
Mother of Us All, The, 288/89
Motian, Paul, (P) 216:s2/2
Motley, Willard, (L) 214:s1/8
Moto Perpetuo (Twelve Virtuoso Studies), 206:s2/2
Moulin Rouge: Boulevard of Broken Dreams, 270:s1/2; *Coffee in the Morning, Kisses in the Night,* 240:s2/1
Mounce, Bill, (P) 287:s2/8
Mountain Ramblers, The, (P) 294:s2/9
Mountjoy, Monte, (P) 287:s2/9
Mount Olivet Regular Baptist Church Congregation, (P) 294:s1/1, 3, 5
Mucci, Louis, (P) 284:s1/8
Much, Marc, (P) 234:s2
Much Too Young to Die, 207:s1/3
Muddy Waters, *see* Waters, Muddy
Mujeres de Borinquen, Las, 244:s2/2
Mullally, W. S., (C) 267:s1/3
Mullen, Daniel, (P) 276:s1/3, s2/1, 3
Müller, Georg Gottfried, (C) 230:s1/2

Mulligan Guard Ball, The: *The Babies on Our Block*, 265:s1/1

Mulligan Guard Nominee, The: *Hang the Mulligan Banner Up*, 265:s1/5

Mulligan's Silver Wedding: *John Riley's Always Dry*, 265:s1/3

Mulvihill, Brendan, (P) 239:s2/11

Munch, Charles, (P) 286:s1

Mundy, Jimmy, (P) 217:s1/4

Munn, Frank, (P) 240:s1/6

Munson, Amos, (C) 255:s1/3

Murcell, Raymond, (P) 220:s1/2, s2/2, 4-5

Murphy, Stanley, (L) 233:s1/4

Murray, Billy, (P) 222:s1/3; 233:s1/8

Murray, Don, (P) 274:s2/3

Murray, James R., (C) 251:s2/5, 10 (L) 251:s2/10

Musical Joke on "Bedelia," A, 282:s1/8

Music Box Revue: *Rock-a-Bye Baby*, 238:s1/4

Music for Saxophone and Piano (Bassett, C), 209:s2/1

Music Goes Round and Round, The, 248:s2/1

Music of Changes, Parts III, IV, 214:s2/1-2

Mussulli, "Boots" (Henry), (P) 275:s1/6

Muzillo, Ralph, (P) 295:s1/5-6

My Blue Heaven, 279:s2/5

My Buddy Blues, 290:s2/8

My Dream of the Big Parade, 222:s1/8

Myers, Mark, (P) 234:s1, s2/2

My Gal Is a High-Born Lady, 265:s2/1

Mygrant, W. S., (C) 266:s2/5

My Guy's Come Back, 222:s2/9

My Heart (*Evangeline*), 221:s1/3

My Honey's Loving Arms, 250:s1/1

My Lord Keeps a Record, 294:s2/9

My Man John, 239:s1/4

My Maryland, 266:s2/5

My Papa's Waltz, 229:s2/11

My Pretty Little Pink, 226:s1/3

My Romance (*Jumbo*), 204:s2/1; 227:s2/3

Mystery Train, 207:s1/9

Nancarrow, Conlon, (C) 203:s2/5-7

Nance, Ray, (P) 274:s2/2

Nancy Jane, 236:s2/6

Nanton, Joe ("Tricky Sam"), (P) 250:s1/2; 272:s2/1

"Na Obi Nogi" Polka ("On Two Feet" Polka), 238:s1/4

Nares, James, (C) 205:s2/4

Nash, Billie, (P) 288/89

Nash, Joey, (P) 240:s2/2

Natalie Polka-Mazurka, 293:s1/5

Natoma: *I List the Trill*, 241:s1/1; *No Country Can My Own Outvie*, 241:s1/2

Navajo Indian, (C,P) 246:s2/2

Navajo War Dance (chorus), 213:s2/1

Navajo War Dance (piano), 213:s2/2

Navarro, "Fats" (Theodore), (C) 271:s2/3 (P) 271:s2/3; 284:s2/6

Na Wesiliu pid Chatoju (At a Wedding under the Eaves), 283:s2/3

Nay, Maccus, Lay Him Down (*The King's Henchman*), 241:s1/4

Nearer, My God, to Thee, 224:s2/7

Neloms, Bob, (P) 204

Nelson, Herbert, (P) 245:s2/6

Nelson, S., (C) 207:s1/1

Nelstones Hawaiians, (P) 245:s2/6

Never No More Blues, 207:s1/2

Nevin, Ethelbert, (C) 206:s1/1

New Arkansas Travelers, (P) 264:s2/1

Neway, Patricia, (P) 241:s2/2

New Brown's Chapel Congregation, Memphis, (P) 252:s2/2, 4

Newburgh, 255:s1/3

Newgrass Revival, The, (P) 225:s2/8

New Harmony, 205:s1/8

New Jersey Percussion Ensemble, (P) 285:s2/1

New Jordan, 255:s1/8

Newman, C., (L) 250:s2/4

Newman, David, (P) 249:s2/7

Newman, Joe, (P) 261:s1/1

New Orleans, 249:s2/9

New Orleans Gang, (P) 250:s2/1

New Orleans Orchestra, (P) 269:s2/3

New Orleans Rhythm Kings, (P) 269:s2/4

New Salty Dog, A, 236:s2/5

Newton, John, (L) 294:s1/2

New World Chamber Ensemble, (P) 273:s2/5

New World Singers, The, (P) 213:s1/3, s2/1

New World String Orchestra, The, (P) 230:s1/8

New York Philharmonic, (P) 241:s2/1, 3; 253:s2; 258:s1; 286:s2

Nica's Dream, 242:s1/3

Nicholas, Albert, (P) 274:s2/1, 6

Nichols, Alberta, (C) 248:s2/2

Nichols, Herbie, (P) 275:s1/1

Nichols, Lester, (P) 217:s1/8

Nichols, "Red" (Loring), (P) 274:s2/7; 279:s2/2

Nie Będę Się Żynił (I Will Not Marry), 283:s1/6

Nigger Blues, 290:s1/8

Night in the Tropics, 208:s2

Night Winds, The (*Three Tone-Pictures*), 273:s2/5

Niles, Nathaniel, (L) 255:s2/3

Ninety and Nine, The, 224:s2/3

Nobody Else But Me (*Show Boat*), 240:s2/6

No coming to God without Christ (*Seven Pious Pieces*), 210:s2/3

No Country Can My Own Outvie (*Natoma*), 241:s1/2

No Irish Need Apply, 267:s1/3

Nolan, Bob, (C) 287:s2/6

No Love, No Nothin', 222:s2/7

No More, My Lord, 252:s2/1

Noone, Jimmie, (P) 274:s1/6

Norden, Betsy, (P) 218:s2/2-4

Norman, Gertrude, (L) 300:s2/4-7

Norris, Ella Vera, (P) 246:s2/1; 297:s1/9-11

North Carolina Ramblers, (P) 236:s2/2

Northern Arapaho Indians, (C,P) 246:s1/3

Northfield, 205:s2/13

North Port, 205:s2/6

North Texas State University Grand Chorus, (P) 234

Northwestern Symphonic Wind Ensemble, (P) 211

Norton, W. George, (L) 269:s1/3

Norvo, Red, (C) 271:s1/1 (P) 250:s1/7; 271:s1/1

Norworth, Jack, (C,L) 215:s2/1

Not for All the Rice in China (*As Thousands Cheer*), 238:s2/3

Noto, Sam, (P) 216:s2/1

Novellette (*Twelve Virtuoso Studies*), 206:s2/1

Nówobielski, Józef, (P) 283:s1/5-9

Now's the Time, 242:s2/2

NRA Blues, 270:s2/4

Nubin, Katie Bell, (P) 224:s1/6

Null, Jimmie Lu, (P) 288/89

Nye, Pearl R., (P) 291:s1/2

Oberek Puławiak (Oberek from Puławy), 283:s1/1

Oceana Roll, 233:s1/1

O'Connor, George, (P) 290:s1/8
O Death, 278:s1/6
Ode on Martyrdom, 255:s2/6
Odes of Shang, The, 219:s2
Offner, Herbert, (P) 216:s1/4
Ogan, Sarah, (P) 245:s1/7
Ogdon, Ina Duley, (L) 224:s2/5
Oh, Blue, 291:s1/3
*Oh, Caesar, Great Wert Thou
    (The King's Henchman)*,
    241:s1/3
*Oh, How I Hate to Get Up in
    the Morning*, 238:s1/1
*Oh, Kay! (Someone to Watch
    over Me)*, 272:s1/5
Oh, Please! (Like He Loves Me),
    272:s1/4
*Oh, You Must Be a Lover of the
    Lord*, 220:s2/2
Ohio, 251:s2/3
Ohman, Phil, (P) 240:s1/1, 6;
    298:s1/2
Oh My Little Darling, 245:s2/1
Ojibwa War Dance Song,
    291:s2/4
O'Keefe, Walter, (C) 233:s2/7
Oklahoma Two-Step, 246:s2/4
Old Age, 225:s1/9
Old Canoe, The, 251:s1/6
Older, Lawrence, (P) 239:s1/8
Old Fashion Love, 269:s2/7
Old Gospel Ship, The, 294:s2/1
Old Grandpaw Yet, 291:s2/7
Old Gray Horse, The, 226:s1/2
Old Joe Clark, 236:s1/2
Old John the Rabbit, 291:s2/6
*Old Man's Love Song, The
    (Three Indian Songs)*,
    213:s1/1, 3
Old Mother Hippletoe, 291:s1/1
Old Original Blues, 252:s1/5
Old Rosin the Bow, 251:s1/4
Old Shellover (Peacock Pie),
    300:s2/1
Oliver, Joe ("King"), (C)
    217:s2/7
Oliver, John, (P) 210:s2/3; 296

Oliver, Sy, (C) 248:s2/7
    (P) 217:s2/7-8
Olsen, George, (P) 240:s1/3
Olson, Phil, (P) 265:s1/1-5
Once a Lady Was Here, 243:s1/3
Once in a While, 248:s2/4
*Once Upon a Time (The
    Children)*, 243:s1/1
O'Neal, Waldo, (C,L) 287:s1/4
O'Neill, Tommy, (P) 284:s1/4
One Mint Julep, 261:s2/3
One Up One Down, 204:s2/2
On Jersey Shore, 266:s2/6
*Only Another Boy and Girl
    (Seven Lively Arts)*, 240:s2/5
*On Patrol in No Man's Land
    (Shuffle Along)*, 260:s2/6
On the Beach at Fontana,
    243:s2/3
On the 5:15, 233:s1/4
*On the Good Ship Lollypop
    (Bright Eyes)*, 270:s1/6
On the Sea, 206:s1/6
*On the Sunny Side of the Street
    (International Revue)*,
    215:s2/2
"On Two Feet" Polka, 283:s1/4
Onyx Club Boys, (P) 248:s2/1
Onyx Club Orchestra, (P)
    250:s1/9
Operti, Giuseppe, (C) 221:s1/1,
    s2/4
Ore, John, (P) 275:s2/1-2
Oregon State University Choir,
    (P) 255
O'Reilly, (C) 267:s1/3
Orem, Preston Ware, (C) 213:s1/2
Original Dixieland One-Step,
    217:s2/4
Original Faubus Fables, 242:s2/4
Original Jazz Hounds, (P)
    269:s2/5
Orioles, The, (C) 261:s2/6
*Ornithological Combat of Kings,
    The*, or *The Condor of the
    Andes and the Eagle of the
    Cordilleros*, 208:s1

Orphans of the Storm, 227:s1/5

Orr, Raymond, (P) 271:s1/5

Orta, Neri, (P) 244:s2/1-4

Orvath, Aviva, (P) 288/89

Ory, "Kid" (Edward),
   (C) 269:s1/7
   (P) 269:s1/7-8

Ory's Creole Trombone,
   269:s1/7

Osborne, R., (C) 205:s2/6

Osborne Brothers, (P) 225:s2/4

Oswald, James, (C) 276:s1/3

Otis, Cynthia, (P) 231:s1/3-4;
   237:s2/1

Otten, Judith, (P) 231:s1;
   299:s1/2

Otto, Lloyd, (P) 216:s1/4

Ottobrino, Carl, (P) 216:s1/4

Our Director, 266:s1/9

Ousley, John Mack, (P)
   232:s1/2-3, 5

Out of Work, 267:s1/2

Overstreet, W. Benton, (C)
   279:s2/1

Over There, 222:s1/4

Oves, Jr., Elam, (C,L) 251:s2/4

Owens, Bonnie, (C) 207:s2/5

Owens, Buck, (C,P) 207:s2/5

Owens, Henry, (P) 261:s1/3

Ozawa, Seiji, (P) 273:s2/1-4;
   296:s1/2

Pacific Railroad, The, 267:s1/1

*Paddy Duffy's Cart (Squatter
   Sovereignty)*, 265:s1/4

Padget, Jimmy, (P) 284:s1/4

Padilla, Vicente, (P) 292:s1/1, 4

Page, Clarence, (P) 217:s2/7-8

Page, "Hot Lips" (Oran), (P)
   217:s2/1; 256:s2/2-3;
   261:s1/8; 295:s1/3

Page, Walter, (C) 256:s2/2
   (P) 217:s2/1; 256:s2/2-3;
   274:s1/1, s2/9; 295:s1/1-2

Pageant, 211:s1/2

Paine, John Knowles, (C) *Fuga
   Giocosa*, 206:s1/3; *Romance*,
   206:s1/4; *Mass in D*, 262/63;

*Fantasia über "Ein' feste
   Burg,"* 280:s2/3

Paladino, Don, (P) 216:s1/4

Palma, Donald, (P) 254:s1/2

Palma, Susan, (P) 285:s1/1

Palmer, Horatio, (C) 224:s1/5

Palmer, Jack, (C) 256:s2/9
   (C,L) 256:s2/9; 274:s1/7

Pantaloon—He Who Gets Slapped,
   300:s2/2

Paradise Orchestra, (P) 256:s1/3

Paratore, Anthony, (P) 208:s2

Paratore, Joseph, (P) 208:s2

Pardon Me, Pretty Baby, 274:s1/5

Paree (At Home Abroad),
   215:s2/4

Parigian, H., (P) 264:s2/5

Parish, Mitchell, (L) 272:s1/6

Parker, Charlie ("Bird") (C)
   Donna Lee, 242:s1/2; *Now's
   the Time*, 242:s2/2; *Shaw
   Nuff*, 271:s1/3; *Parker's
   Mood*, 271:s1/4; *Relaxin' at
   Camarillo*, 271:s1/6; *Ko-Ko*,
   271:s1/8; *Donna Lee*, 284:s1/8
   (L) 271:s1/3
   (P) 271:s1/1-4, 6, 8

Parker, Herman, (C) 207:s1/9

Parker, Horatio William, (C)
   Valse Gracile, 206:s1/7; *Love
   in May*, 247:s1/3; *The Lark
   Now Leaves His Watery Nest*,
   247:s1/4; *Fugue in C Minor*,
   280:s2/2

Parker, Irene, (P) 205:s2/11

Parker, John ("Knocky"), (P)
   226:s2/10

Parker, Leo, (P) 271:s1/2

Parker, Thomas, (P) 288/89

Parker, William, (P) 213:s1/1,
   s2/3; 300

Parker's Mood, 271:s1/4

Parkhurst, Mrs. E. A., (C)
   267:s2/3

Parnell, Dave, (P) 224:s1/2

*Parody upon a Well-known
   Liberty Song*, 276:s2/2

Parrish, Lydia (Mrs. Maxfield),
   (arr.) 278:s2/7
Parshley, Tom, (P) 295:s2/8
Partch, Harry, (C,P) 214:s1
Parton, Dolly, (C) 207:s2/8
Pasquinade, 282:s1/5
Passing Show, The: *Sex Against
   Sex*, 221:s2/1
Passion Flower, 274:s2/2
Pastoral, 264:s2/4
Pastoral Novellette, A, 257:s1/4
Pat, Joe, (P) 283:s1/3
Pathfinder of Panama, The,
   266:s1/3
Pathway of Teardrops, A,
   225:s2/4
Patriot, The, 282:s1/4
Patterson, Joe, (P) 291:s2/1
Paul, Gene de, (P) 295:s1/5-6
Paull, Edward T., (C) 282:s1/9
Pawnee Horses, 213:s2/2
Pay Me, 278:s2/7
Payne, Bennie, (C) 217:s1/7
   (P) 217:s1/6-7
Payne, J. H., (L) 251:s1/2
Paynter, John P., (P) 211
Pazmor, Radiana, (P) 247:s2/9
Peach Tree Blues, 290:s1/1
Peacock Pie: *Cake and Sack*;
   Old Shellover; *The Ship of
   Rio*; *Tillie*, 300:s2/1
Peacock Rag, 226:s2/8
Pearly Dew, 226:s1/7
Pearse, Padraic, (L) 229:s2/8
Pease, F. H., (C) 251:s1/5
Peck, Thomas, (P) 262/63
Pecora, Santo, (C,P) 269:s2/4
Peerless Quartet, (P) 222:s1/8
Pelican Song, 297:s2/2
Pelissier, Victor, (C) 299:s2/4
Pelletier, Wilfred, (P)
   241:s1/5-6; 247:s2/3
Pembroke, C. G., (C) 255:s1/8
Penn, Andrew, (P) 284:s1/7
Pennington, Douglas, (P)
   267:s1/3, s2/1
Pennsylvanians, (P) 240:s1/2;
   279:s1/3

Penque, Romeo, (P) 295:s2/8
Penterman, Carol, (P) 267:s2/2
Pepper, Art, (P) 216:s1/4
Perdido, 284:s2/1
Perez, Kike, (P) 244:s1/5
Perkins, Bill, (P) 216:s2/1
Perkins, Ike, (P) 259:s2/1
Perrin, Curley, (P) 226:s2/10
Perry, Douglas, (P) 288/89
Perry, Richard, (P) 221:s1/2,
   s2/7; 267:s1/2-3, s2/3
Perry, W., (C) 225:s1/6
Perry County Music Makers, (P)
   236:s1/8
Perryman, Lloyd, (P) 287:s2/6
Perryman, Pat, (P) 287:s1/1
Persichetti, Vincent, (C)
   211:s1/1
Peter, Johann Friedrich (John
   Frederik), (C) 230:s1/4
Peters, William C., (C) 251:s1/4,
   s2/6-7
Petersen, Gary, (P) 234:s1/1, s2/1
Peterson, Pete, (P) 250:s1/6-7
Petros, Evelyn, (P) 230:s2/3
Pettiford, Oscar, (P) 242:s1/2;
   284:s1/6
Pettis, Jack, (C) 250:s2/2;
   274:s2/5
Petty, D'Artagnan, (P) 288/89
Petty, Norman, (C) 249:s2/2
Pfeffner, Ralph, (P) 216:s1/1
Phantom of the Opera, The,
   227:s2/7
Philanthropy, 230:s2/3
Phile, Philip, (C) 299:s2/9
Philips, Flip, (P) 216:s1/1;
   271:s1/1
Phillips, Burr, (P) 234:s1/1
Phillips, Harvey, (P) 216:s2/4
Phillips, Sam, (C) 207:s1/9
Phipps, Ernest, (P) 245:s2/8
Phonemena, 209:s1/1-2
Piaf, Edith, (L) 298:s2/6
Piano Concerto No. 1 (Kirchner,
   C) 286:s2
Piano Piece (*Paris 1924*) (Cowell,
   C) 203:s1/3

Piano Sonata (Copland, C) 277:s1

Piano Variations (Copland, C) 277:s2/1

Piantadosi, Al, (C) 222:s1/2

Piatigorsky, Gregor, (P) 281:s2/1

Piazza Navona, 216:s2/4

Piccolo Rag, 235:s1/4

Pickard, Obed, (P) 226:s1/2

Pickin' the Cabbage, 217:s1/6

Pie de este Santo Altar, Al, 292:s1/1

Pied Pipers, (P) 272:s2/3

Piedrera, La, 264:s1/8

Pierce, Jacqueline, (P) 220:s1/5

Pierce, Webb, (C) 225:s2/4

Pieśń Zbójników (Song of the Bandits), 283:s1/5

Pillars, Charles, (P) 256:s2/8-9

Pillars, Hayes, (P) 256:s2/7-9

Pillars, Louis, (P) 256:s2/9

Pinero, Frank, (P) 250:s2/1

Pinetop's Boogie Woogie, 259:s1/4

Piney Brown Blues, 295:s1/3

Pinkard, Maceo,
(C) 279:s1/6; 293:s2/6
(L) 279:s1/6

Pino, Andy, (P) 284:s1/5

Pins and Needles: *Sunday in the Park*, 272:s2/4

Piperakis, Harilaos, (P) 264:s2/7

Pippa's Song, 229:s2/4

Piron, Armand J., (C) 250:s1/4
(P) 269:s2/3

Piston, Walter Hamor, Jr., (C) 284:s1

Pitchford, Lonnie, (P) 291:s2/1

Pitot, Genevieve, (P) 247:s2/9

Pitter Panther Patter, 274:s2/8

Pitts, Kenneth, (P) 226:s2/10

Pitts, Lewis, (P) 256:s2/9

Pixley, Frank, (L) 221:s1/6

Plant, Judith, (P) 293:s1/1, 6-7, 9

Plater, Bobby, (P) 284:s1/7

Plaza Hotel Orchestra, (P) 256:s2/4-5

Pleasure Dome of Kubla Khan, The, 273:s2/1

Pleneros de la 110th Street, (P) 244:s1/1-2

Pletcher, Stew, (P) 250:s1/7

Po' Boy Blues, 252:s1/2

Poco Loco, Un, 271:s2/2

Polca, La, 292:s2/11

Pollack, Lew,
(C) 227:s2/5; 233:s1/7
(L) 227:s2/5

Polo, Danny, (P) 284:s1/8

Polonaise (*Twelve Virtuoso Studies*), 206:s2/12

Pompelli, Rudy, (P) 249:s1/5

Poole, Charlie, (P) 236:s2/2

Poor Drunkard's Dream, The, 245:s2/7

Poor Pilgrim of Sorrow, 294:s1/3

Pope, Alexander, (L) 231:s2/4

Pope, J. D., (P) 236:s1/4

Pope's Arkansas Mountaineers, (P) 236:s1/4

Poplin, China, (P) 235:s2/6

Poprawyny (Second-Day Wedding Feast), 283:s2/7

Porrello, Joseph, (P) 232:s1/2-3, 5

Porter, Cole, (C) *You Do Something to Me*, 227:s1/2; *Only Another Boy and Girl*, 240:s2/5; *What Is This Thing Called Love*, 256:s1/8, 271:s2/5; *Anything Goes*, 272:s2/2; *What Is This Thing Called Love*, 274:s1/3-4; *Begin the Beguine*, 298:s2/3
(L) 240:s2/5
(P) 272:s2/2

Porter, Steve, (P) 222:s1/3

Postlude, 280:s2/4

Poston, Joe, (P) 274:s1/6

Post-Partitions, 209:s2/2

Potter, Martha, (P) 237:s2/2

Potter, Tommy, (P) 271:s1/7

Poulenc, Francis, (P) 229:s1/2-6

Powell, Bud, (C) 271:s2/2
  (P) 271:s1/8; 272:s2/2;
  284:s2/6
Powell, Dick, (P) 270:s1/8
Powell, Ed, (P) 295:s2/8
Powell, Jimmy, (P) 284:s1/6
Powell, John, (C) 228:s2/2
Powell, Lester, (P) 291:s2/8
Powell, Mel, (C) 222:s2/9
Powell, Richie, (P) 271:s2/5
Powell, Rudy, (P) 217:s1/1
Pozo, Chino, (P) 271:s2/3
Prairie Ramblers, (P) 287:s2/1
Praise the Lord and Pass the
  Ammunition, 222:s2/8
Pratcher, Bob, (P) 252:s1/8, 10
Pratcher, Miles, (P) 252:s1/5, 8,
  10, s2/7
Prater, Matthew, (P) 290:s1/3
Pratt, Adam, (P) 246:s2/4
Pratt, Charles E., (C) 220:s2/3
Prayers of Steel, 285:s2/3
Prelude II (Huss, C) 206:s1/2
President's March, The,
  (Herbert, C) 266:s1/8
President's March, The, (Phile
  and Hopkinson, C) 299:s2/9
Presley, Elvis, (P) 207:s1/9
Presson, Nonnie Smith, (C,P)
  236:s1/8
Pretty Girl, A., (Wang) 221:s2/2
Pretty Girl Is Like a Melody, A
  (*Ziegfeld Follies of 1919*),
  238:s1/3
Prévert, Jacques, (L) 298:s2/8
Price, Jesse, (P) 284:s1/1-2
Price, Lloyd, (C,P) 249:s1/7
Price, Ray, (P) 207:s1/3
Price, Sammy, (P) 224:s1/6
Pride of America, The, 266:s2/1
Pride of Erin Orchestra, (P)
  264:s1/5
Priester, Julius (or Julian), (P)
  275:s2/3-4; 295:s2/7
Prima, Louis, (P) 250:s2/1
Prima Donna Waltz, 293:s1/1
Prince, Faith, (P) 267:s2/3

Prince of Pilsen, The: The
  Heidelberg Stein Song,
  221:s1/6
Procope, Russell, (P) 250:s1/4,
  s2/9
Proctor, Willis, (P) 278:s1/1-7,
  s2/1-3, 5, 7-9
Promise of Living, The (*The
  Tender Land*), 241:s2/3
Propps, Louis, (P) 226:s2/7
Providence, 255:s1/7
Pryor, Arthur,
  (C) 266:s2/6; 282:s1/4, 7
  (P) 282:s1/4, 7
Pryor, Herbert, *see* Vallee, Rudy
Pryor Band, The, (P) 282:s2
Puckett, (P) 217:s2/5-6
Puckett, Riley, (P) 226:s1/12;
  236:s2/1
Pueblo Indians, San Juan, *see*
  San Juan Pueblo Indians
Puerta Esta Quebrada, La,
  291:s2/4
Puertorriqueño, El, 244:s2/3
Puisque tout passe (*Mélodies
  Passagères*), 229:s1/2
Purdy, James, (L) 243:s2/6
Purtill, Maurice, (P) 250:s1/7
Purvis, William, (P) 276:s1/1, 3,
  s2/2, 4
Putman, Janet, (P) 295:s2/8
Put My Little Shoes Away,
  220:s2/3
Putnam, Ashley, (P) 288/89
Puttin' On the Ritz, 238:s2/2
Pyle, Thomas, (P) 276:s1/1

Quartet Euphometric, 218:s2/2
Quartet Romantic, 285:s1/1
Queenie's Song (*The Second
  Hurricane*), 241:s2/1
Quillian, Ben, (P) 290:s2/2
Quillian, James, (P) 247:s2/2
Quillian, Rufus, (P) 290:s2/2
Qu'il m'irait bien, 300:s1/8
Quinn, Maud, (P) 205:s1/7
Quintero, Nieves, (P) 244:s2/1-4

Quintetto (Holyoke ?) 299:s1/1
Quivar, Florence, (P) 296

Rabbit Dance, 246:s1/4
Rabbit in the Pea Patch, 291:s2/7
Rabbit Song, 297:s1/3
Rabbitt, 291:s2/6
Race for Space, 275:s1/3
Rachell, "Yank" (James), (C,P) 290:s1/1
Raeburn, Andrew, (P) 230:s1/8, s2/3
Raelets, (P) 249:s2/7
Ragas, H., (C) 250:s1/5; 269:s1/4
Raggy Levy, 278:s2/2
Raglin, Junior, (P) 216:s2/2
Rahmings, Nat, (P) 278:s1/8, s2/4, 6, 10
Railroad Boomer, 287:s2/3
Raines, Ronald, (P) 288/89
Rainger, Ralph, (C) 215:s1/7; 250:s2/3
Rainwater, Floyd, (P) 287:s1/6
Rainwater, Lonnie, (P) 287:s1/6
Raise a Ruckus Tonight, 225:s2/6
Raksin, David, (C) 216:s2/5
Ralph, Cindy Lynn, (P) 299:s1/2, s2/4
Ramona, (P) 240:s1/7
Ramos, Efraim, (P) 244:s1/1
Ramos, Manny, (P) 244:s1/5
Ramsey, Alberta, (P) 278:s1/8, s2/4, 6, 10
Ramsey, Ben, (P) 278:s1/2, 4-7, s2/3, 5, 7-8
Ramsey, Emma, (P) 278:s1/8, s2/4, 6, 10
Rand, Odell, (P) 290:s2/5
Randall, Tony, (P) 202:s2/1
Randy Lynn Rag, 235:s2/8
Raney, Tom, (P) 237:s1/1
Rapee, Erno, (C,L) 227:s2/5
Ratcliff, Henry, (P) 252:s1/1
Rat Riddles, 285:s2/2
Rauch, Billy, (P) 217:s1/2

Ravens, The, (P) 261:s1/9
Raver, Leonard, (P) 230:s1/8
Rayam, Curtis, (P) 220:s1/6
Raye, Don, (L) 295:s1/6
Raye, Martha, (P) 248:s2/4
Raymond, Don, (P) 249:s1/5
Razaf, Andy, (L) 256:s1/7; 272:s1/7; 279:s2/7; 284:s2/2; 298:s2/1
Read, Daniel, (C) 205:s1/1, s2/1; 255:s1/7
Read 'Em John, 278:s1/7
Red and Miff's Stompers, (P) 274:s2/7
Redding, Edward, (C) 295:s2/8
Redding, Joseph Deighn, (L) 241:s1/1-2
Red-Haired Lass, The, 264:s1/6
Redman, Don, (P) 215:s1/6; 256:s1/4; 269:s2/8
Reed, Al, (P) 249:s1/5
Rees, H. S., (C) 205:s1/3
Reese, Marion, (P) 226:s1/1
Reet Petite, 249:s2/4
Reeves, Gerald, (P), 274:s1/2
Reeves, Jim, (C,P), 207:s2/1
Reflections, 209:s1/4
Reg'lar, Reg'lar, Rollin' Under, 278:s2/6
Reid, John, (C) 276:s1/1
Reid, Lyman, (P) 216:s1/1
Reilly and the 400: Maggie Murphy's Home, 265:s1/2
Reinagle, Alexander, (C) 293:s1/3
Reisman, Leo, (P) 215:s2/3; 238:s2/3-4; 240:s1/4; 248:s1/1; 256:s1/8
Relaxin' at Camarillo, 271:s1/6
Relly, James, (L) 255:s2/4
Reminiscences of Sabala, 283:s1/3
Reno, Don, (P) 225:s1/4
Repasz Band March, 282:s2/10
Rescue From Moose River Gold Mine, The, 287:s2/2
Reuben and Cynthia (*Trip to Chinatown*), 221:s2/3
Reuss, Alan, (P) 250:s2/3

Réveillon, Le (Four Impressions), 273:s1/8
Revel, Harry, (C) 240:s1/3
Revival March, 266:s2/3
Reyes, Marcial, (P) 244:s1/1-2
Reynolds, Roger, (C,P) 237:s1/1
Rhapsody in Black: Until the Real Thing Comes Along, 248:s2/2
Rhapsodie Nègre, 228:s2/2
Rhyne, Palmer, (P) 245:s2/2
Rhythm Aces, (P) 256:s1/5-6
Rhythm Boys, The, (P) 279:s2/4
Rhythm Kings, (P) 259:s2/1
Ribbon Dance, 246:s2/2
Riccardi, Andy, (P) 284:s1/5
Ricci, Paul, (P) 295:s1/5-6
Rice, Ben, (P) 223:s1/2
Rice, Edward E., (C) 221:s1/3
Rich, Don, (C) 207:s2/5
Richard Cory, 243:s1/5
Richards, Cynthia, (P) 299:s1/2
Richards, Emil, (P) 214:s1/9
Richards, Walter, Sr., (P) 246:s2/1; 297:s2/4-6
Richardson, Diane, (P) 273:s1/5-8
Richardson, "Snake," (P) 217:s2/7-8
Richman, Al, (P) 216:s2/4
Richman, Harry, (P) 215:s2/2; 238:s2/2
Richman, James, (P) 276:s1/3, s2/2, 4
Richmond, 255:s2/4
Richmond, Dannie, (P) 204; 242:s2/4
Riddle, Almeda, (P) 245:s1/1; 291:s1/1, 3; 294:s2/5
Riddle, Jimmie, (P) 223:s1/1
Riddle Me This, 240:s1/4
Ridgecrest (N. C.) Baptist Conference Center, (P) 224:s2/1-2
Riegger, Wallingford, (C) 285:s1/2
Riley, Mike, (C,P) 248:s2/1

Rilke, Rainer Maria, (L) 229:s1/2-6
Rille Cajun, Le, 226:s2/6
Ring, Blanche, (P) 233:s1/6
Ringing the Pig, 223:s1/1
Rip van Winkle Was a Lucky Man, 265:s2/6
Risselty Rosselty, 223:s1/3
Ritchie, Grandpa Isom, (P) 223:s2/6
Rivera, Hector, (C,P) 244:s1/5
Rivera, Ismael, (P) 244:s1/1-2
Rivers, Earl, (P) 221; 267
Roach, Max, (P) 271:s1/4-5, 7-8, s2/2; 275:s2/3-4; 295:s2/7
Roark, Shortbuckle, (P) 236:s1/1
Robbins, Harold, (P) 217:s2/4
Robbins, Marty, (C,P) 207:s2/2
Robbins Nest, 295:s1/7
Roberta Martin Singers, (P) 224:s1/5
Roberts, George, (P) 216:s2/1
Roberts, James, (P) 245:s2/4
Roberts, Mrs. King, (P) 205:s1/6
Robertson, Dick, (P) 222:s2/4, 6
Robeson, Paul, (P) 247:s2/8, 10
Robin, Leo, (L) 222:s2/7; 250:s2/3
Robin, Sid, (L) 248:s2/5; 261:s1/1
Robin Hood: Song of Brown October Ale, 221:s2/5
Robin Hood and the Peddlar, 291:s1/1
Robinson, Bill ("Bojangles"), (P) 215:s1/6
Robinson, Edward Arlington, (L) 243:s1/5-7
Robinson, Eli, (C) 217:s1/8
Robinson, Fred, (P) 256:s1/2
Robinson, Ikey, (P) 256:s1/5-6
Robinson, J. Russell, (C) 217:s2/4; 250:s2/6
Robinson, James, (P) 269:s2/1-2; 284:s1/7
Robinson, Janice, (P) 204:s1/2, s2/2

Robinson, Jimmy, (P) 261:s2/1
Robinson, Leighton, (P)
    223:s2/1
Robinson, Les, (P) 250:s2/8
Robinson, Robert, (L) 300:s1/2
Robison, Carson J., (C) 287:s2/3
Rock-a-Bye Baby (*Music Box
    Revue*), 238:s1/4
Rockets, (P) 284:s1/1-2
Rock of Ages, 220:s1/7
Rocky Mountain Blues, 250:s1/2
Roddy, Reuben, (P) 256:s2/2-3
Rodeheaver, Homer Alvan, (P)
    224:s2/5-6
Rodgers, Gene, (P) 274:s1/8
Rodgers, Jimmie (James Charles),
    (C) 207:s1/2; 287:s1/2, 4
    (L) 287:s1/4
    (P) 207:s1/2; 261:s2/7;
    287:s1/2, 4
Rodgers, Richard,
    (C) *My Romance*, 204:s2/1;
    227:s2/3; *We'll Be the Same*,
    240:s1/1; *Boys and Girls Like
    You and Me*, 240:s2/4; *Blue
    Moon*, 248:s1/5; *You Are
    Never Away*, 272:s2/5; *Thou
    Swell*, 295:s2/3; *Happy Talk*,
    298:s2/2; *The Most Beautiful
    Girl in the World*, 298:s2/7
    (P) 272:s2/5
Rodney, Red, (P) 271:s2/1;
    284:s1/8
Rodowicz, Frank, (P) 284:s1/5
Rodriguez, Arseño, (P) 291:s1/2
Rodriguez, Quinqu, (P) 291:s1/2
Roefs, Benedict, (C) 202:s1/4
Roethke, Theodore, (L)
    229:s2/9-11
Rogers, Ginger, (P) 238:s2/7
Rogers, Grant, (P) 239:s2/10
Rogers, Shorty, (P) 216:s1/1, 4;
    271:s2/1
Rogers, Walter B., (P)
    282:s1/3, 6
Roland, Walter, (P) 290:s2/4
Rolled and Tumbled, 252:s2/6
Roll 'Em, Pete, 261:s1/2

Rollini, Adrian, (P) 250:s2/2
Rollins, Sonny, (P) 242:s2/2;
    271:s2/5
Rollo, Mario, (P) 284:s1/8
Roly, *see* Rollini, Adrian
Romance (Paine, C) 206:s1/4
Romance (Gottschalk, C)
    257:s2/3
Rome, Harold, (C,P) 272:s2/4
Ronald McDonald, 291:s2/2
Rondelli, Bruno, (P) 284:s1/4
Root, George Frederick, (C) *The
    Haymakers*, 234; *Where Home
    Is*, 251:s1/1; *The Old Canoe*,
    251:s1/6; *The Pacific Railroad*,
    267:s1/1; *Root Cellar*,
    229:s2/10
Rorem, Ned, (C,P) 229:s2
Rosalie: In the Still of the Night,
    270:s1/4
Rosamunde, 300:s1/7
Rose, Billy, (L) 215:s1/5;
    227:s2/4
Rose, Ed, (L) 233:s1/8
Rose, Erma, (P) 234
Rose, Fred, (C,L) 279:s1/7
Rose, Stewart, (P) 237:s2/1;
    285:s1/2
Rose, The (*The Children*),
    243:s1/1
Rose, The (*Eleven Intrusions*),
    214:s1/1
Rose, Vincent, (C) 274:s1/5;
    279:s1/1
Roseman, Ronald, (P)
    276:s1/1, 3, s2/2, 4
Rosenfeld, Sidney, (L) 221:s2/1
Rosenstock, Milton, (P)
    238:s1/1; 240:s2/7
Rose of the Night, The (*Three
    Poems of Fiona MacLeod*),
    273:s2/4
Rosolino, Frank, (P) 216:s2/1
Ross, James, (P) 284:s1/1-2
Ross, Margaret, (P) 216:s2/3
Round to Maryanne's, 291:s1/2
Roundtree, L., (P) 287:s2/6
Rousseau, Charles, (P) 256:s2/6

Roxie Anne, 291:s2/7

Royal, Ernie, (P) 265:s1/1; 271:s2/1

Royal Canadians, (P) 248:s2/3; 279:s1/2

Royal Roost, 284:s2/6

Roybal, Melitón, (P) 292:s2

Royster, Joseph F., (C,L) 249:s2/9

Rubenstein, Bill, (P) 295:s2/5

Rubinowitch, Sam, (P) 216:s1/1

Ruby, Herman, (L) 250:s1/1; 298:s1/1

Ruddick, M., (C) 225:s1/8

Rudziński, Bruno, (P) 283:s1/4

Ruff Scufflin, 256:s2/6

Rugolo, Pete, (C) 216:s1/4

Run, Banjo, 226:s1/6

Rundless, Reverend, (P) 224:s1/3

Running Sun, The, 243:s2/6

Rush, Joe, (P) 246:s2/4

Rushing, James, (C) 295:s1/2 (P) 256:s2/2-3; 295:s1/2

Russ, R. Sebastian, (P) 232:s2/1-2

Russell, Curly, (P) 271:s1/3-4, 8, s2/2-3

Russell, George, (C) 216:s2/2 (P) 216:s2/2; 242:s2/3

Russell, Henry, (C) 251:s2/3

Russell, Luis, (P) 272:s1/3; 274:s2/1

Russell, M., (P) 287:s2/6

Russell, "Pee Wee" (Ellsworth), (P) 250:s2/1

Russell, Robert, (P) 217:s2/4

Russo, Bill, (C) 216:s1/4, s2/1

Rutherford, Rudy, (P) 284:s1/6

Ryan, Jack, (P) 250:s2/1

Rymer's Favorite, 226:s2/5

S., J. N., (arr.) 220:s2/2

Sacred Harp Singers, (P) 245:s2/9

Sadovnik, Konstantin, (P) 264:s1/2

Safacón de la 102 St., El, 244:s1/1

Saint, The, 284:s1/3

St. Clair, Cy, (P) 256:s1/3-4

St. Louis Symphony Chorus, (P) 262/63

St. Louis Symphony Orchestra, (P) 262/63

Sally Died, 291:s2/2

Salome, 291:s2/2

Sam, Archie, (P) 246:s1/5, s2/3

Sam, Eli, (P) 246:s1/5, s2/3

Samel, Morey, (P) 250:s1/6

Sampson, Edgar, (P) 256:s1/3

Sanchez, Armando, (C,P) 244:s2/6

Sandburg, Carl, (L) 285:s2/2-4

San Juan Pueblo Indian, (C,P) 246:s1/1

Sankey, Ira D., (C) 224:s2/3

Santa Fe Opera, The, (P) 288/89

Sant'Ambrogio, John, (P) 262/63:s1/3

Santiago, Adalberto, (P) 244:s1/5

Santisi, Ray, (P) 275:s1/6

Sarfaty, Regina, (P) 229:s2/2

Sargent, Charles, (P) 287:s1/7

Sargon, Merja, (P) 237:s2/2

Sarkisian, Reuben, (C,P) 264:s2/5

Sarkisian, Vart, (P) 264:s2/5

Satepauhoodle, E. R., (P) 246:s2/4

Saukevičius, A., (P) 264:s2/8

Saunders, Gertrude, (P) 260:s1/5, s2/1

Savage, Henry, (P) 217:s2/7-8

Saved by Grace, 244:s2/8

Savitt, Jan, (C) 295:s1/6

Sawyer, Charles Carroll, (L) 202:s2/3

Sayf Lahziq (Your Sword Has Pierced Me), 264:s2/6

Scammel, A. R., (C) 207:s1/4

Scandals: 1922—I'll Build a Stairway to Paradise, 215:s1/4; *1931—Life Is Just a Bowl of Cherries*, 270:s1/3; *1939—Are You Havin' Any Fun*, 215:s2/6

Scanlan, William, (C) 267:s2/1

Schackne, Dave, (P) 216:s1/4

Schaeffer, William, (P) 221:s2/3

Scharre, Kate, (P) 267:s1/3

Schildkraut, Dave, (P) 216:s2/6

Schmidt, Fred, (P) 284:s1/8

Schneider, Alexander, (P) 281:s1/2

Schneider, Edwin, (P) 247:s1/6

Schoebel, Elmer, (C) 250:s2/2; 274:s2/5

Scholtens, Eugene, (P) 299:s1/1, s2/2-3, 5, 8-9

Schonberger, John, (C) 279:s1/1

Schrader, Virginia Dell, (P) 205:s2/4

Schuller, Gunther, (C) 212:s2; 216:s2/3 (P) 216:s2/4; 262/63

Schulte, Rolf, (P) 285:s1/1

Schuman, William, (C) 253:s1

Schuster, Ira, (L) 233:s2/2

Schutt, Arthur, (P) 274:s2/7; 279:s2/2

Schwartz, Arthur, (C) 215:s2/3-4

Schwartz, Jean, (C) *Hello, Central! Give Me No Man's Land*, 222:s1/5; *Rip Van Winkle Was a Lucky Man*, 265:s2/6; *Chinatown, My Chinatown*, 293:s2/3

Schwarz, Gerard, (P) 293:s2/1-3

Scott, Bud, (P) 274:s1/2, 6

Scott, Frederick W., Jr., (P) 297:s2/3

Scott, Howard, (P) 284:s1/6

Scott, Walker, (P) 269:s1/1

Scott, Walter, (L) 231:s1, s2/1-2

Screechowl, Cedo, (P) 246:s1/5, s2/3

Scruggs, Beatrice, (P) 291:s1/3

Scruggs, Earl, (P) 225:s1/2; 235:s2/8

Scruggs, Faye, *see* Adams, Faye

Scruggs, Irene, (P) 291:s1/3

Scruggs, Thelma, (P) 291:s1/3

Seaboy, Joseph, (P) 246:s1/3

Seagle, Oscar, (P) 224:s2/7

Seago, Leon, (P) 287:s2/4

Seagraves, Robert, (L) 205:s2/4

Seagull Song, 297:s1/10

Searcy, (C) 205:s1/11

Sears, Al, (P) 217:s2/7-8

Second-Day Wedding Feast, 283:s2/7

Second-Hand Rose (*Ziegfeld Follies of 1921*), 215:s1/2

Second Hurricane, The: *Jeff's Song*; *Queenie's Song*; *Sextet*; *Two Willow Hill*. 241:s2/1

Sedliacky Zabavny Czardăs (The Farmer's Diversion Czardăs), 264:s1/1

Sedric, "Honey Bear," (P) 250:s2/3

See Aunt Dinah, 278:s2/4

Seeger, Pete, (P) 270:s2/7

Seeger, Ruth Crawford, (C) 285:s2/2-4

See Him, 230:s1/7

Seeley, Blossom, (P) 233:s2/3; 279:s2/3

See That My Gave Is Kept Clean, 294:s2/4

See You Later, Alligator, 249:s1/5

Seguirre, Charles, (P) 269:s2/3

Seitz, Roland F., (C) 266:s2/4

Selic, Leonard, (P) 216:s1/4

Selvin, Ben, (P) 238:s2/5

Seneca Indians, (C,P) 246:s1/2

Senegal Field Song, 252:s1/1

Sensational Mood, 217:s2/3

Septeto Son de la Loma, (P) 244:s2/5-6

Serdab, 201:s1/2

Serenade, The, 266:s2/8

Serenaders, (P) 217:s2/3

Sesquicentennial March, 266:s2/9

Sessions, Roger, (C) 243:s2/3; 296

Setti, Giulio, (P) 241:s1/3-4

Setzer, Philip, (P) 212; 218

Seven Foot Dilly, (P) 226:s2/9

Seven Lively Arts: *Only Another Boy and Girl*, 240:s2/5

Seven Pious Pieces: *Eternitie*; *His Ejaculation to God*; *Mercy and Love*; *No coming to God without Christ*; *The Soule*; *Teares*; *To Death*; *To his ever-loving God*; *Welcome what comes*, 210:s2/3

Sex Against Sex (*Passing Show*), 221:s2/1

Sextet (*The Second Hurricane*), 241:s2/1

Sexteto Criollo Puertorriqueño, (P) 244:s1/1-4

Shake, Rattle and Roll, 249:s1/1

Shake a Hand, 249:s1/4

Shaking the Blues Away (*Ziegfeld Follies of 1927*), 238:s1/5

Shall We Know Each Other There, 220:s1/5

Shamblin, Eldon, (P) 287:s2/9

Shand, Terry, (L) 274:s2/1

Shank, Bud, (P) 216:s1/4

Shannon, Four, The, (P) 222:s1/6

Shapey, Ralph, (C) 254:s2/1

Shapiro, A., (P) 287:s2/6

Shapiro, Artie, (P) 250:s2/5

Shapiro, Eudice, (P) 281:s2/2

Shapiro, Ted, (P) 279:s2/1

Sharp, William, (L) 273:s2/2-4

Shaughnessy, Ed, (P) 295:s2/6

Shaughnessy, Florence, (P) 246:s2/1; 297:s1/12

Shavers, Charles, (C) 248:s2/5 (P) 217:s1/8; 250:s2/9; 274:s1/4

Shaw, Elliot, (P) 222:s1/6

Shaw, Oliver, (C) 231:s2/3; 299:s2/5-6

Shaw, Rosalie, (P) 239:s2/9

Shaw 'Nuff, 271:s1/3

Shayne, J. H. ("Freddie"), (C) 259:s1/2, 8

Shean, Al, (C,P) 215:s1/3

Sheep, Sheep, Don't You Know the Road, 278:s1/3

Sheffield, Leslie, (P) 256:s2/9

Shelor Family, (P) 236:s1/3

Shelton, Allen, (P) 225:s1/6, s2/3

Shenandoah Valley Boys, (P) 225:s1/6

Shepherd, Arthur, (C) 218:s2/2-4

Shepherd Playing the Flute, 283:s2/8

Sheppard, Leo, (P) 284:s1/7

Sherburne, 205:s1/1

Sherman, Al, (C) 233:s2/6

Sherman, James, (P) 250:s1/9

Sherry, Fred, (P) 237:s1/2

Sherwood, Lew, (P) 240:s2/1; 256:s1/8

She's Cryin' for Me, 269:s2/4

Shields, Calvin "Eagle Eye," (P) 261:s2/1

Shields, L., (L) 250:s2/5; 269:s1/4

Shifrin, Seymour, (C) 219:s2

Shilkret, Nathaniel, (C) 227:s2/1 (P) 238:s2/6

Shine on, Harvest Moon (*Ziegfeld Follies of 1931*), 215:s2/1

Ship of Rio, The (*Peacock Pie*), 300:s2/1

Shirelles, The, (C,P) 249:s2/5

Shoe Shine Boy, 248:s1/7

Show Boat: *Nobody Else But Me*, 240:s2/6

Shuffle Along, 260

Shuken, P., (P) 287:s2/6

Shulman, Daniel, (P) 254:s1/2

Shulman, Joe, (P) 284:s1/8

Shutta, Ethel, (P) 240:s1/3

Sichelski, Jan, (P) 283:s1/6, 9

Sidell, Al, (P) 250:s2/2

Siegstein, Sandy, (P) 284:s1/8

Signorelli, Frank, (P) 274:s2/3

Silhouettes, The, (C,P) 249:s2/1

Silleshaw, John, (P) 226:s2/9

Silver, A., (C) 250:s1/8

Silver, Horace, (C,P) 242:s1/3; 271:s2/6

Silver Rain, The, 299:s1/2

Silvers, Louis, (C) 279:s1/2

Silver Spring, 257:s2/6

Silverstein, Joseph, (P) 268

Simeon, Omer, (P) 217:s1/4;
   256:s1/5
Simmon, Bill, (C) 250:s1/2
Simmons, Calvin, (P) 228:s1,
   s2/2
Simmons, John, (P) 271:s2/4;
   284:s2/1; 295:s1/7
Simms, Hector, (P) 246:s2/1;
   297:s1/14
Simon, Maurice, (P) 284:s1/3
Simon, Nahem, (P) 264:s2/6
Simons, Seymour, (L) 248:s1/4
Simpkins, Po, (P) 261:s1/6
Simpson, Cassino, (P) 265:s1/5
Simpson, James, (P) 256:s2/2-3
Sims, Lee, (P) 298:s1/1
Sims, Zoot, (P) 271:s2/1
*Sinbad: Hello, Central! Give Me
   No Man's Land*, 222:s1/5
Sing a Sad Song, 207:s2/7
Singer, Hal, (P) 261:s1/8
Singer, Lou, (C) 250:s2/9
Singer, Sam, (P) 216:s1/4
Singleton, Charles, (C,L)
   261:s2/5
Singleton, Zutty, (P) 256:s1/2
Sinta, Donald, (P) 209:s2/1
Sirone, (P) 201
Sissle, Noble,
   (C) 260:s1, s2/1-4, 6-7
   (P) 260:s1/2-4, s2/3-7
Sisson, Allen, (P) 226:s2/5
Siteiako, 264:s2/7
Six Brown Brothers, (P)
   269:s1/5
*Six Imitations: Ancient Welch
   Air; English Legendary Air;
   German Waltz; Plaintive Irish
   Ditty; Scotch Song; Spanish
   Ballad*, 299:s1/4
Six Men and a Girl, (P) 284:s2/2
Sizzling Syncopators, (P)
   260:s1/2, s2/7
Skelly, Joseph P., (C) 267:s1/3
Skillet Lickers, (P) 235:s2/2;
   236:s2/1
Skrobacs, Lawrence, (P) 202:s1,
   s2/1; 220

Slater, Vernon, (P) 284:s1/3
Slaughter, M. O., (P) 205:s2/1
Slaughter, Marion T., (P) 233:s2/6
Slayden, Anne, (P) 299:s1/1,
   s2/2-3, 5, 9
*Sleepin' Bee, A (House of
   Flowers)*, 272:s2/6
Slippin' Around, 274:s2/7
Sloan, Harry, (P) 261:s1/1
Slovensky, Hudba, (P) 264:s1/1
Small, Paul, (P) 240:s1/3
Smeck, Roy, (P) 245:s1/9
Smiley, Red, (P) 225:s1/4
Smit, Leo, (P) 277:s2/2
Smith, Arthur, (P) 226:s2/8
Smith, Bertha, (P) 224:s1/7
Smith, Bulow, (P) 236:s1/8
Smith, Buster, (P) 256:s2/2-3
Smith, Clara, (P) 290:s1/7
Smith, Clarence ("Pinetop"),
   (C,P) 259:s1/4-5
Smith, Cricket, (P) 269:s1/1
Smith, Don, (P) 216:s2/1
Smith, Emma Pow (Bauder),
   (L) 267:s2/2
Smith, Eugene, (P) 224:s1/5
Smith, Floyd, (P) 284:s2/2
Smith, George, (P) 269:s1/1
Smith, Gipsy, *see* Smith, Rodney
Smith, Hale, (C) 211:s1/2
Smith, Harry B., (L) 221:s2/5;
   272:s1/1
Smith, Hobart, (P) 226:s1/8;
   278:s1/8, s2/4, 6, 10;
   294:s2/2, 4, 7
Smith, Howard, (P) 250:s1/7
Smith, Jabbo (Cladys),
   (C,P) 256:s1/5-6
   (L) 256:s1/6
   (P) 256:s1/7
Smith, Jack, (C,L,P) 279:s1/6
Smith, Jess, (P) 256:s1/8
Smith, Joyce, (P) 205:s1/5
Smith, Leonard, (P) 269:s1/1
Smith, Odell, (P) 236:s2/2
Smith, Preston, (P) 294:s2/2, 7
Smith, Ralph, (P) 287:s2/4
Smith, Rodney, (P) 224:s2/8

Smith, "Stuff" (Hezekiah), (P) 250:s1/9; 256:s2/7-8

Smith, Tab, (P) 217:s1/8

Smith, William H. ("Smitty"), (P) 284:s1/1-2

Smith, William Oscar, (P) 274:s1/8

Smith, William Overton, (C,P) 209:s1/3

Smith, William S., (P) 284:s1/1-2

Smith, Willie May Ford, (P) 224:s1/7

Smith, Willie "The Lion," (P) 274:s1/4; 295:s1/4

Smokey Mountain Boys, (P) 287:s2/3

Snake, 229:s2/9

Snow, Hank, (C) 249:s2/7 (P) 207:s1/4

Soar Away, 205:s1/4

Society Blues, 269:s1/8

Society Orchestra, (P) 269:s1/1-2

Sokoloff, Alan, (P) 265:s2/4-5, 7

Soldier, Rest, 231:s1/2

Soldo, Joe, (P) 284:s1/4

Sollberger, Harvey, (C) 254:s1/1 (P) 254:s1/1-2

Sollberger, Sophie, (P) 254:s2/1

Someone to Watch Over Me (*Oh Kay*), 272:s1/5

Sommer, Teddy, (P) 216:s2/3

Sonata I (Cage, C) 203:s1/4

Sonata V (Cage, C) 203:s1/5

Sonata X (Cage, C) 203:s1/7

Sonata XII (Cage, C) 203:s1/8

Sonata da Camera (Weber, C) 281:s1/2

Sonata for Microtonal Piano (Johnston, C) 203:s2/1-4

Sonata for the Piano Forte with an Accompaniment for a Violin (Taylor, C) 299:s1/6

Sonata in A Minor for Piano and Violin (Beach, C) 268:s1

Sonata in G Minor for Piano and Violin (Foote, C), 268:s2

Sonatas and Interludes (Cage, C): Excerpts, 203:s1/4-8

Sondheim, Stephen, (C,P) 272:s2/7

Song (Copland, C) 243:s2/2

Song from Zakopane, 283:s1/8

Song of an Old Woman, 243:s1/4

Song of Brown October Ale (*Robin Hood*), 221:s2/5

Song of the Bandits, 283:s1/5

Song of the Dagger, 273:s1/9

Song of the Deathless Voice (*Three Indian Songs*), 213:s1/1

Song of the Red Man, The, 267:s1/1

Song of the Shepherd, 283:s1/7

Song on Liberty, 276:s1/2

Song to Stop the Rain, 297:s1/11

Sonnambula Quadrille Number Two, La, 293:s1/9

Sonnier, Lennis, (P) 287:s1/6

Son of the Sheik, The, 227:s1/3

Sons of the Mountaineers, (P) 245:s2/7

Sons of the Pioneers, (P) 287:s2/6

Sosnik, Harry, (P) 270:s1/5

Soule, The (*Seven Pious Pieces*), 210:s2/3

Soul Stirrers, (P) 224:s1/3

Sounds of the Singing School, 251:s2/2

Sour, Robert, (L) 274:s1/8; 275:s1/6

Sour Mash, (L) 267:s2/3

Sousa, John Philip, (C) 266:s1/3, s2/3, 7, 9; 282:s1/1, 3, 6

Sousa Band, The, (P) 282:s1

South, Eddie, (P) 250:s1/3

South American Way (*Streets of Paris*), 215:s2/7

Southern Broadcasters, (P) 236:s1/2

Southern Plains Indians, (C,P) 246:s2/4

Southern Rag, 235:s1/2

Southland Ladies Quartette, (P) 233:s2/5

Spangler, George, (P) 294:s1/4

Spann, Otis, (P) 261:s2/7

Spanish Fandango, 226:s1/5

Sparrow, John, (P) 236:s1/4

Sparrow, Johnny, (P) 284:s1/7

Spaulding, Antonia, (P) 250:s1/3

Spaulding, James, (P) 204:s1/2, s2/2

Specht, Marianne, (P) 267:s2/1, 3

Specht, Paul, (C) 256:s1/1

Spector, Max, (P) 284:s1/5

Speculum Musicae, (P) 285:s2/2-4

Speed, Samuel, (P) 269:s2/6, 8

Speer, G. T., (C) 225:s1/3

Spelling from the Old Blue-Black Speller, 223:s1/2

Spencer, O'Neal, (P) 250:s2/6,9; 295:s1/5-6

Spencer, Tim, (P) 287:s2/6

Spicer, Willie, (P) 222:s2/1

'Spiew Juchasa (Song of the Shepherd), 283:s1/7

Spinney, Bradley, (P) 295:s2/8

Spong, Jon, (P) 273:s1/1-4, 9; 276:s1/2, s2/1

Spooner, Charles, (L) 220:s2/1

Spooney Five, The, (P) 235:s2/4

Spring, 229:s2/5

Spring and Fall, 229:s2/6

Springhill Disaster, 225:s1/8

Squareface, 250:s1/6

Squatter Sovereignty: Paddy Duffy's Cart, 265:s1/4

Squid Jiggin' Ground, 207:s1/4

Stacey, Gladys, (C) 225:s1/2

Stack-o-Barley, 264:s1/5

Staff Necromancer, The (Americana), 219:s1/2

Stafford, George, (P) 256:s1/3-4

Stalin Wasn't Stallin', 222:s2/3

Stambler, Bernard, (L) 300:s2/2

Stamper, I. D., (P) 226:s1/3

Stamps-Baxter School of Music, (P) 223:s2/8

Standin' in the Need of Prayer (Emperor Jones), 241:s1/5

Stanley, Carter, (P) 225:s1/3

Stanley, James, (P) 222:s1/8

Stanley, Ralph, (P) 225:s1/3

Stapp, Olivia, (P) 273:s1/5-8

Star Dust, 272:s1/6

Stark, Bobby, (P) 274:s2/5

Starvation Blues, 256:s2/1

Static Strut, 256:s1/1

Stauffer, Virginia ("Gypsy"), (C) 225:s2/8

Stay in Your Own Back Yard, 265:s1/6

Stebbins, George Coles, (C) 224:s2/8

Steber, Eleanor, (P) 247:s2/2

Steele, Alphonse, (P) 235:s1/7

Steele, John, (P) 238:s1/3

Steele, Pete, (P) 226:s1/5

Steele, Silas, (P) 224:s1/2

Steel Guitar Rag, 235:s2/6

Stein, Gertrude, (L) 229:s2/2; 288/89

"Stella of Washington," *see* Bradley, Nellie H.

Stennet, Samuel, (L) 255:s1/8

Stephens, Haig, (P) 250:s2/6

Stepheson, John, (C) 205:s2/2

Steppin' on the Gas, 269:s2/2

Stept, Sammy, (C) 298:s1/1

Sterkin, D., (P) 287:s2/6

Stevens, Bert, (C) 256:s1/2

Stewart, Dee, (P) 217:s2/1

Stewart, Maeretha, (P) 220:s1/7

Stewart, Rex, (P) 250:s2/7; 256:s1/4

Stewart, Slam, (P) 271:s1/1

Stewart, W., (C) 207:s2/7

Stiles, Danny, (P) 295:s2/6

Stitt, Sonny, (P) 284:s2/6

Stoch, Karol, (P) 283:s1/3, 5-9

Stockard, Ocie, (P) 287:s1/9

Stock Yard Strut, 269:s1/6

Stokes, Richard, (L) 241:s1/6

Stoll, George, (P) 240:s2/4

Stoller, Mike, (C,L) 249:s2/8; 261:s2/4

Stomp Dance, 246:s2/3

Stone, Fred S., (C) 293:s2/2

Stone, Jesse, (C) 249:s1/1; 256:s2/1, 6

Stoneburn, Sid, (P) 250:s2/2

Stone Grinds All, 276:s2/3

Stoneham, Ernest V. ("Pop"), (P) 236:s1/7

Stoneham, Hattie, (P) 236:s1/7

Stoner, Philip, (L) 221:s2/4

Stopka, Craig, (P) 276:s1/3, s2/1, 3

Stop Time, 271:s2/6

Storm, Gail Stoddard, (P) 239:s1/1, 4

Stormy Weather (Cotton Club Parade), 248:s1/1

Stowe, Sandra, (P) 288/89

Straighten Up and Fly Right, 261:s1/4

Straw Hat Revue, The: Anatole of Paris, 215:s2/5

Strayhorn, William (Billy), (C) 250:s2/7; 274:s2/2 (P) 250:s2/7

Street, The (Eleven Intrusions), 214:s1/8

Streets of Paris: South American Way, 215:s2/7

Strength and Sanity, 275:s2/4

Strike Me Pink: Let's Call It a Day, 240:s1/6

Strike Up the Band, 227:s1/1

String Quartet No. 2 (Harris, C) 218:s1

String Quartet No. 2 (Schuller, C) 212:s2

String Quartet No. 4 (Imbrie, C) 212:s1

Strip Polka, 272:s2/3

Strong, Eugene ("Pop"), (P) 224:s1/1

Strong, Jimmy, (P) 256:s1/2

Strong, Joseph, (C) 255:s2/2

Strong, Luther, (P) 226:s2/1

Stuart, Herbert, *see* Wiederhold, Albert

Stubborn Girl, 283:s1/2

Studies for Player Piano (Nancarrow, C) 203:s2/5-7

Sturgis, Ted, (P) 271:s1/2

Styne, Jule, (C) 240:s2/7; 279:s2/2 (L) 279:s2/2

Sublime Process of Law Enforcement, The (Americana), 219:s1/4

Suessdorf, Karl, (L) 295:s2/1-2

Suitcase Blues, 259:s1/3

Suite for Cello and Harp (Harrison, C) 281:s1/1

Suite for Harp and Wood Quintet (Chou Wen-Chung, C), 237:s2/1

Sullivan, Charles, (P) 204

Sullivan, Niki, (P) 249:s2/2

Summer Sequence, 216:s1/1

Summons, 255:s2/7

Sumpka, Robert, (P) 246:s1/5, s2/3

Sumter Rag, 235:s2/6

Sunday, 279:s2/2

Sunday in the Park (Pins and Needles), 272:s2/4

Sunderland, 255:s2/2

Sun Didn't Shine, The, 261:s1/3

Sunflowers, 254:s1/1

Sunny Mountain Boys, (P) 225:s2/2

Sunrise, 300:s1/5

Sunrise Serenade, A, 298:s2/1

Sunshine, Marion, (C,L) 298:s1/5

Sunshine Orchestra, (P) 269:s1/7-8

Sure on This Shining Night, 243:s2/5

Suskind, Milton, (P) 298:s2/7

Sutterfield, Barry, (P) 223:s1/6

Swan, Timothy, (C) 255:s1/6

Swans, 247:s1/5

Swanstrom, Arthur M., (C) 233:s2/1

Sweatman, Wilbur, (C) 269:s1/5

Sweeley, Charles C., (C) 282:s2/10

Sweeney, Patrick, (P) 264:s1/5

Sweeney-Sparrow, Carol, (P) 221:s1/3, s2/1; 267:s1/3, s2/1

Sweet and Low Blues, 256:s1/5

Sweet By and By, 220:s1/1

Sweet Charity: If My Friends Could See Me Now, 272:s2/8

Sweet Fern, 287:s1/3

Sweet Home, 251:s1/2

Sweet Man, 293:s2/6

Sweet Rose of Heaven, 236:s2/7

Sweet William, 245:s1/3

Sweet Wine, 223:s1/4

Swift, Bob, (P) 271:s2/1

Swift, Kay, (C) 295:s2/4

'S Wonderful, 275:s1/1

Swope, Earl, (P) 271:s2/1

Symphonic Raps, 256:s1/2

Symphonic Songs for Band (Bennett, C) 211:s2/3-5

Symphony No. 4 (Diamond, C) 258:s1

Symphony No. 6 (Piston, C) 286:s1

Symphony No. 7, "Variation-Symphony" (Mennin, C) 258:s2

Syracuse Symphony Orchestra, (P) 208:s1

Szanto, Jan, (P) 214:s1/9

Szanto, Jon, (P) 214:s1/9

Sztajer z Góry Baraniej (Dance from the Sheep Mountains), 283:s2/5

Tabasco, 266:s2/2

Tagore, Rabindranath, (L) 218:s2/2-4; 247:s2/3-5

Tailor's Thimble, The, 264:s1/6

'Tain't What You Do, 248:s2/7

Take Your Girlie to the Movies, 233:s1/8

Takvorian, Tak, (P) 284:s1/8

Tangle Eye, (P) 252:s1/3, s2/1

Tanglewood Festival Chorus, (P) 296

Tanner, Arthur, (P) 245:s2/3

Tanner, Elmo, (P) 248:s1/3

Tanner, Gid, (P) 235:s2/2; 236:s2/1

Tanner, Jeanne, (P) 299:s1/6

Tap-Room Gang, (P) 250:s2/2

Ta-Ra-Ra Boom-De-Ay, 267:s2/4

Tarlton, Jimmie, (P) 223:s2/3; 235:s2/1

Tatar, Stanisław, (P) 283:s1/5-9

Tate, Buddy, (P) 295:s1/2

Tate, Erskine, (P), 256:s1/1

Tate, James, (P) 256:s1/1

Taylor, Billy, Sr., (P) 224:s1/6

Taylor, Cecil, (C) 201; 275:s2/1

Taylor, Clarence, (P) 256:s2/6

Taylor, Deems (Joseph Deems), (C) 241:s1/3-4

Taylor, Jack, (P) 287:s2/1

Taylor, Jasper, (P) 269:s1/6

Taylor, Kevin, (P) 239:s2/11

Taylor, Louis, (P) 217:s1/4

Taylor, Oscar, (P) 246:s2/1

Taylor, Raynor, (C) 232: 299:s1/2, 6

Taylor, Rose, (P) 220:s1/4-5, s2/3-5

Taylor, Stephen, (P) 237:s2/1; 285:s1/2

Taylor-Griggs Louisiana Melody Makers, (P) 236:s2/7

Tchornyj Ostrov Polka (Black Island Polka), 264:s1/3

Tea for Two, 284:s2/3

Teares (Seven Pious Pieces), 210:s2/3

Teasdale, Sara, (L) 247:s1/5

Techner, Joe, (P) 284:s1/4

Teddy Bear's Picnic, The, 282:s2/7

Tejeda, Wilfredo ("Moreno"), (P) 244:s1/3-4

Tell 'Em about Me, 259:s2/4

Tell 'Em I'll Be There, 265:s2/3

Temple, Shirley, (P) 270:s1/6

Tender Land, The: It Promises to Be a Fine Night; The Promise of Living, 241:s2/3

Tened Piedad, Dios Mío, 292:s1/5

Tennessee Cut Ups, (P) 225:s1/4

Tenting on the Old Camp Ground, 202:s1/5

Tercera de Noviembre, La (*El Valse*), 292:s2/9

Terrell, Pha, (P) 248:s2/2

Terry, Arnold, (P) 225:s1/6

Texans, (P) 287:s2/4

Texas Playboys, (P) 287:s2/8

Thanks be to Thee, 230:s2/2

Tharpe, Rosetta, (P) 224:s1/6

That'll Be the Day, 249:s2/2

That Lucky Fellow (*Very Warm For May*), 240:s2/3

That's How I Feel Today, 256:s1/4

That's My Rabbit, My Dog Caught It, 226:s2/4

Thawl, Willie, (P) 287:s2/1

Thayer, W. Eugene, (C) 280:s2/1

There'll Be Some Changes Made, 279:s2/1

There'll Come a Time, 287:s1/10

There's a Squabblin', 256:s2/3

There's a Vacant Chair in Every Home Tonight, 222:s1/6

There's Nothing True but Heav'n, 231:s2/3

There's Poison in Your Heart, 207:s1/5

These, My Ophelia, 243:s2/4

They Led My Lord Away, 224:s1/8

Thigpen, Ben, (P) 284:s2/2

Things to Come, 271:s1/5

Think, 291:s2/3

Third Little Show, see Little Show, Third

This Is the Army: I Left My Heart at the Stage Door Canteen, 222:s2/5

Thomas, Duane, (P) 214:s1/9

Thomas, Edward, (P) 224:s1/4

Thomas, Gordon, (P) 271:s1/5

Thomas, Hersal, (C,P) 259:s1/3

Thomas, Jasper, (P) 249:s1/6

Thomas, Jeff, (P) 217:s2/2

Thomas, Michal, (P) 283:s2/6

Thomas, Walter, (P) 217:s1/6-7

Thomas Logge (*Epitaphs*), 243:s1/2

Thompson, Bobby, (P) 225:s2/9

Thompson, Sir Charles, (C) 295:s1/7

Thompson, Chuck, (P) 284:s2/7

Thompson, Marion, (P) 224:s1/1

Thompson, Randall, (C) 219:s1/1-5; 247:s2/6

Thompson, Will Lamartine, (C) 224:s2/2

Thomson, Earl, (P) 284:s2/2

Thomson, Virgil, (C) 288/89

Thornhill, Claude, (P) 250:s1/6; 284:s1/8

Thornton, Willie Mae ("Big Mama"), (P) 261:s2/4

Thornton Regular Baptist Church Congregation, (P) 294:s1/4

Thou Swell, 295:s2/3

Three Blind Mice, 274:s2/3

369th U. S. Infantry ("Hell Fighters") Band, (P) 260:s2/4-6; 269:s1/3-4

Three Indian Songs: Song of the Deathless Voice; Inketunga's Thunder Song; The Old Man's Love Song, 213:s1/1

Three Men They Went A-Hunting, 239:s2/4

Three Poems of Fiona MacLeod, 273:s2/2-4

Three Sketches (Imbrie), 254:s2/2

Three Songs (Seeger), 285:s2/2-4

Three Tone-Pictures: The Lake at Evening; The Night Winds; The Vale of Dreams, 273:s2/5

Three Variations on a Theme (Harris, C) 218:s1

Thumbs Up: Autumn in New York, 298:s2/5

Thumm, Francis, (P) 214:s1/9

Thump, Francis, (P) 214:s1/9

Thurlow, Janet, (P) 216:s1/5

Thy Dark Eyes to Mine (*Three Poems of Fiona MacLeod*), 273:s2/3

Tibbett, Lawrence, (P) 241:s1/3-6

Tibbs, Leroy, (P) 269:s2/6
Tierney, Louis, (P) 287:s2/8
Tigeroo (*Childhood Fables for Grownups*), 300:s2/7
Til, Sonny, (P) 261:s2/6
Tillie (*Peacock Pie*), 300:s2/1
Till Times Get Better, 256:s1/6
Tio, Lorenzo, Jr., (P) 269:s2/3
'Tis an Earth Defiled (*Merry Mount*), 241:s1/6
Titanic, The, 278:s2/10
Tizol, Juan,
(C) 217:s1/1; 284:s2/1
(P) 250:s2/7
Tobacco Auctioneering, 223:s1/2
Tobias, Charles, (L) 222:s2/4
Toby, 217:s2/1
Today Is Monday, 291:s2/5
Todd, Mazy, (P) 236:s1/9
To Death (*Seven Pious Pieces*), 210:s2/3
To God Be the Glory, 244:s2/4
To his ever-loving God (*Seven Pious Pieces*), 210:s2/3
Tolman, Harvey, (P) 239:s1/10
Tolman, Newton F., (P) 239:s1/5
Tolman, Rose, (P) 239:s1/10
Tolowa Indians, (P) 297:s2/2-6
Tombeau dans un parc (*Mélodies Passagères*), 229:s1/4
To Music, 219:s1/6
Toombs, Rudolph, (C) 261:s2/3
Top Hat: Cheek to Cheek, 238:s2/7
Toplady, Augustus Montague, (L) 220:s1/7
To the Willow Tree, 229:s2/7
To This We've Come (*The Consul*), 241:s2/2
Tottle, Jack, (P) 225:s2/6
Touchstone, James, (P) 245:s2/6
Towne, T. Martin, (C) 267:s2/1
To You, 229:s2/3
Transformation, 216:s2/3
Traumerei (*Twelve Virtuoso Studies*), 206:s2/9

Traveling On, 205:s1/7
Travis, Merle, (C) 287:s2/7
(P) 235:s2/7; 287:s2/7
Tree of Level, 224:s1/4
Treigle, Norman, (P) 241:s2/3
"Trent," (L) 270:s1/4
Trent, Alphonso, (P) 256:s2/7-9
Trevathan, Charles E., (C) 221:s1/8
Tribble, Earl, (P) 217:s2/7-8
Trip to Chinatown, A: The Bowery, 221:s2/3; *Reuben and Cynthia*, 221:s2/7
Triptych for High Voice and String Quartet: The Day Is No More; He It Is; Light, My Light, 218:s2/2-4
Tristano, Lennie, (P) 216:s1/3
Trombone Sneeze, 282:s1/7
Trueheart, John, (P) 217:s1/5
Trujillo, Steven, (P) 246:s1/1
Trumbauer, Frankie, (C,P) 274:s2/3
Trusting, 220:s1/6
Try Me One More Time, 207:s1/6
Tubb, Ernest, (C,P) 207:s1/6
Tucker, E., (P) 264:s1/5
Tucker, Henry, (C) 202:s2/2-3
Tucker, Sophie, (P) 279:s2/1
Tudor, David, (P) 214:s2
Turbyfill, Lena Bare, (P) 245:s1/5
Turetzky, Bertram, (P) 254:s1/3
Turk, Roy, (C,L) 279:s1/6
(L) 250:s2/6; 293:s2/6
Turkey in the Straw, 223:s1/3; 292:s2/6
Turner, Claramae, (P) 241:s2/3
Turner, Floyd, (P) 284:s1/3
Turner, Joe,
(C) 261:s1/2; 295:s1/3
(L) 261:s1/2; 295:s1/4
(P) 249:s1/1; 295:s1/4
Twelve Clouds of Joy, (P) 217:s1/3; 248:s2/2
Twelve Virtuoso Studies: Burlesque; Bluette; Elfin Dance; Impromptu; Improvisation; March Wind;

Moto Perpetuo; *Novellette*; *Polonaise*; *Träumerei*; *Valse Triste*; *Wild Chase*, 206:s2

Twenty-One Years, 225:s1/7

II, V, I, 275:s1/4

Two Brothers, The, 239:s1/3

Two Willow Hill (*The Second Hurricane*), 241:s2/1

Two Worms (*Childhood Fables for Grownups*), 300:s2/4

Tyeska, James, (P) 231:s2/4

Tyner, McCoy, (P) 242:s2/1

Tyson, Willie, (P) 290:s1/6

Tyson-Davies, W., (C,L) 250:s1/9

Tyus, Charles, (C,P) 290:s2/1

Tyus, Effie, (C,P) 290:s2/1

Ucil, 204:s1/2

Udall, Lyn, (C) 265:s1/6

Ukrainska Orchestra Michala Thomasa, (P) 283:s2/6

Ukrainska Orchestra Pawla Humeniuka, (P) 283:s2/1-3

Ukrainska Selska Orchestra, (P) 283:s2/4

Ukrainskyj Trisak (Ukranian Trisak), 283:s2/4

Ulmer, Randall, (P) 299:s1/1, s2/2-3, 5, 9

Uncle Sam's Farm, 267:s1/3

Undecided, 248:s2/5

Underwood, Sugar, (P) 235:s1/3

Unemployment Stomp, 270:s1/7

United States Grand Waltz, 257:s1/3

University of Michigan Chamber Choir, (P) 219

University of Michigan Symphony Orchestra, (P) 219

Until the Real Thing Comes Along (*Rhapsody in Black*), 248:s2/2

Upon Julia's Clothes, 229:s2/7

Upton, Brad, (P) 244:s1/5

Urso, Phil, (P) 284:s1/4

Utterback, Sam, (P) 256:s2/6

Vacca, Robert, (P) 299:s2/2-3, 5, 9

Valdez, Vicentico, (P) 244:s2/5-6

Valendez, Marcelino, (P) 244:s2/5-6

Vale of Dreams, The (*Three Tone-Pictures*), 273:s2/5

Vallee, Rudy (Herbert Pryor), (L) 279:s2/6 (P) 270:s1/3; 279:s2/6

Valse, El (*in A*), 292:s2/10

Valse, La (*in G*), 292:s2/1

Valse de Bon Baurche, La, 264:s2/3

Valse de ma coeur, 293:s2/4

Valse du Bambocheur, 264:s2/3

Valse Gracile, 206:s1/7

Valse Triste (*Twelve Virtuoso Studies*), 206:s2/6

Van, Allen, (P) 256:s2/4-5

Van and Schenck, (P) 238:s1/2

Van Arsdale, Paul, (P) 239:s2/1

Van Arsdale, Phil, (P) 239:s2/1

Van Arsdale, Sterl, (P) 239:s2/1

Vanderlinde, Debra, (P) 231:s2/4; 232:s1/4, s2

Vanderpool, Teodoro, (P) 244:s2/5-6

Vandersloot, Carl D., (C) 282:s2/1

Van Loan, James, (P) 249:s1/3

Vanni, Helen, (P) 288/89

Variations on the Russian National Hymn, 280:s2/1

Varsalona, Bart, (P) 216:s1/4

Vass, Ruby, (P) 294:s2/1

Vaughan, Sarah, (P) 271:s1/2; 295:s2/1

Veal, Jimmy, (P) 224:s1/2

Vehanen, Kosti, (P) 247:s1/9

Velez, Lupe, (P) 238:s1/7

Velvet Shoes, 247:s2/6

Vendome Orchestra, (P) 256:s1/1

Venir, Almas Devotas, 292:s1/3

Venuti, Joe, (P) 250:s1/1

Vermillion, Bill, (P) 246:s1/3

Verrechico, Joe, (P) 284:s1/5

Verticals Ascending, 211:s1/3
Very Warm for May: *That Lucky Fellow*, 240:s2/3
Victor, Frank, (P) 295:s1/5-6
Victoria Galop, 293:s1/7
Vie en Rose, La, 298:s2/6
Village School, The, 245:s2/6
Vincent, Eddie, (P) 269:s1/6
Vincent, Nat, (C) 222:s1/1
Violin Blues, 290:s1/3
Virginia Boys, (P) 225:s2/3
Voice of Nature, The: *She Is Condemned*, 299:s2/4
Von Tilzer, Harry, (C) 221:s1/5

Wagner, Larry, (C) 298:s2/1
Wagner, Richard, (P) 299:s2/2-3, 5-6, 8-9
Wain, Bea, (P) 248:s2/6
Wainikainen, Aili, (P) 264:s1/3
Wainikainen, Lyyli, (P) 264:s1/3
Wainwright, Connie, (P) 284:s1/6
Wake Up, Jake, 251:s2/1
Walder, Herman, (P) 256:s2/6
Waldron, Cliff, (P) 225:s2/7
Waldron, Mal, (P) 295:s2/7-8
Walk, Billy Abbot, 278:s2/5
Walk a Little Faster: *Where Have We Met Before?*, 240:s1/5
Walk Around, 224:s1/3
Walker, Aaron ("T-Bone"), (C,P) 261:s1/7
Walker, Earl, (P) 284:s1/7
Walker, Mack, (P) 250:s1/9
Walker, Wayne P., (C) 225:s2/4
Walker, William, (C) 294:s2/3
Walker, William, (C) 205:s1/9
Wall, Enis, (P) 205:s1/11
Wall, Phil, (C) 256:s1/1
Wallace, Barbara, (P) 230:s1/3, 5-6, s2/3; 231:s1/4, s2/2
Wallace, J. C., (C) 202:s2/6
Wallace, Johnny, (C,L) 261:s2/5
Wallace, Oliver, (C) 222:s2/1
Waller, Charlie, (P) 225:s2/5
Waller, "Fats" (Thomas W.), (C) *That's How I Feel Today*, 256:s1/4; *Willow Tree*,

256:s1/7; *Honeysuckle Rose*, 272:s1/7; *Zonky*, 284:s2/2
(P) 256:s1/4; 272:s1/9
Wallington, George (Giorgio Figlio), (P) 271:s2/1
Walter, Cy, (P) 298:s2/2
Walter, Little, *see* Little Walter
Walter Family, (P) 226:s2/4
Waltzing the Blues, 293:s2/6
Wand, Hart, (C,L) 217:s1/3
Wang: *A Pretty Girl*, 221:s2/2
Ward, Billy, (C) 249:s1/3
Ward, Mr. and Mrs. Crockett, (P) 245:s1/2
Ward, Fields, (P) 245:s1/3
Ward, Robert, (C) 300:s2/2
Ward, Wade, (P) 290:s1/5
Ware, Harvey, (P) 246:s2/4
War Gewessen, 242:s2/3
Waring, Fred, (P) 240:s1/2; 279:s1/3
Warnecke, Louis, (P) 269:s2/3
Warren, 276:s2/3
Warren, Earle, (P) 274:s1/1; 295:s1/2
Warren, George William, (C) 257:s1/1
Warren, Harry, (C) *No Love, No Nothin'*, 222:s2/7; *Coffee in the Morning, Kisses in the Night*, 240:s2/1; *The Boulevard of Broken Dreams*, 270:s1/2; *The Gold Diggers' Song*, 270:s1/8
Washboard Sam, (P) 290:s1/1
Washburn, J. H. ("Country"), (P) 287:s2/6
Washington, 255:s2/1
Washington, Dinah, (P) 295:s1/8
Washington, Fred, (P) 269:s1/7-8
Washington, George, (P) 274:s2/1
Washington, Jack, (P) 217:s2/1; 256:s2/1; 274:s1/1, s2/9; 295:s1/2
Washington, Lightnin', (P) 291:s1/3
Washington, Ned, (L) 248:s1/6; 274:s2/4

Washington's March, 276:s2/4

Watchman!, 300:s1/3

Waterfall, The (*Eleven Intrusions*) 214:s1/3

Waters, Benny, (P) 256:s1/3

Waters, Ethel, (P) 238:s2/5; 279:s1/4

Waters, Muddy (McKinley Morganfield), (C,P) 261:s2/7

Watkins, Doug, (P) 242:s1/3; 271:s2/6

Watson, Leo, (P) 295:s1/5-6

Watts, Archie, (P) 217:s2/3

Watts, Howard ("Cedric Rainwater"), (P) 225:s1/1

Watts, Isaac, (L) 205:s1/3, s2/1, 5, 13; 220:s2/2; 224:s2/1; 255:s1/3, 5, s2/1, 5-6

Watts, Samuel, (P) 267:s1/1, s2/1

Watts, Wilmer, (P) 245:s2/2

Wayne, Chuck, (P) 216:s1/1

We Are Coming, Father Abra'am, 202:s1/3

We Are Coming from the Cotton Fields, 202:s2/6

We Are Happy Now, Dear Mother, 220:s1/3

Weatherford, Teddy, (P) 256:s1/1

Weaver, Clint, (P) 256:s2/6

Webb, Chick, (P) 217:s1/5; 248:s2/5

Webb, Clifton, (P) 238:s2/3-4

Webb, Ray, (P) 274:s1/5

Webb, Willie, (P) 224:s1/5

Webber, Lynne, (P) 209:s1/1-2

Weber, Ben, (C) 281:s1/2

Webster, Ben, (P) 217:s2/1; 284:s2/1

Webster, Freddie, (P) 271:s1/2; 284:s1/6

Webster, Henry DeLafayette, (L) 220:s1/2

Webster, Joseph Philbrick, (C) 220:s1/1-2

Weckler, Ellen, (P) 209:s2/1

We Did It Before and We Can Do It Again, 222:s2/4

Weed, Buddy (Harold Eugene), (P) 298:s2/5

Weems, Ted, (P) 248:s1/3

Weeping, Sad and Lonely, 202:s2/3

Weiss, Adolph, (C) 228:s2/1

Weiss, George, (C) 284:s2/4

Weiss, Sam, (P) 250:s2/1

Welborn, Larry, (P) 249:s2/2

Welch, Robert, (P) 217:s2/3

Welcome what comes (*Seven Pious Pieces*), 210:s2/3

Weldon, A. F. ("Fred"), (C) 266:s1/4

Well, Oh Well, 261:s2/1

We'll Be the Same (*America's Sweetheart*), 240:s1/1

Wells, Dickie, (P) 250:s1/4; 274:s2/9; 295:s1/2

Wells, Johnny, (P) 274:s1/6

Wells, Kitty, (P) 207:s1/5

Welsh, Robert, *see* Welch, Robert

Wendlandt, William, (P) 214:s1/4-7

Wendling, Pete, (C) 233:s1/8

We Never Speak as We Pass By, 267:s2/1

We're Marching to Zion, 224:s2/1

Werner, Joe, (P) 287:s1/6

Wesley, Charles, (C) 205:s1/9; 255:s2/8

Wesley, Samuel, (L) 255:s1/4

We Speak, 275:s2/3

West End Blues, 217:s2/7

West Indies Blues, 269:s2/3

Weston, Paul, (P) 272:s2/3

Wethington, Crawford, (P) 217:s1/1; 256:s1/2

Wetmore, Truman S., (C) 255:s2/7

What About Us?, 249:s2/8

What Can You Say in a Love Song? (*Life Begins at 8:40*); 240:s2/2

What Is This Thing Called Love?, 256:s1/8; 271:s2/5; 274:s1/3

What's the Matter Now?,
  290:s1/4
What's the Use?, 250:s2/4
*When Brazen Trumpets from
  Afar*, 299:s2/1
*When I Bring You Coloured
  Toys (Gitanjali)*, 247:s2/4
*When I Have Sung My Songs
  (Gitanjali)*, 247:s2/7
*When Jesus Christ Was Here on
  Earth*, 294:s1/5
*When Johnny Comes Marching
  Home*, 202:s2/5
*When Lilacs Last in the Door-
  yard Bloom'd*, 296
When Malindy Sings, 295:s2/7
*When My Dreamboat Comes
  Home*, 248:s2/3
When the Girls Can Vote,
  267:s2/2
When the Lusitania Went Down,
  222:s1/1
When the Stars Begin to Fall,
  294:s2/2
When You Dance, 264:s2/8
*Where Have We Met Before
  (Walk a Little Faster)*,
  240:s1/5
Where Home Is, 251:s1/1
*Where Is the Song of Songs for
  Me? (Lady of the
  Pavements)*, 238:s1/7
Whetsol, Arthur, (L) 250:s1/2;
  272:s2/1
Whispering, 279:s1/1
White, B. F., (C) 205:s1/11,
  s2/3, 10
White, Bert, (C,L) 298:s1/2
White, Charles Albert, (C)
  220:s1/6
White, Charlie, (P) 261:s2/3
White, Chris C., (P) 246:s2/4
White, Hy, (P) 284:s1/5;
  295:s1/7
White, John, (P) 245:s1/9
White, Johnny, (L) 233:s2/2
White, Leroy ("Lasses"), (C)
  290:s1/8

White Cliffs of Dover, The,
  270:s2/8
*White Dawn Is Stealing, The
  (Four American Indian
  Songs)*, 213:s2/3
Whiteman, Paul, (P) 215:s1/4;
  240:s1/7; 260:s1/7; 279:s1/1,
  s2/4
Whiting, George E., (L) 279:s2/5
Whiting, George Elbridge, (C)
  280:s2/4
Whiting, Richard A., (C) 270:s1/6
Whitloch, Ellis, (P) 217:s2/4
Whitman, Walt, (L) 229:s2/3; 296
Whitted, Ben, (P) 256:s1/3
Who'll Buy? (Temperance),
  251:s2/10
Whoopee-Ti-Yi-Yo, 245:s1/9
Whooping, 223:s1/1
*Who Will Bow and Bend Like a
  Willow?*, 239:s1/9
Why Did You Wander?, 225:s1/1
Why Must I Wear This Shroud?,
  294:s1/4
Whyte, Bubber, (P) 217:s2/7-8
Whyte, Zach, (P) 217:s2/7-8
*Widow Jones, The: May Irwin's
  "Bully" Song*, 221:s1/8
Wiederhold, Albert, (P) 222:s1/1
Wiejska Czwórka "Bracia
  Kuziany," (P) 283:s2/5
Wilcox, Jesse, (P) 217:s2/5-6
Wildcat, Leona, (P) 246:s2/3
Wildcat, Luman, (P) 246:s1/5,
  s2/3
Wildcat, Squirrel, (P) 246:s1/5,
  s2/3
*Wild Chase (Twelve Virtuoso
  Studies)*, 206:s2/3
Wilde, Oscar, (L) 273:s1/5-8
Wilder, Joe, (P) 216:s2/4
Wiley, Jackson, (P) 216:s1/5
Wilkinson, Max, (P) 256:s2/1
Williams, Ben, (P) 217:s1/8
Williams, Bert, (P) 215:s1/1;
  233:s1/7
Williams, C., (arr.) 207:s2/4
Williams, Chocolate, (P) 275:s1/1

Williams, Clarence, (C) *West End Blues*, 217:s2/7; *West Indies Blues*, 269:s2/3; *I've Found a New Baby*, 274:s1/7
(L) 269:s2/3
(P) 269:s2/7
Williams, "Cootie" (Charles), (C) 250:s2/8
(P) 250:s2/8; 274:s1/7
Williams, Devonia, (P) 261:s2/4
Williams, Eddie, (P) 217:s1/8
Williams, Elmer, (P) 217:s1/5
Williams, Fayette, (P) 256:s1/1
Williams, Gus, (C) 265:s2/4-5, 7
Williams, Jimmy, (P) 274:s1/5
Williams, John, (C) 217:s1/3, 8
Williams, Lawrence, (P) 217:s2/4
Williams, Marco, (P) 235:s1/1
Williams, Marion, (P) 224:s1/8
Williams, Mary Lou, (P) 217:s1/3; 284:s2/2
Williams, Nolan, (P) 269:s2/2
Williams, Paul, (P) 225:s1/7, s2/2
Williams, Pearlis, (P) 290:s2/5
Williams, Roger, (P) 298:s2/8
Williams, Spencer, (C,L) 256:s2/9; 269:s2/3
Williams, Walter, (P) 284:s1/7
Williams, Winston, (P) 284:s1/2
Williamson, Billy, (P) 249:s1/5
Williamson, John Lee ("Sonny Boy"), (C) 290:s2/7
(P) 290:s1/1, s2/7
Williamson, Stu, (P) 216:s2/1
Willie's Grave, 220:s1/2
Willingham, Thaddeus C., (P) 245:s2/1
Willis, Alvin, (arr.) 282:s2/3
Willis, Edgar, (P) 249:s2/7
Willow Tree, 256:s1/7
Wills, Billy Jack, (P) 287:s2/8
Wills, Bob, (C) 287:s2/9
(P) 236:s2/6; 287:s2/8
(arr.) 287:s2/8
Wilson, Eric, (P) 212; 218

Wilson, Jackie, (P) 249:s2/4
Wilson, Quinn, (P) 217:s1/4
Wimby, Julius, (P) 249:s1/9
Wind, The (*Eleven Intrusions*), 214:s1/2
Wind Demon, Rhapsodie Caracteristique, The, 257:s2/1
Windom, A. H., (C) 224:s1/2
Wind Quintet (Riegger, C) 285:s1/2
Winfree, D., (C) 250:s1/5
Wilson, Mrs. A. P., (P) 291:s2/5
Wilson, Arlandus, (P) 261:s1/3
Wilson, Carl ("Flat Top"), (P) 261:s1/8
Wilson, Don, (P) 269:s2/5
Wilson, Dick, (P) 284:s2/2
Wilson, Gerald, (C,P) 284:s1/3
Wilson, Gus, (P) 256:s2/10
Wilson, Lonnie, (P) 287:s2/3
Wilson, Ollie, (P) 271:s2/1
Wilson, "Shadow" (Rossiere), (P) 271:s2/4; 275:s1/1; 284:s1/6
Wilson, Teddy, (P) 250:s2/3; 271:s1/1
Wingreen, Harriet, (P) 213:s2/3; 230:s2; 231:s1/1-2, s2
Winner, Septimus, (C) 267:s1/2
Winston, Albert, (P) 261:s2/4
Winter, Lois, (P) 265:s1/1-5
Wise, Chubby, (P) 225:s1/1, s2/2
Wiseman, Mac, (P) 225:s1/5
Witt, L. O. de, (arr.) 293:s2/1
Wiwczar na Supylci (Shepherd Playing the Flute), 283:s2/8
Woltz, DaCosta, (P) 236:s1/2
Wolverine Blues, 274:s2/6
Women's Brush Dance, 246:s2/1
Wondrous Love, 205:s1/6
Wood, Abraham, (C) 276:s2/3, 5
Woodbury, Isaac Baker, (C) 220:s1/3
Woode, Henri, (C) 217:s2/3
Woodman, Britt, (P) 284:s1/7
Woods, Pete, (P) 217:s2/3; 256:s2/6

Woods, Phil, (P) 295:s2/6
Woody'n You, 242:s1/1
Woolum, Dave, (C,P) 225:s1/9
Work, Henry Clay, (C) 267:s1/1
Wormick, Jimmy, (P) 284:s1/7
Worth, Leah, (L) 295:s2/1
Wright, Lammar, (P) 217:s1/6-7
Wright, Wallace, (P) 217:s2/3
Wróbel, Andrew, (P) 283:s1/3
Wspomnienia Sabaly (Reminiscences of Sabala), 283:s1/3
Wulfe, Jack, (P) 216:s1/4
Wuorinen, Charles, (C) 209:s2/3
Wylie, Elinor, (L) 247:s2/6

Yancey, Jimmy, (C,P) 259:s2/3-4
Yancey Special, 259:s1/7
Yankee Doodle Boy, The (*Little Johnny Jones*), 221:s1/2
Yankee Shuffle, 282:s2/6
Yar Ounenal (I Love You), 264:s2/5
Yazzie, Raymond K., (P) 246:s2/2
Yazzie, Sam Jr., (P) 246:s2/2
Yazzie, Sam Sr., (P) 246:s2/2
Year's at the Spring, The, 247:s1/2
Yellen, Jack, (L) 215:s2/6; 256:s1/1
Yes, Sir, That's My Baby, 279:s2/3
Yesterdays, 216:s1/3
Yield Not to Temptation, 224:s1/5
Yip, Yip, Yaphank: Oh, How I Hate to Get Up in the Morning, 238:s1/1
Yodeling Blues, 290:s1/5
Yo Quisiera Ser, 244:s1/5
Yotko, Fr., (P) 264:s2/8
You Are Never Away (*Allegro*), 272:s2/5
You'd Better Wake Up, 225:s1/5
You Do Something to Me (*Fifty Million Frenchmen*) 227:s1/2

You Forgot Your Gloves (*The Little Show*), 240:s1/2
You Gotta Cut That Out, 252:s2/8
Youmans, Vincent, (C) *Great Day*, 227:s2/4; *Like He Loves Me*, 272:s1/4; *I Know That You Know*, 274:s1/6; *Tea for Two*, 284:s2/3; *Carioca*, 298:s2/4 (P) 272:s1/4
You Never Miss the Water Till the Well Runs Dry, 251:s1/7
Young, Dave, (P) 242:s2/3
Young, Ed, (P) 278:s1/8, s2/4, 6, 10; 290:s2/1
Young, Ella, (L) 214:s1/1-3
Young, James, (P) 246:s1/3
Young, Joe, (L) 222:s1/5; 260:s2/5; 279:s1/4
Young, John, (P) 222:s1/3
Young, Lester, (P) 274:s1/1, s2/9; 295:s1/1-2
Young, Lonnie, (P) 252:s1/6
Young, Snooky, (L) 284:s1/3
Young, "Trummy" (James), (C) 248:s2/7 (P) 217:s1/4; 248:s2/7; 284:s1/6
Young, Victor, (C) 248:s1/6; 274:s2/4 (P) 238:s2/7; 240:s1/5
Young Men from the Country, 264:s2/2
You're Not the Kind, 271:s1/2
Your Left, 291:s2/3
Your Old Standby, 225:s1/6
Your Sword Has Pierced Me, 264:s2/6
You Were Meant for Me (*Broadway Melody*), 227:s1/4
Yurok Indians, (C,P) 246:s2/1; 297:s1/1-4, 6-7, 10-12
Yutzy, Philip, (P) 221:s1/4; 267:s1/2

Zakopiańska Picsnka (Song
  from Zakopane), 283:s1/8
Zalim Te Momce (I Saw You,
  Lad), 264:s1/4
Zandy, Eddie, (P) 284:s1/8
Zawzęta Dziewczyna (Stubborn
  Girl), 283:s1/2
Zegler, Manuel, (P) 216:s2/3
Ziegfeld Follies
  1921, *Second-Hand Rose*,
    215:s1/2
  1922, *Mister Gallagher and
    Mister Shean*, 215:s1/3
  1931, *Shine on, Harvest
    Moon*, 215:s2/1

Zing-Zing-Zing, 291:s2/2
Zinzendorf, Christian Renatus
  von, (L) 230:s1/3
Zitano, Jimmy, (P) 275:s1/6
Zlozyw i Widohraw Solo
  Skrypkowe Pawlo Humeniuk,
  (P) 283:s2/7-8
Zonky, 284:s2/2
Zoodiac, 291:s2/2
Żukowsky, Ewgen, (P)
  283:s2/2-3, 7-8

Index to Printed Material

This is a general index to information contained in the liner notes and covers of each album. Included are topics discussed at length in the notes, as well as their authors (record number in boldface) and photographs of individuals (record number in italics). Discussions of those works included on the recordings do *not* appear in this index. The user can assume that if a work is found on a recording it will be covered in the liner notes. The art on each album cover can be located by its creator (indicated as artist) and its title (indicated as cover art).

Acuff, Roy, *207, 287*

Abelman Ida (artist), 264

Abstraction (cover art), 228

Adams Hoover, Cynthia, *see* Hoover, Cynthia Adams

Aerograph (cover art), 285

Afro-American music, *see* black music

alabados, 292

Alabama Sacred Harp Convention, 205

Alexander, Charles McCallom, 224

Almanac Singers, 270

Altman, Harold (artist), 256

Ameen, Ramsey, **201**

America Guided by Wisdom (cover art), 231

American Bandmasters Association, 211

American Folklore Society, 213

American Indian influence, *see* "Indianist" movement

American Revolution, *see* Revolutionary War

American Theatre Wing's Stage Door Canteen, 222

Anderson, Donna K., **273**

Angry Sky (cover art), 216

antiwar songs, 222

Appalachian musical tradition, 225; *see also* bluegrass

Arapaho Indians, 246

Archibald, Bruce, **218, 286**

Armstrong, Louis, 295

Arnold, Eddy, *207*

Artist's Mother, The (cover art), 283

art music, influence on jazz, 216, 228

art songs, *see* songs, art

Asian influences on Western art music, 237

Assembly Church (cover art), 252

Astarte (cover art), 268

Atherton, James, *288/89*

auctioneering, 223

Auerbach-Levy, William (artist), 238

Autry, Gene, *287*

avant-garde, 209, 214
  in piano music, 203

Babbitt, Milton, 209, **240**

Bachleda, Stanislaw, *283*

Bacon, Peggy, (artist), 298

bailes, 292

Baker, David, **228**, *242*

Baline, Israel, *see* Berlin, Irving

ballads, 223, 239, 245

ballet music, 253

band music, 211

bands, 266, 282; *see also* concert bands; jazz bands; school bands

banjo, 225, 226, 236

ban on recordings, *see* recording ban

Baptist hymns, *see* hymns; Protestant hymns

Barber, Samuel, 229, *229*

Barron, David, **208**

Basie, Count, 217

Bassett, Leslie, 209

Bath Scene (cover art), 215

Battle of Lights, Coney Island (cover art), 227

Beach, Mrs. H. H. A., 247

Bearden, Romare (artist), 204, 217

Beardsley, Bethanee, *243*

bebop, 271

Bechet, Sidney, 274, *274*

Beiderbecke, Bix, *274*

Bellows, George (artist), 224

Bennett, Robert Russell, 211

Bennie Moten's Kansas City Orchestra, *217*

Benton, Thomas Hart (artist), 207, 245, 300

Berlin, Edward A., **230, 257**

Berlin, Irving, 238

Bernstein, Leonard, *277*

Bierstadt, Albert (artist), 262/63

big-band jazz, *see* jazz bands

big bands, *see* dance bands

Big Parade, The, 222
Billings, William, 205
Billy Sunday (cover art), 224
Black Crook, The, 221
black music, 201, 228, 260, 261,
  269, 277. 290; *see also*
  boogie-woogie; jazz; musicals,
  black; spirituals
Blake, Eubie, *260*
bluegrass, 225, 226
Bluegrass Boys, *225*
blues, 252, 261, 290; *see also*
  boogie-woogie; piano blues;
  rhythm and blues
Blues Serenaders, *256*
Blumenthal, Bob, 275
Board of Music Trade, 267
Bontecou, Lee (artist), 242
boogie-woogie, 259
Booth, Philip, *288/89*
Boots and His Buddies, *217*
bop, *see* bebop
Boston-dip waltz, *see* waltz,
  Boston-dip
Boston musical life, 268
Bowles, Paul, *243*
Brant, Henry Dreyfuss, 211
Brass Band (cover art), 211
Breinin, Raymond (artist), 253
Brice, Fannie, *215*
broadside ballads, *see* ballads
Broadway (cover art), 240
Broadway songs, *see* songs,
  popular; theater, musical;
  revues, musical
Brooks, William, **231**, 267
Brown-Roach, Inc., 242
Buck, Dudley, 220
Buddhism, *see* Zen Buddhism
Burchfield, Charles (artist), 205,
  294
Burgdorff, Ferdinand (artist),
  213
Burleigh, Harry Thacker, 247
burlesque, 260

Cadman, Charles Wakefield, 213,
  247

Cadmus, Paul (artist), 281
Cage, John, 203, 214
  (artist), 214
cakewalk, 265
Calder, Alexander (artist), 259
Calling of Isaiah, The (cover art),
  255
Calloway, Cab, *217*
calls, dance, *see* dance calls
Canal Market in 1860 (cover art),
  251
Canyon de Chelly (cover art), 213
Capps, Charles Merrick (artist),
  292
Carpenter, John Alden, 228, 247
Carr, Benjamin, 231, 299
Carter, Benny, *274*
Carter, Elliott, 219, *219*
Carter Family, *287*
Casa Loma Orchestra, 217, *217*
Cash, Johnny, *207*
chalk-line walk, *see* cakewalk
Chaloff, Serge, *275*
chance, in music of John Cage,
  214
Chanler, Theodore, *243*
Chapple Publishing Co., 202
Charles, Ernest, 247
Charleston, the, 293
Chase, Gilbert, 212
Cheney, Amy Marcy, *see* Beach,
  Mrs. H. H. A.
Cherokee Indians, 246
Chestnut Street Theatre,
  Philadelphia, 232
Chicago Symphony Orchestra,
  258
children's songs, 291
Chocolate Beau Brummels, *see*
  Zach Whyte's Chocolate Beau
  Brummels
Chop Suey Dancers No. 2 (cover
  art), 279
choral music, 219
Chou Wen-Chung, 237
Christian, Charlie, *274*
Church, Frederick Edwin (artist),
  206, 208, 257

church music, *see* sacred music
Church of God in Christ, 224
Cincinnati, music in, 251
Citkowitz, Israel, *243*
Civil War, 202; *see also* war
  songs
Claude Melnotte [pseud.], *see*
  Kunkel, Charles
Cohan, George M., 221
Cohen, Norm, **236**
Cohn, Lawrence, **235**
Coleman, Cy, **272**
College Band Directors National
  Association, 211
college bands, *see* school bands
concert bands, 211
conservatories, 206
Cook, Will Marion, 265
Coolidge, Elizabeth, Sprague,
  286
cool jazz, 242
Copland, Aaron, 241, *277*
Counce, Curtis, *275*
Country Church (cover art), 294
country-dance, 293
country music, 207, 223, 287
Covert, John (artist), 211
Cowell, Henry, 203, 218, *218*
Cox, Elaine Sherer (artist), 203,
  235, 246, 247, 260, 266,
  271, 273, 276, 280
Crawford, Richard, **255, 276,**
  299
Creek Indians, 246
Cuban music, 243
Curtin, Phyllis, *229*

Dadaism, and John Cage, 214
Damrosch, Walter Johannes, 247
dance, modern, 253
dance bands, 217, 269; *see also*
  territory bands
dance calls, 223
dance music, 256, 269, 293; *see*
  also bailes; country-dance;
  Charleston, the; fox trot;
  galop; gavotte; march;
  mazurka; minuet; polka;

quadrille; ragtime; schottische;
  two-step; waltz; waltz, Boston-
  dip; waltz, hesitation-and-
  Boston; waltz, jazz
Darrell, R. D., 228
Davis, Jefferson, 202
Davis, Richard, *204*
Delmonico Building (cover art),
  277
Dempster, Stuart, *254*
Diamond, David, 258, *258*
Diana Dancing Academy (cover
  art), 248
Dickerson, Carroll, and
  orchestra, *256*
Dies Irae (cover art), 270
Dillard, Bill, *274*
Dodds, Baby, *274*
Dodds, Johnny, *274*
Driggs, Frank, *256, 274*
dulcimer, 225, 226, 239
Dunn, James Philip, 247
Dunn, Johnny, *269*
Dunn, Mignon, *288/89*
Dvořák, Antonin, 213
Dwight, John Sullivan, 257,
  262/63
Dying and Dead Veteran (cover
  art), 296

Easterday, Jess, *287*
Eastman Symphonic Wind
  Ensemble, 211
eephing, 223
electronic music, 237
elementary school bands, *see*
  school bands
Ellington, Duke, 217, 248
emigration to the U.S., 264
Emerson String Quartet, *212*
Emmett, Dan D., 202
Epstein, Dena J., 234
Erickson, Robert, 254
Eskew, Harry, 224
Esty, Alice, 243
Ethical Movement (cover art),
  284
Ethiop, The (cover art), 232

ethnic music, *see* immigrant groups—music

Europe, American musicians in, 206

Evans, David, **290**

Evergood, Philip (artist), 243

Eye (cover art), 254

Fairbank, Janet, 243

Farmer, Michael McKibbin (artist), 291

Farmers Nooning (cover art), 234

Farr, Hugh, *287*

Farr, Karl, *287*

Farwell, Arthur, 206, 213, 218

Feldman, Lou, *274*

Fennell, Frederick, 211

Ferrér, Rafael (artist), 244

fiddle, 225, 226, 236

fife, 226

films, *see* motion pictures

Finney, Ross Lee, 211

First Fruits, The (cover art), 230

Fischer, William G., 220

Flatt, Lester, *225*

Floyd, Troy, *256*

Foerster, Adolph Martin, 206, *206*

folk music, 226, 239, 245, 294; *see also alabados*; *bailes*; blues; country music

folk songs, 236, 245; *see also* auctioneering; ballads; bluegrass; children's songs; country music; dance calls; eephing; games' songs; gospel music; hollering; nonsense songs; sea shanties

folk songs, Anglo-American, 223

folk songs, Irish, 239

folk songs, Scottish, 239

Follies, see Ziegfeld's *Follies*

Ford, Ricky, 204, *204*

Forest (cover art), 258

For Freedon (cover art), 222

Foster, Pops, *274*

foundation commissions, 286

fox trot, 293

Frankenstein, Alfred, **285**

Freed, Alan, 249

Friedman, Robert, **244**

Frightened Faces (cover art), 274

Frizzell, Lefty, *207*

fuging tune, in Sacred Harp music, 205

Gaby, Dan, *274*

Gallagher, Ed, *215*

galop, 293

games' songs, 291

Gardner, Isabella Stewart, 268

Gatti-Casazza, Giulio, 241

gavotte, 293

Gelles, George, **300**

George White's Scandals, 215

Georgia Sea Island Singers, *see* Sea Island Singers

Gibbons, John Sloan, 202

Giddins, Gary, **249**

Gilbert, Henry F., 206, *206*, 228

Gillespie, Dizzy, 271, 284

Gillespie, John Birks, *see* Gillespie, Dizzy

Gilmore, Patrick Sarsfield, 202

Godfrey, Batyah, *288/89*

Godzilla (cover art), 249

Goldman, Richard Franko, 266

Goode, Mort, **298**

Goodman, Benny, 217, *274*

Gorky, Arshile (artist), 283

gospel music, 223, 224; *see also* hymns

Gottschalk, Louis Moreau, 208, 257

Grand Erg Occidental (cover art), 244

Grand Tier at the Metropolitan (cover art), 241

Green, Douglas B., **287**

Green, Stanley, **221**

Greenburg, Samuel (cover art), 222

Griffes, Charles Tomlinson, 247, 273

Gruenberg. Louis, 241
guitar, 236
Gushee, Lawrence, **269**
Guy, Joe, *274*

Hageman, Richard, 247
Hagert, Thornton, **293**
Haidt, John Valentine (artist), 230
Hail America (cover art), 282
Hamilton, David, **277**
Hamm, Charles, **202, 203, 270**
Handel and Haydn Society, 219
Handlin, Oscar, **264**
Hanson, Howard, 241
Harding, A. A., 211
Harman, Carter, **281**
harmonica, 226
Harrigan, Edward "Ned," 265
Harris, Roy, 218
Harrison, Jimmy, *274*
Hart, Charles, 222
Hassler, Bud, *274*
Hawkins, Coleman, 250, *274*
Hayes, Edgar, and His Orchestra, *217*
Heart of the Andes, The (cover art), 257
Heart Songs, 202
Heckman, Don, **261**
Heilbut, Anthony, **224**
Heinrich, Anthony Philip, 208, 213, 230
Helps, Robert, *243*
Henderson, Fletcher, 217
Hentoff, Nat, **250**
Herbert, Victor, 241, *272*
hesitation-and-Boston waltz, *see* waltz, hesitation-and-Boston
Heth, Charlotte, **246, 297**
Hewitt, John Hill, 202
Higginbotham, J. C., *see* Higginbotham, Jay C.
Higginbotham, Jay C., *274*
Hines, Earl, 274
Hines, Earl, and His Orchestra, *217*

Hispanic music, 243; *see also* Cuban music; Latin music; Puerto Rican music
Hitler, Adolph, 222
Hodges, Johnny, *274*
Holiday, Billie, 295
Holiness Church, *see* Church of God in Christ
hollering, 223, 252, 290
Hollywood songs, *see* motion pictures, music in; songs, popular
Holyoke, Samuel, 299
Homer, Louise, *229*
Homer, Winslow (artist), 202
hoodling, *see* eephing
Hoover, Cynthia Adams, **299**
Hopper, Edward (artist), 225, 239
Horizontal Spines (cover art), 259
Hounfor (cover art), 201
Hunter, Lloyd, *217*
Huntington, Daniel (artist), 220
Huss, Henry Holden, 206, *206*
Hutchinson family, 202
Hydroplanes at Rest (cover art), 233
hymns, 224, *294*; *see also* *alabados*; gospel music; Protestant hymns; Sacred Harp music

I Got a Gal on Sourwood Mountain (cover art), 245
Imbrie, Andrew, 212, 254
immigrant groups—music, 244, 264, 292; *see also* black music; Cuban music; Hispanic music; Polish music; Puerto Rican music; Slavic music; Ukranian music
improvisation, 201
and jazz, 204
Indiana, Robert (artist), 288/89
Indian influence in art music, *see* "Indianist" movement
"Indianist" movement, 213

Indians, *see* Arapaho Indians; Cherokee Indians; Creek Indians; Navajo Indians; Plains Indians; Pueblo Indians; Seneca Indians; Tolowa Indians; Yurok Indians
industry, themes in music, 267
instruments, musical, in 18th-century music, 276, 299; *see also* banjo; dulcimer; fiddle; fife; guitar; harmonica; jew's harp; mouthbow; organ; piano
Irving Berlin (cover art), 238
Ives, Charles, 203, 247, 300
Ives, Gene, *288/89*
Ivey, William, **207**

Jackson, Billy Morrow (artist), 269
Jackson, George K., 231
Jackson, Richard, **206, 208, 220**
Jacobson, Wayne, *274*
Jazz (cover art), 250
jazz, 201, 242, 256, 269
    and avant-garde, 216
    and classical music, 216
    improvisation in, 204
    influence on art music, 228
    see also art music, influence on jazz; bebop; cool jazz; dance bands; ragtime; third stream; waltz, jazz
jazz bands, 248, 256; *see also* territory jazz bands
Jazz Messengers, 242
Jazz 1930s: The Savoy (cover art), 217
jazz singing, 295
Jeremiah (cover art), 255
jew's harp, 226
Jim and Jesse, *225*
Johnson, Bunk, 271
Johnson, Charlie, *256*
Johnson, James P., *256, 274*
Johnson, John Rosamond, 247
Johnson, Tom, **237**

Johnston, Ben, 203, **214**
Jolson, Al, 222
Jones, Jo, *274*
Jones, Lindley Armstrong, *see* Jones, "Spike"
Jones, Mary Harris, *see* Jones, "Mother"
Jones, "Mother," *270*
Jones, "Spike," 222
Joplin, Scott, 235
Juggler (cover art), 295

Kaminski, Andrzej, **283**
Kansas City Orchestra, *see* Bennie Moten's Kansas City Orchestra
Kaplan, Justin, **296**
Katz, Leo (artist), 229
Kaufer, Waldo Glover (artist), 254
Kaye, Danny, *215*
Keepnews, Peter, **295**
Kenny, Herbert A., **268**
Keppard, Freddie, *269*
Kimball, Robert, **260**
Kirby, Pete ("Bashful Brother Oswald"), *287*
Kirchner, Leon, 286, *286*
Kish Sklar, Kathryn, *see* Sklar, Kathryn Kish
Korall, Burt, **284**
Koussevitzky, Serge, 286
Kramer, A. Walter, 247
Krisel, Harold (artist), 261
Krushenick, Nicholas (artist), 249
Kuniyoshi, Yasuo (artist), 295
Kunkel, Charles, 220

Ladnier, Tommy, *274*
Lambert, Louis [pseud.], *see* Gilmore, Patrick Sarsfield
Landacre, Paul (artist), 286
Laning, Edward (artist), 267
Lankes, J. J. (artist), 290
Latin music, 244
Law, Andrew, 205
Leather Patch, The (cover art), 265
Lee, George E., *256*
Leppard, Raymond, *288/89*

Levine, Jack (artist), 218
Lewis, Robert Hall, 254
Lewis, William, *288/89*
Lighthouse, The (cover art), 239
Lillie, Beatrice, *215*
lining-out, *see* hymns; spirituals
liturgical music, *see* sacred music
Living Better Without (cover art), 226
Lodwig, Ray, *274*
Lomax, Alan, **205**, **252**, **278**, **294**
Londin, Edwin, **210**
Lowry, Robert, 220
Lunceford, Jimmie, 217
Lusitania, 222

MacDowell, Edward Alexander, 206, *206*, 247
MacIver, Lauren (artist), 210
MacKay, Jean (artist), 278
McKee, Joseph, *288/89*
McNulty, William Charles (artist), 272
Man (cover art), 256
march, 266
March (cover art), 287
marching bands, *see* bands
Marsh, Reginald (artist), 241, 248, 279
Martino, Donald, 210
Martirano, Salvatore, 210
Marx, Robert, **288/89**
Mason, Lowell, 251, 257
Mather, Cotton, 255
Maxwell, Linn, *288/89*
mazurka, 293
Mennin, Peter, *258*
Menotti, Gian Carlo, 241
Mercer, Johnny, *272*
Mercy's Dream (cover art), 220
Mess, George Joseph (artist), 226
Metropolitan Opera, 241
Mezzrow, Mezz, *274*
Miley, James "Bubber," *256*
military bands, *see* bands
Miller, Philip L., 247
Miller, Robert, *203*

Mills Blue Rhythm Band, 217, *217*
Mingus, Charlie, *242*
minstrel shows, 260, 265
minstrelsy, 249, 251
minuet, 293
Mission at Trampas (cover art), 292
Mobile (cover art), 281
modern dance, *see* dance, modern
Modern Jazz Quartet, 242, *242*
Moholy-Nagy, Laszlo (artist), 212
Mole, Miff, *274*
Monroe, Bill, *225*
Monroe Brothers, *287*
monster concerts, 208
Montana, Patsy, *287*
Moody, Dwight L., 224
Moore, Eustice, *274*
Moore, Michael, 227
Moore, Tom, 231
Moravians, 230
Morgan, Robert, **219**
Morgan's Jazz Band, *see* Sam Morgan's Jazz Band
Morgenstern, Dan, **271**
Morris, Robert, 254
Mosler, Henry, Jr. (artist), 251
Moten's Kansas City Orchestra, *see* Bennie Moten's Kansas City Orchestra
motion pictures, 227
music in, 240, 248, 270
Mount, William Sidney (artist), 234
mouthbow, 223
movies, *see* motion pictures
musical revues, *see* revues, musical
musical theater, *see* theater, musical
musicals, black, 260
Music Box Revues, 238
musicians, American in Europe, *see* Europe, American musicians in

My Father Reminisces
(cover art), 264

Nancarrow, Conlon, 203
Nashville, 207
Naumburg Rosenberg, James,
    see Rosenberg, James
    Naumburg
Navajo Indians, 246
Neloms, Bob, *204*
Nesbitt, Jackson Lee (artist),
    236
Nevin, Ethelbert, 206, *206*
New England, *see* northeastern
New Orleans Orchestra, *269*
New Orleans Rhythm Kings, *269*
Newsom, Jon, **251**
New York City Opera, 241
New York Philharmonic, *258*
Night on the Boardwalk (cover
    art), 293
Nolan, Bob, *287*
nonsense songs, 223
Noone, Jimmie, *274*
northeastern music, 239, 255
Northern Arapaho Indians, *see*
    Arapaho Indians
Northern Plains Indians, *see*
    Plains Indians
northwestern music, 297
November Evening (cover art),
    236

O'Callahan, Kevin (artist), 275
Offergeld, Robert, **257**
Offering, The (cover art), 269
opera, 232, 241
Oppenheimer, George, 215, 238
Orem, Preston Ware, 213
organ, 227, 280
Orr, Dee, *274*
Ory, Kid, *269*
Our Banner in the Sky (cover
    art), 206
Owen, Barbara, **280**

Page, Walter, *256*
Paine, John Knowles, 206,
    262/63
Panassie, Hugues, *274*
Pankake, Jon, **245**
Paradise Orchestra, *256*
Parker, Charlie, 271, 284
Parker, Horatio, 206, *206*, 247
Partch, Harry, 203, 214, *214*
Parton, Dolly, *207*
Passage to India (cover art), 267
Paton, Sandy, **239**
patriotic music, 202, 222, 276
Paynter, John P., **211**
Pearson, Henry (artist), 284
Pegasus (cover art), 229
Pennell, Joseph (artist), 233, 282
Pentecostal Church, *see* Church
    of God in Christ
Perry, Douglas, *288/89*
Perryman, Lloyd, *287*
Persichetti, Vincent, 211
Peterdi, Gabor (artist), 216
Peter Ring dem Bells (cover art),
    278
Phantom of the Opera, The, 227
Phillips, Harvey E., **258**
piano, 203
piano blues, 259
piano music, 206, 257, 298
Piron, Armand J., *269*
Piston, Walter, 286, *286*
Plains Indians, 246
player piano, *see* piano
Plaza Hotel Orchestra, *256*
Polish music, 283
political songs, 202
polka, 293
popular music, 220, 240, 267,
    270, 272, 276, 279, 298
"populist" music, 267
Powell, John, 228
Press, The (cover art), 286
Price, Sammy, *274*
Protestant hymns, 205; *see also*
    Church of God in Christ;
    hymns; Moravians
Pryor, Arthur, 282

psalmody, eighteenth-century, 255, 276
Pueblo Indians, 246
Puerto Rican music, 243
Putnam, Ashley, *288/89*

quadrille, 293
quartets, vocal, 224
Quartette (cover art), 218

radio, influence on popular music, 240
Raeburn, Andrew, **262/63**
ragtime, 235, 269, 293; *see also* boogie-woogie
Railroad, The (cover art), 225
Ramey, Phillip, **212**, **229**
Rattner, Abraham (artist), 274
Ray, Man (artist), 250, 285
recitals, song, 243, 247
recording ban, 222
recordings, influence on jazz, 242
Red Votive Lights (cover art), 210
Reisman, Leo, *256*
religious music, *see* sacred music
Revelli, William D., 211
revivalism, 224
Revolutionary War, 276; *see also* war songs
Revue (cover art), 221
revues, musical, 215
rhythm and blues, 261
Richards, Spencer, **201**
Rinzler, Kate, **291**
Ritual Bayou (cover art), 204
Rivers, Larry (artist), 296
rock 'n' roll, 249
and country music, 207
Rodeheaver, Homer Alvan, 224
Rodgers, Jimmie, *287*
Rodriguez, Arsenio, 244
Rollins, Sonny, *242*
Rome, Harold, *272*
Root, Deane L., **221**
Root, George Frederick, 202, 234

Rorem, Ned, 229, *229*, **243**
Rose, Fred, *207*
Rosenberg, James Naumburg (artist), 270
Rosenberg, Neil V., 225
Rushing, Jimmy, *256*
Russell, George, *242*
Russell, Morgan (artist), 228
Russell, Pee Wee, *274*
Ryan, Anne (artist), 237

Sacred Harp music, 205; *see also* shape-note singing
sacred music, 210, 255, 294; *see also alabados*; gospel music; Moravians; psalmody; Sacred Harp music
Salzman, Eric, **209**
Sam Morgan's Jazz Band, *269*
Sanctified Church, *see* Church of God in Christ
Sankey, Ira D., 224
Sargent, John Singer (artist), 268
Scandals, see George White's Scandals
Scheele, Carl H., **222**, **233**
school bands, 211
schottische, 293
Schuller, Gunther, **204**, 212, **212**, 216, **262/63**
Schuman, William, 253
Scruggs, Earl, *225*
Sea Island Singers, 278
sea shanties, 223
secondary school bands, *see* school bands
Seeger, Charles, 218
Seidel, Richard, 242
Seneca Indians, 246
Sessions, Roger, *243*, *296*
Seventeen Drawings by Thoreau (cover art), 214
Shahn, Ben (artist), 258
Shaker songs, 239
shape-note singing, 205, 223
Shapey, Ralph, 254
Shapiro, Nat, **248**, **272**, **279**
Sharp, Cecil, 223

Shaw, Oliver, 231
Shean, Al, *215*
Sheeler, Charles (artist), 277
Shepherd, Arthur, 218, *218*
Sherer Cox, Elaine, *see* Cox,
    Elaine Sherer
Shifrin, Seymour, *219*
Shinn, Everett (artist), 221
Singer, Roberta, **244**
singing-school movement, 219,
    223, 255
Sissle, Noble, *260*
Sklar, Kathryn Kish, **251**
Slavic music, 283
Sloan, John (artist), 293
Smart, James R., **282**
Smith, David (artist), 209
Smith, Hale, 211
Smith, Jabbo, *256*
Smith, Patrick J., **241**
Smith, Richard (artist), 219
Smith, William O., 209
Smoky Mountain Boys, *287*
Social Graces, The (cover art),
    298
Soft Pack (cover art), 219
Sollberger, Harvey, 254, **254**
Sondheim, Stephen, *272*
song recitals, *see* recitals, song
songs, art, 243, 247; *see also*
    Victorian songs
songs, popular, 215, 220, 221,
    233, 240; *see also* Tin Pan
    Alley
Songs of the War (cover art),
    202
Sons of the Pioneers, *287*
sound effects in twentieth-
    century music, 203, 237
Sousa, John Philip, 282
Sousa Band, *282*
Southern music, 226, 236, 245,
    287; *see also* Appalachian
    musical tradition
Southern Plains Indians; *see*
    Plains Indians
southwestern music, 292
Spaulding, James, *204*

Spencer, Tim, *287*
spirituals, 278, 294
Spottswood, Richard, 264, 283
Sprague Coolidge, Elizabeth, *see*
    Coolidge, Elizabeth Sprague
Spring Twilight (cover art), 290
square-dance calls, *see* dance calls
Stage Door Canteen, *see*
    American Theatre Wing's
    Stage Door Canteen
Stark, Richard B., *292*
Stein, Gertrude, 288/89
Steinberg, Michael, **296**
Stella, Joseph (artist), 227
Stern Timbers (cover art), 275
Steven, Tommy, *274*
Stoch, Karol, *283*
Stone, Jesse, *256*
Stone, Peter Eliot, **262/63**
Story Hour (cover art), 291
Strickland, W. (artist), 232
Sudhalter, Richard M., **265**
Sunday-school movement, 224
Sunset in the Yosemite Valley
    (cover art), 262/63
Susman, Warren, **227**
Swing era, 217
symphonic bands, *see* concert
    bands
symphony, 258

Tagore, Rabindranath, 218
Tall White Sun (cover art), 205
Tanner, Benjamin (artist), 231
Tate, Erskine, *256*
Taylor, Cecil, 201
Taylor, Deems, 241
Taylor, J. R., **217**
Taylor, Prentiss (artist), 252
territory bands, 217
territory jazz bands, 256
Terry, Walter, **253**
Texas Playboys, *287*
theater, musical, 202, 221, 232,
    240, 248, 260, 265, 299; *see
    also* cakewalk; vaudeville
theater organ, *see* organ

third stream jazz, 216
and Gunther Schuller, 212
XXXV (cover art), 237
Thompson, Randall, 219, *219*, 247
Thomson, Virgil, 288/89
369th Infantry ("Hell Fighters") Band, 269
Thurston, Ray, *274*
Times Square (cover art), 272
Tin Pan Alley, 248, 270, 279; *see also* songs, popular
Tobey, Mark (artist), 240
Tolowa Indians, 297
Travis, Merle, *287*
Trees in Jamaica (cover art), 208
Trent, Alphonso, and orchestra, *256*
Trottman, Lloyd, *274*
Trumbauer, Frankie, *274*
two-step, 293
Tyler, Royall, 299

Ukranian music, 283
universities and new music, 209
Untamed (cover art), 223
Untitled (cover art), 242, 261
Untitled Abstraction (cover art), 212
Untitled II (cover art), 209
Urban, Joseph (artist), 215
urban music, 224

Valentino, Rudolph, *227*
Vanni, Helen, *288/89*
Varèse, Edgard, 237
vaudeville, 260
Veach, Rachel, *287*
Vendome Orchestra, *256*
Victorian songs, 220
virtuosity, 209, 254
vocal music, 295; *see also* jazz singing; quartets, vocal
vocal quartets, *see* quartets, vocal

Waller, Fats, *256*
waltz, 293
Boston-dip, 293
hesitation-and-Boston, 293
jazz, 293
war songs
Civil War, 202
Revolutionary War, 276
World War I, 222
World War II, 222
Watts, Isaac, 224
Wa-Wan Press, 213
Webb, Chick, and His Orchestra, *217*
Webster, Joseph Philbrick, 220
Weiss, Adolph, 228
Wells, Kitty, *207*
Wengenroth, Stow (artist), 223
West, Benjamin (artist), 255
western (region) music, 287
Wheat (cover art), 300
White, Charles Albert, 220
White, George, 215
Whitman, Walt, 296
Whyte, Zach, 217
Whyte's Chocolate Beau Brummels, *see* Zach Whyte's Chocolate Beau Brummels
Williams, Hank, *207*
Williams, Martin, **259**
Wills, Bob, *287*
Wilson, Lonnie, *287*
Wilson, Mark, **226**
Witham, Charles (artist), 265
Wolfe, Charles, **223**
women, role of
in art music, 243
in gospel music, 224
Women at Piano (cover art), 243
Wood, Grant (artist), 287
Woodbury, Isaac Baker, 220
Work, Henry Clay, 202
World War I, 222
World War II, 222
WSM (Radio Station), *225*
Wuorinen, Charles, 209

Yale University, 206
Yellin, Victor Fell, 232
Youmans, Vincent, *272*
Young, David X. (artist), 201
Young, Lester, 270, 274, *274*
Youth Music (cover art), 207
Yurok Indians, 246, 297

Zach Whyte's Chocolate Beau
    Brummels, *217*
Zen Buddhism, 214
Ziegfeld, Florenz, 215
Ziegfeld, Jr., Florenz, 215
Ziegfeld's *Follies*, 215

Index to Genres and Performing Media

This index contains a systematic classification of the contents of each recording by genres—e.g., cantatas, operas, marches—and by performing media—e.g., dance-band music, choral music.

ART SONGS, *see* SONGS: **Art**

BAND MUSIC (excludes marches for band)

Bonnie Annie Laurie, 266:s1/7
Boston Commandery, 266:s1/2
Chimes of Liberty, The, 266:s1/6
Concerto for Alto Saxophone and Orchestra of Wind Instruments, 211:s2/1
Creole Belles, 282:s1/2
Expansions, 211:s1/2
Gardes du Corps, 266:s2/7
Gate City, 266:s1/4
Glory of the Yankee Navy, 282:s1/6
Governor's Own, The, 266:s1/1
Grandioso, 266:s2/4
His Excellency, 266:s1/5
Musical Joke on "Bedelia," A, 282:s1/8
My Maryland, 266:s2/5
On Jersey Shore, 266:s2/6
Our Director, 266:s1/9
Pageant, 211:s1/1
Pathfinder of Panama, The, 266:s1/3
Patriot, The, 282:s1/4
Pride of America, The, 266:s2/1
Serenade, The, 266:s2/8
Symphonic Songs for Band, 211:s2/2
Tabasco, 266:s2/2
Teddy Bear's Picnic, The, 282:s2/7
Trombone Sneeze, 282:s1/7
Verticals Ascending, 211:s1/3
see also MARCHES

BEBOP, *see* JAZZ

BIG BAND MUSIC, *see* DANCE-BAND MUSIC

BLUEGRASS MUSIC

Blackberry Blossom, 225:s2/1
Blue Ridge Cabin Home, 225:s1/2
Body and Soul, 225:s2/8
Daniel Prayed, 225:s1/3
Diesel Train, 225:s2/3
Dill Pickles Rag, 225:s2/9
Fox on the Run, 225:s2/7
Hills and Home, 225:s2/5
Hold Whatcha Got, 225:s2/2
Love Please Come Home, 225:s1/4
Old Age, 225:s1/9
Pathway of Teardrops, A, 225:s2/4
Raise a Ruckus Tonight, 225:s2/6
Springhill Disaster, 225:s1/8
Twenty-One Years, 225:s1/7
Why Did You Wander?, 225:s1/1
You'd Better Wake Up, 225:s1/5
Your Old Standby, 225:s1/6

BLUES, *see also* RHYTHM AND BLUES

Instrumental

Bass Goin' Crazy, 259:s2/2
Blues on the Downbeat, 259:s2/6
Boogie Woogie Stomp, 259:s2/1
Chicago Stomp, 259:s1/1
Climbin' and Screamin', 259:s2/5
Cuttin' the Boogie, 259:s2/8
Honky Tonk Train, 259:s1/6
Jump Steady Blues, 259:s1/5
Kaycee on My Mind (arr.), 259:s2/7
Mellow Blues, The, 259:s2/3
Mr. Freddie Blues, 259:s1/2
Pinetop's Boogie Woogie, 259:s1/4
Suitcase Blues, 259:s1/3
Tell 'Em About Me, 259:s2/4
Yancey Special, 259:s1/7

BLUES (continued)

Vocal

Beggin' the Blues, 252:s2/5
Berta, Berta, 252:s1/4
Buttermilk, 252:s1/8
Church-House Moan, 252:s2/4
  (choral)
*Death Comes A-Creepin' in My
  Room*, 252:s2/3
Field Song from Senegal,
  252:s1/1
Goin' Down to the Races,
  252:s2/7
House Lady Blues, 290:s2/4
*I'm Gonna Live Anyhow till I
  Die*, 252:s1/10
Jim and John, 252:s1/6
Katie Left Memphis, 252:s1/3
Lining Hymn and Prayer,
  252:s2/2 (choral)
Louisiana, 252:s1/1
Mama Lucy, 252:s1/9
Nigger Blues, 290:s1/8
No More, My Lord, 252:s2/1
Old Original Blues, 252:s1/5
Peach Tree Blues, 290:s1/1
Po' Boy Blues, 252:s1/2
Rolled and Tumbled, 252:s2/6
Violin Blues, 290:s1/3
Yodeling Blues, 290:s1/5
You Gotta Cut That Out,
  252:s2/8

BOOGIE WOOGIE, *see* BLUES:
  Instrumental

CANTATAS

Haymakers, The, 234
*When Lilacs Last in the Door-
  yard Bloom'd*, 296

CHAMBER MUSIC

Duos

Before the Cask of Wine, 214:s1/7
Capriccio for Cello and Piano,
  281:s2/1
Configurations, 254:s2/1
I Am a Peach, 214:s1/5
Intruder, The, 214:s1/4
Midnight Farewell, A, 214:s1/6
Music for Saxophone and Piano
  (Bassett), 209:s2/1
Rose, The, 214:s1/1
Sonata da Camera (Weber),
  281:s1/2
Sonata for the Pianoforte with an
  Accompaniment for a Violin
  (Taylor), 299:s1/6
Sonata in A Minor for Piano and
  Violin (Beach), 268:s1
Sonata in G Minor for Piano and
  Violin (Foote), 268:s2
Street, The, 214:s1/8
Suite for Cello and Harp
  (Harrison), 281:s1/1
Sunflowers, 254:s1/1
Three Sketches (Imbrie), 254:s2/2
Waterfall, The, 214:s1/3
Wind, The, 214:s1/2

Trios

Bassoon Variations (Wuorinen),
  209:s2/3
Concertino a Tre, 281:s2/2
*From Behind the Unreasoning
  Mask*, 237:s1/1
Motet on Doo-Dah, 254:s1/2

Quartets

Air (Shaw), 299:s2/6
Ceremony II ("Incantations"),
  237:s1/2
Quartet Euphometric, 218:s2/1
Quartet Romantic, 285:s1/1
String Quartet No. 2 (Schuller),
  212:s2

CHAMBER MUSIC (continued)

String Quartet No. 4 (Imbrie), 212:s1
Three Variations on a Theme (String Quartet No. 2) (Harris), 218:s1/1-3

Quintets

Quintetto (Holyoke ?), 299:s1/1
Wind Quintet (Riegger), 285:s1/2

Sextets

Suite for Harp and Wind Quintet (Chou Wen-Chung), 237:s2/1

Ensembles

Abongo, The, 284:s2/1
Lovely Nancy, 276:s1/4
Stone Grinds All, 276:s2/3
Three Songs (Seeger), 285:s2/2-4
Three Tone-Pictures, 273:s2/5

CHORAL MUSIC

Americana, 219:s1/1-5
Amsterdam, 205:s2/4
Baptismal Anthem, 205:s2/3
Beauregard's Retreat from Shiloh, 202:s2/1
Blessed Bible, The, 251:s2/8
Cusseta, 205:s2/8
David's Lamentation, 205:s1/2
Firmament, 251:s2/11
Future America, The, 267:s1/1
Greenwich, 205:s1/2
Hallelujah, 205:s1/9
Hand That Holds the Bread, The, 267:s1/1
Haymakers, The, 234
Henry, 251:s2/9
Ho! For Kansas, 251:s1/5
Homeward Bound, 205:s2/11
Hymn on Peace, A, 276:s1/5
I'm a Long Time Traveling Away from Home, 245:s2/9
Independence, 276:s1/5

Ives, 251:s2/4
I Wish I Was in Dixie's Land, 202:s1/1
Jeff in Petticoats, 202:s2/2
Jesus Is All the World to Me, 224:s2/2
Jovial Farmer Boy, The, 251:s1/8
Just as I Am, Without One Plea ("Woodworth"), 224:s2/9
Lamentation Over Boston, 276:s1/1
Last Words of Copernicus, The, 205:s2/9
Loving Jesus, 205:s1/11
March and Chorus "She is Condemned," 299:s2/4
Mass (Martirano), 210:s1, s2/1-2
Mass in D (Paine), 262/63
Melancholy Day, 205:s1/3
Memorial Service, 205:s2/7
Milford, 205:s2/2
Montgomery, 205:s2/5
Morning Trumpet, The, 205:s2/10
Navajo War Dance, 213:s2/1
New Harmony, 205:s1/8
Northfield, 205:s2/13
North Port, 205:s2/6
Odes of Shang, The, 219:s2
Ohio, 251:s2/3
Old Canoe, 251:s1/6
Old Man's Love Song, The, 213:s1/3
Pacific Railroad, The, 267:s1/1
Seven Pious Pieces, 210:s2/3
Sherburne, 205:s1/1
Soar Away, 205:s1/4
Sounds of the Singing School, 251:s2/2
Sweet By and By, 220:s1/1
Sweet Home, 251:s1/2
Tenting on the Old Camp Ground, 202:s1/5
To Music, 219:s1/6
Traveling On, 205:s1/7
Wake Up, Jake, 251:s2/1
Warren, 276:s2/3
We Are Coming, Father Abra'am, 202:s1/3

CHORAL MUSIC (continued)

We Are Coming from the Cotton Fields, 202:s2/6
We Are Happy Now, Dear Mother, 220:s1/3
Weeping, Sad and Lonely, 202:s2/3
We're Marching to Zion, 224:s2/1
When Brazen Trumpets from Afar, 299:s2/1
When Johnny Comes Marching Home, 202:s2/5
When Lilacs Last in the Dooryard Bloom'd, 296
When the Girls Can Vote, 267:s2/2
Who'll Buy (Temperance), 251:s2/10
Willie's Grave, 220:s1/2
Wondrous Love, 205:s1/6

CLARINET MUSIC

Fancies for Clarinet Alone, 209:s1/3

CONCERTOS

Concerto for Alto Saxophone and Orchestra of Wind Instruments, 211:s2/1
Piano Concerto No. 1 (Kirchner), 286:s2

COUNTRY MUSIC

All I Love Is You, 206:s2/6
Blue Yodel No. 11, 287:s1/2
Born To Lose, 287:s2/4
Chant of the Wanderer, 287:s2/6
Coat of Many Colors, 207:s2/8
Cotton Eyed Joe, 287:s2/8
Dark as a Dungeon, 287:s2/7
Don't Let Her Know, 207:s2/5
Dreaming with Tears in My Eyes, 287:s1/4

Fais Pas Ça, 287:s1/6
Fat Boy Rag, 287:s2/9
Forgotten Soldier Boy, 287:s1/8
Georgia Wildcat Breakdown, 287:s1/1
Gospel Ship, 287:s1/5
Help Me Make It Through the Night, 207:s2/9
Ida, Sweet as Apple Cider, 287:s1/9
I'm a Honky-Tonk Girl, 207:s2/3
It Won't Be Long, 287:s2/5
I Wanna Be a Cowboy's Sweetheart, 287:s2/1
Jimmy Martinez, 207:s2/2
Last Roundup, The, 287:s1/7
Little Ole You, 207:s2/1
Lorena, 207:s2/4
Railroad Boomer, 287:s2/3
Rescue from Moose River Gold Mine, The, 287:s2/2
Sing a Sad Song, 207:s2/7
Sweet Fern, 287:s1/3
There'll Come a Time, 287:s1/10

CRETAN MUSIC, *see* IMMIGRANT GROUPS— MUSIC: **European, Western**

CUBAN MUSIC, *see* IMMIGRANT IMMIGRANT GROUPS— MUSIC: **Hispanic**

CZECHOSLOVAKIAN MUSIC, *see* IMMIGRANT GROUPS— MUSIC: **European, Eastern**

DANCE-BAND MUSIC

After You've Gone (arr.), 256:s2/8
A-La-Bridges (arr.), 284:s1/1
Atlanta Low Down, 217:s2/5
Auburn Avenue Stomp, 217:s2/6
Black and Blue Rhapsody, 256:s2/7

DANCE-BAND MUSIC
(continued)

Blue Devil Blues, 256:s2/2
Blues of Avalon, 217:s2/2
Boy in the Boat, The, 256:s1/3
Call It Stormy Monday, 261:s1/7
Caravan, 217:s1/1
Casa Loma Stomp, 217:s1/2
Chase, The, 284:s2/7
Choo Choo Ch'Boogie, 261:s1/6
Dallas Blues (arr.), 217:s1/3
Dameron Stomp (arr.), 284:s1/2
Donna Lee, 284:s1/8
Dreamland Blues I, 256:s2/4
Dreamland Blues II, 256:s2/5
Ebony Silhouette, 217:s1/7
Elevation (arr.), 284:s1/4
Five O'Clock Shadow (arr.), 284:s1/5
Flying Home, 261:s1/1
Good Feelin' Blues, 217:s2/8
Good Jelly Blues, 284:s1/6
Good Rockin' Tonight, 261:s1/8
Heebie Jeebies, 217:s1/5
Hoochie Coochie Man, 261:s2/7
I Can't Get Up the Nerve, 284:s2/4
I've Found a New Baby (arr.), 256:s2/9
Jammin' for the Jackpot, 217:s1/8
Madhouse, 217:s1/4
Mellow Mood, 284:s2/5
Mingus Fingers, 284:s1/7
Original Dixieland One-Step, 217:s2/4
Perdido, 284:s2/1
Pickin' the Cabbage, 217:s1/6
Royal Roost, 284:s2/6
Ruff Scuffling, 256:s2/6
Saint, The, 284:s1/3
Sensational Mood, 217:s2/3
Starvation Blues, 256:s2/1
Static Strut (arr.), 256:s1/1
Straighten Up and Fly Right, 261:s1/4

Sweet and Low Blues, 256:s1/5
Symphonic Raps, 256:s1/2
Tea for Two, 284:s2/3
That's How I Feel Today, 256:s1/4
There's A Squabblin', 256:s2/3
Till Times Get Better, 256:s1/6
Toby, 217:s2/1
Well, Oh Well, 261:s2/1
West End Blues, 217:s2/7
What Is This Thing Called Love (arr.), 256:s1/8
Willow Tree (arr.), 256:s1/7
Zonky (arr.), 284:s2/2
see also **JAZZ**

DANCE MUSIC

Alligator Dance, 246:s1/2
Arkansas Traveler, The, 292:s2/7
At the Mississippi Cabaret, 293:s2/4
Butterfly Dance, 246:s1/1
Chinatown, My Chinatown, 293:s2/3
Chotis, El, 292:s2/13
Country Fiddle Music, 293:s1/4
Cutilio, El, 292:s2/2-5
Eagle Dance, 246:s1/3
Eliza Jane McCue, 293:s2/1
Fall River Legend, 253:s2
Flirt Polka, The, 293:s1/8
Flying Cloud Schottische, 293:s1/6
Gar Dance, 246:s1/5
Hiawatha, 293:s2/2
Hold Me, 293:s2/5
Indita, La, 292:s2/12
Irresistible, El, 293:s2/3
Jenny Lind Polka, 293:s1/2
Kansas City Blues, 293:s2/5
Ladies Walpole Reel, 239:s1/5
Lady Hope's Reel, 276:s2/1
Listen to the Mockingbird, 292:s2/8
Ma Ragtime Baby, 293:s2/2
Minuet and Gavotte, 293:s1/3

DANCE MUSIC (continued)

Natalie Polka-Mazurka, 293:s1/5
Oklahoma Two-Step, 246:s2/4
Polca, La, 292:s2/11
Prima Donna Waltz, 293:s1/1
Rabbit Dance, 246:s1/4
Ribbon Dance, 246:s2/2
Sonnambula Quadrille Number Two, La, 293:s1/9
Stomp Dance, 246:s2/3
Sweet Man, 293:s2/6
Tercera de Noviembre, La, 292:s2/9
Turkey in the Straw, 292:s2/6
Undertow, 253:s1
Valse, El, 292:s2/1, 10
Valse de Ma Coeur, 293:s2/4
Victoria Galop, 293:s1/7
Waltzing the Blues, 293:s2/6
Women's Brush Dance, 246:s2/1

DOUBLE-BASS MUSIC

Inflections I, 254:s1/3

DUOS, *see* CHAMBER MUSIC: **Duos**

EASTERN EUROPEAN MUSIC, *see* IMMIGRANT GROUPS— MUSIC: **European, Eastern**

ELECTRONIC MUSIC

Phonemena, 209:s1/2
Reflections, 209:s1/4

ENGLISH MUSIC, *see* IMMIGRANT GROUPS— MUSIC: **European, Western**

ENSEMBLES, CHAMBER, *see* CHAMBER MUSIC: **Ensembles**

FILM SONGS, *see* SONGS: **Musical Theater**

FOLK MUSIC

Instrumental

Banjo Pickin' Girl, 236:s2/8
Bibb County Hoedown, 226:s2/9
Bigfooted Nigger, 226:s2/3
Billy Grimes, the Rover, 236:s1/3
Blues, 226:s1/8
By the Cottage Door, 236:s1/8
Carve that Possum, 236:s1/9
Cherish the Ladies, 239:s2/11
Corrina, Corrina, 236:s2/3
Cotton-Eyed Joe, 236:s1/6
Emmaline, Take Your Time, 252:s1/7
Fe Fe Ponchaux, 226:s1/11
Flowers of Edinburgh, The, 239:s2/1
George Washington, 236:s1/4
Going Down the Valley, 236:s1/7
Granny Went to Meeting with Her Old Shoes On, 226:s1/4
Groundhog, 226:s1/1
Hunky Dory, 226:s2/2
I Truly Understand, You Love Another Man, 236:s1/1
Jig, 226:s2/10
Katie Dear (Silver Dagger), 236:s2/4
Kimball House, 226:s1/12
Knit Stockings, 239:s2/7
Ladies' Walpole Reel, 239:s1/5
Last of Sizemore, The, 226:s2/1
Lights in the Valley, 226:s1/9
Little Maggie, 236:s2/9
Little Maud, 236:s1/5
Lost Boy Blues, 226:s1/10
Lost Indian, 226:s2/7
Medley of Scottish Fiddle Tunes, A, 239:s1/10
Milwaukee Blues, 236:s2/2
Molly Put the Kettle On, 236:s2/1
My Pretty Little Pink, 226:s1/3

FOLK MUSIC (continued)

Nancy Jane, 236:s2/6
New Salty Dog, A, 236:s2/5
Old Gray Horse, The, 226:s1/2
Old Joe Clark, 236:s1/2
Peacock Rag, 226:s2/8
Pearly Dew, 227:s1/7
Rille Cajun, Le, 226:s2/6
Run, Banjo, 226:s1/6
Rymer's Favorite, 226:s2/5
Spanish Fandango, 226:s1/5
Sweet Rose of Heaven, 236:s2/7
*That's My Rabbit, My Dog
    Caught It*, 226:s2/4
*Untitled Fife Tune with
    Clapping Accompaniment*,
    291:s2/1
see also BLUEGRASS MUSIC

Vocal

Ain't I Right, 278:s2/3
All Hid, 291:s2/4
And Now, Old Serpent, 239:s1/9
Apple Tree Song, 291:s2/1
B-A-Bay, 291:s2/5
Banjo Pickin' Girl, 236:s2/8
Barbara Allen, 223:s1/5
*Been a Long Time Traveling
    Here Below*, 223:s2/6
Been on the Job Too Long,
    245:s2/2
Beulah Land, 278:s1/8
Billy Grimes, the Rover,
    236:s1/3
Black Sheep, The, 223:s2/3
Blue Ridge Cabin Home,
    225:s1/2
Bobby Halsey, 291:s1/1
Body and Soul, 225:s2/8
*Bold McCarthy, or The City of
    Baltimore*, 223:s1/4
Brave Boys, 239:s1/6
Bright and Morning Star,
    223:s2/2
Bump, Bump, Bump, 291:s2/2
Buzzard Lope, The, 278:s2/1

By the Cottage Door, 236:s1/8
Carrie Belle, 278:s2/8
Carve that Possum, 236:s1/9
Catfish, 291:s2/1
Chariot, 291:s2/4
Cheering Is My Game, 291:s2/3
Chick-A-Li-Lee-Lo, 245:s1/1
Come All You Coal Miners,
    245:s1/7
Come Up, Horsey, 291:s2/8
Corrina, Corrina, 236:s2/3
Cotton-Eyed Joe, 236:s1/6
Cotton Mill Blues, 245:s1/8
Crawling and Creeping, 245:s2/4
Daniel, 278:s1/5
Daniel Prayed, 225:s1/3
Diesel Train, 225:s2/3
Diez Perritos, 291:s1/2
Dr. Ginger Blue, 245:s2/3
*Don't Put Off Salvation Too
    Long*, 223:s2/5
Dors, Dors, 'tit Bebe, 291:s2/8
Dos y Dos Son Cuatro, 291:s2/5
Dreadnaught, The, 239:s2/3
Dynomite, 291:s2/3
Eephing, 223:s1/1
Erin-Go-Bragh, 239:s2/5
Fair Fannie Moore, 239:s1/7
*Farmer Is the Man that Feeds
    Them All, The*, 245:s1/6
Farmer's Curst Wife, The,
    239:s1/2
Fox on the Run, 225:s2/7
Frog He Would A-Wooing Go, A,
    239:s1/1
Frog Went A-Courtin', 291:s1/1
George Washington, 236:s1/4
George Washington, 291:s2/2
*Give an Honest Irish Lad a
    Chance*, 239:s2/6
Going Down the Valley, 236:s1/7
*Good Old Days of Adam and
    Eve*, 239:s2/9
Good Old State of Maine, The,
    239:s2/2
Go to Sleep, Little Baby, 291:s2/8

FOLK MUSIC (continued)

Gray Goose, The, 291:s1/3
Hanging Johnny, 223:s2/1
Haunted Road Blues, 245:s2/5
Hey Hey, I'm Memphis Bound, 223:s2/4
Hills and Home, 225:s2/5
Hold Whatcha Got, 225:s2/2
Hollerin', 223:s1/1
Hollywood Now Swingin', 291:s2/3
I Am O'ershadowed by Love, 223:s2/8
If the Light Has Gone Out in Your Soul, 245:s2/8
I'll Hit the Road Again, Boys, 239:s2/10
I'm a Long Time Traveling Away from Home, 245:s2/9
I'm on My Journey Home, 223:s2/7
I'm Runnin' on the River, 291:s2/4
I Truly Understand, You Love Another Man, 236:s1/1
Jam on Gerry's Rock, The, 239:s1/8
Je Me Suis Mis-t-à Courir, 291:s1/2
Jim Crack Corn, 291:s1/2
Johnstown Flood, The, 239:s2/8
Katie Dear (Silver Dagger), 236:s2/4
King William Was King George's Son, 245:s1/2
Kneebone, 278:s1/2
Late One Evening, 223:s1/6
Laz'rus, 278:s2/9
Lexington Murder, The, 245:s1/4
Lily Schull, 245:s1/5
Little Maggie, 236:s2/9
Little Maud, 236:s1/5
Little Rooster, 291:s1/3
Little Sally Water, 291:s1/2
Live Humble, 278:s1/4

Love Please Come Home, 225:s1/4
Milwaukee Blues, 236:s2/2
Mister Rabbit, 291:s2/6
Molly Put the Kettle On, 236:s2/1
Mon Cherie Bebe Creole, 245:s1/10
Moses, 278:s1/1
My Man John, 239:s1/4
Nancy Jane, 236:s2/6
New Salty Dog, A, 236:s2/5
O Death, 278:s1/6
Oh, Blue, 201:s1/3
Oh My Little Darling, 245:s2/1
Ojibwa War Dance Song, 291:s2/4
Old Age, 225:s1/9
Old Grandpaw Yet, 291:s2/7
Old Joe Clark, 236:s1/2
Old John the Rabbit, 291:s2/6
Old Mother Hippletoe, 291:s1/1
Pathway of Teardrops, A, 225:s2/4
Pay Me, 278:s2/7
Poor Drunkard's Dream, The, 245:s2/7
Puerta esta Quebrada, La, 291:s2/4
Rabbit, 291:s2/6
Rabbit in the Pea Patch, 291:s2/7
Raggy Levy, 278:s2/2
Raise a Ruckus Tonight, 225:s2/6
Read 'em, John, 278:s1/7
Reg'lar, Reg'lar, Rollin' Under, 278:s2/6
Ringing the Pig, 223:s1/1
Risselty Rosselty, 223:s1/3
Robin Hood and the Peddler, 291:s1/1
Ronald McDonald, 291:s2/2
Round to Maryanne's, 291:s1/2
Roxie Anne, 291:s2/7
Sally Died, 291:s2/2
Salome, 291:s2/2
See Aunt Dinah, 278:s2/4
Sheep, Sheep, Don't You Know the Road, 278:s1/3

FOLK MUSIC (continued)

Spelling From the Old Blue-Back Speller, 223:s1/2
Springhill Disaster, 225:s1/8
Sweet Rose of Heaven, 236:s2/7
Sweet William, 245:s1/3
Sweet Wine, 223:s1/4
Think, 291:s2/3
Three Men They Went A-Hunting, 239:s2/4
Titanic, The, 278:s2/10
Tobacco Auctioneering, 223:s1/2
Today Is Monday, 291:s2/5
Turkey in the Straw, 223:s1/3
Twenty-One Years, 225:s1/7
Two Brothers, The, 239:s1/3
Village School, The, 245:s2/6
Walk, Billy Abbot, 278:s2/5
Whoopee-Ti-Yi-Yo, 245:s1/9
Whooping, 223:s1/1
Who Will Bow and Bend Like a Willow?, 239:s1/9
Why Did You Wander?, 225:s1/1
You'd Better Wake Up, 225:s1/5
Your Left, 291:s2/3
Your Old Standby, 225:s1/6
Zing-Zing-Zing, 291:s2/2
Zoodiac, 291:s2/2
see also IMMIGRANT GROUPS —MUSIC

FRENCH MUSIC, *see* IMMIGRANT GROUPS— MUSIC: European, Western

HYMNS

Al Pie de Este Santo Altar, 292:s1/1
Amazing Grace, 294:s1/2
Babe of Bethlehem, The, 220:s2/6
Been A Long Time Traveling Here Below, 223:s2/6
Brighten the Corner Where You Are, 224:s2/5

Buenos Dias, Paloma Blanca, 292:s1/6
Canaan Land, 224:s1/2
Considera, Alma Perdida, 292:s1/2
Cusseta, 205:s2/8
Daniel in the Lion's Den, 244:s1/6
Dividido et Corazón, 292:s1/4
Don't Put Off Salvation Too Long, 223:s2/5
Dulce Esposo de Mi Alma, 292:s1/7
Give Me Wings, 224:s1/7
God Shall Wipe All Tears Away, 224:s1/1
Guide Me, O Thou Great Jehovah, 294:s1/1
Homeward Bound, 205:s2/11
Hymn on Peace, A, 276:s1/5
I Love To Tell the Story, 220:s2/4
I'm a Long Time Traveling Away From Home, 245:s2/9
In the Garden, 224:s2/6
Invitation, 255:s1/5
Jesus Is All the World to Me, 224:s2/2
Just as I Am, Without One Plea ("Woodworth"), 224:s2/9
Last Hymn, The, 220:s2/5
Loving Jesus, 205:s1/11
Macedonia, 255:s2/5
Middletown, 255:s2/8
Morning Trumpet, The, 205:s2/10
Nearer, My God, To Thee ("Bethany"), 224:s2/7
New Jordan, 255:s1/8
Ninety and Nine, The, 224:s2/3
Oh, You Must be a Lover of the Lord, 220:s2/2
Poor Pilgrim of Sorrow, 294:s1/3
Rock of Ages, 220:s1/7
Saved by Grace, 224:s2/8
Shall We Know Each Other There?, 220:s1/5
Tened Piedad, Dios Mío, 292:s1/5

HYMNS (continued)

There's Nothing True But Heav'n, 231:s2/3
They Led My Lord Away, 224:s1/8
To God Be the Glory, 224:s2/4
Traveling On, 205:s1/7
Tree of Level, 224:s1/4
Venir, Almas Devotas, 292:s1/3
Walk Around, 224:s1/3
We're Marching to Zion, 224:s2/1
When Jesus Christ Was Here on Earth, 294:s1/5
Yield Not to Temptation, 224:s1/5
see also SPIRITUALS; RELIGIOUS MUSIC

IMMIGRANT GROUPS–MUSIC

Asian: Armenia, Syria

Sayf Lahziq, 264:s2/6
Yar Ounenal, 264:s2/5

European, Eastern: Czechoslovakia, Lithuania, Poland, Russia, Yugoslovia

Bohacki Zaruczyny, 283:s2/2
Dye Se Doťu Białka, 283:s1/9
Hutzulka w Semereczyni, 283:s2/6
Kasakka Polką, 264:s1/3
Kozak Zawydija, 283:s2/1
Kuomet Šokis, 264:s2/8
Malenky Barabanshtchik, 264:s1/2
"Na Obi Nogi" Polka, 283:s1/4
Na Wesiliu pid Chatoju, 283:s2/3
Nie Będę Się Żynił, 283:s1/6
Oberek Puławiak, 283:s1/1
Pieśń Zbójników, 283:s1/5
Poprawyny, 283:s2/7
Sedliacky Zabavny Czardaš, 264:s1/1
'Spiew Juchasa, 283:s1/7

Sztajer z Góry Baraniej, 283:s2/5
Ukrainskyj Trisak, 283:s2/4
Wiwczar Na Supylci, 283:s2/8
Wspomnienia Sabaly, 283:s1/3
Zakopiańska Picsnka, 283:s1/8
Zalim Te Momce, 264:s1/4
Zawzięta Dziewczyna, 283:s1/2

European, Western: British Isles, Crete, France, Italy

I Tickled 'Em, 264:s2/1
Jeuns Gens Compagnard, 264:s2/2
Pastorale, 264:s2/4
Red-Haired Lass, 264:s1/6
Tailor's Thimble, The, 264:s1/6
Valse de Bon Baurche, La, 264:s2/3

Hispanic: Cuba, Mexico, New Mexico, Puerto Rico

Al Pie de Este Santo Altar, 292:s1/1
Amor a la Virtud, 244:s2/5
Arkansas Traveler, The, 292:s2/7
Bomba Calindé, 244:s1/2
Borinquen, 244:s2/1
Buenos Dias, Paloma Blanca, 292:s1/6
Chotis, El, 292:s2/13
Coco-Cancion, El, 264:s1/7
Considera, Alma Perdida, 292:s1/2
Cuna de Mis Amores, La, 244:s2/4
Cutilio, El, 292:s2/2-5
Dividido et Corazón, 292:s1/4
Dulce Esposo de Mi Alma, 292:s1/7
Emi ra obini le wa, 244:s1/3
Guajira del Mayoral, 244:s2/6
Indita, La, 292:s2/12
Listen to the Mockingbird, 292:s2/8
Loteria, 244:s1/4
Mujeres de Borinquen, Las, 244:s2/2

IMMIGRANT GROUPS—MUSIC (continued)

Piedrera, La, 264:s1/8
Polca, La, 292:s2/11
Puertorriqueño, El, 244:s2/3
Safacón de la 102nd St., El, 244:s1/1
Tened Piedad, Dios Mío, 292:s1/5
Tercera de Noviembre, La, 292:s2/9
Turkey in the Straw, 292:s2/6
Valse, El, 292:s2/1, 10
Venir, Almas Devotas, 292:s1/3
Yo Quisiera Ser, 244:s1/5

INDIAN MUSIC

Alligator Dance, 246:s1/2
Basket Song, 297:s1/6
Brush Dance Song, 297:s1/7-8
Butterfly Dance, 246:s1/1
Ceremonial Dance, 297:s2/5-6
Eagle Dance, 246:s1/3
Gambling Song, 297:s1/4, s2/1, 3-4
Gar Dance, 246:s1/5
Grizzly Bear War Song, 297:s1/2
Hunting Song, 297:s1/12
Love Song, 297:s1/1, 5, 9
Oklahoma Two-Step, 246:s2/4
Pelican Song. 297:s2/2
Rabbit Dance, 246:s1/4
Rabbit Song, 297:s1/3
Ribbon Dance, 246:s2/2
Seagull Song, 297:s1/10
Song to Stop the Rain, 297:s1/11
Stomp Dance, 246:s2/3
Women's Brush Dance, 246:s2/1

IRISH MUSIC, *see* IMMIGRANT GROUPS—MUSIC: **European, Western**

ITALIAN MUSIC, *see* IMMIGRANT GROUPS— MUSIC: **European, Western**

JAZZ

Aerolinos, 204:s2/3
A-La-Bridges, 284:s1/1
Beale Street Mama, 250:s2/6
Blowtop Blues, 295:s1/8
Blues in My Condition, 250:s2/8
Blues March, 242:s2/1
Blues Peru, 204:s1/3
Body and Soul, 274:s1/8
Body and Soul, 275:s1/6
Bogulousa Strut, 269:s2/1
Bugle Blues, 269:s2/5
Bugle Call Rag, 250:s2/2
Bugle Call Rag, 274:s2/5
Bugler's Dilemma, 250:s2/9
Can't We Be Friends, 295:s2/4
Careless Love, 295:s1/4
Castle House Rag, 269:s1/1
Castle Walk, 269:s1/2
Chase, The, 284:s2/7
Chasing Shadows, 250:s1/8
China Boy, 250:s1/5
Clarinet Marmalade, 250:s2/5
Clarinet Marmalade, 269:s1/4
Clothed Woman, The, 216:s1/2
Concerto for Billy the Kid, 216:s2/2
Congo Blues, 271:s1/1
Dameron Stomp, 284:s1/2
Dexter, 204:s1/4
Diane's Melody, 275:s1/5
Donna Lee, 242:s1/2
Donna Lee, 284:s1/8
Down Home Rag, 269:s1/5
Dunn's Cornet Blues, 269:s2/6
Eclipse, 216:s1/5
Egdon Heath, 216:s2/1
Elevation, 284:s1/4
End of a Love Affair, The, 295:s2/8
Embraceable You, 271:s1/7

JAZZ (continued)

Every Tub, 274:s1/1
Five O'Clock Shadow, 284:s1/5
Good Jelly Blues, 284:s1/6
Hejre Kati, 250:s1/3
Holiday en Masque, 201:s2/1
*I Ain't Gonna Play No Second
    Fiddle*, 269:s2/8
I Can't Get Started, 295:s1/1
I Can't Get Up the Nerve,
    284:s2/4
I Double Dare You, 274:s2/1
Idut, 201:s1/1
I Got Rhythm, 250:s1/7
I Know That You Know,
    274:s1/6
I Left My Baby, 295:s1/2
In a Little Gypsy Tearoom,
    250:s2/1
Into the Orbit, 275:s1/2
Introspection, 275:s2/2
It's the Tune That Counts,
    295:s1/6
I've Found a New Baby,
    274:s1/7
[*I Wish That I Could Shimmy
    Like My*] *Sister Kate*, 250:s1/4
Ja-Da, 295:s1/5
Jahbero, 271:s2/3
Jive at Five, 274:s2/9
Jungle Love, 250:s2/3
Key Largo, 295:s2/1
Knock, Knock, 250:s1/9
Ko-Ko, 271:s1/8
Laura, 216:s2/5
Lemon Drop, 271:s2/1
Louise, 275:s2/1
Love, 295:s2/6
Love Me Tonight, 274:s2/4
Loxodonta Africana, 204:s1/1
Melancholy, 274:s1/2
Mellow Mood, 284:s2/5
Memphis Blues, 269:s1/3
Mingus Fingers, 284:s1/7
Mirage, 216:s1/4
Misterioso, 271:s2/4
Misty, 295:s2/5

Moonlight in Vermont, 295:s2/2
My Honey's Loving Arms,
    250:s1/1
My Romance, 204:s2/1
Nica's Dream, 242:s1/3
Now's the Time, 242:s2/2
Old Fashion Love, 269:s2/7
One Up, One Down, 204:s2/2
Original Faubus Fables, 242:s2/4
Ory's Creole Trombone, 269:s1/7
Pardon Me, Pretty Baby, 274:s1/5
Parker's Mood, 271:s1/4
Passion Flower, 274:s2/2
Perdido, 284:s2/1
Piazza Navona, 216:s2/4
Piney Brown Blues, 295:s1/3
Pitter Panther Patter, 274:s2/8
Race for Space, 275:s1/3
Relaxin' at Camarillo, 271:s1/6
Robbins Nest, 295:s1/7
Rocky Mountain Blues, 250:s1/2
Royal Roost, 284:s2/6
Saint, The, 284:s1/3
Serdab, 201:s1/2
Shaw 'Nuff, 271:s1/3
She's Cryin' for Me, 269:s2/4
Slippin' Around, 274:s2/7
Society Blues, 269:s1/8
Squareface, 250:s1/6
Steppin' on the Gas, 269:s2/2
Stock Yard Strut, 269:s1/6
Stop Time, 271:s2/6
Strength and Sanity, 275:s2/4
Summer Sequence, 216:s1/1
'S Wonderful, 275:s1/1
Tapioca, 250:s2/7
Tea for Two, 284:s2/3
Things to Come, 271:s1/5
Thou Swell, 295:s2/3
Three Blind Mice, 274:s2/3
Transformation, 216:s2/3
II, V, I, 275:s1/4
Ucil, 204:s1/2
Un Poco Loco, 271:s2/2
War Gewessen, 242:s2/3
We Speak, 275:s2/3
West Indies Blues, 269:s2/3

JAZZ (continued)

What Is This Thing Called Love?,
  271:s2/5; 274:s1/3-4
What's the Use?, 250:s2/4
When Malindy Sings, 295:s2/7
Wolverine Blues, 274:s2/6
Woody'n You, 242:s1/1
Yesterdays, 216:s1/3
You're Not the Kind, 271:s1/2
Zonky, 284:s2/2
see also DANCE-BAND MUSIC

LITHUANIAN MUSIC, *see*
  IMMIGRANT GROUPS—
  MUSIC: **European, Eastern**

MARCHES

Alagazam March, 282:s2/5
Amazon's March, 221:s1/1
At a Georgia Camp Meeting,
  282:s1/3
Battleship Connecticut March,
  282:s2/4
*Ben-Hur Chariot Race March,
  The*, 282:s1/9
Brickmaker, March, The,
  276:s1/1
British Grenadiers, 276:s1/2
Down the Field March, 282:s2/8
Falcon March, 282:s2/9
Federal March, 282:s1/1
First Grand March, 299:s2/7
General Mixup, U. S. A.,
  282:s2/2
General Pershing March,
  282:s2/1
General Scott's March, 276:s1/3
Gov. Arnold's March, 299:s2/5
Jolley's March, 299:s2/8
Kennebec March, 299:s2/3
*March and Chorus "She is
  Condemned,"* 299:s2/4
March for the 76th Regt.,
  276:s2/2
*March for the 3rd Regt. of Foot,
  Lord Amherst's*, 276:s1/1

March of the 35th Regiment,
  276:s2/1
March Shannon, 282:s2/3
Pasquinade, 282:s1/5
President's March, The, 299:s2/9
Repasz Band March, 282:s2/10
Revival March, 266:s2/3
Sesquicentennial March, 266:s2/9
Trombone Sneeze, 282:s1/7
Turkish Quickstep, 299:s2/2
Washington's March, 276:s1/4
*When Brazen Trumpets from
  Afar*, 299:s2/1
Yankee Shuffle, 282:s2/6

MASSES

Mass (Martirano), 210:s1, s2/1-2
Mass in D (Paine), 262/63

MEXICAN MUSIC, *see*
  IMMIGRANT GROUPS—
  MUSIC: **Hispanic**

MORAVIAN MUSIC, *see*
  RELIGIOUS MUSIC

MOVIE SONGS, *see* SONGS:
  Musical Theater

MUSICAL THEATER SONGS,
  see SONGS: **Musical Theater**

NEW MEXICAN MUSIC, *see*
  IMMIGRANT GROUPS—
  MUSIC: **Hispanic**

OPERAS (complete or excerpted)

Consul, The, 241:s2/2
Emperor Jones, The, 241:s1/5
Haymakers, The, 234
King's Henchman, The, 241:s1/3-4
Merry Mount, 241:s1/6
Mother of Us All, The, 288/89
Natoma, 241:s1/1-2

OPERAS (continued)

Second Hurrican, The, 241:s2/1
Tender Land, The, 241:s2/3

ORCHESTRAL MUSIC

American Life, 228:s2/1
Dance in Place Congo, The, 228:s1/2
Dreamer That Remains, The, 214:s1/9
Fall River Legend, 253:s2
First Grand Minuet, 299:s2/7
Krazy Kat, 228:s1/1
Ornithological Combat of Kings, The, 208:s1
Pleasure-Dome of Kubla Khan, 273:s2/1
Rhapsodie Nègre, 228:s2/2
Symphony No. 4 (Diamond), 258:s1
Symphony No. 6 (Piston), 286:s1/1
Symphony No. 7 ("Variation-Symphony") (Mennin), 258:s2
Undertow, 253:s1

ORGAN MUSIC

Charmaine (arr.), 227:s2/5
Fantasie über "Ein' feste Burg," 280:s2/3
For Heaven's Sake, 227:s2/2
Fugue in C Minor (Parker), 280:s2/2
Grand Sonata in E Flat (Buck), 280:s1
Great Day (arr.), 227:s2/4
Intolerance, 227:s2/6
Jeannine, I Dream of Lilac Time (arr.), 227:s2/1
My Romance (arr.), 227:s2/3
Orphans of the Storm, 227:s1/5
Phantom of the Opera, The, 227:s2/6
Postlude, 280:s2/4

Son of the Shiek, The, 227:s1/3
Strike Up the Band (arr.), 227:s1/1
Variations on the Russian National Hymn, 280:s2/1
You Do Something to Me (arr.), 227:s1/2
You Were Meant for Me (arr.), 227:s1/4

PIANO MUSIC

Adieu, 257:s2/4
Aeolian Harp, 203:s1/2
American Indian Rhapsody, 213:s1/2
Andes, Marche Di Bravoura, The, 257:s1/1
Aquellos Ojos Verdes, 298:s1/6
Autumn in New York (arr.), 298:s2/5
Autumn Leaves (arr.), 298:s2/8
Banshee, The, 203:s1/1
Begin the Beguine (arr.), 298:s2/3
Canadian Capers (arr.), 298:s1/2
Carioca (arr.), 298:s2/4
Danzón Cubano, 277:s2/2
Dixiana, 257:s1/6
Dream Land, 257:s1/2
Etude in Form of a Scherzo, 206:s1/1
Four Piano Blues, 277:s2/3
Frankfort Belle, 251:s2/6
Fuga Giocosa, 206:s1/3
Galop, 251:s2/5
Grande Polka de Concert, 257:s2/5
Happy Talk (arr.), 298:s2/2
I'm Always Chasing Rainbows (arr.), 298:s1/4
In Memoriam L. M. G., 257:s1/5
It Had To Be You (arr.), 298:s1/7
Laurel Waltz, 257:s2/2
Louisville March & Quick-Step, 251:s2/7
Love Me Tonight (arr.), 274:s2/4
Lover's Lullaby, A (arr.), 298:s2/1

PIANO MUSIC (continued)

Mazurka (Gilbert), 206:s1/5
Mine, All Mine (arr.), 298:s1/1
Most Beautiful Girl in the World (arr.), 298:s2/7
Music of Changes Part III, 214:s2/1
Music of Changes Part IV, 214:s2/2
Navajo War Dance, 213:s2/2
Night in the Tropics, 208:s2
Old Rosin the Bow, 251:s1/4
On the Sea, 206:s1/6
Pastoral Novellette, A, 257:s1/4
Pawnee Horses, 213:s2/2
Piano Pieces (Paris 1924), 203:s1/3
Piano Sonata (Copland), 277:s1
Piano Variations (Copland), 277:s2/1
Post-Partitions, 209:s2/2
Prelude II (Huss), 206:s1/2
Reflections, 209:s1/4
Rhapsodie Nègre, 228:s2/2
Romance (Paine), 206:s1/4
Romance (Gottschalk), 257:s2/3
Second Interlude, 203:s1/6
Silver Spring, 257:s2/6
Six Imitations, 299:s1/4
Sonata for Microtonal Piano, 203:s2/1-4
Sonata I (Cage), 203:s1/4
Sonata V (Cage), 203:s1/5
Sonata X (Cage), 203:s1/7
Sonata XII (Cage), 203:s1/8
Studies for Player Piano, 203:s2/5-7
Sunrise Serenade, A (arr.), 298:s2/1
Twelve Virtuoso Studies (MacDowell), 206:s2
United States Grand Waltz, 257:s1/3
Valse Gracile, 206:s1/7
Vie en Rose, La (arr.), 298:s2/6
Wind Demon, Rhapsodie Caracteristique, The, 257:s2/1

POLISH MUSIC, *see* IMMIGRANT GROUPS— MUSIC: **European, Eastern**

POPULAR SONGS, *see* SONGS: **Popular**

PSALMODY, *see* RELIGIOUS MUSIC

PUERTO RICAN MUSIC, *see* IMMIGRANT GROUPS— MUSIC: **Hispanic**

QUARTETS, *see* CHAMBER MUSIC: **Quartets**

QUINTETS, *see* CHAMBER MUSIC: **Quintets**

RAGTIME

Atlanta Rag, 233:s1/5
Barn Dance Rag, 235:s2/5
Bugle Call Rag, 235:s2/7
Cannon Ball Rag, 235:s2/7
Chinese Rag, 235:s2/4
Dallas Rag, 235:s1/1
Dew Drop Alley, 235:s1/3
Dill Pickles Rag, 225:s2/9
Entertainer, The, 235:s1/7
Fat Boy Rag, 287:s2/9
Guitar Rag, 235:s2/3
Hawkins Rag, 235:s2/2
Kill It Kid, 235:s1/6
Maple Leaf Rag, 235:s1/8
Mexican Rag, 235:s2/1
Peacock Rag, 226:s2/8
Piccolo Rag, 235:s1/4
Randy Lynn Rag, 235:s2/8
Southern Rag, 235:s1/2
Sumter Rag, 235:s2/6

RELIGIOUS MUSIC

Abide in Me, 230:s1/6
Amsterdam, 205:s2/4
And Thou Shalt Know It, 230:s1/8
Anthem of Praise, An, 255:s1/1
Baptismal Anthem, 205:s2/3
Chesterfield, 255:s1/2
Crucifixion, 255:s1/4
David's Lamentation, 205:s1/2
Dying Christian's Last Farewell, The, 255:s1/9
Dying Christian to His Soul, 231:s2/4
Gehet in dem Geruch Seines Bräutigams-Namens, 230:s1/5
Greenwich, 205:s1/2
Hallelujah, 205:s1/9
Heroism, 255:s2/3
How Greatly Doth My Soul Rejoice, 230:s2/1
Ich bin in meinem Geiste, 230:s1/3
Last Words of Copernicus, The, 205:s2/9
Leite mich in Deiner Wahrheit, 230:s1/4
Meine Seele erhebet dem Herrn, 230:s1/1
Mein Heiland geht ins Leiden, 230:s1/2
Melancholy Day, 205:s1/3
Memorial Service, 205:s2/7
Milford, 205:s2/2
Montague, 255:s1/6
Montgomery, 205:s2/5
Newburgh, 255:s1/3
New Harmony, 205:s1/8
Northfield, 205:s2/13
North Port, 205:s2/6
Ode on Martyrdom, 255:s2/6
Providence, 255:s1/7
Richmond, 255:s2/4
See Him, 230:s1/7
Seven Pious Pieces, 210:s2/3
Sherburne, 205:s1/1
Soar Away, 205:s1/4
Summons, 255:s2/7
Sunderland, 255:s2/2
Thanks Be to Thee, 230:s2/2
There's Nothing True but Heav'n, 231:s2/3
Washington, 255:s2/1
Why Must I Wear This Shroud?, 294:s1/4
Wondrous Love, 205:s1/6
see also HYMNS; MASSES; SPIRITUALS

RHYTHM AND BLUES

Call It Stormy Monday, 261:s1/7
Choo Choo Ch'Boogie, 261:s1/6
Crying in the Chapel, 261:s2/6
Flying Home, 261:s1/1
Give Me a Simple Prayer, 261:s1/9
Good Rockin' Tonight, 261:s1/8
Hello, Central, 261:s2/2
Hoochie Coochie Man, 261:s2/7
Hound Dog, 261:s2/4
I Wonder, 261:s1/5
Mama, He Treats Your Daughter Mean, 261:s2/5
One Mint Julep, 261:s2/3
Roll 'Em, Pete, 261:s1/2
Straighten Up and Fly Right, 261:s1/4
Sun Didn't Shine, The, 261:s1/3
Well, Oh Well, 261:s2/1
see also BLUES

ROCK 'N' ROLL

At My Front Door, 249:s2/6
Clock, The, 249:s1/2
Every Hour, 249:s1/9
Get a Job, 249:s2/1
Good Golly Miss Molly, 249:s2/3
Have Mercy Baby, 249:s1/3
I Can't Go On, 249:s1/8
I Met Him on a Sunday, 249:s2/5

ROCK 'N' ROLL (continued)

I'm Movin' On, 249:s2/7
Mailman Blues, 249:s1/7
Maybellene, 249:s1/6
New Orleans, 249:s2/9
Reet Petite, 249:s2/4
See You Later, Alligator, 249:s1/5
Shake, Rattle and Roll, 249:s1/1
Shake a Hand, 249:s1/4
That'll Be the Day, 249:s2/2
What About Us, 249:s2/8
see also RHYTHM AND BLUES

RUSSIAN MUSIC, *see* IMMIGRANT GROUPS— MUSIC: **European, Eastern**

SACRED MUSIC, *see* RELIGIOUS MUSIC

SEXTETS, *see* CHAMBER MUSIC: **Sextets**

SONGS

Art Songs

Am Kreuzweg wird begraben, 273:s1/2
An den Wind, 273:s1/1
At Dawning, 247:s2/1
At the River, 300 s1/1
Auf geheimem Waldespfade, 273:s1/4
Ballad from Pantaloon, 300:s2/2
Bitterness of Love, 247:s1/6
By a Lonely Forest Pathway, 247:s2/2
Camp Meeting, The, 300:s1/4
Chamber Music: Five Songs from, 243:s2/1
Chanson de Florian, 300:s1/6
Childhood Fables for Grownups: Four Songs from, 300:s2/4
Children, The, 243:s1/1

Danny Deever, 247:s1/7
Deep River, 247:s1/10
Do Not Go, My Love, 247:s2/3
Dover Beach, 229:s1/1
Early in the Morning, 229:s2/1
Earthlight, 237:s2/2
Elégie, 300:s1/9
Flight from Heaven (excerpts), 229:s2/7
Four American Indian Songs, 213:s2/3
Four Impressions, 273:s1/5-8
General William Booth Enters into Heaven, 247:s2/9
Go Down Moses, 247:s1/8
Heav'n, Heav'n, 247:s1/9
His Exaltation, 300:s1/2
I Am Rose, 229:s2/2
Lady of the Lake, The, 231:s1/1-4, s2/1-2
Lark Now Leaves His Watery Nest, The, 247:s1/4
Light, My Light, 247:s2/5
Listeners, The, 300:s2/3
Lit'l Gal, 247:s2/8
Long Ago, Sweetheart Mine, 247:s1/1
Love in May, 247:s1/3
Luke Havergal, 243:s1/6
Lullaby of the Woman of the Mountain, 229:s2/8
Maid Sings Light, A, 247:s1/1
Meeres Stille, 273:s1/3
Mélodies Passagères, 229:s1/2-6
Miniver Cheevy, 243:s1/7
Moo Is a Cow, 243:s1/1
My Papa's Waltz, 229:s2/11
Once a Lady Was Here, 243:s1/3
Once Upon a Time, 243:s1/11
On the Beach at Fontana, 243:s2/3
Peacock Pie, Four Rhymes from, 300:s2/1
Philanthropy, 230:s2/3
Phonemena, 209:s1/1-2
Pippa's Song, 229:s2/4
Qu'il m'irait bien, 300:s1/8

SONGS: **Art** (continued)

Richard Cory, 243:s1/5
Root Cellar, 229:s2/10
Rosamunde, 300:s1/7
Rose, The, 243:s1/1
Running Sun, The, 243:s2/6
Snake, 229:s2/9
Song (Copland), 243:s2/2
Song of an Old Woman,
    243:s1/4
Song of the Dagger, 273:s1/9
Spring, 229:s2/5
Spring and Fall, 229:s2/6
Sunrise, 300:s1/5
Sure on This Shining Night,
    243:s2/5
Swans, 247:s1/5
*There's Nothing True But
    Heav'n*, 231:s2/3
Thomas Logge, 243:s1/2
Three Indian Songs, 213:s1/1
Three Poems of Fiona MacLeod,
    273:s2/2-4
Three Songs, 285:s2/2-4
To You, 229:s2/3
Triptych, 218:s2/2-4
Velvet Shoes, 247:s2/6
Watchman!, 300:s1/3
*When I Bring You Coloured
    Toys*, 247:s2/4
When I Have Sung My Songs,
    247:s2/7
Year's at the Spring, 247:s1/2

Musical Theater Songs

All in Down and Out Blues,
    270:s2/1
All I Want, 270:s2/7
Anatole of Paris, 215:s2/5
Anyone Can Whistle, 272:s2/7
Anything Goes, 272:s2/2
Are You Havin' Any Fun?,
    215:s2/6
Are You Making Any Money,
    240:s1/7
Babies on Our Block, The,
    265:s1/1

Baltimore Buzz, 260:s1/6, s2/7
Bandana Days, 260:s1/1, 4
*Boulevard of Broken Dreams,
    The*, 270:s1/2
Bowery, The, 221:s2/7
Brother, Can You Spare a Dime,
    270:s1/1
Can't You Just See Yourself,
    240:s2/7
Cat Song, 265:s2/5
Charmaine, 227:s2/5
Cheek to Cheek, 238:s2/7
Coal Loading Machine, 270:s2/3
*Coffee in the Morning, Kisses in
    the Night*, 240:s2/1
*Cup of Coffee, A Sandwich and
    You, A*, 215:s1/5
*Daddy, Won't You Please Come
    Home*, 260:s1/5
Darktown Is Out Tonight,
    265:s2/2
Death of Mother Jones, The,
    270:s2/6
Doin' the New Low-Down,
    215:s1/6
*Don't Give De Name a Bad
    Place*, 265:s2/7
Enchantress, The, 272:s1/1
*Ethiop, or The Child of the
    Desert, The*, 232:s2
Fifteen Miles from Birmingham,
    270:s2/2
Flight, The, 260:s2/2
For Heaven's Sake, 227:s2/2
*Gee, I'm Glad That I'm from
    Dixie*, 260:s2/3
German 5th, The, 265:s2/4
Gold Diggers' Song, The, 270:s1/8
Golden Wedding, De, 265:s1/7
Great Day, 227:s2/4
Gypsy Blues, 260:s1/7
Hang the Mulligan Banner Up,
    265:s1/5
Heat Wave, 238:s2/5
Honeysuckle Rose, 272:s1/7
Hoops, 215:s2/3
How Do You Do It, 240:s1/4

SONGS: **Musical Theater**
(continued)

How's Chances, 238:s2/4
How Ya' Gonna Keep 'Em Down on the Farm, 260:s2/5
I Ain't Got No Home in This World Anymore, 270:s2/5
I Can't Do the Sum, 221:s2/8
I'll Build a Stairway to Paradise, 215:s1/4
I'm Craving For That Kind of Love, 260:s2/1
I'm Just Wild about Harry, 260:s1/1
Indian Princess, or La Belle Sauvage, The, 232:s1
In Honeysuckle Time, 260:s1/2, 6
In the Still of the Night, 270:s1/4
Intolerance, 227:s2/6
It All Belongs to Me, 238:s1/6
Jeannine, I Dream of Lilac Time, 227:s2/1
John Riley's Always Dry, 265:s1/3
Let Me Sing and I'm Happy, 238:s2/1
Let's Call It a Day, 240:s1/6
Life Is Just a Bowl of Cherries, 270:s1/3
Like He Loves Me, 272:s1/4
Louisiana Purchase, 238:s2/8
Love Walked In, 270:s1/5
Love Will Find a Way, 260:s1/3
Lullaby, 221:s2/6
Maggie Murphy's Home, 265:s1/2
Mandy, 238:s1/2
Mirandy, 260:s2/4
Mister Gallagher and Mister Shean, 215:s1/3
Moanin' Low, 215:s1/7
Moon Shines on the Moonshine, The, 215:s1/1
My Gal Is a High Born Lady, 265:s2/1

My Romance, 227:s2/3
Nobody Else But Me, 240:s2/6
Not for All the Rice in China, 238:s2/3
NRA Blues, 270:s2/4
Oh, How I Hate to Get Up in the Morning, 238:s1/1
Only Another Boy and Girl, 240:s2/5
On Patrol In No Man's Land, 260:s2/6
On the Good Ship Lollypop, 270:s1/6
On the Sunny Side of the Street, 215:s2/2
Orphans of the Storm, 227:s1/5
Paddy Duffy's Cart, 264:s1/4
Paree, 215:s2/4
Phantom of the Opera, The, 227:s2/6
Pretty Girl Is Like a Melody, A, 238:s1/3
Puttin' On the Ritz, 238:s2/2
Riddle Me This, 240:s1/4
Rip Van Winkle Was a Lucky Man, 265:s2/6
Rock-a-Bye Baby, 238:s1/4
Second-Hand Rose, 215:s1/2
Shaking the Blues Away, 238:s1/5
Shine On, Harvest Moon, 215:s2/1
Sleepin' Bee, A, 272:s2/6
Someone to Watch Over Me, 272:s1/5
Song of Brown October Ale, 221:s2/5
Son of the Shiek, The, 227:s1/3
South American Way, 215:s2/7
Stay in Your Own Backyard, 265:s1/6
Tell 'Em I'll Be There, 265:s2/3
That Lucky Fellow, 240:s2/3
Unemployment Stomp, 270:s1/7
We'll Be the Same, 240:s1/1
What Can You Say in a Love Song?, 240:s2/2

SONGS: **Musical Theater**
(continued)

Where Have We Met Before?,
     240:s1/5
*Where Is the Song of Songs for
     Me?,* 238:s1/7
White Cliffs of Dover, 270:s2/8
You Are Never Away, 272:s2/5
You Do Something to Me,
     227:s1/2
You Forgot Your Gloves,
     240:s1/2
You Were Meant for Me,
     227:s1/4

Popular Songs (excludes Musical
     Theater Songs)

After the Fair, 267:s2/4
Ain't Misbehavin', 279:s2/7
Alabamy Bound, 233:s2/3
*Alknomook, or the Death Song
     of the Cherokee Indians,*
     299:s1/3
All Alone, 233:s2/4
All in Down and Out Blues,
     270:s2/1
All of Me, 248:s1/4
And So to Bed, 240:s1/3
Angels' Visits, 220:s2/1
Anti-Monopoly War Song, The,
     267:s1/1
April Showers, 279:s1/2
Aquellos Ojos Verdes, 298:s1/6
*Argentines, the Portuguese and
     the Greeks, The,* 233:s2/1
Autumn in New York, 298:s2/5
Autumn Leaves, 298:s2/8
Begin the Beguine, 298:s2/3
Blowtop Blues, 295:s1/8
Blue Moon, 248:s1/5
*Boys and Girls Like You and
     Me,* 240:s2/4
*Broadway, Opera and Bowery
     Crawl,* 221:s2/4
Buckets of Gore, 221:s1/4
Canadian Capers, 298:s1/2

Can't We Be Friends, 295:s2/4
Careless Love, 295:s1/4
Carioca, 298:s2/4
*Chinese, the Chinese, You Know,
     The,* 267:s1/3
Collegiate, 279:s1/3
*Come, Josephine, in My Flying
     Machine,* 233:s1/6
Crooked Whiskey, 267:s2/3
Cypress Wreath, The, 299:s1/5
'Deed I Do, 279:s1/7
Deep Night, 279:s2/6
Dinah, 279:s1/4
Drill, Ye Tarriers, Drill, 267:s1/2
Eight Hours, 267:s1/2
End of a Love Affair, The,
     295:s2/8
Enlloro, 298:s1/5
*Everybody Wants a Key to My
     Cellar,* 233:s1/7
Fatherhood of God, The,
     267:s2/2
*Father's A Drunkard, and Mother
     Is Dead,* 267:s2/3
Flee as a Bird, 220:s1/4
Future America, The, 267:s1/1
Ghost of a Chance, 248:s1/6
*Gimme a Little Kiss, Will Ya
     Huh,* 279:s1/6
Girl on the Magazine Cover, The,
     233:s1/2
Good Man Is Hard To Find, A,
     279:s1/5
Hand That Holds the Bread, The,
     267:s1/1
Happy Talk, 298:s2/2
Heartaches, 248:s1/3
Heart and Soul, 248:s2/6
*He'd Have to Get Under, Get
     Out and Get Under,* 233:s1/3
Heidelberg Stein Song, The,
     221:s1/6
Hello, Frisco, 233:s1/5
Hello! Ma Baby, 272:s1/2
*Henry's Made a Lady out of
     Lizzie,* 233:s2/7

SONGS: **Popular** (continued)

How Deep Is the Ocean,
238:s2/6; 248:s1/2
How'd You Like to Spoon with Me?, 221:s1/7
I Can't Get Started, 295:s1/1
If I Had a Talking Picture of You, 233:s2/8
If My Friends Could See Me Now, 272:s2/8
I Left My Baby, 295:s1/2
I'm Always Chasing Rainbows, 298:s1/4
It Had To Be You, 298:s1/7
It's the Tune That Counts, 295:s1/6
I Wants to Be a Actor Lady, 221:s1/5
Ja-Da, 295:s1/5
Jim Fisk, 267:s2/1
Key Largo, 295:s2/1
Kick Him When He's Down, 267:s2/1
Kitten on the Keys, 298:s1/3
Laborer You See, and I Love Liberty, A, 267:s1/2
Laura, 216:s2/5
Life in the West, A, 251:s1/3
Lindbergh, 233:s2/6
Little Ah Sid, 267:s1/3
Little Brown Jug, 267:s2/3
Little White House, The, 233:s2/5
Love, 295:s2/6
Loveless Love, 272:s1/3
Lover's Lullaby, A, 298:s2/1
Ma! Ma! Where's My Pa?, 267:s2/3
May Irwin's "Bully" Song, 221:s1/8
Mine, All Mine, 298:s1/1
Mississippi Mud, 279:s2/4
Mr. Radio Man, 233:s2/2
Misty, 295:s2/5
Mood Indigo, 272:s2/1
Moonlight in Vermont, 295:s2/2

Most Beautiful Girl in the World, 298:s2/7
Music Goes Round and Round, The, 248:s2/1
My Blue Heaven, 279:s2/5
My Heart, 221:s1/3
No Irish Need Apply, 267:s1/3
Oceana Roll, 233:s1/1
Once in a While, 248:s2/4
On the 5:15, 233:s1/4
Out of Work, 267:s1/2
Pacific Railroad, The, 267:s1/1
Piney Brown Blues, 295:s1/3
Pretty Girl, A, 221:s2/2
Reuben and Cynthia, 221:s2/3
Robbins Nest, 295:s1/7
Sex Against Sex, 211:s2/1
Shoe Shine Boy, 248:s1/7
Silver Rain, The, 299:s1/2
Song of the Red Man, The, 267:s1/1
Star Dust, 272:s1/6
Stormy Weather, 248:s1/1
Strip Polka, 272:s2/3
Sunday, 279:s2/2
Sunday in the Park, 272:s2/4
Sunrise Serenade, A, 298:s2/1
'Tain't What You Do, 248:s2/7
Take Your Girlie to the Movies, 233:s1/8
Ta-Ra-Ra Boom-De-Ay, 267:s2/4
There'll Be Some Changes Made, 279:s2/1
Thou Swell, 295:s2/3
Trusting, 220:s1/6
Uncle Sam's Farm, 267:s1/3
Undecided, 248:s2/5
Until the Real Thing Comes Along, 248:s2/2
Vie en Rose, La, 298:s2/6
We Never Speak as We Pass By, 267:s2/1
What Can You Say in a Love Song, 240:s2/2
When Malindy Sings, 295:s2/7

SONGS: **Popular** (continued)

When My Dreamboat Comes Home, 248:s2/3
When the Girls Can Vote, 267:s2/2
Whispering, 279:s1/1
Yankee Doodle Boy, The, 221:s1/2
Yes, Sir, That's My Baby, 279:s2/3
see also BLUES: **Vocal**; COUNTRY MUSIC; FOLK MUSIC: **Vocal**; RHYTHM AND BLUES; ROCK 'N' ROLL; SONGS: **War**

War Songs

All Quiet Along the Potomac Tonight, 202:s1/2
American Vicar of Bray, 276:s1/4
Beauregard's Retreat from Shiloh, 202:s2/1
Drummer Boy of Shiloh, The, 202:s1/6
Fuehrer's Face, Der, 222:s2/1
Goodbye, Mama (I'm Off to Yokohama), 222:s2/6
Hello, Central; Give Me No Man's Land, 222:s1/5
He's 1-A in the Army and He's A-1 in My Heart, 222:s2/2
I Didn't Raise My Boy to Be a Soldier, 222:s1/2
I Left My Heart At the Stage Door Canteen, 222:s2/5
I'm a Good Old Rebel, 202:s2/4
I've Got My Captain Working for Me Now, 222:s1/7
I Wish I Was in Dixie's Land, 202:s1/1
Jeff in Petticoats, 202:s2/2
Junto Song, 276:s1/3
King's Own Regulars, The, 276:s1/4
Lamentation Over Boston, 276:s1/1

Let's All Be Americans Now, 222:s1/3
Liberty Song, 276:s2/1
Mother, Is the Battle Over?, 202:s1/4
My Dream of the Big Parade, 222:s1/8
My Guy's Come Back, 222:s2/9
No Love, No Nothin', 222:s2/7
Over There, 222:s1/4
Parody Upon a Well-Known Liberty Song, 276:s2/2
Praise the Lord and Pass the Ammunition, 222:s2/8
Song on Liberty, 276:s1/2
Stalin Wasn't Stallin', 222:s2/3
Tenting on the Old Camp Ground, 202:s1/5
There's a Vacant Chair in Every Home Tonight, 222:s1/6
We Are Coming, Father Abra'am, 202:s1/3
We Are Coming from the Cotton Fields, 202:s2/6
We Did It Before and We Can Do It Again, 222:s2/4
Weeping, Sad and Lonely, 202:s2/3
When Johnny Comes Marching Home, 202:s2/5
When the Lusitania Went Down, 222:s1/1

SPANISH MUSIC, see IMMIGRANT GROUPS— MUSIC: **Hispanic**

SPIRITUALS

Airplane Ride, The, 294:s2/8
Amsterdam, 205:s2/4
Baptismal Anthem, 205:s2/3
Cusseta, 205:s2/8
David's Lamentation, 205:s1/2
Deep River, 247:s1/10
Go Down Moses, 247:s1/8
Greenwich, 205:s1/2

SPIRITUALS (continued)

Hallelujah, 205:s1/9
Heav'n, Heav'n, 247:s1/9
Hicks' Farewell, 294:s2/3
Homeward Bound, 205:s2/11
I Am a Poor Wayfaring Stranger, 294:s2/5
Jim and Me, 294:s2/7
Last Words of Copernicus, The, 205:s2/9
Little Family, The, 294:s2/6
Loving Jesus, 205:s1/11
Melancholy Day, 205:s1/3
Memorial Service, 205:s2/7
Milford, 205:s2/2
Montgomery, 205:s2/5
Morning Trumpet, The, 205:s2/10
My Lord Keeps a Record, 294:s2/9
New Harmony, 205:s1/8
Northfield, 205:s2/13
North Port, 205:s2/6
Old Gospel Ship, The, 294:s2/1
See That My Grave Is Kept Clean, 294:s2/4
Sherburne, 205:s1/1
Soar Away, 205:s1/4
Traveling On, 205:s1/7
When the Stars Begin to Fall, 294:s2/2
Wondrous Love, 205:s1/6
see also HYMNS

STRING QUARTETS, *see*
    CHAMBER MUSIC: **Quartets**

SYMPHONIES, *see*
    ORCHESTRAL MUSIC

THEATER, MUSICAL—SONGS, *see* SONGS: **Musical Theater**

TRIOS, *see* CHAMBER MUSIC: **Trios**

TROMBONE MUSIC

General Speech, 254:s2/3

UKRANIAN MUSIC, *see*
    IMMIGRANT GROUPS—
    MUSIC: **European, Eastern**

VOCAL MUSIC, *see* BLUES:
    Vocal; FOLK MUSIC: **Vocal**;
    CHORAL MUSIC; SONGS;
    and specific headings, e.g.,
    OPERA; ROCK 'N' ROLL;
    etc.

WAR SONGS, *see* SONGS: **War**

WESTERN EUROPEAN MUSIC, *see* IMMIGRANT GROUPS—
    MUSIC: **European, Western**

WIND MUSIC, *see* BAND MUSIC

YUGOSLAVIAN MUSIC, *see*
    IMMIGRANT GROUPS—
    MUSIC: **European, Eastern**

Chronological Index

For purposes of historical overview, the albums are here arranged by the composition dates of their recorded selections. If works belong to an oral tradition, they are listed by the date of recording.

1770s	The Birth of Liberty	276
1770-1840	Make a Joyful Noise	255
1776-1835	Music of the Federal Era	299
18th-19th cent.	The Flowering of Vocal Music in America: Vol. 1	230
18th-19th cent.	The Flowering of Vocal Music in America: Vol. 2	231
1790s-1925	Come and Trip It	293
early 19th cent.	John Bray/Raynor Taylor	232
1843-1877	*Angels' Visits*	220
1857	George F. Root: *The Haymakers*	234
1859-1867	John Knowles Paine: *Mass in D*	262/63
mid 19th cent.	*Where Home Is*	251
mid 19th cent.	A. P. Heinrich/Louis M. Gottschalk	208
1860s	Songs of the Civil War	202
mid 19th cent.	*The Wind Demon*	257
mid to late 19th cent.	Fugues, Fantasia, and Variations	280
mid to late 19th cent.	Don't Give the Name a Bad Place	265
1865-1893	*The Hand That Holds the Bread*	267
1866-1906	*I Wants to Be a Actor Lady*	221
1876-1926	*The Pride of America*	266
1880s-1920s	Works by Arthur Farwell, Preston Ware Orem, Charles Wakefield Cadman	213
1892-1902	Malcolm Frager Plays	206
1896-1900s	Mrs. H. H. A. Beach/Arthur Foote	268
1900-1940	*When I Have Sung My Songs*	247
1901-1926	The Sousa and Pryor Bands	282
1803-1918	Charles Tomlinson Griffes	273
1906-1921	John Alden Carpenter, Henry F. Gilbert, Adolph Weiss and John Powell	228
1910-1929	*Come Josephine in My Flying Machine*	233
1909-1974	*Brighten the Corner Where You Are*	224
1911-1954	Toward an American Opera	241
1912-1973	And Then We Wrote	272
1913-1927	*Steppin' on the Gas*	269
1915-1946	*Praise the Lord and Pass the Ammunition*	222
1916-1935	The Mighty Wurlitzer	227
1916-1942	*Let's Get Loose*	290
1916-1955	Old-Country Music in a New Land	264
1917-1930s	Chamber Works by Arthur Shepherd, Henry Cowell, Roy Harris	218
1919-1924	Sissle and Blake's *Shuffle Along*	260
1919-1942	Follies, Scandals, and Other Diversions	215
1920s	*Sweet and Low Blues*	256
1920-1929	*Yes Sir, That's My Baby*	279

234   *Index to New World Records*

1920s	Works by Henry Cowell, Wallingford Riegger, John J. Becker, and Ruth Crawford	285
1920s-1940s	*Jive at Five*	274
1920s-1950s	*It Had To Be You*	298
1923-1959 (recorded)	*Oh My Little Darling*	245
1923-1965	Sound Forms for Piano	203
1925-1940	The Vintage Irving Berlin	238
1926-1938	*Going Down the Valley*	236
1926-1941	*Cuttin' the Boogie*	259
1926-1948	Aaron Copland: Works for Piano	277
1926-1975	Harry Partch—John Cage	214
1927-1964	*Maple Leaf Rag*	235
1927-1973	*That's My Rabbit, My Dog Caught It*	226
1928-1950	*'Spiew Juchasa/Song of the Shepherd*	283
1928-1971	*I'm On My Journey Home*	223
1929-1949	Country Music: South and West	287
1930s	*Jammin' for the Jackpot*	217
1930s	Little Club Jazz	250
1930-1960	But Yesterday Is Not Today	243
mid 20th cent.	Songs of Charles Ives, Theodore Chanler, Norman Dello Joio, Irving Fine, Robert Ward	300
1930s-1960s	Songs of Samuel Barber and Ned Rorem	229
1930s-1970s (recorded)	*Old Mother Hippletoe*	291
1930-1939	*The Music Goes Round and Around*	248
1931-1941	*Brother, Can You Spare a Dime?*	270
1931-1947	*Where Have We Met Before?*	240
1932-1962	Choral Works by Randall Thompson, Elliott Carter, Seymour Shifrin	219
1938-1953	*Straighten Up and Fly Right*	261
1938-1961	*When Malindy Sings*	295
1940s	*The Mother of Us All*	288/89
1940s	Chamber Music by Lou Harrison, Ben Weber, Lukas Foss, Ingolf Dahl	281
1940s	Jazz in Revolution	284
1940s	Bebop	271
mid 1940s	William Schuman/Morton Gould	253
1940s-1970s	Country Music in the Modern Era	207
1940-1970 (recorded)	Dark and Light in Spanish New Mexico	292
1945-1964	David Diamond/Peter Mennin	258
1938-1961	*Mirage*; Avant-Garde and Third Stream Jazz	216
1946-1976	*Hills and Home*	225

1947-1959 (recorded)   The Roots of the Blues   252
1952-1961   Introspection   275
1952-1962   *Shake, Rattle & Roll*   249
1953-1967   Winds of Change   211
1955-1956   Walter Piston/Leon Kirchner   286
1955-1964   *Nica's Dream*   242
1959 (recorded)   The Gospel Ship   294
1959 (recorded)   White Spirituals from *The Sacred Harp*   205
1960-1961   Georgia Sea Island Songs   278
1960-1972   Gunther Schuller/Andrew Imbrie   212
1959-1976   Salvatore Martirano/Donald Martino   210
1963-1977 (recorded) *Brave Boys*   239
1968-1970   New Music for Virtuosos   209
1960s-1970s   New Music for Virtuosos/2   254
1960s-1970s   Works by Paul Chihara, Chou
                        Wen-Chung, Earl Kim and
                        Roger Reynolds   237
1970s (recorded)   Songs of Earth, Water, Fire and Sky   246
1970s (recorded)   Songs of Love, Luck, Animals, and
                        Magic   297
1977 (recorded)   Caliente = Hot   244
1970   Roger Sessions: *When Lilacs Last in
                        the Dooryard Bloom'd*   296
1977   *Loxodonta Africana*   204
1977   Cecil Taylor   201

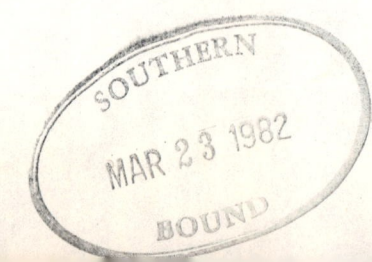